The Margins of Late Medieva

1430–1540

New Historical PERSPECTIVES

New Historical Perspectives is a book series for early career scholars within the UK and the Republic of Ireland. Books in the series are overseen by an expert editorial board to ensure the highest standards of peer-reviewed scholarship. Commissioning and editing is undertaken by the Royal Historical Society, and the series is published under the imprint of the Institute of Historical Research by the University of London Press.

The series is supported by the Economic History Society and the Past and Present Society.

P&P

ECONOMIC HISTORY SOCIETY 1926

The Margins of Late Medieval London, 1430–1540

Charlotte Berry

LONDON
ROYAL HISTORICAL SOCIETY
INSTITUTE OF HISTORICAL RESEARCH
UNIVERSITY OF LONDON PRESS

Published by
UNIVERSITY OF LONDON PRESS
SCHOOL OF ADVANCED STUDY
INSTITUTE OF HISTORICAL RESEARCH
Senate House, Malet Street, London WC1E 7HY

Available to download free or to purchase the hard copy edition at https://www.sas.ac.uk/publications.

ISBNs
978 1 914477 01 0 (hardback edition)
978 1 914477 02 7 (paperback edition)
978 1 914477 04 1 (epub edition)
978 1 914477 03 4 (pdf edition)

DOI 10.14296/202202.9781914477034

RHS
New Historical
PERSPECTIVES

Cover image: Master of Alkmaar, Polyptych with the Seven Works of Charity, 1504. Object Number: SK-A-2815. Courtesy of Rijksmuseum.

Contents

List of figures

List of tables

List of abbreviations

BL	British Library, London
Jor.	Journals of the common council of the city of London. LMA, COL/CC/01/01
LMA	London Metropolitan Archives
P&M Rolls	Thomas, A.H. (ed.), *Calendar of Plea and Memoranda Rolls of the City of London* (London, 1926–61)
TNA	The National Archives, London

Acknowledgements

I find myself writing these acknowledgements in the cafe at the Barbican Centre overlooking, appropriately enough, the remnants of London's medieval wall and the fifteenth-century parish church of St Giles Cripplegate. It's an inspiring spot and one I've come to several times on the journey of research and writing which has led to this book, so it is a good place to look back and reflect on that journey. Getting here has taken a decade and more and I have been helped along the way by many people to whom I am supremely grateful.

I first became fascinated with fifteenth-century London and its people as an undergraduate at the University of York, inspired by the teaching of Sarah Rees Jones. I particularly owe my love of the neighbourhood politics and minutiae of daily life found in the wardmote courts to her special subject course on York and London. Years later, she and Vanessa Harding were encouraging examiners of my thesis, and this book is far better for their suggestions on how to develop my work. As a masters student at the Institute of Historical Research, it was conversations with Matthew Davies that first got me thinking about ways to look at the city beyond the perspectives of its citizens and government. I am extremely grateful to Matthew for the many ways in which he has helped me develop my work and thoughts over the past ten years, most of all for his patient and wise supervision of my thesis and his continued support as I embarked on the process of writing this book. I thank him for always being generous with his time and encouraging me to be ambitious and think expansively. I also owe a great debt to Mark Merry, my second thesis supervisor. This book would not be what it is without many conversations with Mark about how to put my work in a longer-term perspective and how to find the best digital approaches to sources. I could not have embarked on a PhD without the generous AHRC studentship I received through the London Arts and Humanities Partnership.

As a student and scholar of late medieval London, I have been lucky to be part of a friendly community centred on the IHR Medieval and Tudor London seminar convened by Caroline Barron, Vanessa Harding and Julia Merritt. My thanks to all the members of the seminar, past and present, from whose expertise, thoughtful questions and comments on papers by myself and others I have learnt much. I should particularly like to thank

Justin Colson and Kit French, who have always been generous with advice, encouraging feedback and archival leads.

It was also through the seminar that I met Shannon McSheffrey, and I really cannot thank Shannon enough for all her encouragement, suggestions for the development of the themes of this book and help, including sharing pre-publication drafts of her work and transcripts of the consistory court deposition books. Shannon, Ian Forrest and Rosa Salzberg were readers of an earlier version of this book and I am very grateful for the thought-provoking discussions we had at the author workshop which immeasurably improved it. My thanks also to Tom Johnson, who kindly read and gave many helpful comments on an earlier draft of Chapter Five. I am very grateful to all those at University of London Press who have made the process of publishing this book a pleasure, in particular Elizabeth Hurren and Jane Winters. Special thanks go to Ian Forrest who went above and beyond as an editor, not just helping me navigate the practicalities of publication but also being generous with his time and considerable expertise through comments on early drafts and participation in the author workshop.

The scholarship on which this book is based would have been impossible without the hard work and commitment of staff at the London Metropolitan Archives, National Archives, British Library and Institute of Historical Research. I am also indebted to colleagues in and out of academia over the last three years who have been encouraging and supportive of my work on this book alongside post-doctoral positions, particularly Tracey Hill and the staff of the Goldsmiths' Company Library.

The journey has been a bumpy one, and I really could not have got here without the love and support of my friends and family. To Will Attwood, Amy Jessop and Harriet Robinson, my thanks for always being sources of laughter and kindness when I needed it most. I hope to repay you all in kind. The same too to Marie Southall and Barney Harper, and also my immense gratitude goes to them for giving me a calm and welcoming space in their home so that I could write during the turbulent summer of 2020. All my love and thanks to my family, to whom I owe so much; my parents John and Alison Berry and my sister Liz.

Finally, this book is dedicated to all the early career scholars I have met along the way, all of whom have been brilliant, smart and passionate about their work in the face of immense pressures and uncertain futures.

September 2021

Introduction

In 1432, poet John Lydgate was commissioned to commemorate the triumphal entry of Henry VI to London. Setting the scene, Lydgate wrote of 'this Citee with laude, pris, and glorie/For joye moustred lyke the sonne beem'.[1] He described the participants in this civic muster in terms of their clothing: the mayor in red velvet, the sheriffs and aldermen in scarlet furred cloaks and 'the citizenis echoon [each one] of the Citee' wearing a white livery and ranked in their crafts.[2] Lydgate paused also 'forto remembre of other alyens',[3] naming the great merchants of Genoa, Florence, Venice and the 'Esterlings' (of the Hanseatic League) who joined the procession to meet the king outside the city at Blackheath. This was an orderly image of the city, represented by its body politic and its wealthy international traders. This was the London that dominated not only ceremonial occasions like the one Lydgate commemorated but also the records of the civic government. It was the city as represented by, in the language of the time, 'the more sufficient', 'the more wise and discrete' or the trustworthy men (*probi homines*). Because of its prominence in the civic records, it is also the version of the city that looms largest in histories of late medieval London. This book looks past the ranked citizens and officers in white and red to the crowds who thronged the route in 1432 and yet whom Lydgate's poem, much like the civic records, pays little regard.

In order to look past the urban body politic, this history of late medieval London puts at its heart places on the city's fringe which are similarly absent from its contemporary and modern representations. We have few contemporary visual representations of late medieval London – the Agas map (Figure 0.2) is a mid-sixteenth-century image of a city undergoing transformational growth. In the fifteenth century, cities were often represented as walled fortresses with little beyond their bounds. Yet for the largest of European urban centres in the middle ages, and indeed for many smaller ones too, the city overspilled its walls. These extramural neighbourhoods might have been geographically

[1] J. Lydgate, 'Henry VI's triumphal entry into London', in *Mummings and Entertainments*, ed. C. Sponsler, TEAMS Middle English Texts (Kalamazoo, MI, 2010), ll. 24–5 <https://d.lib.rochester.edu/teams/text/sponsler-lydgate-mummings-and-entertainments-henry-vi-triumphal-entry-into-london> [accessed] 8 Jan. 2021].

[2] Lydgate, 'Henry VI's triumphal entry into London', l. 36.

[3] Lydgate, 'Henry VI's triumphal entry into London', l. 43.

marginal but for city dwellers they were essential places, for the production of food, for recreation and for spiritual foundations which saved citizens' souls. To understand better the course of urban history, we need to consider the suburbs as crucial parts of the city and pay close attention to their role in urban development. In this book, I argue that in marginal neighbourhoods the full range of urban society, from the 'wise and discrete' citizens to the casual day labourer and the poor widow, lived alongside one another in communities which were adjacent to urban institutional structures and the body politic but which were not defined by them. Poverty, work, landscape, mobility, regulation of behaviour and reputation were all important forces in these communities, which must be centred in order to understand the full complexity of urban life.

In London before the mid-sixteenth century, citizenship was limited to just a quarter of the male population. Even if we take a more generous definition and include wives and widows of citizens as *de facto* beneficiaries of their husbands' status, we are still left with a majority of Londoners largely marginalized in most of the existing histories of the city. In focusing on the social and spatial fringes of the city, this book presents a new view of the late medieval city beyond this relative social elite. It also contributes to a growing recognition of the importance of spatial difference and of neighbourhood in urban history. Classically, historians defined medieval cities through their institutional structures, particularly guilds and civic governments or magistracies which centrally organized the city around a body of citizens who thereby accrued wealth and power.[4] However, scholars in recent years have begun to centre space and spatial difference as defining features of the medieval and early modern city. The shift is rooted in revised conceptual understandings of cities, influenced by geographers, which recognize plurality of jurisdiction and diversity of land use as essential to the city rather than aberrations. By spatializing the social history of late medieval London, I focus on its inhabitants as primarily neighbours, new arrivals or, occasionally, suspected outsiders rather than through the institutional binary of citizen and non-citizen.

[4] See e.g. C. Phythian-Adams, *Desolation of a City: Coventry and the Urban Crisis of the Later Middle Ages* (Cambridge, 1979); S. Rappaport, *Worlds within Worlds: Structures of Life in Sixteenth-Century London* (Cambridge, 1989).

Margins and marginality

Relating the social to the spatial margins of the city is no anachronism; it was a relationship which medieval people often drew themselves.[5] Civic authorities decreed that those who threatened both the health of citizens' bodies and the welfare of the community were to be turned away from city gates or live on the urban fringe. Such regulations affected lepers and prostitutes but also laundresses and those in polluting industries.[6] London's gates were closed each night to prevent the movement of thieves and other malefactors into the city. Over the early modern period, the growth of the city's suburbs contributed to the breakdown of the livery companies' economic control,[7] but even in the late medieval period we can locate anxiety about ungoverned suburbs. As Frank Rexroth has argued, the city's government implicitly considered its extensive extramural neighbourhoods less important, legally part of the city and yet in a realm not governed by civic morals.[8] Definitions of centre and margin were reinforced by ceremonial uses of city space, where civic celebrations, royal procession routes and sites of official proclamations converged on urban commercial hubs such as marketplaces and central shopping streets.[9] The use of the same sites for prestigious events and high-value commerce reflects key aspects of Henri Lefebvre's theories about space and place. According to Lefebvre, the use of space by people (social space) and the concepts of and depiction of space (representational space) are highly interrelated, producing one another.[10] The conduct of public executions on waste ground at city fringes and royal processions through the busiest shopping streets reinforced the symbolic roles of those respective spaces in the cityscape – and who belonged there. As we shall see, social and economic reality was far more complex but, in

[5] K. D. Lilley, *City and Cosmos: the Medieval World in Urban Form* (London, 2009), ch. 5; M. Wedell, 'Marginalität und Raumsemantik: Zur Einleitung', *Das Mittelalter: Perspektiven mediävistischer Forschung*, xvi (2011), 8–16, at pp. 11–12.

[6] C. Rawcliffe, *Urban Bodies: Communal Health in Late Medieval English Towns and Cities* (Woodbridge, 2013), pp. 27, 111–12, 199; Lilley, *City and Cosmos*, pp. 152–7.

[7] Rappaport, *Worlds within Worlds*, p. 213; J. R. Kellett, 'The breakdown of gild and corporation control over the handicraft and retail trade in London', *Economic History Review*, x (1958), 381–94. at pp. 381–3.

[8] F. Rexroth, 'Grenzen der Stadt, Grenzen der Moral: der urbane Raum im Imaginarium einer vormodernen Stadtgesellschaft', in *Die Stadt und ihr Rand*, ed. P. Johannek (Cologne, 2008), pp. 147–65.

[9] S. J. Minson, 'Political Culture and Urban Space in Early Tudor London' (unpublished Oxford University DPhil thesis, 2013); B. A. Hanawalt, *Ceremony and Civility: Civic Culture in Late Medieval London* (Oxford and New York, 2017), pp. 5–6, 19–21.

[10] H. Lefebvre, *The Production of Space* (Oxford, 1991), p. 116.

terms of symbolic uses of space by urban elites, the centre–periphery divide reinforced an urban moral topography privileging certain town-dwellers over others.[11]

Within urban society, the boundary between the centre and the margins is far more complex to establish. The concept of social marginality has been debated and nuanced by generations of historians. Bronisław Geremek's *The Margins of Society in Late Medieval Paris*, originally published in 1976, defined the social margins of the city in two ways: those who were socially excluded due to the unpalatability of their activities and those who engaged in criminal activity.[12] He thus relied on legal records as a means to identify marginal individuals and study their lives. Similarly, Frank Rexroth's work on deviance in London worked within the parameters set by the civic government itself.[13] While Geremek's work has been very influential, his conception of marginality has come in for some criticism. One problem with identifying marginality on the basis of court records is that socially marginal categories and identities 'invariably pre-exist those that inhabit them'.[14] A good example is that classic marginal figure, the prostitute. In England, there were few places with formally sanctioned brothels, and women in all kinds of extramarital sexual relationships were indicted in court records as 'whores' (*meretrices* in the Latin of the court records).[15] The identity of a prostitute was one which courts ascribed to all kinds of women with different lives, the accusation 'whore' being an interpretation of their behaviour rather than necessarily a profession. Practices of exclusion by authorities could be influenced by stereotypes drawn from literature, which, for example, drew connections between begging and bawdry.[16] A criminal or legal definition of marginal groups can only be part of the story: how people came to be marginalized was down to the interpretation within local communities of the laws made by mayors and magistrates.

[11] Lilley, *City and Cosmos*, pp. 144–5.

[12] B. Geremek, *The Margins of Society in Late Medieval Paris* (Cambridge, 1987), pp. 7–8.

[13] F. Rexroth, *Deviance and Power in Late Medieval London*, Past and Present Publications (Cambridge, 2007).

[14] D. Duncan, 'Margins and minorities: contemporary concerns?', in *At the Margins: Minority Groups in Premodern Italy*, ed. S. J. Milner (Minneapolis, 2005), pp. 21–35, at p. 30.

[15] R. M. Karras, *Common Women: Prostitution and Sexuality in Medieval England* (Oxford, 1998), p. 27; P. J. P. Goldberg, 'Pigs and prostitutes: streetwalking in comparative perspective', in *Young Medieval Women*, ed. K. J. Lewis, N. Menuge and K. M. Philips (Stroud, 1999), pp. 172–93, at pp. 178–9.

[16] K. Simon-Muscheid, 'Randgruppen, Bürgerschaft und Obrigkeit: der basler Kohlenburg, 14.–16. Jahrhundert', in *Spannungen und Widersprechen: Gedenkschrift für František Graus*, ed. S. Burghartz (Sigmaringen, 1992), pp. 203–25, at p. 208.

If legal categories need to be set in a broader social context, then another approach is to relate marginality to the organizing structures of the pre-modern city. Much twentieth-century scholarship of pre-modern cities, implicitly or explicitly, centred Marxist structuralist models to describe urban society. Urban historians worked within a paradigm where towns were organized through institutional structures, particularly guilds, overseen from the top by a wealthy governing class of merchants.[17] Institutional exclusion as a definition of marginality was implicit in Geremek's *Margins of Society*, in which he included study of casual labourers as marginal figures and excluded artisans on the basis that their guild membership drew them into mainstream society.[18] Guilds provided not just craft regulation and support for training but also political rights and important opportunities for socializing. In London from the early fourteenth century, citizenship was predicated on guild membership and so not belonging to a guild meant exclusion from the city's wider legal and economic privileges.[19] As social historians have increasingly adopted the concept of social capital from sociologists, guilds have been reinterpreted as institutions which assisted urban dwellers in the accrual of personal credit.[20] Pierre Bourdieu defined social capital as 'the aggregate of the actual and potential resources which are linked to … membership in a group', a framework which fits well with the benefits of guild membership.[21] As a result, guilds have retained their explanatory power even as urban historians have shifted away from Marxist structural models of the city, towards approaches influenced by network and actor–network theory.[22] Other institutional roles available in the city, such as religious fraternities, civic offices and parish governance, were often

[17] Examples which adopt this model for English cities include Rappaport, *Worlds within Worlds*, ch. 9; H. Swanson, *Medieval Artisans: an Urban Class in Late Medieval England* (Oxford and New York, 1989); S. H. Rigby and E. Ewan, 'Government, power and authority, 1300–1540', in *The Cambridge Urban History of Britain*, ed. D. M. Palliser (Cambridge, 2000), i, 291–312, doi:org/10.1017/CHOL9780521444613.014.

[18] Geremek, *The Margins of Society in Late Medieval Paris*, pp. 2–3.

[19] C. M. Barron, *London in the Later Middle Ages: Government and People, 1200–1500* (Oxford, 2004), pp. 204–6.

[20] G. Rosser, *The Art of Solidarity in the Middle Ages: Guilds in England 1250–1550* (Oxford and New York, 2015); S. Ogilvie, *Institutions and European Trade: Merchant Guilds, 1000–1800* (Cambridge, 2011), pp. 6–13.

[21] P. Bourdieu, 'The forms of capital', in *The Sociology of Economic Life*, ed. M. Granovetter and R. Swedberg, 3rd edn (Boulder, Colo., 2011), pp. 78–92, at p. 84.

[22] B. D. Munck, 'Re assembling actor–network theory and urban history', *Urban History*, xliv (2017), 111–22, doi:org/10.1017/S0963926816000298; J. Colson and A. van Steensel, 'Introduction', in *Cities and Solidarities: Urban Communities in Pre-Modern Europe* (London and New York, 2017), pp. 1–24.

occupied by guild members, and these overlaps created networks of personal connections through which individuals might accrue both enhanced personal reputation and business opportunities.[23] All these groups were dominated politically by men, even where women were able to participate, and the interchange of social capital from one context to another was highly gendered, anchored in an understanding of good governance (of money, a household or a community) as part of ideal masculinity.[24] These overlaps mean that urban historians, often influenced by the work of sociologist Barry Wellman, have adopted the concept of the network as a means to account for the role of institutions in urban prosperity.[25] This has become far more prevalent in the last two decades as Social Network Analysis (SNA) software has become more accessible, enabling historians to visualize and quantify those networks.[26] It is thus tempting to define marginality in terms of those excluded from the institutional networks which formed the core of urban life.

However, an institutional definition of marginality can only go so far in accounting for the lived experience of urban life, especially in medieval London. Around three quarters of adult men living in fifteenth-century London were not citizens, making institutional inclusion the exception

[23] C. Berry, '"To avoide all envye, malys, grudge and displeasure": sociability and social networking at the London Wardmote Inquest, *c.*1470–1540', *London Journal*, xlii (2017), 201–17, doi:org/10.1080/03058034.2017.1378058; C. M. Barron, 'The parish fraternities of medieval London', in *The Church in Pre-Reformation Society: Essays in Honour of F. R. H. Du Boulay*, ed. C. Harper-Bill and C. M. Barron (Woodbridge, 1985), pp. 13–37; R. Goddard, 'Medieval business networks: St Mary's Guild and the borough court in later medieval Nottingham', *Urban History*, xl (2013), 3–27, doi:org/10.1017/S0963926812000600.

[24] S. McSheffrey, 'Jurors, respectable masculinity and Christian morality: a comment on Marjorie McIntosh's "Controlling Misbehavior"', *Journal of British Studies*, xxxvii (1998), 269–78; S. McSheffrey, 'Man and masculinity in late medieval London civic culture: governance, patriarchy and reputation', in *Conflicted Identities and Multiple Masculinities: Men in the Medieval West*, ed. J. Murray (New York, 1999), pp. 243–78.

[25] P. Craven and B. Wellman, 'The network city', *Sociological Inquiry*, xliii (1973), 57–88, doi:org/10.1111/j.1475-682X.1973.tb00003.x; on the history of historians' adoption of networks as a concept see J. Innes, '"Networks" in British History', *East Asian Journal of British History*, v (2016), 51–72; M. Düring and U. Eumann, 'Historische Netzwerkforschung: ein neuer Ansatz in den Geschichtswissenschaften', *Geschichte und Gesellschaft*, xxxix (2013), 369–90.

[26] For examples of institutional network analysis see J. Colson, 'Local communities in fifteenth century London: craft, parish and neighbourhood' (unpublished Royal Holloway, University of London PhD thesis, 2011); M. Burkhardt, 'Networks as social structures in late medieval and early modern towns: a theoretical approach to historical network analysis', in *Commercial Networks and European Cities, 1400–1800*, ed. A. Caracausi and C. Jeggle (London, 2014), pp. 13–43.

rather than the rule.[27] The primary route to guild membership (and thus citizenship) was apprenticeship, but dropout rates for apprentices were very high, with more than half not completing their training.[28] For many, the benefits of joining guilds seem not to have justified tolerating a long period in unpaid service. It was perfectly possible to get by in the city without any formal role in its central institutions. Many, both householders and servants, worked in an institutional grey area as tolerated unenfranchised or semi-incorporated labour on the fringes of guilds.[29] Yet others would have been like the 'unsettled' poor discussed by Patricia Fumerton who came to the city as casual labourers in droves in the later sixteenth and seventeenth centuries with no foothold at all in institutions.[30] Institutional marginality thus covered people of very different statuses, modes of employment and wealth. On the other hand, the idea of the institution as a network should not obscure the very real power differentials that existed even among 'insiders': guild members themselves were divided between livery and yeomanry, with differing levels of influence, even if ostensibly connected by joint membership. Status and wealth mattered in medieval society and all people did not have equal access to networks, nor could being part of a network alone guarantee social inclusion in all contexts.

As a case in point, a focus on institutional membership and non-membership as definitions of inclusion and marginality is highly problematic with regards to the position of half the urban population – women. Women were very active in the economy, either on the fringes of institutional structures or in informal settings: some learned and practised trades and many more were engaged in retail. The idea that there was a 'golden age' of economic opportunity for women in towns in the late fourteenth and early fifteenth century, which was proposed principally by Jeremy Goldberg

[27] C. M. Barron, 'London 1300–1540', in *The Cambridge Urban History of Britain, 600–1540*, ed. D. M. Palliser (Cambridge, 2000), i, 395–440, at p. 400.

[28] C. Minns and P. Wallis, 'Rules and reality: quantifying the practice of apprenticeship in early modern England', *Economic History Review*, lxv (2012), 556–79, doi:org/10.1111/j.1468-0289.2010.00591.x; S. R. Hovland, 'Apprenticeship in later medieval London (*c*.1300–*c*.1530)' (unpublished Royal Holloway, University of London PhD thesis, 2006), pp. 233–6.

[29] M. Davies, 'Citizens and "foreyns": crafts, guilds and regulation in late medieval London', in *Between Regulation and Freedom: Work and Manufactures in European Cities, 14th–18th Centuries*, ed. A. Caracausi, L. Mocarelli and M. Davies (Newcastle upon Tyne, 2018), pp. 1–21; C. Berry, 'Guilds, immigration and immigrant economic organization: alien goldsmiths in London, 1480–1540', *Journal of British Studies*, lx (2021), 534–62.

[30] P. Fumerton, *Unsettled: the Culture of Mobility and the Working Poor in Early Modern England* (Chicago, Ill., 2006), ch. 2.

and Caroline Barron, has been treated with scepticism in recent literature.[31] More recent work emphasizes that formal barriers to inclusion held firm: few women became citizens, and in London only widows of freemen were technically allowed to continue their husbands' occupations, so women were on most counts institutionally marginalized despite their evident engagement in the economy more broadly.[32] Similarly, women socialized in ways which sometimes intersected with masculine networks and social capital, particularly in their role within the parish, but often did not.[33] To focus solely on marginality based on exclusion from citizenship and governance would be to ignore the more complicated experience of the vast majority of the city's population, who had to secure their place in the city through other means. There were also those who lived in the city who did not need citizenship to get by or advance in their careers, particularly the clergy, who would have been very numerous, but also smaller groups such as members of the gentry and aristocracy. Some were simply ineligible for full citizenship, such as the 6–10 per cent of Londoners who had immigrated from outside the kingdom of England.[34] Simply put, the circumstances of those marginalized from the city's institutional networks were diverse, with wildly different levels of social capital.

In the face of these many exceptions, what is needed, as Barbara Hanawalt suggests, is a conception of marginality as a multifaceted and flexible category.[35] The concept has been very much nuanced by the scholarship of the last two decades. The work of Simona Cerutti has been very important

[31] P. J. P. Goldberg, *Women, Work and Life Cycle in a Medieval Economy: Women in York and Yorkshire c.1300–1520* (Oxford and New York, 1992); C. M. Barron, 'The "golden age" of women in medieval London', *Reading Medieval Studies*, xv, 35–58.

[32] B. A. Hanawalt, *The Wealth of Wives: Women, Law and Economy in Late Medieval London* (Oxford, 2007), chs. 8 and 9; S. R. Rees Jones, 'Women and citizenship in later medieval York: a case study', in *The Routledge History Handbook of Gender and the Urban Experience*, ed. D. Simonton (Abingdon, Oxon and New York, 2017), p. 169.

[33] K. L. French, 'Women in the late medieval English parish', in *Gendering the Master Narrative: Women and Power in the Middle Ages*, ed. M.C. Erler and M. Kowaleski (Ithaca, NY, 2003), pp. 156–73; T. Reinke-Williams, *Women, Work and Sociability in Early Modern London* (Basingstoke, Hampshire and New York, 2014), pp. 127–9.

[34] J. L. Bolton, 'The alien population of London in the fifteenth century: a reappraisal', in *The Alien Communities of London in the Fifteenth Century: the Subsidy Rolls of 1440 and 1483–4* (Stamford, 1998), pp. 1–40; J. Lutkin, 'Settled or fleeting?: London's medieval immigrant community revisited', in *Medieval Merchants and Money: Essays in Honour of James L. Bolton*, ed. M. Allen and M. Davies (2016), pp. 137–56, at pp. 150–51.

[35] B. A. Hanawalt, 'Introduction', in *Living Dangerously: On the Margins in Medieval and Early Modern Europe*, ed. B. A. Hanawalt and A. A. Grotans (Notre Dame, Ind., 2005), pp. 1–7, at p. 1.

in francophone early modern urban history, emphasizing as she does the difference between an essentialist view of marginality rooted in personal characteristics and the condition of exteriority which was produced by the structures of *ancien régime* society.[36] Recently, scholarship in history and geography has acknowledged that individuals with no formal rights in the city were nonetheless able to instrumentalize knowledge of urban space to make, in the words of Eleonora Canepari and Elisabetta Rosa, a 'quiet claim to citizenship'.[37] The work of Erik Spindler, who focused on marginality in late fourteenth and early fifteenth-century London and Bruges, provides a useful framework for reimagining marginality.[38] He foregrounded the importance of networks and connections in achieving inclusion but also the pervasive instability of medieval life. Thus, a visiting merchant might have wealth and influential friends at home but through misfortune might find himself imprisoned and friendless in London. On the reverse of the coin, Spindler also rejected the notion that those in supposed marginal groups had a permanent marginalized status. For those who resorted to prostitution 'marginality was not an inevitable result of involvement in the sex industry'[39]: women might do so as a way to avoid worse outcomes, or combine sex work with other kinds of occupation and be fined rather than forced out of business. 'Marginality … is most usefully defined as a situation of simultaneous jeopardy and instability,' according to Spindler.[40] Institutional networks and accrued social capital were important buffers against the effects of instability, while undesirable occupations and criminal activity clearly left individuals vulnerable to prosecution and chastisement by their neighbours. However, there were other kinds of network – kinship and friendship not dependent on institutional contexts – which could also

[36] S. Cerutti, *Étrangers: Étude d'une condition d'incertitude dans une société d'Ancien Régime* (Montrouge, 2012). Cerutti's work and its influence were brought to my attention late in the writing of this book and, owing to the COVID-19 pandemic, it has not been possible for me to read this important study.

[37] E. Canepari and E. Rosa, 'A quiet claim to citizenship: mobility, urban spaces and city practices over time', *Citizenship Studies*, xxi (2017), 657–74, doi:org/10.1080/13621025.2017.1341654; A. Roy, 'Slumdog cities: rethinking subaltern urbanism', *International Journal of Urban and Regional Research*, xxxv (2011), 223–38, doi:org/10.1111/j.1468-2427.2011.01051.x.

[38] E. Spindler, 'Marginality and social relations in London and the Bruges area, 1370–1440' (unpublished University of Oxford DPhil thesis, 2008); E. Spindler, 'Were medieval prostitutes marginals? Evidence from Sluis, 1387–1440', *Revue Belge de philologie et d'histoire*, lxxxvii (2009), 239–72, doi:org/10.3406/rbph.2009.7673; E. Spindler, 'Between sea and city: portable communities in late medieval London and Bruges', in *London and Beyond: Essays in Honour of Derek Keene*, ed. M. P. Davies, J. A. Galloway and D. Keene (London, 2012), pp. 181–200.

[39] Spindler, 'Were medieval prostitutes marginals?', p. 269.

[40] Spindler, 'Were medieval prostitutes marginals?', p. 241.

act as support structures. As Derek Duncan argued, historians of the 'fringes' of society ought to be alert to 'the shifting parameters within which power operates and the provisional contingency of identity in a given situation'.[41] This is just as true of spaces as it is of individuals and groups. Just as a drop in fortunes could turn a respected craftsman into a seeker of alms, so an economic decline might turn busy urban streets into overgrown lanes.[42] To be marginal and marginalized meant to suffer a hardship which could not be mitigated by one's existing social resources.

Suburbs and extramural spaces

Marginality is an explicitly spatial term, and one of the central issues of this book is whether, as influential urban historian Derek Keene thought, the fringes of a city were dominated by socially marginal people. This was something Keene felt applied widely across Europe[43] as well as within medieval England, of which he said that

> In the larger towns the fringes were perhaps too remote from markets and hiring places for all but the unemployed, the disabled, and those carters, drovers, gardeners and tanners whose trade suited a suburban environment.[44]

However, as with understandings of the social fringe, historians have done much since to nuance the meaning and understanding of suburbs and peripheral urban spaces. Urban history has experienced a marked spatialization in which 'places previously accorded a bricks-and-mortar inertness are viewed as alive with generative capacity'.[45] Increased application of Geographic Information System (GIS) mapping to historical sources and digital humanities approaches more generally has opened up the possibilities for closer attention to the texture of urban space and easier analysis of spatial

[41] Duncan, 'Margins and minorities: contemporary concerns?', p. 31.

[42] See e.g. the dramatic effect of the removal of the royal courts on Winchester's townscape. D. Keene, 'The medieval urban environment in written records', *Archives*, xvi (1983), 137–44, at pp. 138–9.

[43] D. Keene, 'Introduction: segregation, zoning and assimilation in medieval towns', in *Segregation – Integration – Assimilation: Religious and Ethnic Groups in the Medieval Towns of Central and Eastern Europe*, ed. D. Keene, B. Nagy and K. Szende (Farnham, Surrey, 2009), pp. 1–14, at pp. 9–10.

[44] D. Keene, 'The medieval urban landscape, ad 900–1540', in *The English Urban Landscape* (Oxford, 2000), p. 93.

[45] P. Arnade, M. Howell and W. Simons, 'Fertile spaces: the productivity of urban space in Northern Europe', *Journal of Interdisciplinary History*, xxxii (2002), 515–48, at p. 526.

aspects of the urban economy such as property prices and craft clustering.[46] In turn, as Colin Arnaud has argued, sociability and the strength of interaction with neighbours could be sharply contrasting from area to area of the same city.[47] Influenced particularly by Lefebvre and others, a conceptually nuanced approach to the urban fringe has emerged among historians of pre-modern cities.[48] As Lefebvre wrote, 'visible boundaries such as walls or enclosures in general give rise for their part to an appearance of separation between spaces where in fact what exists is an ambiguous continuity'.[49] A re-examination of the role of suburbs for several European cities has located this 'ambiguous continuity' in the economic importance of the city's immediate hinterland and the mobility of people between urban areas.[50] In Bremen, the *vorstadt* performed many essential urban functions, including housing craftsmen and their workshops, labourers and farmers producing for the city market.[51] In seventeenth-century Rome, the fringes of the city were distinctive for the mobility of their population and for their semi-rural economy based in viticulture, in which people from the city centre were often non-resident property owners and investors.[52] Nuancing the picture even further, Boris Bove argued in his work on medieval Paris that using measures such as population density and types of occupation practised, places within the city's walls could also be peripheral.[53] Greater understanding of the essential functions of peripheral spaces led Moritz Wedell, reviewing the literature on German cities, to argue that the connection between social and spatial

[46] C. Casson and M. Casson, 'Property rents in medieval English towns: Hull in the fourteenth century', *Urban History*, xlvi (2019), 374–97; J. Colson, 'Commerce, clusters and community: a re-evaluation of the occupational geography of London, *c.*1400–*c.*1550', *Economic History Review*, lxix (2016), 104–30, doi:org/10.1111/ehr.12104.

[47] C. Arnaud, 'Mapping urban communities: a comparative topography of neighbourhoods in Bologna and Strasbourg in the late middle ages', in *Cities and Solidarities: Urban Communities in Pre-Modern Europe*, ed. J. Colson and A. van Steensel (London and New York, 2017), pp. 60–78, at p. 60.

[48] P. Clark and D. Menjot, *Subaltern City? Alternative and Peripheral Urban Spaces in the Pre-Modern Period.* (Turnhout, Belgium, 2019)

[49] Lefebvre, *The Production of Space*, p. 87.

[50] C. Arnaud, 'Mapping Urban Communities', pp. 64–6.

[51] T. Hill, 'Die Stadt und ihr Rand im Mittelalter: das Beispiel Bremen', in *Die Stadt und ihr Rand*, ed. P. Johannek (Cologne, 2008), pp. 167–90, at pp. 176–8.

[52] E. Canepari, 'An unsettled space: the suburban parish of San Giovanni in Laterano and its inhabitants (1630–1655)', *Quaderni Storici*, mmxvi (2016), 113–35, doi:org/10.1408/84143.

[53] B. Bove, 'Penser les périphéries: l'apport du concept d'urbain pour Paris au XIVe siècle', in Clark and Menjot, *Subaltern City? Alternative and Peripheral Spaces in the Pre-modern Period*, pp. 67–94.

marginality is primarily a semantic one rather than a reflection of the social reality of suburbs.[54]

The spatial turn has also had a significant impact on legal history and on understandings of how urban governance was spatialized. For geographers Ananya Roy and Nezar Al Sayyad, medieval cities were models of the spatialization of citizenship with many parallels to modern experience.[55] Cities were distinguished from surrounding territory by the privileges which attached to membership of their institutions, and within urban space there was a patchwork of different sovereignties, the contestation of which was a crucial part of the articulation of citizenship.[56] Historians have begun to see this multiplicity of jurisdictions and patchwork texture as an essential part of defining the pre-modern city.[57] For English cities, the recent work of Tom Johnson, Christian Liddy and Shannon McSheffrey highlights how these multiple jurisdictions worked alongside one another, often uneasily.[58] This is a point at which social marginality, or at least institutional marginality, intersected with urban space. The concept of sanctuary, expanded vastly in the fourteenth and fifteenth centuries, enabled immigrants ineligible for guild membership and citizenship to reside in and practise trades in the precincts of urban religious houses, often living alongside those escaping prosecution for debt or felonies.[59] More broadly, as Johnson observes, 'spatial order, enforced by law, was foundational to the way that late medieval townspeople imagined the legal community in which they lived'.[60]

The focus on plurality invites a reassessment of the role of suburbs, because they were places where matters of jurisdiction were particularly

[54] Wedell, 'Marginalität und Raumsemantik', pp. 12–14.

[55] N. Alsayyad and A. Roy, 'Medieval modernity: on citizenship and urbanism in a global era', *Space & Polity*, x (2006), 1–20.

[56] C. Liddy, *Contesting the City: the Politics of Citizenship in English Towns, 1250–1530* (Oxford and New York, 2017), pp. 53–7.

[57] P. Clark and D. Menjot, 'Introduction', in their *Subaltern City? Alternative and Peripheral Spaces in the Pre-Modern Period*, pp. 9–22.

[58] T. Johnson, *Law in Common: Legal Cultures in Late medieval England* (Oxford and New York, 2020); S. McSheffrey, 'Sanctuary and the legal topography of pre-Reformation London', *Law and History Review*, xxvii (2009), 483–514; S. McSheffrey, 'Liberties of London: social networks, sexual disorder and independent jurisdiction in the late medieval English metropolis', in *Crossing Borders: Boundaries and Margins in Medieval and Early Modern Britain*, ed. K. J. Kesselring and S. Butler (Leiden, 2018), pp. 216–36; C. Liddy, *Contesting the City*, ch. 3.

[59] S. McSheffrey, *Seeking Sanctuary: Crime, Mercy and Politics in English Courts, 1400–1550* (Oxford and New York, 2017).

[60] Johnson, *Law in Common*, p. 57.

pressing. European cities varied considerably in the extent and nature of the jurisdiction they held outside their walls.[61] Outside London's wall was a zone extending as far as the city 'bars', wooden barriers across the road, at most a few hundred metres from the gates, which nominally marked the end of the civic government's jurisdiction. However, the area was dotted with the precincts of religious houses and open ground. In some parts, residents of this extramural zone belonged to parishes which extended out of the city's jurisdiction and into the surrounding county of Middlesex, meaning they were simultaneously residents of the city and neighbours of those not bound by its governance. Throughout this book, I prefer the term 'extramural' to 'suburban' and 'extramural neighbourhoods' to 'suburbs'. The simple reason for this is that London had two well-defined suburban settlements, Southwark to the south of the river and Westminster, along the Thames to the west, which had clear jurisdictional independence from the city. Both had their own focuses of development while benefiting economically from their proximity to the city. These have been the subject of extensive study by Gervase Rosser, Martha Carlin and Katherine French and so will not be re-examined here.[62] In using the term 'extramural', my field of study is confined to the neighbourhoods which immediately surrounded the city walls. It is this area that forms the focus of this book, although such neighbourhoods were intimately connected to London's wider region, which will form a key part of discussion in Chapter Three.

Late medieval London

London was a city of some 50,000 souls in the fifteenth century. The population had been perhaps as high as 100,000 before the Black Death, but the city experienced terrible mortality in the plague of 1348–50 and smaller outbreaks which recurred into the fifteenth century.[63] Neighbourhoods outside the city's western and eastern walls were remodelled by plague as vast burial sites were hastily established. Soon after, religious houses were

[61] P. Clark, *European Cities and Towns: 400–2000*, repr. edn (Oxford and New York, 2009), pp. 78–80.

[62] G. Rosser, *Medieval Westminster: 1200–1540* (Oxford, 1989); M. Carlin, *Medieval Southwark* (London, 1996); K. L. French, 'Loving friends: surviving widowhood in late medieval Westminster', *Gender & History*, xxii (2010), 21–37, doi:org/10.1111/j.1468-0424.2010.01576.x; K. L. French, 'Rebuilding St Margaret's: parish involvement and community action in late medieval Westminster', *Journal of Social History*, xlv (2011), 148–71, doi:org/10.1093/jsh/shr017.

[63] V. Harding, 'Families in later medieval London: sex, marriage and mortality', in *Medieval Londoners: Essays to Mark the Eightieth Birthday of Caroline M. Barron*, ed. E. A. New and C. Steer (London, 2019), pp. 11–36, at p. 13.

built alongside them to pray for the city's dead, adding to London's already numerous hospitals, friaries and priories.[64] The spiritual welfare of city inhabitants was also attended to by over a hundred parish churches. By 1548, when totals of communicants were collated for Edward VI's chantry commissioners, the city's parishes were estimated to vary greatly in size, from 98 to 3,400 people in receipt of communion.[65] For administrative purposes, from 1394 London was divided into twenty-five wards.[66] Each ward was governed by an alderman, elected from among the wealthiest citizens, and each year one alderman was elected as mayor. The mayor was the point of contact between city and crown, ranking equal to an earl during his term of office, and by the early sixteenth century was often knighted on his exit from the post. London was the principal city of the kingdom and provided much revenue to the king through taxation and loans, so the crown took a keen interest in city politics and would intervene in mayoral elections where it suited royal interests.[67] In return, the city had a range of privileges, including jurisdiction over a wide range of disputes normally heard in the royal courts and the annual election of the sheriff of London and Middlesex, the king's legal representative, with the power to try felonies.[68] In the fourteenth and fifteenth centuries, social distinctions in the civic hierarchy were becoming more marked, an experience common to many urban and rural communities in the period.[69] Only rarely were citizens from artisan guilds elevated to the aldermanry and the guilds themselves developed more hierarchical structures.[70] Although all guild members were citizens, power was increasingly reserved to the livery, a subset of the membership who were

[64] S. Pfizenmaier, *Charterhouse Square: Black Death Cemetery and Carthusian Monastery, Meat Market and Suburb* (London, 2016), pp. 20–25.

[65] These numbers in receipt of communion are highly estimated. For a discussion of their problematic relationship to population see the introduction to *London and Middlesex Chantry Certificates, 1548*, ed. C. J. Kitching (London, 1980), pp. 60–81. *British History Online* <http://www.british-history.ac.uk/london-record-soc/vol16/pp60-81> [accessed 23 June 2020].

[66] Previously there were twenty-four: in 1394 Farringdon was divided into separate intra- and extramural wards.

[67] Barron, *London in the Later Middle Ages*, ch. 1.

[68] P. Tucker, *Law Courts and Lawyers in the City of London, 1300–1550* (Cambridge, 2007).

[69] I. Forrest, *Trustworthy Men: How Inequality and Faith Made the Medieval Church* (Princeton and Oxford, 2018); S. H. Rigby and E. Ewan, 'Government, power and authority, 1300–1540', i.

[70] D. Harry, *Constructing a Civic Community in Late Medieval London: the Common Profit, Charity and Commemoration* (Woodbridge, 2019), pp. 21–36.

usually older, wealthier and required nomination to join.[71] The majority of the membership began to be referred to as the yeomanry or the 'young men', notwithstanding that they might spend their whole career without achieving the livery. These institutional hierarchies developed in a situation of relative population stability. High mortality ensured that the population remained stable from around 1370 until the final quarter of the fifteenth century, when there are indications of recovery, and increased by around 40 per cent in the first half of the sixteenth century.[72] By 1550, London was home to about 70,000 people, a total which was to more than double before the turn of the seventeenth century.[73]

One of the main contentions of this book is that many of the patterns of expansion and coping mechanisms seen in the early modern city were established in the fifteenth century and developed in the early sixteenth. The extramural zone is a good place to look for such patterns, as it was to be these neighbourhoods which experienced the most radical transformation in the course of the early modern period as they accommodated the majority of the city's swelling population.[74] My period also coincides with that in which historians have argued that urban decline set in across many regions of England. This was one of the major debates in urban history in the late twentieth century, much influenced by Charles Phythian-Adams's work on Coventry.[75] A recent return to the issue by archaeologist Ben Jervis, incorporating insights from the spatial turn, argued that decline versus growth is an unhelpful dichotomy where we might more usefully focus on the ways in which towns and cities adapted to the new economic realities

[71] Barron, *London in the Later Middle Ages*, pp. 211–16.

[72] Harding, 'Families in later medieval London', p. 9.

[73] Harding, 'The population of London, 1550–1700: a review of the published evidence', *London Journal*, xv (1990), 111–28, doi:org/10.1179/ldn.1990.15.2.111.

[74] P. Baker and M. Merry, '"The poore lost a good frend and the parish a good neighbour": the lives of the poor and their supporters in London's eastern suburb, *c.*1583–*c.*1679', in *London and Beyond: Essays in Honour of Derek Keene*, ed. D. Keene, J. A. Galloway and M. Davies (London, 2012), pp. 155–80; Rappaport, *Worlds within Worlds*, p. 62; I. W. Archer, *The Pursuit of Stability: Social Relations in Elizabethan London*, Cambridge Studies in Early Modern British History (Cambridge, 1991), pp. 12–13.

[75] Phythian-Adams, *Desolation of a City*; A. Dyer, '"Urban decline" in England, 1377–1525', in *Towns in Decline, ad 100-1600*, ed. T. R. Slater (Aldershot, 2000), pp. 266–88; K. D. Lilley, 'Urban planning after the Black Death: townscape transformation in later medieval England (1350–1530)', *Urban History*, xlii (2014), 1–21, doi:org/10.1017/S0963926814000492; R. B. Dobson, 'Urban decline in late medieval England', *Transactions of the Royal Historical Society*, xxvii (1977), 1–22, doi:org/10.2307/3679185; For an overview of the debate up to the late 1980s see D. M. Palliser, 'Urban decay revisited', in *Towns and Townspeople in the Fifteenth Century*, ed. J. A. F. Thomson (Gloucester, 1988), pp. 1–21.

of the post-Black Death era.[76] This new economic situation certainly seems to have benefited London, and the city cemented its dominance of the country's urban hierarchy. From the late fourteenth century onwards international trade, particularly the lucrative export of wool, became more concentrated in the capital and its share of the burden of national taxation was greatly increased.[77] Despite this, the city's central Cheapside neighbourhood appears not to have experienced much investment in the fifteenth century,[78] a paradox which suggests the potential spatiality of the city's economic fortunes and the need to re-examine the periphery as potential alternative spaces of expansion. Explanations of London's early modern transition to one of the largest cities in Europe with relatively little social unrest have focused almost exclusively on the institutional structures of the government and guilds.[79] Steve Rappaport's *Worlds within Worlds*, published in 1989, argued that there was a massive expansion of access to citizenship in the 1530s which accounts for the way in which the city's economy was able to integrate huge numbers of new migrants in the later sixteenth century. In many ways this present book has been influenced by Rappaport's approach to the sixteenth century. However, this book explores how people navigated life in the city before citizenship became a majority status and emphasizes the importance of spatial difference in urban development. The city's development in the fifteenth century was foundational to the assumption of its early modern role as an engine of world trade, colonization and social mobility.

The spatial and social margins of the late medieval city have been relatively little explored, despite London having considerable surviving primary sources. Those sources were produced largely by the institutions which shaped city life, particularly the civic government and guilds, and to an extent those institutions have created the history of the medieval city in their own image. The wide-ranging work of Caroline Barron from the 1970s to date has meticulously elaborated the workings of the city's government and the lives of its mercantile elite, men and women, who held political

[76] B. Jervis, 'Decline or transformation? Archaeology and the late medieval "urban decline" in southern England', *Archaeological Journal*, clxxiv (2017), 211–43, doi:o rg/10.1080/00665983.2017.1229895.

[77] Barron, *London in the Later Middle Ages*, pp. 304–5.

[78] Palliser, 'Urban Decay Revisited', pp. 9–10; D. Keene, 'A new study of London before the Great Fire', *Urban History*, xi (1984), 11–21, at pp. 18–19.

[79] Archer, *The Pursuit of Stability*; Rappaport, *Worlds within Worlds*.

power.[80] As Barron observed in an article on London's 'small people', even artisans of modest means with citizenship left few archival traces, despite being a comparatively small elite in the wider population.[81] The lives of those even further down the social scale are largely lost to the historian's view. However, it is not impossible to explore their experiences; there have been excellent studies of individual non-citizen groups and the relationship between the unenfranchised and civic institutions.[82] What these have in common, however, is that they tend to focus on one group in isolation or on the civic government's approach to those groups rather than placing them in the wider context of experience of life outside the citizenry. Frank Rexroth's *Deviance and Power in Late Medieval London* considered marginality beyond a single group but nonetheless focused on the rhetorical construction of a criminal underworld by the city's ruling class as a bolster to their own power; he was ambivalent about whether such a connected underworld actually existed.[83] Historians have utilised the records of London's myriad courts to explore Londoners' lives beyond their guild halls, counting houses and civic government, particularly in terms of the regulation and experience of sex and marriage. Studies by Shannon McSheffrey and Martin Ingram have illuminated the legal instruments of punishment and how they intersected with civic culture.[84] This book reconsiders many of the same records and concepts, particularly in Chapters Four and Five, with the intention of looking from the other end of the telescope at what they can tell us about the lives of those who were marginalized and places which were considered, as Rexroth argued, outside the city's moral boundary.

Topographic histories of the city have tended to focus on its wealthiest parts. In the 1980s, Derek Keene and Vanessa Harding conducted a massive

[80] For a bibliography of Barron's works see *London and the Kingdom: Essays in Honour of Caroline M. Barron: Proceedings of the 2004 Harlaxton Symposium*, ed. M. P. Davies and A. Prescott (Donington, 2008).

[81] C. M. Barron, 'Searching for the "small people" of medieval London', *Local Historian*, xxxviii (2008), 83–94.

[82] On non-citizens and the guilds and government, see Hanawalt, *Ceremony and Civility*, ch. 6; Davies, 'Citizens and "foreyns"'. Good examples of studies of individual groups include R. A. Wood, 'Poor widows, c.1393–1415', in *Medieval London Widows, 1300–1500*, ed. C. M. Barron and A. F. Sutton (London and Rio Grande, Ohio, 1994), pp. 55–70; J. M. Bennett and C. Whittick, 'Philippa Russell and the wills of London's late medieval singlewomen', *London Journal*, xxxii (2007), 251–69; see also the extensive literature on London's alien population cited in Ch. Two.

[83] Rexroth, *Deviance and Power in Late Medieval London*, p. 305.

[84] M. Ingram, *Carnal Knowledge: Regulating Sex in England, 1470–1600* (Cambridge and New York, 2017); S. McSheffrey, *Marriage, Sex and Civic Culture in Late Medieval London* (Philadelphia, 2006).

survey of the wealthy Cheapside neighbourhood, mapping all its properties and documenting their histories up to the Great Fire of 1666.[85] A follow-up project on the extramural parish of St Botolph Aldgate was begun but never completed, the unpublished findings of which were consulted in the process of research for this book.[86] More recently, the innovative work of Justin Colson demonstrates that the Bridgehead neighbourhood was a social and economic hub for the city's fishmongers, who invested in its property as well as conducting their economic and social lives in the area.[87] The extramural area is, however, well represented in the work of archaeologists, largely due to excavations undertaken during the extensive redevelopment of the city since the 1990s. The sites of plague burial grounds, medieval hospitals and religious houses have been excavated, and many of the findings published by the Museum of London Archaeology Service and used by Nick Holder in his history of London's medieval friaries.[88] Chapter One draws on this scholarship to make important connections between urban development and the economic profile of extramural neighbourhoods.

Localities were more than collections of buildings; they were social spaces in which people worked, lived and died, all in close proximity to other Londoners. There were several potential city communities to which people could belong, with varying levels of spatiality: neighbourhood, parish, guild, citizenry. Community can be something of a fraught term, controversial among historians because of its sometimes implicit assumption of social harmony and inclusivity and association with the now outdated notion that the late medieval period was a paradise of neighbourliness destroyed by the Reformation.[89] Even the spiritual community of the parish, ostensibly a grouping of all Christian souls within particular geographic boundaries, was not all-embracing. As Clive Burgess has shown, formal participation through the roles of churchwarden and assistant was restricted to those

[85] *Historical Gazetteer of London before the Great Fire*, ed. D. J. Keene and V. Harding (Cambridge, 1987).

[86] M. Carlin, *St Botolph Aldgate Gazetteer* (London, 1987). The unpublished typescript is available at the Institute of Historical Research, London.

[87] Colson, 'Local communities in fifteenth-century London'; J. Colson, 'Reinterpreting space: mapping people and relationships in late medieval and early modern English cities using GIS', *Urban History*, 2020, 1–17, doi:org/10.1017/S0963926820000164.

[88] N. Holder, *The Friaries of Medieval London: From Foundation to Dissolution* (Woodbridge, 2017).

[89] M. Rubin, 'Small groups: identity and solidarity in the late middle ages', in *Enterprise and Individuals in Fifteenth-Century England*, ed. J. Kermode (Stroud, 1991), pp. 132–50; K. Wrightson, 'The "Decline of Neighbourliness" revisited', in *Local Identities in Late Medieval and Early Modern England*, ed. N. L. Jones and D. Woolf (London, 2007), pp. 19–49.

who were fairly wealthy and socially ambitious.[90] This sense of a restricted hierarchy has been somewhat tempered by Katherine French, who argues that there were multiple informal ways in which others could participate in the parish.[91] Nonetheless, even in a spiritual community, hierarchies still meant that the majority were excluded from decision-making, even if they could participate in wider ritual and celebratory aspects of the parish. This was a marked feature of English society in the period, as Ian Forrest has argued; after the Black Death, communities across the country developed hierarchies which were more rigid, in which a group of 'trustworthy men' held considerable sway. These men were usually wealthier than their neighbours, and their increasing prosperity allowed them to cement their local influence.[92] In towns this group might be called burgesses and they had a distinctive material culture to match their modestly elevated social position.[93] As we have already seen, hierarchies were a marked feature of other urban communities in the fifteenth century. When the terms 'community' and 'neighbourhood' are used in this book, then, these are not meant to imply groups of equals. Community was a stratified and contested thing in the medieval and early modern city and a Londoner might belong to multiple communities, some of which overlapped.[94] In Chapter Three and Chapter Five, I will discuss in more depth these multiple communities and the processes of social differentiation which went on within them, particularly as it served to marginalize certain individuals.

This book contends that by using a nuanced concept of marginality, in its social and spatial senses, the totality of urban life comes more sharply into focus. In a city where exclusion from citizenship was the norm for men and women alike, it is only by thinking with margins and marginality that we can make sense of how people got by and made their lives. Even for those who ended up as citizens, migration into the city was the majority experience. Almost everyone had to work to get from the outside in, but they did so

[90] C. Burgess, 'Shaping the parish: St Mary at Hill, London, in the fifteenth century', in *The Cloister and the World: Essays in Medieval History in Honour of Barbara Harvey*, ed. J. Blair and B. Golding (Oxford, 1996), pp. 246–85.

[91] French, 'Rebuilding St Margaret's'.

[92] Forrest, *Trustworthy Men*.

[93] F. Riddy, '"Burgeis" domesticity in late medieval England', in *Medieval Domesticity: Home, Housing and Household in Medieval England.*, ed. P. J. P. Goldberg and M. Kowaleski (Cambridge, 2008), pp. 14–36.

[94] Archer, *The Pursuit of Stability*, pp. 58–61; Rubin, 'Small groups: identity and solidarity in the late middle ages', pp. 133–6; B. A. Kümin, *The Shaping of a Community: the Rise and Reformation of the English Parish, c.1400–1560*, trans. D. Nicholson-Smith (Brookfield, 1996), p. 181.

from differing positions of privilege in terms of social connections, personal status, wealth and origin. Likewise, the complex and ambiguous status of the city's extramural neighbourhoods made them places where people could benefit from the urban economy and society while navigating difficulties around their own legal status and financial resources. This approach is a break from previous scholarship, which has usually (though, as we have seen, not always) followed the surviving sources in their concentration on citizens, guilds and the mechanisms of government. In order to realize this new conceptual approach, the book utilizes a mixture of qualitative and quantitative methodologies which extract the maximum information about topics on which the records are often silent or obtuse. This includes digital methodologies, such as mapping and social network analysis, which establish overarching spatial and social patterns. The elusive nature of the subject means I also on occasion extrapolate from the very individual circumstances of those who fortuitously wandered from the obscurity of the social margins into the written record of late medieval London, to imagine how a brief glimpse might fit with wider experience. I make no apology for being a methodological magpie because big conceptual questions about elusive subjects require answers from multiple angles.

Sources and approaches

The sources and methodologies employed will be discussed as they arise, so for the moment it will suffice to give a brief overview and establish some of the basic background to each, which may be useful to the reader. There are three core types of sources used in this book: wills, property records and legal records drawn from a variety of courts. These have been chosen for their capacity to illuminate details of the lives of Londoners on the city's social and spatial margins.

The following two chapters make extensive use of testamentary evidence. Enrolments of last wills and testaments survive plentifully from some, but sadly not all, of the church courts which covered the city. Technically, the term 'will' referred to the testator's written disposal of their movable goods and 'testament' to their property but, in practice, documents combined these functions. Testamentary records discussed in this book are drawn from two of the higher ecclesiastical courts which handled probate administration in the period, the bishop of London's commissary court and the archbishop of Canterbury's prerogative court. The prerogative court of Canterbury handled wills from estates with property in more than one diocese, or with wealth above £10. The commissary court handled wills for many London parishes, while others were proved in the archdeacon's court or, for larger estates, the bishop of London's consistory court. The archdeaconry and consistory records survive only patchily for the fifteenth century and have therefore not been used here. Wills were presented in one of these courts by the executors of the deceased, who paid a fee and were formally given dispensation to carry out the wishes of the testator. Any disputes over how the estate was handled were heard in the same courts. Wills are limited sources for social history as they naturally reflect a group with goods and property to bequeath and are certainly not complete records of individual estates. Nonetheless, their depth of description about the occupation and status of testators and the fact that they often give clues to not just the parish someone was living in when they died but also the places they had lived through their life make wills highly relevant to several key topics of this book: patterns of wealth, poverty, mobility and the extramural economy.

Also plentiful but rather more scattered are the records of property in the city, which play a significant role in Chapter One. London property was a lucrative income source for many institutions and private individuals, then as now. Urban property in cities and towns across England was divided into plots known as tenements. The arrangement of a tenement might vary hugely, however, and a single tenement might contain multiple houses or other structures.[95] Records of the buying and selling of tenements survive from the twelfth century onwards and rentals showing residents and tenants survive periodically in the archives of institutions.[96] Records of property transactions in fifteenth-century London fall into three main categories: deeds, leases and rentals or accounts.[97] The first two give information about a property at a particular point of time, in the case of deeds when a tenement changed ownership and of a lease when a new tenant agreed to pay what was known as 'firm' rent for the property for a specified length of time. Rentals and accounts of estate management record a quarterly or annual view of the income and tenants of a property owner's tenements, vacancies and any repairs made. Structures of property ownership were highly complex, with property owners usually being non-resident and often themselves owing annual duties called quit rents to institutions and

95 J. Schofield, *Medieval London Houses* (New Haven, Conn., and London, 1995).

96 'Introduction', in *A Survey of Documentary Sources for Property Holding in London before the Great Fire*, ed. Derek Keene and Vanessa Harding (London, 1985), pp. xi–xv. *British History Online* <http://www.british-history.ac.uk/london-record-soc/vol22/xi-xv> [accessed 25 June 2020].

97 Other kinds of record which are less common within the period include the valor, an overview of an institution's estate, and the ground plan, which was usually drawn up to support a lease or deed and of which only a few surviving examples are known for London before the later sixteenth century. See J. H. Harvey, 'Four 15th-century London plans', *London Topographical Record*, xx (1952), 1–8.

individuals.[98] Moreover, sub-letting of all or parts of a property by tenants was widespread, which makes it hard to be certain that even a named tenant in a lease or rental was actually resident. Many people, especially those who were poor, probably held tenancies at will rather than drawing up a formal lease with their landlord and had few formal rights in their property.[99] All of these complications are a caveat to the certainty of reconstructing society from records of property. Nonetheless, leases and rentals are the closest we can get to understanding the homes and workplaces of extramural residents, so these form the focus of my analysis.

Chapters Three, Four and Five mainly make use of legal records. Those used are drawn from two very different kinds of court: the civic courts, particularly the city's wardmotes, and the ecclesiastical courts, with supplementary material from manor courts which had jurisdiction over liberties. These courts operated in different legal systems, although with many overlaps in subject matter and status of those appearing as witnesses or jurors.[100] Manor courts worked in the English common law tradition, relying on the appointment of local juries. Ecclesiastical courts adhered to canon law, a very different legal tradition with its roots in Roman law. City courts worked on a mixture of civic custom and common law.[101] Wardmotes, while a civic tradition, shared much in common with manor courts in being essentially local, overseen by one external authority figure (an alderman in London and a lord elsewhere) and with business presented by juries who reported offences carried out by their neighbours.[102] Ecclesiastical courts were staffed by trained canon lawyers and presided over by members of the clergy, who judged the outcomes of cases.[103] Their remit included matters pertaining to the welfare of the soul, but in many areas these overlapped with the interests of common law and civic courts, particularly debt and sexual indiscretions. These were by no means all the courts that operated in late medieval London, but they are the ones which give us some of the most detailed information about how people got along with their neighbours,

[98] D. Keene, 'Landlords, the property market and urban development in medieval England', in *Power, Profit and Urban Land: Landownership in Medieval and Early Modern Northern European Towns*, ed. F.-E. Eliassen and G. A. Ersland (Aldershot, Surrey, 1996), pp. 93–109; Colson, 'Reinterpreting space'.

[99] S. Rees Jones, *York: the Making of a City 1068–1350* (Oxford and New York, 2013), pp. 272–3.

[100] Johnson, *Law in Common*, ch. 6.

[101] Tucker, *Law Courts and Lawyers*, pp. 31–3.

[102] M. K. McIntosh, *Controlling Misbehavior in England, 1370–1600* (Cambridge, 1998).

[103] Ingram, *Carnal Knowledge*, pp. 79–82.

conducted their lives and the quotidian business of keeping order. They thus shed light on issues around social marginality which are central to this book.

In order to make the most of the available sources, I have taken a range of approaches in my analysis. Quantification of information from sources is useful to give a broad overview of the character of neighbourhoods. Admittedly, this is not without its problems, since many of the record sets are incomplete, shaped by both chance loss of documents during the past half millennium and the choices of contemporaries about what was worthy of preservation. However, particularly in the case of wills, the volume of survivals is consistent enough that the approach is justified and indeed necessary to discern patterns of difference around the city and of change over time. I have endeavoured throughout to make this book transparent about the number of records used in quantification and, where a sample is small, to use multiple kinds of evidence to test and reinforce the arguments I make. The process of quantification was greatly aided by building databases for each set of records, which in turn enabled the application of digital methodologies in the analysis. In Chapters Three and Four, social network analysis and GIS have been applied and are key to the arguments surrounding extramural sociability and mobility. The ability to make connections between records over time and thus to pull together scattered information about individuals makes databases particularly useful to a study focused on the social margins, where prosopography is all the more difficult to undertake. While some chapters rely more heavily on quantification to give an overview of social and economic conditions, this is a book which tries to get to the heart of lived experience. Throughout, therefore, I have tried to balance these general views with the individual and particular, nowhere more so than in Chapters Three to Five, which mainly draw on witness statements given in the bishop of London's consistory court. Writing a history of the social and spatial margins of the city requires this balance of approaches, if the inherent institutional perspective of each set of records is to be overcome.

Preview

This book focuses on three extramural neighbourhoods and two parishes which were just inside the walls of the city. The three beyond the walls all had parish churches dedicated to the same saint: St Botolph Aldgate, St Botolph Bishopsgate and St Botolph Aldersgate. These lay, respectively, outside the east, north-east and north-west of the city and are marked on Figure 0.1. Chapters One and Two also include evidence from parishes within the walls: All Hallows on the Wall, St Katharine Cree and St Lawrence Jewry.

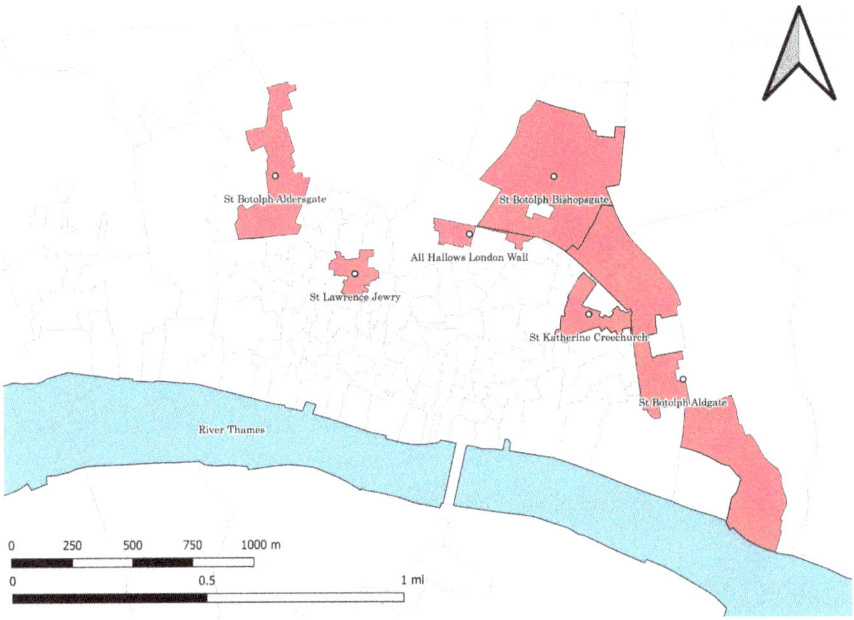

Figure 0.1 Parishes of the City of London, *c.*1520. The primary parishes discussed in this book are highlighted.

Figure 0.2 Sheet from the 'Agas' map of London showing the north-east of the city, including Bishopsgate Street and Aldgate Street, *c.*1561. Published *c.*1633. Image © London Metropolitan Archives (City of London).

All Hallows was a small parish containing no major thoroughfares in the city's north-eastern corner while St Katharine lay just inside Aldgate, along a busy street leading to the city centre. St Lawrence Jewry was at the heart of the city, near the Guildhall and the mercantile Cheapside district and is discussed in this book mainly as a point of comparison to the other parishes. Spatial marginality was by no means confined to the city's extramural area, many of the features which made these places marginal being shared by neighbourhoods just inside the city walls.

In Chapter One, these parishes and the areas adjoining them are the focus of an exploration of the economic, topographic and social characteristics of marginal neighbourhoods. The chapter addresses whether such areas were always poorer than the city centre and the levels of citizenship and occupations of their residents. It argues that the picture is far more complex than has been hitherto acknowledged, with each neighbourhood having a different social character and none being homogeneously poor. This chapter also argues the importance of religious houses in the development of the extramural area, which had an impact on the form of the city's early modern expansion. Chapter Two goes on to discuss in depth the social and spatial networks shaping the lives of those living on the urban periphery, questioning how marginal their lives were to the structures of the city. Focused on an innovative social network analysis of wills made by residents of the same parishes, it establishes the influence of institutional and other connections in shaping sociability, drawing residents into the wider city but also tying them to London's region. Chapter Three looks at this theme of connections in the context of a much broader social spectrum, focusing on the nature and experience of mobility on the fringes of the city. In doing so, it provides an important augmentation to previous scholarship, which has focused on apprentice migration, arguing instead that mobility was a near-universal experience. Drawing on evidence from a wider range of neighbourhoods, it establishes the central role of mobility outside the city walls and its effects on the lives and reputations of the poor, for whom it was a necessity which left them vulnerable to marginalization. Chapter Four establishes further how neighbourhoods policed themselves and determined who was to be socially excluded. The chapter concerns the role of the wardmote and ecclesiastical courts but sets these alongside the informal authority exercised by some prosperous Londoners which both underlay and derived from them. These systems overlapped as part of the constant negotiation of the centre and the periphery of the local community. Chapter Five looks at these processes from the other side, exploring the ways in which people who found themselves on the end of communal judgement could rebuild their reputations or mitigate the effects of punishment. Central to this process, as the chapter argues, was the careful use of space to manage the spread of gossip, and the extramural neighbourhoods provided multiple opportunities for doing so. The book thus progresses from a close focus on the extramural neighbourhoods to a broader view of social networks and marginality and how they intersected with urban space.

1. Landscape and economy

A walk through fifteenth-century London, from its centre to its very fringes, would have taken less than half an hour. If our traveller began her journey at London's heart, the conduit in Poultry where three major city streets converged, she would have found herself amid the cries of a busy market and the bustle of incessant cart traffic. Travelling north-east, she would have followed many of these carts and their horses clattering towards one of the city's gates, dodging under low-hanging roof corners and weaving between the huckster women who carried bread and ale door to door. As she approached Bishopsgate, the pace of traffic would have slowed as the road narrowed between the ancient city walls. Past the gate, much would have seemed similar to the city within the walls. She would have seen a parish church immediately to her left and a mix of large and small houses lining the street, some with alleyways running between them, the sounds and smells of craftsmen working in their shops emerging from them. But our traveller could not have failed to have noticed that this was a different kind of neighbourhood. For one thing, the smell of discarded waste in the city ditch would have hit her as soon as she passed through the gate. Visible behind the churchyard and beyond the houses lay the open spaces of marshy Moorfields to the west and pastures to the east. There were two large, walled hospital complexes a hundred or so metres apart on either side of the road. If she had kept walking, she would have seen the houses becoming more widely spaced. Carts would have trundled along the ancient route, taking their loads to and from places in the countryside many miles away. She would have made her way beyond the bars marking the end of the city's legal boundary and through the village of Shoreditch before completely open countryside dominated her view.

This chapter will unpick what it was that marked out Bishopsgate and other extramural neighbourhoods as distinctive places in the cityscape in geographic and economic terms and sketch out the structures which shaped local society. As they were on the periphery of the city, natural features played a part in shaping the character and contours of these neighbourhoods. Much of the economic activity which provided the most lucrative aspects of the urban economy, such as markets and wharves, were sited elsewhere. However, it would be a mistake to assume that the extramural neighbourhoods were uniformly poor places. Their society was economically stratified and their marginal location provided opportunities for economic activity difficult to carry out within the more cramped city centre. These were important factors in the development of London as a whole, particularly the transition from the late medieval to the early modern city. The city's northern and eastern peripheries were to become extremely populous and challenged by high levels of poverty in the sixteenth and seventeenth centuries. Until the end of the period considered here, demographic pressures were not a major factor in peripheral development, and yet in the economic topography of the fifteenth-century city lay the structures of inequality which produced early modern London.

Sources for local economic and social structure

The focus of this chapter is on establishing the character of extramural spaces, whether extramural areas were generally poorer than the city centre, what kinds of people lived there and what were the distinctive features of the extramural economy. It does so through a focus on two main sources: testamentary and property records, carefully selected and sampled. As discussed in the introduction, most of the property records used are drawn from estate rentals, which are excellent sources of evidence for economic trends in cities. Catherine and Mark Casson have demonstrated for fourteenth-century Hull how differences in rent levels around the city related to the relative desirability of neighbourhoods.[1] The analysis of 'firm' rents, which were the amounts actually owed by tenants as opposed to quit rents and other duties associated with property, has the advantage of suggesting the demand for property not as an investment for the owner but as a place of residence. Even though it is likely that some of the tenants recorded were not resident, the amount of firm rent owed on a property will have borne relation to the ability of tenants to pay and thus to the wealth of those who could afford to live in a given area. My analysis refers to rents across the whole period of study for this book, 1370 to 1540. This is a very long period over which to consider a cost like rent, but there are some justifications for doing so. Uneven distribution of records across the time period would hinder any attempt to consider rent in time series which could be adjusted for inflation: there is no consistency in the volume of records surviving from year to year and far more records exist for the final fifty years of the period, owing to the seizure of monastic property and associated documentation in the 1530s. Moreover, this was a period

[1] C. Casson and M. Casson, 'Property rents in medieval English towns: Hull in the fourteenth century', *Urban History*, xlvi (2019), 374–97

of relative stability: Keene and Harding's study of Cheapside rents showed little change from around 1400 until the mid-sixteenth century, and national price and wage series suggest similar stability.[2] Patchy survival of data is a problem for any historical quantitative analysis, especially when relying on the records of many institutions over such an extended duration. Proceeding with caution and paying attention to the nuances and gaps in the data is the best way to work with what we have rather than do nothing for lack of more perfect sources.

Extracting meaningful data about rent levels from the surviving sources requires some careful reading and handling of the records. Firstly, rentals often exist without deeds or leases to provide precise details of what property each tenant's rental payment referred to. Indeed, some of the smallest sums probably related to tenancies-at-will for small units of an overall tenement plot, for which such documents most likely never existed. Secondly, these smaller units might change in their constitution and value over time, as they were periodically knocked together to be let as larger properties or subdivided into smaller ones, or the whole plot could be let out to a tenant who might or might not have sublet the smaller units. These issues create uncertainty, which presents challenges for long-running quantitative analysis, but these are not insurmountable. As part of the research for this book, a relational database was built to record information about the rents, leases, repairs and vacancies for properties in several areas of London from the late fourteenth to the early sixteenth centuries. Some properties were tagged as 'multiple' where it was clear that a rental charge covered a property with a number of units. All the information was linked over as many years as possible with a single property record. Where it was hard to trace a single property year to year (for instance, because both rental amounts charged and tenants names changed), to err on the side of caution a new property record was created each time a 'new' rental unit could not be connected to any other previous property. Where contextual information is available from leases and deeds, the database entry for properties was augmented with details such as whether they were in a thoroughfare or alleyway, whether they had a garden and clues to their economic function, such as a brewhouse or oven.

Throughout this book, I use a range of terms to describe parts of the city: 'neighbourhoods', 'parishes', 'zones' and 'wards'. Some have more

[2] V Harding, 'Houses and households in Cheapside *c.*1500 1550', in *London and Beyond. Essays in Honour of Derek Keene.*, ed. M. P. Davies, J. A. Galloway and D. Keene (London, 2012), pp. 135–51, at pp. 138–9; J. Humphries and J. Weisdorf, 'The wages of women in England, 1260–1850', *Journal of Economic History*, lxxv (2015), 405–47, at pp. 417–18, doi:org/10.1017/S0022050715000662.

Table 1.1: Zones grouping together property records

Zone name	Parishes and other neighbourhoods included
East Without	St Botolph Aldgate, St Mary Whitechapel, East Smithfield
East Within	St Katharine Cree
North Without	Barbican, St Giles Cripplegate
North-east Without	St Botolph Bishopsgate, Norton Folgate, St Leonard Shoreditch
North-east Within	All Hallows London Wall, Bevis Marks
North-west Without	St Botolph Aldersgate, West Smithfield

precision than others. 'Parishes' and 'wards' were contemporary terms and both had recognized legal boundaries, but 'neighbourhood' is an elastic term, rooted in people's individual perceptions of their local social space. 'Neighbourhood' is nonetheless no anachronism: court depositions indicate that people spoke of their 'neybors', or *vicini*, and of their *vicinia* (neighbourhood), as it was rendered in the Latin of the records. What court deponents meant by 'neighbourhood' was contextual and malleable, as will be seen in Chapter Four.[3] While 'parish' or 'ward' might be precise terms, it would be misleading to stick too firmly to institutional units of space: after all, a parish might contain a hundred people or two thousand people, while a ward spanned multiple parishes. Social and economic space did not map precisely within such arbitrary bounds. In researching this chapter, in order to make the most of the surviving property records and to understand underlying trends in rent levels, records of properties which lay in eastern and northern areas of the city in and around the parishes which form the main focus of this book were gathered and grouped into zones. This reflects the fact that some properties were described by local landmarks or by their street rather than by their parish. Zones are divided within or without the walls, and the parishes and streets each zone covers are shown in Table 1.1. 'Zone' is my own term, applied as a means of grouping the records and this reflects the fact that parts of the city had differing economic characteristics and fortunes which did not conform to institutional boundaries.

The records of fourteen different estates that held property in these areas have been used: six were religious houses, four were parish churches and the remainder consisted of a craft guild, a cathedral, a chantry and a civic endowment. Since the records of properties held by individuals have rarely

[3] See p. 164 below.

survived, institutional estates are far better represented. It could be that institutions charged higher or lower rents than individuals, were more or less active in maintaining property or attracted tenants of greater or lesser status. It may also be that the types of properties held by institutions were unrepresentative of their neighbourhoods as a whole.

However, given that many properties came to institutions via testamentary bequests from individuals, it seems unlikely that the properties described here were exceptional. Using the example of one group of properties that passed from private to institutional management suggests some of the possible differences and similarities between private and institutional management of property. The Black Horse (off Aldersgate Street) was in private hands until the 1480s, when it became part of the estate managed by the local churchwardens of St Botolph Aldersgate. Deeds from the 1430s copied into the records of the parish estate show that it was formed of a large street-front property with an alleyway containing multiple dwellings behind. The alley had a communal privy and well. The deeds also set out that the alley, hitherto managed by an individual as one sublet property, was to be divided in two between two owners, although it was reunited when given to the churchwardens.[4] Larger properties may have presented more of a burden for individuals to maintain, particularly where multiple poor residents had to be chased for rent, as in Black Horse Alley. The churchwardens' accounts reveal that they maintained the existing subdivision of the property. In the early sixteenth century they made an ill-fated attempt to farm the alley out to one individual, Gilbert Alanson, who was to collect rent from residents and pay the full annual rent regardless of vacancies. This attempt to reduce the burden of administration in fact proved an expensive mistake when the churchwardens had to take Alanson to court to recover some of the money.[5] In sum, both private and institutional managers of the Black Horse maintained its subdivided arrangement and attempted to farm out the difficult business of rent collection to a single subtenant. Perhaps the greatest difference was in organizing and paying for repairs, which remained the responsibility of the churchwardens during Alanson's subtenancy. This aspect of property management was perhaps the least attractive for individuals, whereas the churchwardens and other London institutions could simply use the same labourers who worked on their church or wider estate.

While individual inhabitants can be difficult to identify in property records, this chapter uses them alongside wills, which give a far better picture of individual residents of a parish. As with all analyses based on

4 LMA, P69/BOT1/D/002/MS06641.

5 LMA, P69/BOT1/B/013/MS01454/031-036.

testamentary bequests, the results will be representative of a small section of society that was wealthier than the broad population. Information about the individuals named in a will, even the testator themself, can be frustratingly incomplete: in a sizeable number of wills, the testator gave no indication of their occupation. For example, the 1440 will of William Curle from St Katharine Cree makes no reference to his occupation, nor to his being a citizen, and yet he very probably was one, since he left the custody of his underage children's inheritance to the mayor and aldermen.[6] Nonetheless, this is not too great a hindrance to the purpose of drawing a broad outline of local social structure. While a raft of lower-status occupations and individuals are likely to be under-represented in the results, there were will-makers in the sample who worked in a range of artisanal, mercantile and service trades. Despite their limitations, wills are some of the best sources for establishing urban economic and spatial patterns.[7]

As with property records, the analysis in this chapter draws on a relational database of 450 wills drawn from four sample periods (1390–1410, 1430–50, 1465–95, 1515–40).[8] Each will was identified either within the document itself or in the margin of the register as made by a testator who lived in a parish either outside or just inside the city walls: St Botolph Aldgate, St Botolph Aldersgate, St Botolph Bishopsgate and St Katharine Cree. A smaller set of wills was collected for the parish of St Lawrence Jewry for the period 1465–95 and 1515–40 to provide a point of comparison. It has not been assumed that St Lawrence Jewry was in any sense a 'typical' central parish or that its wills form a neutral 'control group'. Nonetheless, the comparison with a central location helps to develop a sense of the distinctiveness of peripheral neighbourhoods and to provide a reference point for the analysis of differences between them. This chapter explores what this dataset reveals about the economic and social structure of extramural neighbourhoods; Chapter Two uses this information in the analysis of sociability and social networks. This chapter also draws on archaeological investigations and local court and taxation records, which provide considerable depth to the picture of topography and economy in fifteenth-century London.

[6] LMA, DL/C/B/004/MS09171/004, fos. 57–57v.

[7] J. Colson, 'Commerce, clusters and community: a re-evaluation of the occupational geography of London, *c.*1400–*c.*1550', *Economic History Review*, lxix (2016), 104–30, doi:org/10.1111/ehr.12104.

[8] Time spans for these samples vary in order to take advantage of shifts in survival levels of wills in the different courts.

Table 1.2 Proportions and reductions of city fifteenth and tenth assessments and loans to the king by ward (in percentages)[9]

	Assessment proportions (as % of total city assessment)					**Reductions (as % of ward assessment)**			
	1441	**1449**	**1453**	**1462**	**Mean**	**1441**	**1449**	**1453**	**Mean**
Aldersgate	0.9	0.9	0.9	1.9	*1.2*	0.0	0.0	0.0	*0.0*
Aldgate	0.8	0.8	0.8	1.5	*1.0*	0.0	0.0	0.0	*0.0*
Bishopsgate	3.0	2.4	3.0	3.0	*2.8*	18.2	50.0	36.4	*34.8*
Portsoken	1.2	1.2	1.1	1.2	*1.2*	33.3	50.0	37.5	*40.3*
Bassingshaw	0.9	0.9	0.9	1.2	*1.0*	0.0	0.0	0.0	*0.0*
Billingsgate	4.3	4.3	4.3	5.9	*4.7*	0.0	0.0	0.0	*0.0*
Bread Street	5.0	5.0	5.0	4.6	*4.9*	0.0	0.0	0.0	*0.0*
Bridge	6.7	6.7	6.7	6.8	*6.7*	0.0	0.0	0.0	*0.0*
Broad Street	3.6	3.6	3.6	3.8	*3.7*	0.0	0.0	0.0	*0.0*
Candlewick Street	2.2	2.2	2.1	3.1	*2.4*	0.0	0.0	0.0	*0.0*
Castle Baynard	1.6	1.6	1.6	2.3	*1.8*	0.0	0.0	0.0	*0.0*
Cheap	9.8	9.8	9.8	8.0	*9.3*	6.6	27.5	27.5	*20.5*
Coleman Street	2.6	2.6	2.6	3.3	*2.8*	10.5	15.8	16.6	*14.3*
Cordwainer Street	9.8	9.8	9.8	5.8	*8.8*	24.7	27.5	27.5	*26.6*
Cornhill	2.2	2.2	2.1	2.8	*2.3*	0.0	0.0	0.0	*0.0*
Cripplegate	6.7	6.7	6.7	9.7	*7.5*	4.0	1.7	20.0	*8.6*
Dowgate	4.8	4.9	4.8	2.5	*4.3*	22.2	27.8	0.0	*16.7*
Farringdon Within	7.3	7.3	7.3	5.6	*6.9*	9.3	2.8	7.4	*6.5*
Farringdon Without	4.7	4.7	4.7	5.1	*4.8*	0.0	0.0	0.0	*0.0*
Langbourne	2.8	2.8	2.8	4.4	*3.2*	0.0	0.0	0.0	*0.0*
Lime Street	0.3	0.3	0.3	1.0	*0.5*	0.0	0.1	0.1	*0.1*
Queenhithe	2.7	2.7	2.7	3.2	*2.8*	10.0	0.0	0.0	*3.3*
Tower	5.9	6.2	6.2	5.8	*6.0*	23.0	39.1	43.5	*35.2*
Vintry	4.8	4.9	4.8	2.9	*4.4*	30.6	41.7	46.3	*39.5*
Wallbrook	5.4	5.4	5.4	4.4	*5.1*	11.3	33.3	21.7	*22.1*

9 LMA, Jor. 3, fo. 115v; Jor. 5, fos. 18v–24v, 127v; Jor. 7, fos. 1–2.

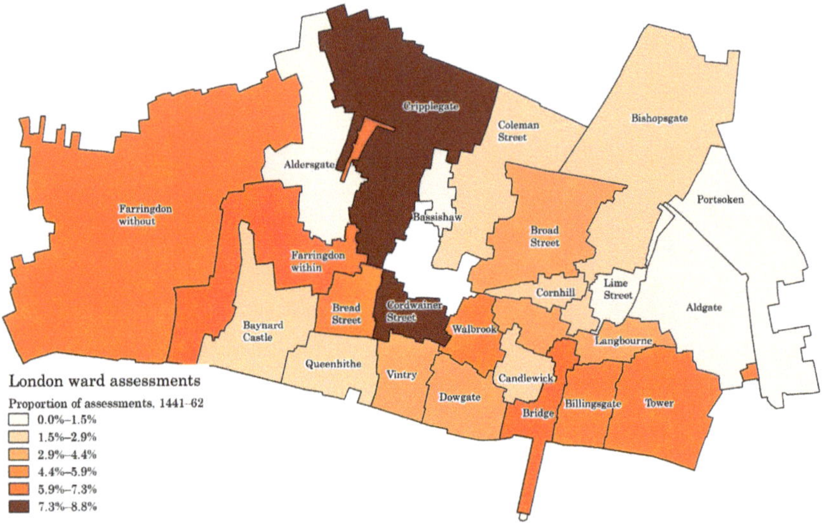

Figure 1.1 Map of mean proportionate ward assessments, 1441–62

Wealth and poverty

At the outset, it is important to address one of the main assumptions about the extramural neighbourhoods that historians have made: that they were poor parts of the city.[10] Was this the case? There are a number of different approaches through which we can assess the relative poverty or wealth of London's neighbourhoods, none of them perfect. One of the most appealing is through records of taxation and levies for loans to the crown, which were, in the fifteenth century, administered by delegation to each ward of the city. The standard form of taxation was the fifteenth and tenth, charged in London at a rate of a fifteenth of a citizen's moveable goods. The same principle of collection was applied for raising loans or grants to the crown and other sums.[11] Wards were granted reductions to the amount they owed based on pleas of poverty. These are a very tempting means by which to assess relative wealth since, in theory, all areas were assessed against their inhabitants' property. Similar records have been used elsewhere in the country in this way, with Mark Forrest utilizing

[10] See Introduction, pp. xxiv–xxvi.

[11] C. M. Barron, *London in the Later Middle Ages: Government and People 1200–1500* (Oxford, 2004), p. 12. For instance, the city raised a fifteenth for buying land at Billingsgate in 1449. LMA, Jor. 3, fo. 41.

fifteenth and tenth returns for the south-west to track economic decline during the fifteenth century.[12] Forrest paid attention to the reductions allowed to settlements, arguing that commissioners used local knowledge of changes in wealth to determine where allowances would be made.[13] Table 1.2 shows proportionate assessments for fifteenths (or parts of fifteenths) and loans or aids to the crown in London made between 1441 and 1462, drawn from assessments by ward which were copied into the journals of the city's common council. Information about reductions is available only for the three earlier assessments. Figure 1.1 maps the average proportion of assessments borne by city wards. In general, there was a disparity between wards within and without the walls as well as between the west and the east of the city. Thus, Farringdon Without and Cripplegate in the west were the most heavily assessed extramural wards, while both Aldgate and Portsoken wards in the east were among the most lightly assessed in the city. The commercial centres of the city around Cheapside and London Bridge were where a greater proportion of assessed wealth lay.

The reductions applied to the assessments in the 1440s and 1453 give nuance to this pattern. Although Portsoken and Aldersgate were given very similar levels of assessment, Portsoken each time received a reduction to its contribution ranging between a third and a half. Aldersgate was apparently able to meet its assessment comfortably and saw its share double in the 1462 assessment. Cheap and Cordwainer Street were the most heavily assessed wards in the city, but they received considerable reductions of up to 27.5 per cent. Out of all the wards deemed to have 4 per cent or more of the city's assessed wealth, only Farringdon Without, Bridge and Billingsgate were apparently able to pay their assessment with no reduction, and by the 1460s all three had duly seen their share of the assessment increase. The commercial districts near St Paul's Cathedral and London Bridge and the attraction of wealthy customers to areas around the Inns of Court and routes to Westminster seem to have determined where the assessed wealth resided. The neighbourhoods focused on in this book all had a lesser share of those eligible for tax. Aldgate, Bishopsgate, Portsoken and Aldersgate wards, where the sample parishes lay, were in the lower half of wards for all the assessments studied. Their combined assessments contributed less than 10 per cent of London's total. The pattern indicated in Figure 1.1 shows a striking similarity to the spread of hearth tax assessments in the city in 1666,

[12] M. Forrest, 'Patterns of economic change in the south-west during the fifteenth century: evidence from the reductions to the fifteenths and tenths', *Economic History Review*, lxx (2017), 423–51, doi:org/10.1111/ehr.12373.

[13] Forrest, 'Patterns of economic change', pp. 445–7.

suggesting that the broad distribution of wealth in the city was resilient even as the sixteenth and seventeenth centuries wrought great changes in London.[14]

However, ward level assessments are very crude measures of patterns of wealth. Since fifteenths assessed moveable goods but not wages, they are probably most effective at indicating the distribution of wealthy merchants around the city rather than the prosperity of the wider population. As a result, assessment levels could be dependent on a very small number of wealthy local residents contributing. The 1449 assessment in the ward of Portsoken was gathered from just six local residents, of whom Henry Jordan paid more than a third (twenty shillings) of the total assessment.[15] The lay subsidy of 1512, which included wage-earners over fifteen years old, showed a similar distribution of assessment across the city to the earlier fifteenths, albeit that the proportionate assessment of extramural wards was slightly higher (around 3 per cent each), as would be expected from a wider base of payers.[16] It is clear with the fifteenths that it was common practice to charge prominent citizens with the deficit left by ward reductions. Notes after the 1441 assessment indicate that Nicholas Blome, the mayor Robert Clopton and John Houghton paid the deficit of Tower, Langbourn and Aldgate wards respectively.[17] This suggests that we should be cautious about how comprehensive the recorded reductions to fifteenths are, as deficits might have been paid personally without being recorded in the city's journals. However, the most important limitation to taxation evidence, demonstrated by Figure 1.1, is the inability to distinguish between different areas of a ward. This is a particular problem for Bishopsgate and Cripplegate wards, which extended from busy intramural shopping streets to extramural areas, and it seems likely (but is impossible to prove) that their assessed wealth was heavily concentrated within the walls. Wards or parishes might contain pockets responding to very different economic stimuli, especially where part of them lay outside the walls. The evidence from assessments can only ever be indicative, and the differences which could exist even within an administrative unit such as the ward or parish require consideration.

Utilizing evidence from property records gives a different and more geographically precise view of patterns of wealth around the city, although the information still requires sensitive handling. Table 1.3 indicates the

[14] A. Wareham, 'The unpopularity of the hearth tax and the social geography of London in 1666', *Economic History Review*, lxx (2017), 452–82, at pp. 461–4, doi:org/10.1111/ehr.12376.

[15] LMA, Jor. 5, fo. 21.

[16] LMA, Jor. 11, fo. 5.

[17] LMA Jor. 3, fo. 115v.

Table 1.3 Median and mean rent levels by zone of property

Zone	Median (d)	Mean (d)	No. of records
North-east Without	96	132.62	394
North-east Within (mural)	80	95.58	378
North Without	160	226.42	144
North-west Without	48	173.13	208
East Without	96	228.19	578
East Within (thoroughfare)	200	265.64	88

mean and median annual rent values of properties found in each zone. This data excludes years when reported rent for a property was zero because it was vacant and also excludes properties that were clearly multiple dwellings being let to a single tenant who most likely sublet them to others. This latter exclusion has some impact on the average values but does allow for the best possible view of the costs of letting a single dwelling for an inhabiting tenant or household. There are significant divergences between the median and mean values of rents in many areas, most dramatically in the eastern extramural zone, which is indicative of the effect that small numbers of high-value properties have on the mean. The median takes into account the quantity of given values in a dataset and is thus a more appropriate measure, but even here caution is required.

Property records give a far more detailed picture of patterns of wealth and poverty than taxation. In the eastern part of the city there was a clear gap between the cost of renting in intramural St Katharine Cree than in the neighbouring areas outside the city wall. Living within the walls here cost more than double living without. In the north-east the picture is different because the intramural area studied was of a different character. Rental values were highly dependent on street frontage and were highest on the busiest thoroughfares.[18] All Hallows on the Wall and St Augustine Papey followed the line of the city defences and, as a result, the median rental values were similar and even lower than in the neighbouring area outside Bishopsgate. It is important to recognize that all of these rental figures are far below those in the Cheapside area, the commercial heart of the city, where it was the norm to let substantial houses for over £3 (720 pence)

[18] Casson and Casson, 'Property rents in medieval English towns', pp. 390–92; J. Colson, 'Local communities in fifteenth century London: craft, parish and neighbourhood' (unpublished Royal Holloway, University of London PhD thesis, 2011), p. 109.

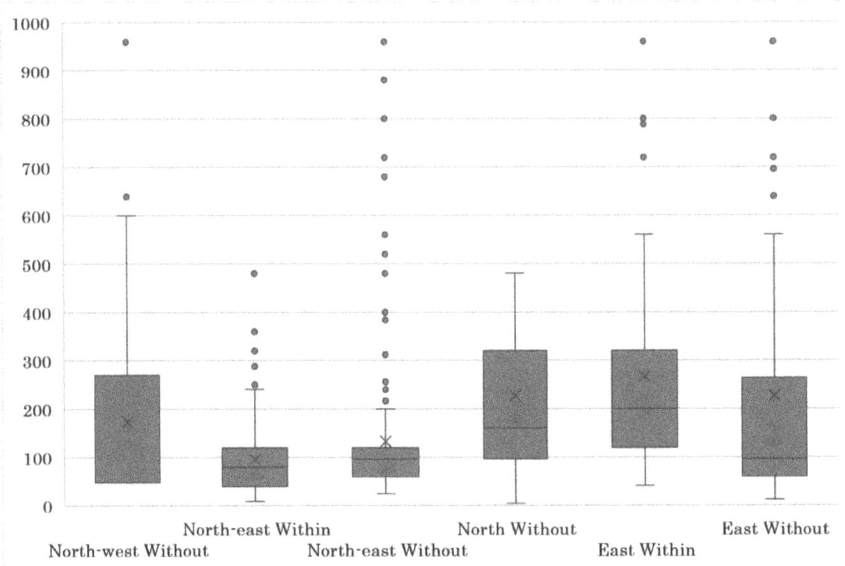

Figure 1.2 Box and whisker plot of distributions of rent in all zones. The median is shown as a solid line within the box and the mean as a cross.

a year.[19] Rather than subdivide those properties into cheaper units when demand was low, landlords preferred to keep Cheapside properties as large complexes in the hope of attracting wealthy tenants.[20] It can be reasonably concluded that rents were lower at the periphery of the city but that there was considerable variance between properties and areas. An intramural area without a major thoroughfare such as All Hallows on the Wall could, at a broad average, be as inexpensive as an extramural location. Moreover, there were significant differences in cost within and between extramural neighbourhoods which, to be fully explained, demand a much closer look at the distribution of rent costs within each zone.

The box and whisker chart in Figure 1.2 plots the spread of annual rent instances within each zone up to 1,000 pence per year. The solid box area reflects the range of costs in which half of the rents fell (the second and third quartiles of values), while the whiskers show the range of distribution of 99 per

[19] Harding, 'Houses and households in Cheapside *c.*1500–1550', pp. 138–43. See eg the properties named St Mary le Bow 104/24, St Mary le Bow 104/14 and All Hallows Honey Lane 11/5 in D. J. Keene and V. Harding, ed., *Historical Gazetteer of London before the Great Fire Cheapside* (London, 1987), *British History Online* <https://www.british-history.ac.uk/no-series/london-gazetteer-pre-fire> [accessed 4 June 2020].

[20] Harding, 'Houses and households in Cheapside *c.*1500–1550', pp. 139–40.

cent of the rents, excluding outlying values, which are plotted as small circles. The mean value is shown with a cross and the median with a line. Effectively, the smaller the area covered by the box, the more homogeneous rental values were within that zone, and the larger the box, the greater were local disparities of cost. There are considerable differences between the box plots for each zone which reflect far more complex patterns of rental cost than simple averages. Most strikingly, the North-east Without zone was far more homogeneous in its low rents than any other area, while North-west Without, despite an overall lower median rent, had a much wider spread of costs. In effect, outside Bishopsgate, tenants tended to pay rents of a similar low value, while outside Aldersgate there were lots of tenants paying low rents living alongside many who paid much higher sums. The box plot also helps to clarify the similarities and differences between the Eastern Within and Eastern Without zones. While their average values were quite different, the range of rents was similar within and without Aldgate. In other words, there were proportionately more low-value rents outside Aldgate, but there were also many tenants paying higher costs similar to those inside the walls. The reasons for these patterns will be explored in the course of this chapter, but for the moment it suffices to say that while tenants on the city's periphery seem to have paid lower rents on the whole, some neighbourhoods, such as the city's north-west, were highly stratified, with dwellers of high- and low-value properties side by side.

This sense of stratification within neighbourhoods and real differentiation between areas outside the city walls is reinforced by evidence from wills. Testamentary records cannot be considered simple proxies for wealth. As Clive Burgess argued, many or even most wills are only a partial representation of a testator's final wishes, as it was common to made pre-mortem verbal arrangements.[21] This was made clear by one testator, a pinner named Geoffrey Wade, who in his will warned his children against suing one another over his estate 'in so much that I [have] given and bequeathed unto [them] … their parts of my goods afore this time beside the bequests'.[22] However, by comparing conventional bequests that are shared in common across many wills it is possible to make something of an assessment of wealth. It was customary for testators to leave a sum to their parish church for tithes forgotten or underpaid in their lifetime, and this has been used as a rough measure of testator wealth in studies of

[21] C. Burgess, 'Late medieval wills and pious convention: testamentary evidence reconsidered', in *Profit, Piety and the Professions in Later Medieval England*, ed. M.A. Hicks (Gloucester, 1990), pp. 14–33, at pp. 15–17.

[22] LMA, DL/C/B/004/MS09171/005, fo. 388.

London and Bury St Edmunds.[23] Robert Dinn's analysis of Bury found a high degree of correlation between forgotten tithe bequests and individual subsidy assessments,[24] which suggests that we can be fairly confident in them as a measure of personal wealth.

While not all wills included a sum for forgotten tithes, the lack of these sums can be indicative of interesting social patterns. Although Robert Wood assumed that a lack of a bequest for tithes indicated extreme poverty,[25] the wills of the 165 testators who left no tithe in the sample gathered in the course of research for this book suggest there may have been many other reasons for their omission. John Newport, Esquire, left no tithe to his parish church of St Botolph Aldersgate. He was no pauper, however, but a man with land at Calais and Chrishall Magna in Essex as well as in Golding Lane outside Aldersgate who requested burial in the chapel of Roger Walden, future archbishop of Canterbury, at St Bartholomew's hospital. He seems to have been a minor official in royal administration who would thus have been very mobile and probably just happened to die at his London home in a parish to which he had little personal attachment.[26] Indeed, the parish of St Botolph Aldersgate had the highest level of failure to make a bequest for forgotten tithes, at 46 per cent of all wills. It was probably the significant presence of London houses of the gentry and aristocracy in the neighbourhood that drove this trend. St Lawrence Jewry had the lowest level, at 23 per cent, and the remaining parishes all fell in the range of 36–40 per cent. Forgotten tithe sums were usually fairly small in the context of other bequests, so it seems unlikely that their lack was always related to poverty. Particularly for those with otherwise large estates, not leaving money for forgotten tithes is more likely to indicate that a testator did not feel they owed their final parish of residence such an obligation.

The box and whisker graph at Figure 1.3 plots the sums for forgotten tithes, excluding wills where no such bequest was made, in a similar manner to the treatment of rents in Figure 1.2. The amount of data here is smaller than for rents, but there are interesting similarities which suggest a pattern.

[23] R. A. Wood, 'Poor widows, *c.*1393–1415', in *Medieval London Widows, 1300–1500*, ed. C. M. Barron and A. F. Sutton (London and Rio Grande, Ohio, 1994), pp. 55–70, at p. 34; R. B. Dinn, 'Popular religion in late medieval Bury St Edmunds' (unpublished University of Manchester Ph.D., 1990), pp. 62–9.

[24] Dinn, 'Popular religion', pp. 63–6.

[25] Wood, 'Poor widows, *c.*1393–1415'. Since Wood's sample is drawn entirely from wills proved in the lower archdeacon's court it may well be that such an assumption holds true only for the very smallest estates.

[26] LMA, DL/C/B/004/MS09171/001, fo. 370. Newport and Walden were jointly responsible for taking lands into the king's hands in Calais. TNA, C 47/24/13/18.

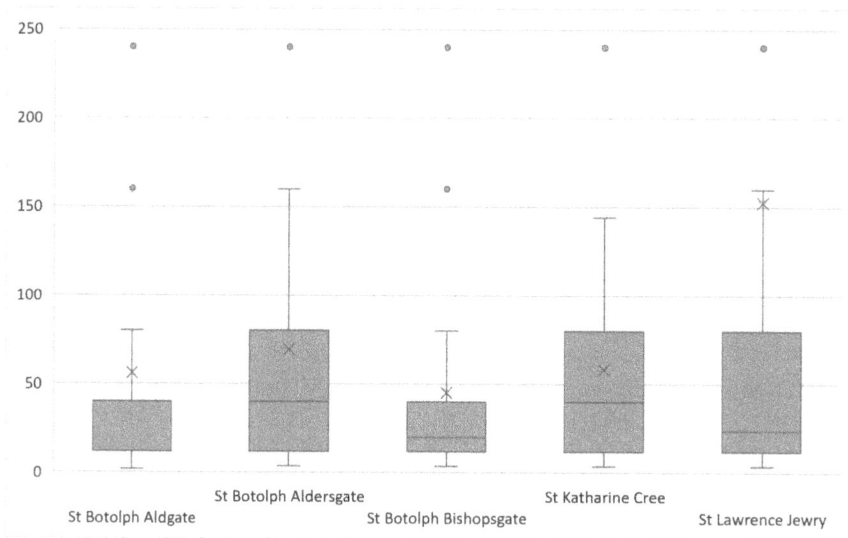

Figure 1.3 Box and whisker plot of distribution of sums for forgotten tithes bequeathed in wills up to 250 pence

The parish of St Botolph Bishopsgate, which made up the bulk of the North-east Without rental data, again has the narrowest spread indicating homogeneously lower sums bequeathed for forgotten tithes than elsewhere. Combined with evidence from rents, it can be said with some confidence that this parish had a population which was, on the whole, poorer than other neighbourhoods and without great disparities of wealth. The pattern at St Botolph Aldersgate also echoes the stratification of rents, with a wider range of forgotten tithe sums than in other extramural parishes. The central parish St Lawrence Jewry looks far more similar to St Botolph Aldersgate and St Katharine Cree in its distribution than to the remaining extramural parishes, albeit that Aldersgate had a wider total range than either. The difference in the east between the parishes within and without the walls was more pronounced than with rents, with a far more homogeneous band of low forgotten tithe amounts in St Botolph Aldgate than in St Katharine Cree.

The peripheral areas were generally less wealthy than parishes within the walls by each of these measures. While, taken in isolation, each source has its pitfalls, in combination they give a nuanced impression of the distribution of wealth around the city. The neighbourhood outside Aldersgate was home to some of the wealthiest residents, while still containing property affordable to far humbler Londoners. Bishopsgate, at the other end of the spectrum, was on the whole the least wealthy of the three extramural areas. This suggests the problems inherent in the evidence of ward taxation assessments as, in these, Bishopsgate ward (which had a significant proportion within the walls) was assessed quite highly in comparison to other extramural wards. The exceptionally low taxation assessments for the area outside Aldgate are not fully reflected by other measures of wealth but, as we shall see, this was a neighbourhood with a very varied social composition. The city within the walls, as represented by St Lawrence Jewry and St Katharine Cree, was wealthier, but the low value of rental properties in the North-east Within zone are a reminder that there were places where poorer Londoners could afford to live. No single parish was homogeneously poor or wealthy, but there were real differences in relative wealth which underpinned many of the social and economic characteristics of the neighbourhoods.

The natural and built environment

The natural and built environment of the urban periphery was distinctive. Roads, walls and watercourses differentiated the margins of the city from the centre visually and economically. In turn, the buildings, gardens and open spaces in extramural areas reflected the particular economy of the city's fringe. The evidence of property records as well as local wardmote and assize of nuisance presentments, which dealt with complaints about shoddily built structures and incursions on to public land, reveal a wealth of detail about the local environment and the ways in which it was used by Londoners. More so than poverty, it was the character of extramural space which defined its marginal nature between city and countryside.

London's wall and gates were an imposing feature of the fifteenth-century city, although not much called on for military defence. Participants in both the Jack Cade (1450) and Warwick (1470–71) rebellions approached the city from the south of the Thames and were kept out by defences on London Bridge.[27] The notable failure of London's defences during the 1381 Rising was due to the opening of the city's gates to the rebels by Londoners. Even during the intermittent civil war of the fifteenth century, military defence for Londoners never seems to have been taken all that seriously and the walls were allowed to fall into disrepair several times.[28] This is perhaps a sign of

[27] M. Mercer, 'A forgotten Kentish rebellion, September–October 1470', *Archaeologia Cantiana: Being Contributions to the History and Archaeology of Kent*, cxxii (2002), 143–51, at pp. 146–7; A. L. Kaufman, 'Jack Cade's rebellion of 1450 and the London midsummer watch', *Nottingham Medieval Studies*, li (2007), 143–66, at pp. 151–2, doi:org/10.1484/J.NMS.3.411.

[28] The postern gate by the tower subsided into a ditch and was never fully rebuilt. D. Whipp, *The Medieval Postern Gate by the Tower of London*, MoLAS Monograph, 29 (London, 2006), p. 14. The repair of walls was ordered in response to immediate threats eg during Warwick's rebellion. LMA, Jor. 7, fos. 221-21v.

the co-dependency of city and crown: what point would there be in a rival for the crown sacking London, after all, when it was so important for the national economy and the royal coffers? The walls fell into decay from the later fourteenth century and were substantially rebuilt in the late fifteenth century with an enlarged entry at Moorgate and the addition of supports to protect against cannon fire.[29] The defensive ditch which surrounded the walls had to be frequently re-cut owing to its use by Londoners as a rubbish dump.[30] Far more common than defensive need, however, was the use of the gates by the city government as sites to demonstrate their authority and to police incomers. Civic-appointed wardens guarded the gates and were responsible for denying entry to those considered undesirable. In 1454, these men (who in most cases were also ward beadles) were sworn to prevent lepers and vagrants from entering the city. The list of those sworn suggests that at four gates (Aldgate, Bishopsgate, Aldersgate and Newgate) there was an additional assistant warden (*custos valletus*).[31] These were presumably the busiest gates, where greater traffic necessitated an extra pair of eyes. The wardens' position at the city's gates also marked the symbolic importance of the wall as a moral boundary. Prostitutes expelled from the city were paraded to the city gates, not its bars, by civic officers, and felons and heretics were executed beyond the walls at Smithfield. The city beyond the gates was left undefended militarily and, symbolically, was surrendered to those who might corrupt the city with disease or immorality.

Waterways were also important elements of the extramural environment. The Walbrook stream was covered and built over within the walls but ran openly to the north of the city.[32] It created a large area which seems to have been too damp and prone to flooding to be much developed in this period. To the west of the stream Moorfields was pastureland completely free of building until the later sixteenth century, with just an access causeway to

[29] C. Thomas, *The Archaeology of Medieval London* (Thrupp, Stroud, Gloucestershire, 2002), p. 127.

[30] J. Lyon, *Within These Walls: Roman and Medieval Defences North of Newgate at the Merrill Lynch Financial Centre, City of London*, MoLAS Monograph, 33 (London, 2007), p. 75. For example, at the Portsoken wardmote in 1467, Thomas Dyrwyn was indicted for 'casting out of straw and dung into the town ditch'. C. L. Winter, 'The Portsoken presentments: an analysis of a London ward in the 15th century', *Transactions of the London and Middlesex Archaeology Society*, lvi (2005), 97–162, at p. 112.

[31] LMA, Jor. 5, fo. 208.

[32] D. Keene, 'Issues of water in medieval London to *c*.1300', *Urban History*, xxviii (2001), 161–79, at p. 162.

Moorgate constructed in 1511 and tentergrounds for the stretching of cloth.[33] Archaeological excavation on the west side of Bishopsgate Street near the stream has revealed that, up until *c.*1400, this was vacant ground with a pond which regularly flooded.[34] It was not until after 1450 that the landlord, the hospital of St Mary Bishopsgate, constructed brick buildings, including one which covered the former pond. Yards, gardens and cesspits were in use here in the last quarter of the fifteenth century.[35] The character of the area north of the city wall was shaped by the Walbrook stream, encouraging the retention of open ground here and making its development uneconomical until there was sufficient demand in the late fifteenth century. To the east of the city, too, the numerous streams and the marshy ground were initial reasons why suburban development was sparser there than in the west.[36] Here, the moat of the Tower of London was filled by the Thames and, according to complaints at the Portsoken wardmote court, attracted an 'accumulation of refuse, filth and other fetid matter on Tower Hill, whereby the air [was] foully corrupted and vitiated and the lives of those dwelling or passing there were endangered'.[37] On the Thames itself, St Katharine's Wharf and Tower Wharf allowed ships to dock while stairs enabled locals to collect water from the river and do their washing. The commercial activity associated with the wharves provided lucrative income for St Katharine's Hospital and the holder of the farm of Tower Wharf.[38] The noxious fumes produced by rubbish dumped in the city ditch and the presumed disorderliness of gathering laundresses at extramural

[33] 'Historical introduction: Moorfields', in *Survey of London: Volume 8, Shoreditch*, ed. James Bird (London: Survey of London, 1922), pp. 88–90, *British History Online* <http://www.british-history.ac.uk/survey-london/vol8/pp88-90> [accessed 24 July 2017]; John Stow, 'Gates in the wall of this Citie', in *A Survey of London. Reprinted from the Text of 1603*, ed. C. L. Kingsford (Oxford, 1908), pp. 27–44, in *British History* online <http://www.british-history.ac.uk/no-series/survey-of-london-stow/1603/pp27-44> [accessed 14 Dec. 2017]. For tenterfields see the map of London *c.*1520, in M. D. Lobel, *The City of London from Prehistoric Times to c.1520*, The British Atlas of Historic Towns (Oxford, 1989), iii.

[34] D. Swift, *Roman Burials, Medieval Tenements and Suburban Growth: 201 Bishopsgate, City of London* (London, 2003), pp. 34–8.

[35] Swift, *Roman Burials, Medieval Tenements and Suburban Growth*, pp. 40–41.

[36] Keene, 'Issues of water', p. 165.

[37] 'Roll A 17: 1371–72', in *Calendar of the Plea and Memoranda Rolls of the City of London: Volume 2, 1364–1381*, ed. A. H. Thomas (London, 1929), pp. 132–49, in *British History* online, <http://www.british-history.ac.uk/plea-memoranda-rolls/vol2/pp132-149> [accessed 28 July 2017].

[38] For instance, see licence for the farm of Tower Wharf in 'Close rolls, Edward IV: 1464', in *Calendar of Close Rolls, Edward IV: Volume 1, 1461–1468*, ed. W. H. B. Bird and K. H. Ledward (London, 1949), pp. 263–4, in *British History Online*, <http://www.british-history.ac.uk/cal-close-rolls/edw4/vol1/pp263-264> [accessed 15 Aug. 2017].

water sources served to underline the association between extramural areas and 'dirt, prostitution, poverty and disorderly conduct'.[39]

More than either the walls or the waterways, it was roads that dominated the topography and economy of extramural areas. Despite the beginnings, described above, of more intensive development in the later fifteenth century, the roadway at Bishopsgate appears to have retained its status as the dominant draw for development well into the sixteenth century. The map of London known as the copperplate or 'Agas' map (dated to *c.*1560) in Figure 0.2 still shows a neighbourhood where the land behind the street-facing houses was mainly gardens and tenteryards.[40] The parish of St Botolph Aldersgate was similar in that its institutional boundaries followed the course of the approach road, and land behind houses to the east of the street was laid out as gardens. Unlike Bishopsgate, however, lanes to the west connected the parish to well-developed neighbourhoods around Smithfield and Clerkenwell. Ribbon development drew urbanization out along the approach roads in a manner which complicates our view of where London itself can be deemed to end. At Whitechapel and Norton Folgate, urban development extended past the bars marking the end of the city's jurisdiction. To the north-west it was Smithfield market, rather than a major entry to the city, that attracted development across jurisdictional boundaries.[41]

The infrastructure of mobility

Routes of transport also profoundly shaped the economy of the city's periphery by connecting it with the economy of the wider region. Over the course of the fifteenth century, the area of the River Lea valley in Essex and Hertfordshire to London's north and east became far more commercialized in supply of the city's markets.[42] Commercialization was driven by the demand of London markets but also by the active investment of Londoners in pasture and crop-growing land in the hinterland.[43] Produce

39 C. Rawcliffe, 'A marginal occupation? The medieval laundress and her work', *Gender & History*, xxi (2009), 147–69, at pp. 155–6, 158, 163, doi:org/10.1111/j.1468-0424.2009.01539.x.

40 'Plan of London (circa 1560 to 1570)', in *Agas Map of London 1561*, in *British History* online, <http://www.british-history.ac.uk/no-series/london-map-agas/1561/map> [accessed 10 Aug. 2017].

41 Development here extended into Middlesex at Clerkenwell Street and the liberty of St John's Street, held by the prior of the hospital of St John of Jerusalem.

42 K. G. T. McDonnell, *Medieval London Suburbs* (London, 1978), pp. 17, 34, 72–3.

43 C. A. Martin, 'Transport for London, 1250–1550' (unpublished Royal Holloway, University of London Ph.D., 2008), pp. 37–8; M. K. McIntosh, 'Money lending on the periphery of London, 1300–1600', *Albion*, xx (1988), 557–71, at pp. 564–5; L. R. Poos, *A Rural Society after the Black Death: Essex 1350–1525* (Cambridge, 1991), pp. 41–3.

and livestock from the region were transported via Ermine Street, which ended at Bishopsgate, or were conveyed down the River Lea, transferred to carts at Stratford some three miles from the city and then transported on the approach road terminating at Aldgate, with livestock taken for sale and slaughter at East Smithfield market.[44] To the north-west, droving routes from the midlands ended at Clerkenwell and West Smithfield market. The livestock markets necessitated pastureland in the immediate environs of the city and other goods were simply more convenient to process outside the walls. On Aldgate Street, a property described as a timberyard contained a yard and two storehouses would have been well positioned to process wood coming in via the route from Stratford. At just five shillings rent per year this kind of land use would perhaps have been profitable only in an extramural area with less intensive development.[45]

Large properties in extramural neighbourhoods often seem to have had facilities for keeping horses. The Axe without Aldgate had a stable, as did a number of other large properties with multiple functions such as the Hert's Horn, which was on the same street and also had shops, a melting house and a 'sopehouse', and a tenement owned by St Paul's in Barbican which, in addition to a stable, had its own mill.[46] The nature of the records means that it is difficult to tell whether stables were solely used by the tenants or if they served as livery stables. Nonetheless, stables were also rented as standalone properties in George Alley outside Bishopsgate and within London Wall in the parish of All Hallows.[47] Stabling, pasturing and storage were necessitated by the flow of goods and people along city approach roads and were important effects of routes of transit on the extramural built environment and economy.

Roads outside city walls were so busy that they struggled to handle the volume of traffic. The maintenance of the road surface was a constant difficulty, owing to the lack of central organization of paving. Instead the city relied on householders or tenants to repair the section of road lying outside their house. This system was particularly difficult to enforce on wide extramural approach roads, where the demand on individuals to repair heavily trafficked highways to a point a couple of metres before their front door was unworkable.[48] As a result, complaints about broken pavements and highways full of dangerous potholes were the most numerous indictments

44 Martin, 'Transport for London, 1250–1550', pp. 37–8.

45 TNA, SC 11/955.

46 TNA, E 303/9/197. The mill is mentioned in repairs to the property undertaken in 1455. LMA, CLC/313/L/D/001/MS25125/080.

47 TNA, SC 11/975; LMA, CLA/007/FN/02/003.

48 Martin, 'Transport for London, 1250–1550', pp. 93–133.

in the returns of Bishopsgate and Farringdon Without wardmotes in 1421–3, with more complaints in Bishopsgate ward than in the rest of the city combined.[49] Sometimes, as in this extract from the presentment of the Aldersgate wardmote jury in 1510, one can gain a sense of the scale of the problem from the volume and geographical specificity of the complaints:

> Seint Botollph [Aldersgate]
> Item we pressente the pamentt before the parsonage and a chimney ayen the parsonage. Item we pressent the paments before John Bone gardeyn to the Spittyll rente. Item we pressente the pament of the Spyttyll rents fro John Honys garden unto thynke [sic] before Seint Bartylmews gate. Item we pressent all the pentyse and the paments of the Bolle rents. Item we pressent all the pament of the Lyon Rentys to the Brethered [brotherhood] halle. Item we pressent all the pament fro the Blakehorsse to the Pryorie of Hownselow rents. Item we pressent al the paments fro the Pekoc to Henmarsshe howse. Item we pressent all the paments of Master Darnolde rents fro the barrys [city bars] to the Anteloppe corner.[50]

And so it goes on. The task which faced wardmote juries in the periphery attempting to ensure the maintenance of roads was formidable. It was perhaps made harder by the lower value of property, which may have made landlords unwilling to invest in expensive repairs to larger expanses of road than would have been necessary within the walls.

All that traffic produced a huge demand in the extramural neighbourhoods for lodgings. These ranged from officially sanctioned inns to informal hostelries and lodgings for the sick, including lepers, who would have been turned away by the wardens on the gates. Innkeeping was held by the civic government to be a position of great responsibility: all those who lodged a newcomer beyond a day and a night were to stand surety for their guest's good behaviour.[51] In larger towns and cities, innkeepers were generally men of substance and in London were expected to be members of the guild of hostellers (incorporated as the Innholders Company from 1516).[52] Though we lack numbers, London undoubtedly had the largest concentration of inns of any city in England:

[49] See p. 146ff. for discussion of the wardmote courts. *Calendar of Plea and Memoranda Rolls Preserved among the Archives of the Corporation of the City of London at the Guild-Hall: ad 1413–1437*, ed. A. H. Thomas (Cambridge, 1943), pp. 121–6.

[50] LMA, CLC/W/FA/005/MS01499.

[51] B. A. Hanawalt, 'The host, the law and the ambiguous space of medieval London taverns', in *Medieval Crime and Social Control*, ed. B. A. Hanawalt and D. Wallace (Minneapolis and London, 1999), pp. 204–23, at p. 216.

[52] J. Hare, 'Inns, innkeepers and the society of later medieval England, 1350–1600', *Journal of Medieval History*, xxxix (2013), 477–97, at p. 494, doi:org/10.1080/03044181.2013.833132.

Southwark south of the city had twenty-two inns alone at the time of the 1381 poll tax.[53] Identifiable inns close to the city gates in extramural neighbourhoods include the George and the Harp outside Bishopsgate and the Axe outside Aldgate.[54] Inns were substantial premises, requiring serious investment from their owners and tenants to maintain facilities, and at the highest end catered for the city's visiting gentry. There was, however, considerable demand for cheaper lodgings and for accommodation for those whom innkeepers, in their role as part of the city's surveillance system, would be unwilling to take in. Such places were known by the early sixteenth century as 'petty hostries', and they are best documented in complaints about them at the wardmote. In 1528 George Brown of St Anne and St Agnes parish, within Aldersgate ward, was complained of for keeping 'petty ostry' and the resorting of men's servants to his house.[55] In a presentment dated *c.*1512–24, in the same ward Thomas Burger and his wife were indicted for 'keeping of petty ostry of seke and laser people [i.e. lepers]', and Alice Epps and John Bott were complained of for 'keeping of people of the poxe and other diseased persons'.[56] There were regulations, discussed above, which ordered the city gate wardens to turn away those suspected of leprosy and other diseases, though, intriguingly, all these presentments were from parishes in the small portion of Aldersgate ward *within* the city walls, suggesting that the wardens were not particularly effective. Perhaps sick people came to the city hoping for lodging in one of its many hospitals and, unable to enter one, turned to lodging houses near the gates. The shadowy world of petty hostelries is difficult to recover, but taking in a weary traveller or two would undoubtedly have been an attractive business on the fringes of a city like London, particularly for the poor, if they had the space. Taking in lodgers was a common strategy for widows and single women seeking to supplement their incomes in the medieval and early modern periods.[57] It is important to remember that the infrastructure

[53] Hare, 'Inns, innkeepers and the society of later medieval England, 1350–1600', pp. 483–5.

[54] The George and the Harp were part of the hospital of St Mary Bishopsgate's estate on Bishopsgate Street, the former described as a *hospicium* in 1468–9 (TNA SC 11/972) and the latter as leased by hosteller John Garle in 1454–5 (TNA, SC 11/974). See below, p. 25, for further discussion of the Axe.

[55] LMA, CLC/W/FA/006/MS01500, recto.

[56] LMA, CLC/W/FA/007/MS01501, recto.

[57] C. S. Schen, 'Strategies of poor aged women and widows in sixteenth century London', in *Women and Aging in British Society since 1500*, ed. P. Thane and L. Botelho (Harlow, 2001), pp. 13–30, at p. 22; D. Postles, 'Migration and mobility in a less mature economy: English internal migration, *c.*1200–1350', *Social History*, xxv (2000), 285–99, at p. 294, doi: org/10.1080/030710200050143329.

of mobility was just as much made up of the economy of makeshifts, the hundreds of people taking one or two newcomers into their homes leaving no documentary trace, as it was by the large inns and wide roads that fell into civic oversight. The fundamental mobility of extramural neighbourhoods, discussed in Chapter Three, relied on the presence of this infrastructure.

Open spaces and gardens

Alongside the busy roads and impromptu rubbish dumps, there were aspects of extramural space which were more pleasant and even semi-rural in character. Until the later seventeenth century, there was a ring of open spaces and gardens around the city.[58] Southwark's 1381 Poll Tax return numbers a small but significant proportion of gardeners among residents, and gardens were a feature of that neighbourhood until their development in the sixteenth century.[59] North of the river, evidence from cases brought under the assize of nuisance suggests that space dedicated to gardens declined within the walls across the fifteenth century, making it a more distinctive feature of the city fringe. In cases heard between 1370 and 1431 where a garden was mentioned, six of twenty-eight of the properties in question were outside the walls, compared to twelve of fifteen viewers' reports that mention gardens in 1500–1530.[60] As a result, there was a demand for dedicated market gardening plots outside the city walls. There were gardens on Tower Hill owned by the churchwardens of St Mary at Hill from at least the late fifteenth century, composed of a mixture of cottages with gardens, small gardens, a tennis court and a 'great garden'.[61] Gardens were also a feature of St Botolph Bishopsgate. Rentals from the local hospital of St Mary grouped rents from the gardens and other open plots of land into a separate list. In 1468, there were eleven tenants, some of whom leased more than one garden, with a variety of occupations. Richard Bray, fuller, rented two gardens, and the widow of John Thorp, scrivener, paid 2s 6d for her

[58] D. J. E. Marsh, 'The gardens and gardeners of later Stuart London' (unpublished Birkbeck, University of London Ph.D., 2005), pp. 173–5, 185–99.

[59] Carlin, *Medieval Southwark*, pp. 58–60, 172, 180.

[60] *London Viewers and Their Certificates, 1508–1558: Certificates of the Sworn Viewers of the City of London*, ed. Janet Senderowitz Loengard (London, 1989), *British History online* <http://www.british-history.ac.uk/london record soc/vol26> [accessed 4 June 2020]; *London Assize of Nuisance, 1301–1431: a Calendar*, ed. Helena M Chew and William Kellaway (London, 1973), *British History Online* <http://www.british-history.ac.uk/london-record-soc/vol10> [accessed 4 June 2020].

[61] LMA, P69/MRY4/B/005/MS01239/001/001.

garden for a year.[62] John Roke, butcher, rented a pasture from the hospital called 'Wodelane' at Whitechapel.[63] In a couple of cases, it is clear that the gardens were let by those who lived elsewhere in the city: Roke's will shows that he was resident in St Botolph Aldgate, and another garden tenant is named as 'Baker bocher in Eschepe [Eastcheap]'.[64]

It was not just gardens which brought people out to the city fringe: recreation was an important aspect of their utility to the wider city. Much of this was informal. John Stow remembered that people went to the city's eastern fringe during his childhood in the 1530s 'therein to walke, shoote, and otherwise to recreate and refresh'.[65] There were also commercial venues for leisure here. In a 1511 consistory court case, St Botolph Aldersgate's parishioners complained that one of their parish chaplains neglected his duties and instead 'attended cock fights in the house of Master Pikton and inside Aldgate and at "le boutts" [archery butts] also in the cemetery in the same place'.[66] The best-documented commercial leisure activities at the fringes of the city were those that catered to London's large Dutch-speaking community. Closhbanes were playing areas for a bowls-like game which originated in the Low Countries.[67] In the Portsoken wardmote presentments, closhbanes were indicted thirty-four times between the 1460s and 1480s.[68] Closhbanes or alleys were also frequently noted in the court rolls of the liberty of Norton Folgate along Bishopsgate Street. Simon Richard was fined multiple times in the 1440s for keeping a closhbane in his garden, a notorious local dive described as the cause of many affrays which local residents were ordered not to visit in 1442 on pain of a 20-shilling fine.[69] Richard himself was an immigrant, probably from the Low Countries,[70] and given that the city's eastern suburbs and Norton Folgate both had considerable immigrant communities, as discussed below, it is unsurprising that closhbanes should proliferate.

[62] TNA, SC 11/972.

[63] TNA, SC 11/972; SC 11/973.

[64] TNA SC11/975; LMA, DL/C/B/004/9171/006, fo. 172.

[65] John Stow, 'Portsoken warde', in *A Survey of London. Reprinted from the Text of 1603*, ed. C. L. Kingsford (Oxford, 1908), pp. 120–29, *British History Online* <http://www.british-history.ac.uk/no-series/survey-of-london-stow/1603/pp120-129> [accessed 27 Jan. 2015].

[66] LMA, DL/C/206, fo. 65v.

[67] 'closh, n.1.' *OED* online <oed.com/view/Entry/34631> [accessed 20 May 2020].

[68] Winter, 'Portsoken presentments', p. 149.

[69] LMA, CLC/313/L/A/047/MS25287, rots. 2–3.

[70] He was taxed in the alien subsidies together with his wife Katherine in 1440–44. *England's Immigrants* <https://www.englandsimmigrants.com/person/39500> [accessed 2 June 2020].

The urban margins could provide space and recreation to those who lived within the walls. That extra space also influenced the size and character of the buildings. Although we lack plans for extramural properties at this early date, it is evident that some properties were large, with multiple potential commercial functions. For example, the Axe, a tenement on Aldgate Street just outside the gate, was an inn with a brewhouse and a bakehouse. The dean and chapter of St Paul's Cathedral owned the property as part of John of Gaunt's chantry, and their workmen were responsible for maintaining the fabric of the building as well as the fittings, such as vats, barrels, taps and the oven, which enabled the tenants to carry on their business.[71] Four of the Axe's fifteenth-century tenants were brewers, and John Brice, who leased the property in the 1470s and 1480s, was a butcher. Given that repairs in 1456 note fourteen shillings paid to three carpenters for 'repairs and amendments of diverse of the houses and chambers in the same place', it is most likely that even the brewers did not occupy the whole of the Axe and sublet a number of other domestic units on the property to tenants of whom we have no record.[72] Other large extramural properties could be very fine houses rather than commercial properties; an early sixteenth-century house excavated on the west side of Bishopsgate Street was well built with a mixture of cream Flemish and red London bricks and backed on to gardens and yards.[73] It is difficult to gauge the grandeur of such houses from their description in property records, but it is easy to imagine that, for example, the great inn with hall, several chambers, a mill, solar, garden and stable at Barbican which the dean and chapter of St Paul's regularly spent large sums repairing from the 1390s to the 1470s was probably impressive.[74]

The *rus in urbe* quality of London's extramural neighbourhoods was enhanced by the style of its buildings. In Portsoken, by far the most numerous wardmote charges in the late fifteenth century were against sheds covered with reeds and wooden chimneys, which Christine Winter argued evidences a preoccupation with risk from fire.[75] However, given the sparse population of Portsoken, it also suggests the persistence of construction materials that were better suited to rural areas, in spite of building regulations against such

[71] See for instance 'Baryngton for his fixed rent owing at le Axe Bakhous' in 1470–71. LMA, CLC/313/L/D/001/MS25125/090. Payment for new millstone and tap hose, solder for the great iron in the furnace in 1465–6. LMA, CLC/313/L/D/001/MS25125/087.

[72] LMA, CLC/313/L/D/001/MS25125/81.

[73] Swift, *Roman Burials, Medieval Tenements and Suburban Growth*, p. 40.

[74] LMA, CLC/313/L/D/001/MS25125/25-95.

[75] Winter, 'The Portsoken presentments', p. 106.

practices being long established in London.[76] Perhaps, although jurors were aware that the wardmote precepts bound them to report roofs of thatch and wooden chimneys,[77] the inhabitants and landlords of Portsoken did not perceive their neighbourhood as a dense urban space in need of protection from fire. This would explain the very large number of charges – 449 across the Portsoken presentments, which equates to 19 per cent of all charges of any type for the period 1373–1528 – and their continuance of complaints year after year with seemingly little change.

Housing the poor

In some neighbourhoods outside the walls, additional space was used to build complexes of alleyway housing which led away from major roads. These small, cheap properties were to become a dominant feature of London's development as population pressure prompted subdivision across the city in the sixteenth century.[78] Commonly, the alley was placed behind a larger property which occupied valuable street frontage. The whole complex was often named for the sign that hung on its street front. This was the case for the Black Horse, the property discussed above which was owned by the churchwardens of St Botolph Aldersgate. In the 1490s it contained three properties along Aldersgate Street with annual rents between ten shillings and 13*s* 4*d* which were arranged across a gateway to an alley behind and where there were fourteen rents let for four shillings per annum each.[79] These fourteen small houses had a communal well and privy.[80] In the neighbourhood outside Bishopsgate, the hospital of St Mary had built at least one alleyway on its lands on the main road by the 1460s and five by the 1490s, named as George, Bell, Harp and Stuard alleys, and one simply known as the alley 'before the well'.[81] Rents were uniformly four or five shillings per annum, compared to costs ranging from five shillings to £3 for properties

[76] On the use of thatch in extramural areas and roof coverings more generally see J. Schofield, *Medieval London Houses*, pp. 96–8.

[77] John Carpenter, *Liber Albus: the White Book of the City of London*, ed. Henry Thomas Riley (London, 1861), pp. 288–9.

[78] L. C. Orlin, 'Temporary lives in London lodgings', *Huntingdon Library Quarterly*, lxxi (2008), 219–42, at pp. 219–24; I. W. Archer, *The Pursuit of Stability: Social Relations in Elizabethan London*, Cambridge Studies in Early Modern British History (Cambridge, 1991), pp. 81–2.

[79] LMA, P69/BOT1/B/013/MS01454/018; P69/BOT1/D/002/MS06641, fos. 155–91.

[80] Copies of deeds related to Black Horse Alley with descriptions of its amenities are found in LMA, P69/BOT1/D/002/MS06641, fos. 155–91.

[81] TNA, SC 11/971; SC 11/975.

Table 1.4 Occupation levels for properties in Bishopsgate Street (North-east Without) and the Black Horse (North-west Without), 1493–1506

Location Type	Total	Vacant		Occupied	
Thoroughfare	161	47	29.2%	114	70.8%
Alley	237	47	19.8%	190	80.2%

in front of the alleys or elsewhere along Bishopsgate Street. A number of these alleys led to the hospital's garden plots.[82] Detailed rentals in 1493–1506 for the Black Horse and the hospital of St Mary's Bishopsgate properties allow insight into patterns of vacancy and occupation during that time. As Table 1.4 indicates, vacancies were 10 per cent more common among thoroughfare properties than those in alleyways. London's population was beginning to rise in this period, but it was small properties that were most in demand. At Cheapside, property owners preferred to maintain large tenements rather than subdivide into small houses, so repaired and kept them vacant until a tenant could be found for the whole property.[83] As the city's precipitous population rise got under way in the sixteenth century, it was to be these modest dwellings that housed the majority of newcomers. The pace of development was different across the city, with alleyways first appearing in St Botolph Aldgate in the 1540s.[84] The changes in fifteenth-century Bishopsgate Street with its increasing number of alleys were a microcosm of later patterns of urban development and of how property owners would cater to poor newcomers. At four or five shillings per annum, extramural alleyway 'rents' were affordable in the late fifteenth and early sixteenth centuries, even for day labourers who might earn £3 in a good year in the same period.[85]

Religious houses and their impact

Directing much extramural urban development were London's religious houses, which lay mainly outside or at the edges of the walled city. Many houses owned much of the property surrounding their precincts: in 1539, Holy Trinity Priory's estate had eighty-one named tenants in the surrounding parish of St Katharine Cree.[86] Growing from sometimes just a single tenement

[82] TNA, SC 11/975.

[83] Harding, 'Houses and households in Cheapside *c.*1500–1550', pp. 137–9.

[84] M. Carlin, *St Botolph Aldgate Gazetteer* (London, 1987), pp. 36–38.

[85] C. Phythian-Adams, *Desolation of a City: Coventry and the Urban Crisis of the Later Middle Ages* (Cambridge, 1979), pp. 132–4.

[86] TNA, SC 12/26/61.

plot, over time they acquired neighbouring land and accrued property elsewhere within and outside the city, often by gifts and bequests from the laity, which provided rental income to support the religious community and its activities.[87] Extramural houses acted as nuclei for local urban development in London and other cities but were also, crucially, active in the shaping of the local property market.[88] In the fifteenth century, many houses and hospitals increasingly looked to lay tenants as a source of income. Within the precincts, this resulted in a proliferation of structures built or repurposed for the use of lay tenants. At the hospital of St Mary Bishopsgate, areas of the outer precinct which had previously been used for crops and grazing animals were instead built on and leased out.[89] By the time the Cistercian abbey of St Mary Graces, East Smithfield, was built in the late fourteenth century, it was evidently thought unnecessary to construct many buildings for ancillary activities (such as food processing) traditionally included in religious precincts and by at least 1425 it had lay tenements.[90] Initially tenants were of high status, attracted by large tenements with special access to church services in the precinct.[91] Lay tenements became common in almost all houses and hospitals by the early sixteenth century, by which time they had become a lucrative income stream.[92] In this later period, development of low-status housing became a common strategy in their estate management. As we have already seen, the hospital of St Mary Bishopsgate used its lands in the parish of St Botolph Bishopsgate

[87] For greater detail on this process see N. Holder, *The Friaries of Medieval London: From Foundation to Dissolution* (Woodbridge, 2017).

[88] On religious houses as nuclei for development see J. Schofield and R. Lea, *Holy Trinity Priory, Aldgate, City of London: an Archaeological Reconstruction and History*, MoLAS Monograph, 24 (London, 2005), pp. 155–6; S. Anthony, *Medieval Settlement to 18th-/19th-Century Rookery: Excavations at Central Saint Giles, London Borough of Camden, 2006–8* (London, 2011), p. 7; in *Die Stadt und ihr Rand*, ed. P. Johannek (Cologne, 2008), pp. 167–90, at pp. 178–9.

[89] C. Thomas, B. Sloane and C. Phillpotts, *Excavations at the Priory and Hospital of St Mary Spital, London*, MoLAS Monograph (London, 1997), pp. 85–7, 99.

[90] I. Grainger and C. Phillpotts, *The Cistercian Abbey of St Mary Graces, East Smithfield, London*, MoLA Monograph, 44 (London, 2011), pp. 35–8, 113.

[91] E. C. Roger, 'Blakberd's treasure: a study in fifteenth-century administration at St Bartholomew's Hospital, London', in *Exploring the Evidence: Commemoration, Administration and the Economy*, ed. L. Clark, The Fifteenth Century, 13 (Woodbridge, 2014), pp. 81–107, at pp. 88–9, 97–8; Holder, *The Friaries of Medieval London*, pp. 299–302; C. M. Barron, 'A virtual London parish: the Precinct of St Bartholomew's Hospital in the fifteenth century' (presented at the Harlaxton Medieval Symposium: Church and City in the Middle Ages, Harlaxton Manor, 2017).

[92] Holder, *The Friaries of Medieval London*, p. 300.

to build alleyways containing cheap, probably small houses called 'rents'.[93] It also built a set of alms houses between the precinct wall and Bishopsgate Street called Crown Rents.[94] At Austin Friars, parts of the outer precinct were developed into small tenements in the later fifteenth century.[95] On a similarly cramped intramural plot, Holy Trinity Priory had also added lay housing to the fringes of its precinct by 1500.[96] In parishes like St Botolph Bishopsgate and St Katharine Cree, where a single local institution also owned much of the land, there was great potential for the priorities of a house or hospital to shape the character of a neighbourhood through its building programme and the kinds of tenants it chose to attract. Their legal privileges, discussed further below, allowed for the continuation of prostitution as well as the residence of those avoiding craft regulations such as immigrants, who were (officially at least) barred from citizenship of London.

The houses would have consumed considerable provisions and other resources which they could not wholly source from their estates in the countryside or produce within their increasingly crowded precincts. Westminster Abbey, whose accounts have been well studied, provides a model which was probably similar to London's extramural houses. The abbey generally preferred to buy in London's main markets rather than rely on local middlemen in Westminster. A notable exception was meat, where the abbey made use of local butchers, and it seems likely that this pattern may have been repeated in neighbourhoods such as those outside Aldgate and Aldersgate with suburban butchers' markets.[97] Economic ties with religious houses could also be reciprocal. In 1524, the renter of the Abbey of St Mary Graces noted two tenants who paid their rents not in cash but in the products of their crafts: Owen Williams, a baker who gave his full annual rent of £4 13s 4d to the abbey in bread, and Peter Curteys, pewterer, who gave 32s 8d worth of vessels.[98] Direct employees might also be their tenants. In a 1473 rental for the hospital of St Mary Bishopsgate, a tenant called Deonisia (Denise?) was described as a former porter or gatekeeper of the hospital (*nuper servientem ianitorem hospitalis*). She paid four shillings per

[93] TNA, SC 11/975.

[94] Thomas, Sloane and Phillpotts, *Excavations at the Priory and Hospital of St Mary Spital, London*, p. 78.

[95] N. Holder, 'The medieval friaries of London: a topographic and archaeological history, before and after the Dissolution' (University of London, 2011), pp. 155–6.

[96] Schofield and Lea, *Holy Trinity Priory*, p. 141

[97] B. F. Harvey, 'Westminster Abbey and Londoners, 1440–1540', in *London and the Kingdom: Essays in Honour of Caroline M. Barron*, ed. M. P. Davies and A. Prescott, Harlaxton Medieval Studies, 16 (Donington, 2008), pp. 12–37, at pp. 27–32.

[98] TNA, SC 12/11/43, fos. 5v–6.

annum for a property in St Botolph Bishopsgate parish.[99] Another possible employee was a tenant described as 'Floraunce Porter', in the 1524 rental for the Abbey of St Mary Graces, who also paid a low rent (five shillings).[100] While not plentiful, the surviving evidence is suggestive of the existence of economic ties between the houses and their surrounding lay communities. More broadly important for the extramural economy is that religious houses' property-management strategies would have had a real impact on who could afford to live in a neighbourhood and what occupations were practised there, particularly when they were landlords for large parts of the area. It is likely that they used some of their properties for charitable purposes, which blurred the line between alms houses and cheap 'rents', of which the case of the former porter may be an example. In sixteenth-century Venice, the charitable use of property by landlords is well documented and endowments for the provision of housing to poor people were a relatively common bequest among the city elites.[101] In the absence of the information networks that developed through print culture in the early modern period, finding property to rent must have relied on word of mouth and thus pre-existing connections to an institution seem a probable means through which to find accommodation.[102]

Another tangible impact of religious houses on the city's periphery was the persistence of prostitution there. The legal exemptions which removed religious houses from civic and royal jurisdiction allowed the continuance of the sex trade as well as other illicit activities. Prostitution in Southwark has been well studied by historians, with its regulated brothels and ordinances governing the contractual relationship between pimps and prostitutes.[103] Westminster, too, developed districts associated with prostitution.[104] Closer to the city, the precinct of St Katharine's Hospital and the Abbey of St Mary Graces, both near Tower Hill, seem to have been particular hotspots, with a 'stewhouse' mentioned in the court roll of the abbey's precinct for 1434, together with many complaints about prostitutes in both institutions'

[99] TNA, SC 11/973.

[100] TNA, SC 12/11/43, fo. 3.

[101] P. Fortini Brown, 'Not one but many cities: housing diversity in sixteenth-century Venice', in *Home and Homelessness in the Medieval and Renaissance World*, ed. N. Howe (Notre Dame, Ind., 2004), pp. 13–44, at pp. 25–33.

[102] D. Postles, 'Migration and mobility in a less mature economy', pp. 290–92.

[103] R. M. Karras, 'The regulation of brothels in later medieval England', *Signs; Journal of Women in Culture & Society*, xiv (1988), 399–433; Carlin, *Medieval Southwark*, ch. 9; P. J. P. Goldberg, 'Pigs and prostitutes: streetwalking in comparative perspective', in *Young Medieval Women*, ed. K. J. Lewis, N. Menuge and K. M. Philips (Stroud, 1999), pp. 172–93, at pp. 180–86.

[104] G. Rosser, *Medieval Westminster: 1200–1540* (Oxford, 1989), pp. 143–44.

liberties.[105] London's civic authorities banned prostitution within the city, although when they conceded that not all prostitution could be kept out of their jurisdiction it was to the suburbs that they looked as the appropriate space for a limited area of tolerated brothels (Cock Lane in the parish of St Sepulchre without Newgate).[106] Even beyond liberties, prostitution seems to have been more common outside the walls. This sense is suggested in the records of the London commissary court, an ecclesiastical court to which sexual misdemeanours were sometimes referred from the wardmote.[107] Out of 104 cases heard at the commissary between March and June 1515, thirteen were for offences relating to prostitution and pimping; ten were in extramural parishes, with six in St Botolph Aldgate alone.[108] Extramural parishes including St Botolph Aldgate and St Botolph Bishopsgate dominated accusations of sexual misdemeanours at the commissary court more generally.[109] The proximity of liberties and, in the east, the maritime community at St Katharine's may well have been the cause. The extramural neighbourhoods may have offered venues where it was easier to evade detection, an issue which will be discussed further in Chapter Five. However, not all those living outside the walls accepted pimping and prostitution as part of the local economy. As Martin Ingram has argued, even in Southwark local householders frequently complained about and sought to end their neighbours' brothel-keeping.[110] The embeddedness of religious houses in the fabric of extramural neighbourhoods is a recurring theme in this book. Their local role is a powerful reminder of how inextricable institutional, social and economic ties were in the city.

Household and economy

Turning from the institutions which shaped extramural neighbourhoods towards their society and economy requires a return to the analysis of property and wills. Of course, the limitations outlined at the start of this chapter about the surviving property records and wills mean we cannot

[105] TNA, SC 2/191/56, rot. 2; S. McSheffrey, 'Liberties of London: social networks, sexual disorder and independent jurisdiction in the late medieval English metropolis', in *Crossing Borders: Boundaries and Margins in Medieval and Early Modern Britain*, ed. K. J. Kesselring and S. Butler (Leiden, 2018), pp. 216–36.

[106] Karras, 'The regulation of brothels in later medieval England', pp. 408–10.

[107] M. Ingram, *Carnal Knowledge: Regulating Sex in England, 1470–1600* (Cambridge and New York, 2017), p. 225.

[108] LMA, DL/C/B/043/MS09064/011, fos. 224v–246.

[109] Ingram, *Carnal Knowledge*, p. 180.

[110] Ingram, *Carnal Knowledge*, pp. 160–72.

be sure that, for example, named tenants in rentals were in fact resident, and the poorest households are no doubt under-represented. There are nonetheless meaningful observations which can be made on society and economy outside the walls. The gender balance among tenants is one such area where limited sources can lead to interesting conclusions about the kinds of households occupying the urban margins. Women made up 12 per cent of the 1842 tenants in the sample, men 87 per cent, and a small number were not identifiable based on their name. Since named tenants were most likely heads of household, if they were resident, this imbalance is to be expected. Women named as tenants would probably have been widows or single women who had never married heading their own households, rather than wives.[111] In every neighbourhood, women paid lower rents than men as shown in Figure 1.4. The median annual rent where a woman was named as tenant was 48 pence (four shillings) against 108 pence (nine shillings) for men. Lower rents among women probably indicate smaller houses, fewer people in their households and smaller means of support. This pattern recurs across all the neighbourhoods, but with great variation in the size of the gender gap. The greatest gap was in the North-east Within zone, where women paid just 39 per cent of the rent that men did, but the smallest difference was just over the wall in the area outside Bishopsgate, where women paid 83 per cent of the median rent for male tenants. In other neighbourhoods, women paid between roughly a half and two thirds.

This gender rent gap had many causes, one of which was probably the charitable use of housing by institutions. The female tenants in the North-east Within zone almost all had the same landlord, the Carpenters' Company. All but three of the properties they rented were part of the company's cheap 'rents within the Hall', costing less than six shillings per year in the parish of All Hallows on the Wall. These were part of a complex of properties attached to the company hall, and many or even most of the tenants were most likely company members or their widows. Of 106 tenants named in 1440–1500 within the company accounts, 30 per cent were mentioned as receiving or making payments in various other roles such as enrolling apprentices, receiving alms or paying for their freedom. Many tenants were widows who, if they had a connection to the company through their husbands, would be unlikely to feature in the records before their widowhood, suggesting that this is a significant undercount. Until 1458, these chambers were described

[111] On the prevalence of single women in late medieval London see J. M. Bennett and C. Whittick, 'Philippa Russell and the wills of London's late medieval singlewomen', *London Journal*, xxxii (2007), 251–69.

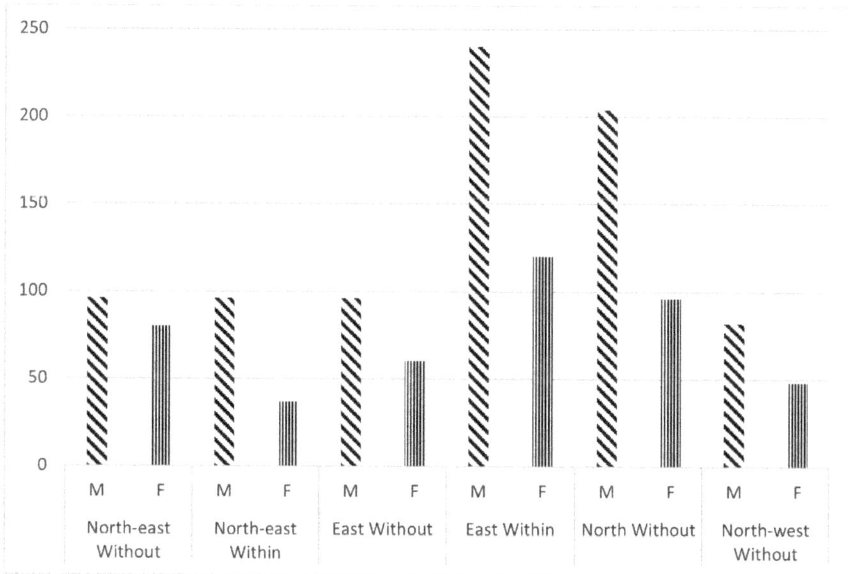

Figure 1.4 Median rents in pence by zone for male and female tenants

in the company accounts as an alms house.[112] Even after this date, the properties still served a charitable function. The company was an extremely lenient landlord: many tenants 'within the hall' were permitted to pay rent 'old and new' at the same time, gave sums in part payment, or even had their rent paid for them by other tenants. In at least one case, a tenant paid with household goods in lieu of cash.[113] The women living here, then, were poor, probably company widows, and were housed partly out of charity, and poor widows often made use of institutional connections to support them in their old age.[114] The Carpenters' rents also had male tenants, but the average rent for men in the North-east Within zone as a whole is raised by the amounts paid for properties elsewhere, including a house with a

[112] *Records of the Worshipful Company of Carpenters. Vol. 2 Warden's Account Book 1438–1516*, ed. B. Marsh (Oxford, 1914), p. 27.

[113] See eg 1506: 'Received of Maud Gervys of rent old and new – 4s.; Received of Harry Brayne of old rent – 4s.; Received of Elizabeth Creyke in party of payment – 19d'; 1486: 'Item received of Margery Albryght for rent by the hands of Steven Scales – 5s. 10d'; 1501: 'Received of Guy Birchfeld for Mother Sage – 16d'; 1508: 'Item received of William Pudsey for certain stuff of household prised for rent 16d.' LMA, CLC/L/CC/D/002/MS04326/001.

[114] Schen, 'Strategies of poor aged women and widows in sixteenth century London', pp. 23–5.

garden and stable and a number of cottages with gardens.[115] The same kind of difference drove the disparity between men and women elsewhere; in the North-west Without zone, thirty-five of the forty-two female tenants lived in Black Horse Alley. While both men and women of small means rented cheap properties, men on the whole had access to greater resources and therefore were more likely to find themselves in a position to occupy larger houses with greater amenities and the potential to house more servants or a workshop. The same was true in Coventry, where Charles Phythian-Adams found that the poorest houses were more likely to be female-headed and with an average household size of just 1.8 people.[116] Sarah Rees Jones has described similar small properties, typically in alleyways, in York as 'a form of dormitory style housing provided for people who were expected to sell their labour to others'. In York, too, they had a higher than usual number of female-headed households.[117] She argued that these tenants were excluded from the late medieval urban polity and were denied the status of householder, making a clear connection between access to domestic space and urban social status.[118] For the women who lived here, however, their residency could be viewed more positively as enabling them to live in a city which was often hostile to female labour as well as perhaps giving them a sense of safety and community in the enclosed space of the alleyway.

The women of the neighbourhood outside Bishopsgate provide a fascinating and somewhat contrasting case. In this area, women made up the joint highest proportion of testators (22 per cent), and 14 per cent of all testators were explicitly described as widows. Women constituted 18 per cent of all tenants, a little higher than in the total sample. However, as the median rent disparity for this area shown in Figure 1.4 suggests, women paid rents dramatically closer to those of men than in other neighbourhoods. What was so unusual about these women and their households? Many seem to have been widows: fifteen of the forty-six women tenants were described as widows in the rentals and others probably were too, without this identification being made in the property records. Avice Shrewsbury, whose will was proved in 1489, twenty-eight years after that of her husband, John, was a Bishopsgate tenant in her widowhood, although this status was never mentioned in rentals. She is in fact emblematic of the more varied

[115] LMA, CLA/007/FN/02/003.

[116] Phythian-Adams, *Desolation of a City*, p. 243.

[117] S. Rees Jones, *York: the Making of a City, 1068–1350* (Oxford and New York, 2013), pp. 272–3; P. J. P. Goldberg, 'Space and gender in the later medieval English house', *Viator*, xlii (2011), 205–32, at p. 224, doi:org/10.1484/J.VIATOR.1.102250.

[118] Rees Jones, *York*, p. 273.

kinds of property that women rented in this area. In 1469 she rented a tenement on Bishopsgate Street for £1 per year, and Agnes Buckby leased an inn called the George on the same street for five shillings; the pair also paid 13*s* 4*d* between them for a third tenement on the street.[119] By 1473, Agnes was no longer mentioned, but Avice paid 33*s* 4*d* 'for her rent'.[120] Avice's tenement was probably the 'shop with all its instruments and necessaries pertinent to it' left to her by her husband, who was a blacksmith. Under John Shrewsbury's will, Avice was allowed to retain his shop and tools 'from which to sustain her and her children' so long as she remained unmarried.[121] She seems to have done so until her death, and through co-tenancy with Agnes Buckby was perhaps engaged in some kind of commercial partnership on the side of her business as a blacksmith.[122] Other women with more modest means also lived in the neighbourhood, many clustered in the alleys which ran away from the main street. For instance, in Stuard Alley in 1505, four of the six occupied houses had female tenants (Margaret Brown, Elene Thorpe, Margaret Luffdale and Joan Nutte), all paying an annual rent of four shillings.[123] What was different about Bishopsgate Street, however, was that women rented properties with a range of costs which were fairly similar to those of local men: for every Margaret Brown in a cheap 'rent' there was an Agnes Buckby occupying a major thoroughfare property. Probably because of its general cheap housing, female artisans such as Avice Shrewsbury could afford to make the choice to keep their own households here and preserve the resources left to them in their widowhood.

This was a more general pattern among all Bishopsgate tenants, male and female. There were only five tenants who worked as servants in the whole sample; four were labourers and one was a retired porter, and all lived in the area outside Bishopsgate. The most expensive property between them was rented by labourer John Bramsgrove outside George Alley for ten shillings a year.[124] Lower property values made housing affordable for those with the most precarious occupations as well as those who, despite moderate resources, might have struggled to find city-centre accommodation.

[119] TNA, SC 11/972.

[120] TNA, SC 11/973.

[121] TNA, PROB 11/4/388

[122] Avice's will of 1489 mentions a 'John Bokby and Joan his spouse' in the list of souls to be prayed for in masses after her death, so Agnes may have been a kin relation or family friend. LMA DL/C/B/004/MS09171/003, fo. 291v.

[123] TNA, SC 11/971.

[124] TNA, SC 11/971.

Table 1.5 Male and female testators with marital status

	Total testators (n)	**Male testators (n)**	**Living wife (n)**	**Proportion men married (%)**	**Female testators (n)**	**Named widow (n)**	**Proportion women widows (%)**
St Botolph Aldersgate	61	50	36	72	11	7	64
St Botolph Aldgate	123	104	81	78	19	12	63
St Botolph Bishopsgate	111	87	70	80	24	16	67
St Katharine Cree	100	76	58	76	24	14	58
St Lawrence Jewry	66	61	47	77	5	4	80

There were, however, many in more prosperous households living outside the walls, which corresponded far more closely with the medieval urban ideal. The 'model' late medieval household, headed by a married couple engaged in a trade and also perhaps containing children, servants, apprentices and journeymen, required at least a modest amount of capital or stable occupation (or mix of occupations) in order to support its members.[125] As Table 1.5 indicates, over 70 per cent of male testators named a living wife in their will. Some households were very large, with numerous servants as well as a married couple. While we cannot be certain any children named in a will were resident, numbers of servants named can give an impression of household size. William Boste, a glover from St Botolph Aldgate with a large estate, left money to a maid and two apprentices; since he also named a living wife, Boste's household numbered at least five individuals. Boste's will was later subject to a consistory court case, when one of the apprentices sued his widow.[126] The household of William Marow, alderman

[125] On the model artisan household structure of the late medieval period see F. Riddy, '"Burgeis" domesticity in late medieval England'; S. Rees Jones, 'Household, work and the problem of mobile labour: the regulation of labour in medieval English towns', in *The Problem of Labour in Fourteenth-Century England*, ed. P. J. P. Goldberg, W. M. Ormrod and J. Bothwell (York, 2000), pp. 133–53; M. Kowaleski and P. J. P. Goldberg, 'Introduction', in *Medieval Domesticity: Home, Housing and Household in Medieval England*, ed. M. Kowaleski and P. J. P. Goldberg (Cambridge and New York, 2008), pp. 1–13.

[126] TNA, PROB 11/8/380. The ex-apprentice's suit is discussed in Chapter Three, at pp. 109–10.

of Bishopsgate ward, must have been exceptionally large, given the eleven servants, including a cook, named in his will.[127] Phythian-Adams's study of Coventry found that citizens' households contained an average of four or five people, with only victuallers and merchants having households any larger.[128] Although lacking material as in depth as Coventry's 1522 census, households in London appear to have followed a very similar pattern.

Sometimes wills reveal more unusual domestic arrangements. Nicholas Long, a butcher from St Botolph Aldgate, left the house in which they dwelled to his wife for the term of her life, and described it as lying between the highway in the south and 'the tenement brewhouse that John Raulyn and Anne my daughter hold on the west side'.[129] It seems likely that with his daughter and son-in-law so close by, the boundaries between their properties may have been legal formalities. As Long's example suggests, the descriptions of household relationships in wills often seem to simplify a complex reality. Margaret Brere of St Botolph Bishopsgate left an exceptionally large amount of household goods in her 1438 will to a woman described as her servant named Agnes Fulk. The bequests included the bed she slept in, soft furnishings, silverware and kitchen apparatus. Margaret's will was also unusual in that she named her occupation as a weaver, and she left Agnes 'two instruments together of my craft called the looms with all their apparatus'.[130] Although Margaret described Agnes as a servant, it does not seem too great a leap to imagine that the relationship between these two women was in fact much closer. Household arrangements very different to the late medieval ideal are perhaps buried beneath the wording of many wills from neighbourhoods all over the city.

More distinctive to the areas outside the city walls, however, were communities of immigrants from outside England, known as aliens. Only a handful of surviving wills could be identified as made by aliens, but this is to be expected, given the profile of immigrant communities in London. There was a constant stream of new arrivals to the city, of whom only a minority became permanent residents.[131] Immigrants were often young and thus would be less likely to either becomes heads of household or die

[127] TNA, PROB 11/5/139.

[128] Phythian-Adams, *Desolation of a City*, p. 242.

[129] LMA, DL/C/B/004/MS09171/001 fos. 319v–320.

[130] LMA, DL/C/B/004/MS09171/003 fo. 517v.

[131] J. Lutkin, 'Settled or fleeting?: London's medieval immigrant community revisited', in *Medieval Merchants and Money: Essays in Honour of James L. Bolton*, ed. M. Allen and M. Davies (2016), pp. 137–56, at pp. 150–54.

in their London parish.[132] Service migration, such as the system of artisan training known as the *wanderjahr*, brought craftsmen to the city for a few years before moving on elsewhere to hone their skills.[133] The impact of their presence can be felt in local court records, such as the complaints about closhbanes, and in taxation. Analysis of the fifteenth-century alien subsidy records has shown that the east of the city was particularly favoured by 'Doche' (Dutch- and German-speaking) migrants and that the community in Portsoken grew across the fifteenth century to become by far the largest in the city.[134] This population was very much still in evidence in the eastern extramural zone in the early sixteenth century. Of ninety-seven inhabitants of East Smithfield liberty assessed for the 1524 subsidy, two thirds (sixty-four) were classed as aliens.[135] Norton Folgate, which probably had a population of around one hundred people, was the residence of seventeen aliens taxed in the 1440 subsidy.[136] Liberties were important hubs for immigrant communities, partly because they enabled alien craftsmen to continue their business without interference from London's guilds but also perhaps because living surrounded by those who spoke one's language was comforting.[137] Moreover, we should not draw too hard and fast a line between immigrants and guilds, since by the later fifteenth and early sixteenth centuries several London companies had oversight of immigrants' work and even offered quasi-guild member status to trusted craftsmen.[138] The imperative to escape guild control thus depended on the circumstances of individual trades rather than being experienced by all aliens. Immigrants were an integral part of extramural society and as such they will recur throughout this book.

[132] J. L. Bolton, 'The alien population of London in the fifteenth century: a reappraisal', in *The Alien Communities of London in the Fifteenth Century: the Subsidy Rolls of 1440 and 1483–4* (Stamford, 1998), pp. 1–40, at pp. 26–8.

[133] C. Berry, 'Guilds, immigration and immigrant economic organization: alien goldsmiths in London, 1480–1540', *Journal of British Studies*, lx (2021), 534–62, at pp. 536–7, 545–6.

[134] Bolton, 'The alien population of London', p. 11.

[135] TNA, E 179/141/113, m. 8.

[136] *England's Immigrants 1330–1550*, <http://www.englandsimmigrants.com/search/results?col1=name&col2=nationality&col3=residence&col4=date&col5=origin&esSort=col1&esSortDir=asc&page=1&residenceWard=Norton%20Folgate&taxCollection_untouched_facet=1440-1> [accessed 4 June 2020].

[137] S. McSheffrey, 'Stranger artisans and the London sanctuary of St Martin Le Grand in the Reign of Henry VIII', *Journal of Medieval and Early Modern Studies*, xliii (2013), 545–71.

[138] M. Davies, 'Aliens, crafts and guilds in late medieval London', in *Medieval Londoners: Essays to Mark the Eightieth Birthday of Caroline M. Barron*, ed. E. A. New and C. Steer (London, 2019), pp. 119–48; Berry, 'Guilds, immigration and immigrant economic organization: alien goldsmiths in London, 1480–1540'.

In the later fifteenth century, anxiety about non-citizens trading illicitly without the freedom of the city seems to have increased. It is hardly a coincidence that this coincided with a period in which English religious houses began to more actively acquire privileges for those living in their precincts.[139] The tensions which built up are evident in the increasing complaints about foreign workers in guild ordinances of the later fifteenth century and the complaints about non-English immigrants which resulted in both the Evil May Day riots of 1517 and the city's dogged legal challenge of St Martin le Grand's sanctuary in the 1530s.[140] The sanctuary at St Katharine's and liberty at the hospital of St Mary Bishopsgate were also subject to civic complaints from the mid-fifteenth century.[141] This hardening of attitudes does not seem to have produced specific complaints against all the other extramural houses and their lay populations. It may be that residents infringing the franchise here were seen as part of a wider problem with those living in the ribbon development that led up to the city bars. Indeed, from the 1480s the city claimed rights to regulate all craft production within two miles, a power it sporadically enforced.[142]

Despite the expansion of the city and companies' rights beyond the bars, historians traditionally assumed that the economy of London's extramural neighbourhoods was based on avoidance of civic regulations, the responsibilities of citizenship and control exerted by guilds.[143] However, wills provide a salutary reminder that there was a community of citizens outside the walls, even if overall levels of citizenship here were lower. Following the 1413 Statute of Additions, which required suitors at law to declare their occupation and status, it became more common for individuals to declare personal details in all kinds of other legal documents. Testators frequently began their wills with the formula 'citizen and [occupation/guild affiliation] of London'. As demonstrated in Table 1.6, statements of citizenship were noticeably less common outside the walls; while over 55 per cent of testators said they were citizens in central St Lawrence Jewry, only 31–42 per cent did so in the extramural parishes and St Katharine Cree. Statements about what craft a testator practised (a good indicator of guild membership) followed a

[139] S. McSheffrey, *Seeking Sanctuary: Crime, Mercy and Politics in English Courts, 1400–1550* (Oxford and New York, 2017), pp. 11, 94–6, 190.

[140] McSheffrey, *Seeking Sanctuary*, ch. 5; M. Davies, 'Citizens and "foreyns": crafts, guilds and regulation in late medieval London', in *Between Regulation and Freedom: Work and Manufactures in European Cities, 14th–18th Centuries*, ed. A. Caracausi, L. Mocarelli and M. Davies (Newcastle upon Tyne, 2018), pp. 1–21, at pp. 19–20.

[141] McSheffrey, *Seeking Sanctuary*, pp. 61–2.

[142] McSheffrey, *Seeking Sanctuary*, p. 125.

[143] See the Introduction for discussion of this literature.

Table 1.6 Citizenship declared by testators, 1390–1540

	Total	**Citizen**		**Not specified**	
St Botolph Aldersgate	*55*	17	31%	38	69%
St Botolph Aldgate	*110*	36	33%	74	67%
St Botolph Bishopsgate	*106*	45	42%	61	58%
St Katharine Cree	*97*	36	37%	61	63%
St Lawrence Jewry	*64*	35	55%	29	45%
Totals	*432*	*169*		*263*	

similar pattern. Seventy-five per cent of St Lawrence Jewry testators named their occupation, compared to 42–57 per cent outside the walls. Citizens and guild members were thus residents outside the walls, but in lower numbers.

Far from evading regulation, many of these non-citizens were either ineligible for guild membership or did not need it to support themselves. In this period, guild membership was a prerequisite for citizenship of London and the gap between the numbers of those with a declared occupation and those with citizenship is to an extent accounted for by those with occupations which simply lacked a guild. These included two minstrels and a gardener in St Botolph Bishopsgate and a corser (horse dealer) and mariner in St Botolph Aldgate. Aside from the minstrels, it should be noted that, given the proximity of major roads and gardens, these were occupations where living at the fringe of the city would have been an advantage. Members of the gentry and people with positions reliant on royal and aristocratic patronage also lived in peripheral areas, particularly in St Botolph Aldersgate and St Katharine Cree. These included esquires and gentlemen in both parishes, as well as Robert Biggerstaff, clerk of the earl of Northumberland's kitchen, who lived outside Aldersgate. Aside from within liberties, evasion of city regulations was not a significant facet of the appeal of living in the city's immediate environs, especially after 1470, when guild jurisdiction extended two miles beyond London. Lower property values, access to major roads and larger properties encouraged those whose occupations were either precarious or unincorporated into the civic hierarchy to live there. Citizens, many of them prosperous, still formed a sizeable portion of the resident population. The rest of the population was diverse. Much of the non-citizen population either lacked the resources to participate in a craft or earned their living in ways which meant civic and craft institutions were of limited relevance. As we saw in the introduction, citizenship was a minority status in the city as a whole before the 1530s and guilds were increasingly hierarchical organisations in the fifteenth century. The labourers who did much of the work in London were peripheral to or excluded from institutional membership. London's poor were not evading citizenship; it was simply not intended to include them. The urban economy was simply too complex for guilds to fully encompass it, a fact which attention to the extramural neighbourhoods brings sharply into focus. As the complex situation of alien workers in relation to the companies demonstrates, to frame all urban work in terms of either guild-control or evasion is to assume a rigidity of institutions which was simply impractical.

Nonetheless, there were economic advantages to be gained from living outside the walls for people with certain occupations. Food producers seem to have chosen to locate themselves in extramural neighbourhoods in significant numbers. In both St Lawrence Jewry and St Katharine Cree, bakers, brewers, butchers, cooks and similar workers formed 3 per cent or less of testators, while in all the extramural parishes they formed 15 per cent or more of the total. This is largely accounted for by the number of brewers in the sample from St Botolph Aldersgate (ten), St Botolph Aldgate (thirteen) and St Botolph Bishopsgate (fourteen). From the early part of the fifteenth century, brewing moved away from being a primarily domestic activity to one of commercial scale as beer overtook ale in popularity, and London's brewing industry was commercialized to a far greater degree than other towns.[144] The larger premises available outside the walls, such as the aforementioned Axe outside Aldgate, would have been able to produce beer in profitable quantities. Dutch and Flemish immigrants also brought significant brewing expertise, and no doubt made up much of the workforce in this industry.[145] Butchers were the second-largest group with a named occupation in the St Botolph Aldgate sample. They may partly have lived there because of availability of large premises but most important was probably the flesh market at nearby East Smithfield and the availability of local pasturing; we have already seen that John Roke, butcher, leased pastureland in Whitechapel from the hospital of St Mary Bishopsgate. Butchers' bequests, discussed in more detail in Chapter Two, indicate that they had family and business connections related to the trade in livestock to the east and north of London and that extramural residence was also attractive owing to the ease of transport outwards.

Tenants were far less likely to have a named occupation than testators, but what information can be gleaned from property records is helpful

[144] J. M. Bennett, *Ale, Beer and Brewsters in England: Women's Work in a Changing World, 1300–1600* (New York, 1996), ch. 5; Hanawalt, 'The host, the law and the ambiguous space of medieval London taverns', pp. 206–7.

[145] Bolton, 'The alien population of London', pp. 18–19; Bennett, *Ale, Beer and Brewsters in England*, pp. 79–84.

Table 1.7 Median annual rent costs (pence) within and without the walls by occupation group of tenant

	Within (d)	Sample size	Without (d)	Sample size
Assistant	-	0	48	9
Building trades	2160	2	168	12
Clerical	58	8	268	4
Food distribution	380	2	132	9
Food preparation	80	6	240	21
Mercantile	-	0	132	2
Metalworking	-	0	88	12
Nobility/gentry	3040	1	440	13
Other distribution	-	0	713	2
Other manufacture	120	2	160	7
Other	-	0	216	10
Services	36	2	120	11
Textile distribution	308	2	48	3
Textile manufacture	2160	1	80	29
Unknown	108	255	96	684
Weaponry manufacture	-	0	480	1
Widow	36	7	54	38

in understanding the complex series of factors which both pushed and pulled those with certain occupations to the peripheries of the city. Table 1.7 compares the rent levels paid by different kinds of trade in parishes within and without the city walls. Those working in food preparation outside the walls (brewers, bakers, butchers, cooks, etc.) paid on average over eleven shillings (160 pence) per year more than those who produced clothing and textiles (dyers, weavers, cappers, shearmen, etc.). Residential patterns at the margins were created by a localized balance of push and pull factors, with some opting to spend more to live outside the walls. Food producers without Aldgate rented properties costing a median of 560 pence a year, while the same group outside Bishopsgate paid a median of 96 pence, a pattern repeated with metalworkers, textile manufacturers and those providing services. Metalworking had a long association with the area and the desirability of specialized premises for this purpose was vividly demonstrated in a 1511 consistory court case. William Culverdon, a brazier, had secured lease of a house in St Botolph Aldgate from the prior of Holy Trinity apparently against the wishes of the sitting inhabitant, William Smyth, who made defamatory complaints, including exclaiming 'cokwold [cuckold] knave bawde and hormonger thow hast hired my howes ower my hede'.[146] The prior's rent collector and a canon evicted Smyth, his wife and children by accessing the property through the yard of the neighbouring 'Belhouse', leased to bellfounder Thomas Bullesdon, 'where there were new bells suspended and hanging'.[147] The area outside Aldgate seems to have been quite attractive, pulling in artisans who needed sizeable premises and clustering those with shared occupations. Some trades actively paid more to live in extramural neighbourhoods. This is particularly notable for those in manufacturing trades, such as chandlers, tawyers and dyers, whose processing activities were noxious and who were encouraged to remove to extramural areas.[148] Tenants with high social status, like gentlemen Bartholomew Willesdon and Thomas Cavendish, paid large sums for extramural properties which might provide them with a convenient London residence when needed. Both were tenants, in the 1480s and 1500s respectively, of a large tenement with three shops and a garden called Rothes Place on Aldersgate Street, paying between £1 13s 4d and £2 for the privilege.

There were multiple economic reasons why people lived in extramural neighbourhoods. Attempting to carry on a trade outside guild regulation was probably not a significant one outside of liberties. A combination of push and pull factors created neighbourhoods where clusters of prosperous artisans existed alongside those whose existence was precarious. The precarious are no doubt under-represented in the surviving sources, but what we can tell is that they by no means made up the total extramural population. Those who could afford the space and had less need to live close to the commercial networks of the city might choose residence in the extramural areas, and different neighbourhoods appealed to different groups. Religious houses held considerable potential power over the shape of the extramural economy, which can be most clearly seen in their influence over the property market via investment in lay housing within and outside their precincts. On the whole, as with patterns of wealth, each parish was varied, but the occupational structure of peripheral neighbourhoods suggests that

[146] LMA, DL/C/0206, fo. 44.

[147] LMA, DL/C/0206, fos. 45v–46.

[148] C. Rawcliffe, *Urban Bodies: Communal Health in Late Medieval English Towns and Cities* (Woodbridge, 2013), pp. 206–10.

they were loosely bound to the economic basis of civic structure – the guilds. In the following chapter, the social effects of this disengagement from civic life will be outlined.

A balance of choice and necessity shaped the society and economy of extramural neighbourhoods. These areas were for many a resort of necessity. Lower average rents meant that the poor could establish a home while remaining close to the markets and social networks offered by the city. However, residence outside the walls was also desirable to some. The availability of open space afforded flexibility in land use which produced both cheap alley rents as well as gardens and larger houses. Larger houses were desirable for those who could afford to invest in practising their craft on a large scale, such as brewers and founders, as well as those who wanted an impressive home for reasons of status. The differences between localities at the periphery were caused by the weighting of the balance of desirability and necessity; while nowhere was homogeneous, that balance influenced the overall character of the neighbourhood.

Spatial marginality was marked by diversity of land use, economic functions and plurality of jurisdictions. The variation represented even within the small number of neighbourhoods discussed here shows the importance of thinking of the pre-modern city as a place of great texture and spatial differentiation. There were no homogeneous 'quarters' dedicated to a particular economic function in London, but subtle differences of topography and economy marked each neighbourhood. In the large parish of St Botolph Aldgate, availability of open space produced sizeable premises and gardens alongside humbler dwellings. As a result, it was characterized by occupations and land uses that required space or took advantage of its outward connections via Aldgate Street. Its neighbour within the walls, St Katharine Cree, was wealthier and had higher property values. The small parish of All Hallows London Wall provides a useful contrast; despite its mural location, the fact that it contained no major thoroughfare produced a built environment similar to peripheral urban spaces and lower property values. Its extramural neighbour St Botolph Bishopsgate was poorer but provided opportunities for women and others of modest and comfortable means to set up home. At St Botolph Aldersgate there was a neighbourhood of even more dramatic contrasts. A significant minority of testators were exceptionally wealthy but lived alongside alleyways of poorer residents, a stratification also borne out in the wills of its inhabitants. The overriding similarity between all the peripheral parishes lies in weakened connection between testators and the institutions of citizenship, highlighted by the contrast to St Lawrence Jewry. Whether by choice or not, residents at the peripheries were more likely to be those outside such institutions. The differentiation of extramural from intramural space, and the smaller gradations of social space and jurisdictional boundaries which divided neighbourhoods, had tangible social consequences which are demonstrated in greater detail in Chapters Three and Five. In particular, the economic power of the religious houses in their immediate neighbourhood underlay and reinforced their role as alternative poles of authority on the fringe of the city.

The religious houses and other property owners were active in developing these neighbourhoods in the fifteenth century in ways which set the pattern for the poor suburbs of the later sixteenth and seventeenth centuries. By the later fifteenth century, they had seen the profitable potential of developing small extramural dwellings to serve the city's poor. The landlords who acquired the houses' estates after the Dissolution created suburbs characterized by small, cheap housing in alleyways and courts.[149] Religious houses also pockmarked the city government's legal territory beyond the walls, and even the surrounding neighbourhoods that lay within the mayor's jurisdiction were by no means civic-controlled spaces, in the sense that the great majority of their inhabitants were not citizens and had little say in London's government. Their mixed economies, accompanied by lower citizenship levels, are a salutary reminder of just how much of the urban economy took place adjacent to or outside guild-regulated trade even before the decline of the livery companies' control of the economy in later centuries. Spatial patterns of society and economy were evident in the late medieval period and would be exacerbated and intensified by the population boom of the mid- to late sixteenth century. The non-citizen-dominated suburbs of the fifteenth century set a pattern for urban expansion which was to take place largely after the expansion of citizenship in the 1530s. A focus on the urban margins shows that the framework of expansion came not just from guilds and institutional membership, as shown by Steve Rappaport, but also in the generative potential of extramural space.

[149] P. Baker and M. Merry, '"The poore lost a good frend and the parish a good neighbour": the lives of the poor and their supporters in London's eastern suburb, *c.*1583–*c.*1679', in *London and Beyond: Essays in Honour of Derek Keene*, ed. D. Keene, J. A. Galloway and M Davies (London, 2012), pp. 155–80, at pp. 156–9.

2. Socio-spatial networks

Neighbourhoods are not just points on maps but are formed by social interactions rooted in a particular place.[1] As we saw in the previous chapter, neighbours often had much in common with one another, whether they were communities of women sharing an alleyway or butchers living and working near the same market. Londoners' experience of the city was shaped by the friendships they made with their neighbours, the churches they worshipped in and the work they did; all drew them into social networks which were associated with particular urban spaces. Some networks were rooted in the neighbourhood and others encompassed the entire city. The social lives of Londoners living beyond the city walls reveal how far they were drawn into the centralizing forces of urban life. However, social lives are ephemeral things; few of the records left to us by medieval people about their world explicitly tell us about their friendships and acquaintances. Even fewer can tell us much about social life outside of institutions. Presented with this problem, the approach here is to take a relatively abundant and well-used source – last wills and testaments – and apply the methodologies of social science to extract answers about patterns of sociability among those on the urban margins. By doing so, I trace the effects of places and networks in people's lives as inscribed in their testamentary wishes.

In a book concerned with marginality, it may seem strange to devote so much attention to documents such as wills which reflected the propertied section of society. However, the socio-spatial networks found in wills tell us much about the fundamental nature of marginal neighbourhoods, and especially the complex sense in which they related to the urban whole. They indicate the networks that carried the greatest social capital in the extramural areas and set the stage for closer attention to wider neighbourhood society. They also give a nuanced picture of the differences between parishes outside the city walls, which were similar, but by no means homogeneous. The groups of people who lived in each had slightly different patterns of affiliation to central aspects of the city: institutions, neighbourliness and mobility.

[1] H. Lefebvre, *The Production of Space* (Oxford, 1991), p. 129.

Between networks: neighbourhood, city, region

London's society was a patchwork of neighbourhoods and institutions; while some institutions were based within a locality, others operated across the whole city. All were vital parts of the medieval 'civil society', as Gervase Rosser has argued, in which individuals acted collectively to negotiate their position.[2] These institutions were integrative of locals and newcomers and inculcated common civic values, a necessity in cities because of the high number of immigrants needed to maintain a stable urban population.[3] Collective endeavours that knitted together urban society included craft and fraternity organizations, worship in the parish church, local jury service and participation in parish administration and civic government.[4] There were thus multiple kinds of social networks which Londoners participated in, seeking to find and cement their place in the city. In this chapter, we will see how Londoners from the city's margins interacted with neighbourhood social networks as well as the networks which connected the whole city. Social network analysis and mapping of testamentary bequests illustrate these socio-spatial networks. Being spatially peripheral did not preclude engagement with civic and craft institutions, although, as we saw in Chapter One, citizens were less prevalent in extramural neighbourhoods. People's interactions with the central institutions of urban life affected the character of sociability in their neighbourhood and influenced what kind of relationships they formed.

Social networks of all kinds were, moreover, no trivial matter. Gervase Rosser argues that support networks could be so strained by the instability and risk of medieval life that building trusting relationships was vital to people's survival.[5] Trusting relationships were essential for a whole range of socio-economic purposes: to gain access to monetary credit, to enable

[2] G. Rosser, *The Art of Solidarity in the Middle Ages: Guilds in England 1250–1550* (Oxford and New York, 2015), ch. 1.

[3] B. A. Hanawalt, *Ceremony and Civility: Civic Culture in Late Medieval London* (Oxford and New York, 2017), pp. 2–3.

[4] D. Durkee, 'A cursus for craftsmen? Career cycles of the worsted weavers of late medieval Norwich', in *Cities and Solidarities: Urban Communities in Pre-Modern Europe*, ed. J. Colson and A. van Steensel (Abingdon, 2017), pp. 151–68; G. Rosser, 'Finding oneself in a medieval fraternity: individual and collective identities in the English guilds', in *Mittelalterliche Bruderschaften in Europäischen Städten: Funktionen, Formen, Akteure*, ed. M. Escher-Apsner (Frankfurt am Main and Oxford, 2009), pp. 29–46; B. A. Kümin, *The Shaping of a Community*; C. M. Barron, 'Lay solidarities: the wards of medieval London', in *Law, Laity and Solidarities: Essays in Honour of Susan Reynolds.*, ed. J. Martindale, P. Stafford and J. L. Nelson (Manchester, 2001), pp. 218–33.

[5] Rosser, *The Art of Solidarity in the Middle Ages*, p. 149.

the collaborative production of goods and to avoid the pariah status attached to the marginalized 'stranger'.[6] To build a social network and establish a 'creditworthy' reputation was thus highly important in order to insulate oneself against the vicissitudes of medieval life. Perhaps the most obvious opportunity for social networks were those based on locality, the neighbourhood and the parish. Scholars have argued that the concept of the parish community in London was a relatively restricted one, the term 'parishioners' referring to a group of householders of some standing in the local area and office-holders being drawn from a small select group.[7] Therefore, although the sources used here are grouped by parish, it is important to make a distinction between the parish as a local institution and the neighbourhood as a community based on spatial proximity. The will-making section of the population naturally consisted of the better-off, so those considered senior parishioners are more likely to be represented within the sample. Some networks will therefore have been formed or reinforced through common involvement in parish institutions. However, simply the act of being neighbours will have formed yet other connections, and in some cases may make the artificially designated bounds of the parish meaningless in terms of social networks. In some extramural parishes, bounded by the city walls on one side and sparsely populated areas at their fringes, this complication may be less applicable. While only a minority of witnesses, executors and supervisors (hereafter referred to as testamentary officials) are identified by parish of residence, of the 339 (out of a total 1,649) whose residence was identified, 276 (81 per cent) lived in the same parish as the testator. Locality was thus one of the focal points around which the social networks of testators formed.

The remaining witnesses, executors and supervisors reflect social connections created in other ways. The craft guilds (known as companies by the later part of the period) had firmly established their central role in controlling access to and supporting the political power of the civic government in the fourteenth century.[8] The majority of citizens gained their

[6] Rosser, *The Art of Solidarity in the Middle Ages*, ch. 5; E. Spindler, 'Marginality and social relations in London and the Bruges area, 1370–1440' (unpublished University of Oxford DPhil thesis, 2008), p. 249; R. W. Scribner, 'Wie wird man Außenseiter? Ein- und Ausgrenzung im frühneuzeitlichen Deutschland', in *Aussenseiter zwischen Mittelalter und Neuzeit: Festschrift für Hans-Jürgen Goertz zum 60. Geburtstag*, ed. N. Fischer and M. Kobelt-Groch (Leiden, 1997), pp. 21–46, at pp. 30–32; I. Forrest, *Trustworthy Men: How Inequality and Faith Made the Medieval Church* (Princeton and Oxford, 2018), pp. 36–40.

[7] See Introduction.

[8] C. M. Barron, *London in the Later Middle Ages: Government and People 1200–1500* (Oxford, 2004), pp. 232–34.

entrance to the freedom of the city through apprenticeship in one or other craft; on successful completion of their term of service they became both a freeman of the city and a member of a company. Companies and guilds actively fostered social and economic bonds between members through both the institutions of apprenticeship and office-holding and in communal activities such as feasting and the attendance of one another's funerals.[9] Craft was thus another focal point for strong social networks that provided access to the kind of respectable men likely to act as testamentary officials. While there were some small craft clusters within the marginal parishes, none was dominated by a single trade, and so craft guilds were on the whole 'central' London institutions to which individuals belonged, although the Fishmongers who concentrated in the parishes north of London Bridge were a notable exception.[10] The small groups with shared occupations in parishes outside the walls suggest the potential overlap between local and central social networks. In such cases, where the same group of respectable men occupied office-holding positions in both craft and parish, social capital could be transferred between contexts. Nonetheless, guild connections represent an important means through which residents of the margins participated in social networks that extended across London.

Social connections might also be maintained into London's hinterland and beyond. The high levels of in-migration London experienced and its widespread economic connections are reflected in bequests. In the sampled wills, 18 per cent of bequests to institutions were to those which lay outside London. Some were explicitly directed towards the parish where the testator was born, such as the forty shillings left for works to the nave of St Mary's Church at Allingbourne, Sussex, by the widow Sibyl Bret of St Botolph Aldersgate.[11] Such specificity in the reason for a bequest is unusual, however. John Jacob, a brewer also from Aldersgate, requested that 'five marks are spent on the church of the parish of St Hilary, Cornwall where I was born', but also made bequests of land at West Ham, Essex, a house at Stanbridge, Bedfordshire and left twenty shillings' worth of charcoal to the

[9] G. Rosser, 'Finding oneself in a medieval fraternity', pp. 34–8; G. Rosser, 'Going to the fraternity feast: commensality and social relations in late medieval England', *Journal of British Studies*, xxxiii (1994), 430–46, doi:org/10.1086/386064.

[10] J. Colson, 'London's forgotten company? Fishmongers: their trade and their networks in later medieval London', in *The Medieval Merchant: Proceedings of the 2012 Harlaxton Symposium*, ed. C. M. Barron and A. F. Sutton (Donington, 2014), pp. 20–40, at pp. 29–34; J. Colson, 'Commerce, clusters and community: a re-evaluation of the occupational geography of London, *c*.1400–*c*.1550', *Economic History Review*, lxix (2016), 104–30, doi:org/10.1111/ehr.12104, pp. 117–19.

[11] LMA, DL/C/B/004/MS09171/003, fos. 382–382v.

poor of the parish of Tottenham, Middlesex.[12] Jacob's property and charity show the connections he had developed to places close to London but far removed from his original home. As we shall see in this chapter, bequests outside London might reflect business interests and social connections built up over the testator's lifetime as well as their place of birth. London's central role in the economy of England prompted both migration and the building of long-distance business networks.[13] These connections, while more patchily recorded, suggest that in addition to local and city-wide networks the hinterland also exerted an influence on the sociability of residents at the margins.

Analysing testamentary networks

The main sources used in this chapter are the wills and testaments of people who lived in the extramural parishes of St Botolph Aldgate, St Botolph Aldersgate and St Botolph Bishopsgate, St Katharine Cree just inside London's wall and, for comparison, the wealthy central parish of St Lawrence Jewry. Chapter One described the samples selected for the period 1390–1540, and the same wills, sampled in twenty- to–thirty-year cohorts, are utilised here. Their interpretation in this chapter is primarily undertaken with digital methodologies, the most important of which is Social Network Analysis (SNA). SNA is a quantitative methodology for the analysis of interactions between a set of 'nodes' (points within the network) which enables both the visualization of those interactions as a network graph and the statistical expression of a network's characteristics. Originally developed by social scientists for research into contemporary human interactions, SNA is a methodology with much to offer historians.[14] Although a historian cannot interview medieval people about their subjective experience of personal relationships in the same way as a sociologist would when building a picture of a social network, for certain kinds of formal interaction historians with archival sources are at an advantage.[15] Putting together the archival traces of social actions can open up a new explanatory

[12] TNA, PROB 11/8/34.

[13] See for instance the connections between the west midlands and London demonstrated in C. Dyer, *A Country Merchant, 1495–1520: Trading and Farming at the End of the Middle Ages* (Oxford, 2012).

[14] The case for SNA's utility to the historian is argued succinctly in C. Wetherell, 'Historical Social Network Analysis', *International Review of Social History*, xliii (1998), 125–44, doi:org/10.1017/S0020859000115123.

[15] This point is argued in C. Lemercier, 'Formal network methods in history: why and how?', in *Social Networks, Political Institutions and Rural Societies*, ed. G. Fertig (Turnhout, 2015), pp. 281–310, at p. 285.

paradigm for historical phenomena. A classic example is John Padgett and Christopher Ansell's study of the rise of the Medici, which used SNA to demonstrate that the family consolidated its power by building marriage alliances, patronage and business networks which spanned the fault lines in Florence's political elites.[16]

While SNA is not yet a common tool among urban historians, the idea of the network as a driver of urban social relations is quite widely diffused; the language of SNA ('network', 'ties', 'embeddedness') has become popular in historical analysis even among those not using its formal methods.[17] Its ascendance has primarily been at the expense of structural approaches to the medieval city, which centred on the power of institutions. The decline of structural explanations has had two strands. First, historians have stressed the caveats to institutional power and the compromises they made. The membership of institutions such as the London livery companies is now seen not to have played such an all-encompassing role in granting economic opportunity as previously thought, and the key route to membership – apprenticeship – was as likely to result in dropouts as it was to produce new freemen.[18] Second, the focus shifted to the power of interpersonal connections. The work of Justin Colson on the Fishmongers, for instance, suggests that while the company acted as an integrative body enabling the economic advancement of members, it also had a split structure reflecting two spatially and socially separate groups of fishmongers.[19] Thus, urban historians utilizing network analysis are able to produce nuanced answers to questions about the role of structure and institutions in city life.[20] This chapter considers networks with a spatial element by centring on the range of types of connections which a Londoner might make: neighbourly, urban and regional. It also uses the quantitative potential of networks to compare and contrast how neighbours acted as a group in the different parishes. This

[16] J. F. Padgett and C. K. Ansell, 'Robust action and the rise of the Medici, 1400–1434', *American Journal of Sociology*, xcviii (1993), 1259–319, doi:org/10.1086/230190.

[17] J. Innes, '"Networks" in British History', *East Asian Journal of British History*, v (2016), 51–72, at pp. 52–3; Lemercier, 'Formal network methods in history', pp. 282–3.

[18] C. Minns and P. Wallis, 'Rules and reality: quantifying the practice of apprenticeship in early modern England', *Economic History Review*, lxv (2012), 556–79.

[19] Colson, 'London's Forgotten Company?', pp. 29–40.

[20] M. Burkhardt, 'Networks as social structures in late medieval and early modern towns: a theoretical approach to historical network analysis', in *Commercial Networks and European Cities, 1400–1800*, ed. A. Caracausi and C. Jeggle (London, 2014), pp. 13–43; E. Jullien, 'Netzwerkanalyse in der Mediävistik: Probleme und Perspektiven im Umgang mit mittelalterlichen Quellen', *Vierteljahrschrift für Sozial- und Wirtschaftsgeschichte*, c.2013, 135–53, at pp. 143–50.

is a real strength of network analysis for the historian, as it makes it possible to set the particular and the personal in the context of the behaviour of a group and then to compare the ways that different groups act.

Testamentary data lends itself well to the use of SNA since wills describe a range of interactions between a testator and their social group, whether individuals acted as beneficiaries to wills, executors or supervisors of the testator's estate or as witnesses to the act of making a will itself. Beneficiaries listed in wills were, as noted in Chapter One, probably an incomplete picture of those benefiting from an estate. Therefore this chapter primarily uses testators and their witnesses, supervisors and executors, since even the shortest will named at least an executor to ensure its contents were carried out. Each will describes what is, in network terms, an 'egocentric network' for its testator. In network analysis terms, the people named in wills (including testators, witnesses and executors) are nodes and the relationships between them edges. The drawback in focusing on testamentary officials is that they were more likely to have been drawn from the better-off, respectable sections of society. This was due to the fact that executors and supervisors were expected to be trustworthy and, ideally, to have experience in handling money. In addition, respectable people were favoured as witnesses so that in the event of the will being disputed their testimony would be accepted in court.[21] This serves to exaggerate the tendency of testamentary evidence to represent the better-off by excluding those who may have been socially close to a testator but not considered suitable to act as an official. However, the great advantage of the approach is that it provides a sense of who those 'central' individuals were who could be relied upon to act as officials in any parish. We can thus approach the question of whether, when testators came to make a choice about who would best represent their interests after death, they relied upon their respectable neighbours or on relationships formed through other means.

In answering this question, the analysis uses the modularity score of different cohorts of testators as a means of comparison. Modularity is the measurement of the extent to which nodes in a network graph can be divided into densely connected communities known as modules. A lower modularity score indicates that connections are spread more evenly through a network, while a higher score means that nodes fall into modular groups which are internally well connected but weakly connected to the wider network. Scores fall on a range between –1 (least modular) and 1 (most modular). Scores are comparable between networks of different

[21] K. L. French, 'Loving friends: surviving widowhood in late medieval Westminster', *Gender & History*, xxii (2010), 21–37, doi:org/10.1111/j.1468-0424.2010.01576.x, pp. 24–7.

sizes, and the statistically defined modules are represented in each graph by assigned colours. Another advantage of modularity is that it effectively tests statistical significance as part of the calculation, since the score is derived by comparing the number of connections for each node against the expected number of connections if edges were distributed randomly. Testamentary networks are naturally modular, since testators named as their officials people with a personal connection to them, some of whom were unlikely to feature in the wills of others, particularly surviving widows and other family members. Similarly, even samples taken at twenty-year intervals cannot fully account for the fact that many of the officials named may have died early in the sample period or reached their majority or moved to the parish only late within it. Thus, the circumstances of will-making and the sampling process make it highly unlikely that any neighbourhood would have equal connections between all testators and officials and thus a modularity score close to –1.

Modularity is highly relevant for the analysis of wills, since it essentially expresses the degree of overlap between the communities found in each will within a parish. Admittedly, the chance loss of wills over time means there is a degree of uncertainty and imprecision; we will never know if lost wills might have named individuals who now appear unimportant in their parish networks. Some wills could have been proved in error in one of the London archdeaconry courts whose records are now lost. Archival loss as well as the natural modularity of testamentary networks means that modularity scores will tend to bunch at the higher end: the parish samples

Table 2.1 Modularity of testamentary network graphs by sample and parish

	1390–1410		**1430–50**		**1465–95**		**1515–40**		**Mean**
	No. of edges	**Modularity**	**Edges**	**Mod.**	**Edges**	**Mod.**	**Edges**	**Mod.**	
St Botolph Aldersgate	50	0.893	50	0.930	61	0.812	59	0.756	0.848
St Botolph Aldgate	78	0.914	70	0.917	123	0.859	132	0.916	0.902
St Botolph Bishopsgate	89	0.783	57	0.923	86	0.825	170	0.791	0.831
St Lawrence Jewry	-	-	-	-	162	0.875	97	0.890	0.883
St Katharine Cree	31	0.864	105	0.844	93	0.860	124	0.873	0.860

presented here all fall in a range between 0.76 and 0.93. With these caveats in mind, the main focus in this chapter is the comparison of the whole network's qualities and the use of those comparisons to ask questions about the relationship between testamentary networks and underlying patterns of social interaction, identifying the different varieties of social experience which influenced testators.

This is, admittedly, a narrow range of scores, but it provides a useful focus point for understanding the differences between parishes and the will-making behaviour of different kinds of people. Figures 2.1–3 show graphs for three parish samples and provide good examples of different network structures. Figure 2.1, which depicts the network for St Botolph Aldgate testators in 1515–40, has the highest modularity score of the three networks, at 0.916. The lowest of the three is the network for St Botolph Aldersgate in 1465–95, with a score of 0.812. What principally drove the higher modularity of the Aldgate sample was the number of wills that did not overlap with any others, that is, did not name another testator as an official or share an official with a fellow parishioner. This was the case for fifteen of the thirty wills in the sample. The score was also affected by the exceptionally large number of officials named by brazier William Culverden (twelve), of whom only one was shared with a neighbour. This effect is also seen in Figure 2.2, with the will of Bishopsgate's alderman William Marow. Marow named ten officials, none of whom appeared in the wills of his fellow parishioners.[22] His circle of officials was so large that it increased the modularity score of the whole St Botolph Bishopsgate 1465–95 sample from 0.803, which would have been the lowest score in that sample period, to 0.825. The lower score in the St Botolph Aldersgate sample in Figure 2.3 is down to the size of the 'giant component' in the network: that is, the largest number of nodes that can be connected together. Seven of the fifteen wills fell in this group. While a similar proportion of the wills were isolated with no shared connections to the Aldgate network in Figure 2.3, what made the difference in score is that when Aldersgate testators in this sample were connected to another person it was most likely to be a connection that had onward links to many other wills. More important than individual scores, however, are the reasons for these differences, which can be revealed only by looking more closely at individual testators, officials and their backgrounds. For instance, in Figure 2.3 the goldsmith John Friend was named by two testators. Reference to the register of the parish fraternity shows that he and the two testators who named him (Thomas White and John Jacob) were all members of the local Fraternity of SS Fabian and Sebastian, and that Jacob and Friend acted as wardens together in

[22] TNA, PROB 11/5/139.

1482–3.[23] By contrast, the will of Nicholas Bailey, gentleman, from the same sample shows that while he, too, was a member of the parish fraternity, he apparently did not choose his officials from among its membership.[24] Bailey, Friend and Jacob were all connected by a local institution, but they were Londoners of different statuses who made different kinds of choice about their testamentary officials. The graphs and scores thus provided a stepping-off point in researching parish testamentary networks, inviting further research to explain and contextualize the connections between individuals and of the group as a whole.

Influences on social interactions

All of the parishes were complex social spaces, part of socio-spatial networks at the level of the neighbourhood, city and region. Testamentary social networks are an indication of the strength of local ties. As we saw in Chapter One, there were some broad socio-economic similarities among parishes beyond the walls. However, testamentary networks reveal important local differences. There were several social circumstances which will be used as explanations for modularity scores in this chapter. These can be divided into three broad categories:

1. Neighbourly integration: the effect of informal sociability prompted by proximity and formal local institutions such as parish and ward in creating a basic cohesiveness in local social networks.
2. Cultural connections/disconnections: the influence of social and cultural differences in creating modularity in local networks. These differences might centre on differences of language or social status. In some cases, cultural differences may be closely related to the third category – occupational connections – particularly where trades which required a high degree of mobility mitigated against neighbourly integration.
3. Occupational connections/disconnections: craft and trade ties around which social networks were formed and which thus limited or enhanced neighbourly integration. Occupation often appears to have competed against locality as a focus for ties, but the presence of a trade cluster might in some instances decrease local modularity where elements of a trade's infrastructure were present.

[23] 'Appendix: membership and office-holding (141–3),' in Parish Fraternity Register Fraternity of the Holy Trinity and SS Fabian and Sebastian (Parish of St Botolph Without Aldersgate), ed. Patricia Basing (London, 1982), pp. 82–6, in *British History Online* <http://www.british-history.ac.uk/london-record-soc/vol18/pp82-86> [accessed 11 May 2016].

[24] LMA, DL/C/B/004/MS09171/007 fo. 49–49v. Bailey left two wax torches to the fraternity to be burned next to his body during his funeral.

Testamentary networks in each parish were impacted by a balance of these factors, meaning that no two places were the same.

Neighbourhood ties

Trying to quantify something as nebulous as social interaction poses a formidable challenge for any historian, let alone one with such imperfect sources standing at half a millennium's remove from their subjects. However, one thing is quite clear: people in different parishes relied on their neighbours as testamentary officials to quite different extents. We have seen how modularity scores can indicate the quality of connections between people in a network: lower scores show more even ties across a whole network; higher scores indicate more isolated will communities. Table 2.1 shows the modularity scores for each graph produced from the will samples. On average, St Botolph Bishopsgate had the lowest score and St Botolph Aldgate the highest, followed by St Lawrence Jewry. St Botolph Aldersgate's testators changed their habits over time, with far more even connections between their wills in the early sixteenth century than a hundred years before. St Katharine Cree testators, by contrast, were quite consistent over time and fell in the middle of most samples. The historical circumstances which caused these results were complex and need to be carefully teased out to throw light on the relationship between quantification of testamentary networks and real social interactions.

It is very important to bear in mind that this kind of analysis does not directly measure sociability but the *practices involved in making a will.* While much can be inferred about society from will-making, circumstances out of a testator's control could also influence their actions. Given that most wills were made when death was shortly anticipated (rather than in advance), we might expect conditions of epidemic disease and high mortality to be just such a circumstance. Evidence from both chronicles and bonds of debt suggest that the 1430s was a period of recurrent plague in London, exacerbated by food shortages.[25] Perhaps as a result, sample 2 is an anomaly in most parishes, with generally higher modularity scores despite an increase in the sample sizes of testators from sample 1. Within the sample, modularity was higher in every parish in 1430–39 than in 1440–50.[26]

[25] C. Creighton, *A History of Epidemics in Britain*, 2nd edn, 2 vols (London, 1965), i, pp. 223, 227–9; P. Nightingale, 'Some new evidence of crises and trends of mortality in late medieval England', *Past & Present*, 2005, 33–68, at pp. 48, 53.

[26] St Botolph Aldgate (1430–39: 0.885; 1440–50: 0.875); St Botolph Aldersgate (1430–39: 0.891; 1440–50: 0.809); St Botolph Bishopsgate (1430–39: 0.896; 1440–50: 0.866); St Katharine Cree (1430–39: 0.882; 1440–50: 0.769).

There are several potential ways in which epidemic disease could change will-making practices. A testator's first choice of executor or supervisor might have already died, forcing them to use other friends to fulfil these positions. Higher mortality could also reduce the overlap between wills, with important local contacts named by one testator dying before they could be named by another neighbour. There is even some indication that people named fewer officials in this period, perhaps because wills had to be written at shorter notice.[27] While there were notable periods of epidemic disease during other samples, in particular in the 1460s and during the first sweating sickness of 1485, the longer time span of the later samples may serve to even out the effects. The effect of epidemic disease is an important reminder that this chapter considers *testamentary* networks and not complete *social* networks, and indicates how cautious the historian must be not to conflate the two.

Nonetheless, the modularity of testamentary networks does offer us some important clues to the wider context of social relationships. In Bishopsgate, the dense connections between testators and executors were relatively evenly distributed through the sample, when compared to other parishes. Figure 2.2 shows the network graph for Bishopsgate in 1465–95. Seven individuals named in two or more wills form important nodes in the network, including a parish chaplain, William Nolath, a notary public, who would have assisted in writing wills, William Chant and a prominent brewer (later sergeant of the king's larder), Henry Rycroft. However, also important to the linkages through the sample are a number of testators who were named by others as officials (and thus have an in-degree of one) such as two more brewers, John Wilcox and Robert Broad, and the minstrel John Ingham. This suggests that people living in Bishopsgate tended to look to their neighbours to act as testamentary officials and, perhaps, that social relationships were quite closely tied to the neighbourhood. This was the case from the earliest to the latest wills, and so seems to have been a long-standing characteristic of will-making in Bishopsgate.

[27] In Aldersgate the number of connections per testator fell from 3.8 in sample 1 to 2.6 in sample 2; in Aldgate parish from 2.8 to 2.4; and in Bishopsgate from 3.9 to 1.8. Only in St Katharine Cree, where modularity decreased, did the number remain stable at 3.1 to 3. This pattern is mirrored within the sample, as numbers of officials per testator was lower in the 1430s than in the 1440s by 4–7 per cent except at St Katharine Cree, where it was higher by 5 per cent.

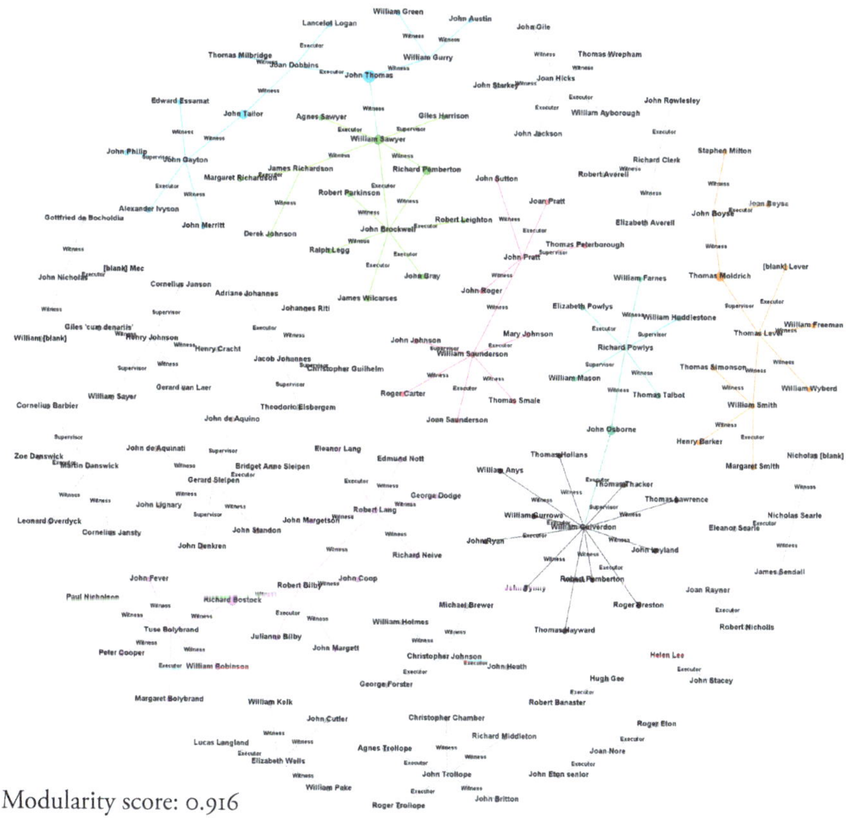

Modularity score: 0.916

Figure 2.1 Network graph for St Botolph Aldgate testators sample 4 (1515–40)[28]

How can we relate this tendency back to neighbourhood society more generally? Some assistance is provided by the exceptionally unconnected will of William Marow, grocer and alderman of Bishopsgate ward. As noted above, this is despite his naming ten testamentary officials. In fact, Marow's will shows greater overlap with the contemporary sample from St Lawrence Jewry, since he named as one of his executors the city recorder, Thomas Urswick. Marow's estate was large and, in addition to bequests to the church and clergy of St Botolph Bishopsgate, he left money for forgotten

[28] Important information about a network is represented visually in the network graphs. In the graphs used in this chapter, the statistically determined 'modules' are shown in different colours. The edges (connections) between each node have an arrow indicating the direction of the relationship from testator to official. The number of connections inwards (that is, the number of times an individual was cited as an official) is expressed as the In-degree of their node. All nodes have been sized relative to their in-degree, highlighting the individuals who figure most prominently in the wills of others.

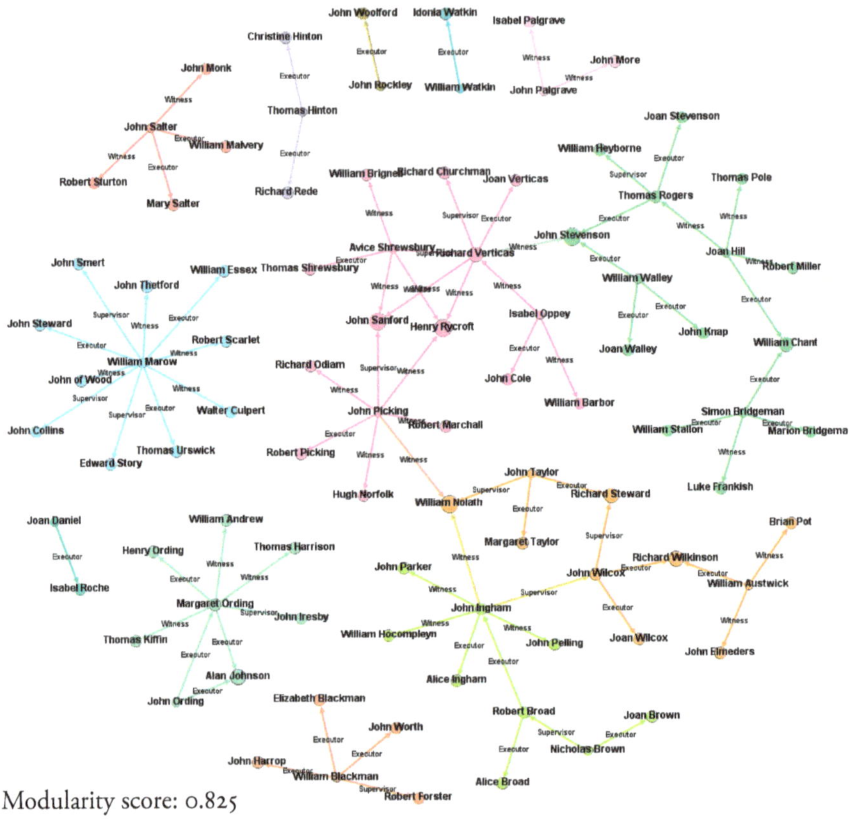

Modularity score: 0.825

Figure 2.2 Network graph for St Botolph Bishopsgate testators sample 3 (1465–95)

tithes to the parish of St Mary at Hill, indicating prior residence there, as well as bequests to the poor of Essex, Kent and Stepney, Middlesex. As a prominent man in city politics and a successful merchant, Marow's social connections extended well beyond Bishopsgate. It was, as mentioned in Chapter One, the poorest of the parishes considered in this book. While its testators would still have been of middling wealth, they were certainly lower status than Marow and less wealthy as a group than in other parishes, hence they relied on trusting relationships with their neighbours rather than higher-prestige connections which spanned the city. Marow's style of will-making contrasted sharply with his neighbours' but was similar to Aldersgate's aristocratic and gentry residents, as discussed below, so it was perhaps typical of the most wealthy and well-connected individuals. While perhaps an extreme example, it serves to illustrate the point that the wealthier an individual was, the less reliant they were probably to be on local networks.

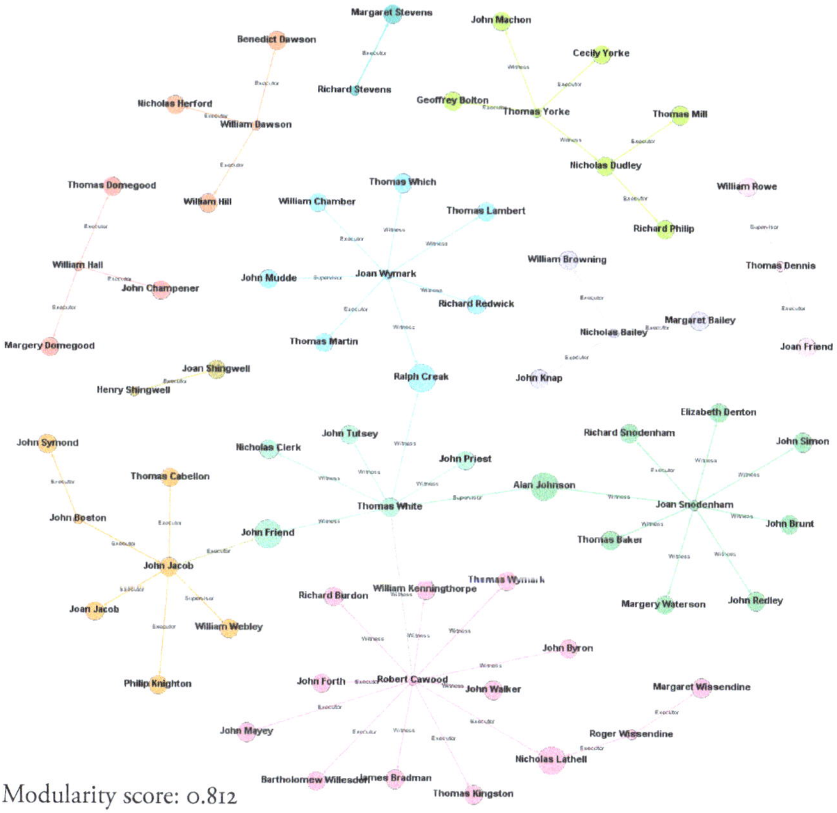

Figure 2.3 Network for St Botolph Aldersgate testators sample 3 (1465–95)

Local institutions underlay and supported neighbourhood sociability. This can be seen at Aldersgate, which has surviving churchwardens' accounts, wardmote inquest returns and a parish fraternity register. The third sample of wills from St Botolph Aldersgate is shown in Figure 2.3, when the parish had the lowest modularity of any in the sample period. Several of those featured had leading roles within local institutions. Alan Johnson and Nicholas Lathell, both of whom were named twice by fellow parishioners, feature in the churchwardens' accounts for the parish: Johnson was churchwarden many times between 1468 and his death while in the post in 1497–8, and Lathell was fined for absence from the presentation of the accounts in 1487–8. Lathell and Johnson were also both sometime wardens of the parish fraternity of SS Fabian and Sebastian. Other men named as officials who also feature as parishioners, churchwardens or fraternity wardens include Thomas Wymark, John Symond and William

Keningthorpe.[29] Jury service at the wardmote in both St Botolph Aldgate (that is, in Portsoken ward) and Aldersgate was a powerful creator of social connections, enabling social mobility and forging friendships.[30] For many men, officiating a neighbour's will was the endpoint of associations that had lasted throughout their adult lives.

This middling sort who were highly engaged with the parish's institutions, was evidently strong in the late fifteenth century at St Botolph Aldersgate. However, the parish seems to have undergone significant social change over the period, which can be charted through its testamentary networks. In 1390–1410, there were no shared officials at all between wills. In 1430–50, the only connections were in the wills of John and Felicia Mason, a married couple who both selected the same executors, and John Clement, tailor, who appeared both as a testator and as executor to the widow Margaret Morris. Accordingly, modularity was higher in these earlier samples than in the late fifteenth and early sixteenth centuries. This is an intriguing contrast, and setting this shift alongside the economic and social circumstances of the parish provides some answers as to why it might be as indication of a wider pattern of social relations. Aldersgate was a popular location for the grand city houses of the aristocracy and gentry, who had few neighbourly ties in the area and so were isolated within testamentary networks. This group remained present throughout the fifteenth century, but their effects on the social network graphs is mitigated in the latter part of the period by their far more connected, middling neighbours who, on the whole, had a similar profile to will-makers in Bishopsgate. By the later fifteenth century, the make-up of the parish's population seems to have changed, gaining a more prominent group of those of middling but comfortable status.

The importance of local institutions is also demonstrated by the prominence of parish fraternities in the wills of those from every neighbourhood. Fraternities in receipt of bequests were by and large those within the testator's parish itself or in parishes close by. Caroline Barron suggested that parish fraternities were particularly popular and important in extramural areas and perhaps performed some of the functions of local government.[31] It seems safe to assume that those leaving bequests to fraternities had been members in

[29] St Botolph Aldersgate churchwardens' accounts, LMA, P69/BOT1/B/013/MS01454/001-024.

[30] See C. Berry, '"To avoide all envye, malys, grudge and displeasure": sociability and social networking at the London Wardmote Inquest, *c.*1470–1540', *London Journal*, xlii (2017), 201–17, doi:org/10.1080/03058034.2017.1378058.

[31] C. M. Barron, 'The parish fraternities of medieval London', in *The Church in Pre-Reformation Society: Essays in Honour of F. R. H. Du Boulay*, ed. C. Harper-Bill and C. M. Barron (Woodbridge, 1985), 13–37, at pp. 28–9.

life, some bequests giving details which confirm this. For example, John de Bee of St Katharine Cree left to the parish fraternity a hood of their livery, and John Jacob of St Botolph Aldersgate ten marks 'for the payment of my debts' to the local fraternity of SS Fabian and Sebastian, of which he had been a warden.[32] In St Botolph Aldgate, the largest number of fraternity bequests (twenty-one) went to the Jesus Fraternity based in the parish church, although three testators left money to the Corpus Christi fraternity in neighbouring St Mary Matfelon, Whitechapel. At St Botolph Aldersgate fourteen testators left money to a variety of fraternities based in the parish (the number of which appears to have changed over time) and four to fraternities based nearby: the fraternity of Holy Mary at St Bride, St Giles at St Giles Cripplegate, St Lucy at St Nicholas Shambles and Holy Mary of Graces at St Paul's Cathedral. In St Botolph Bishopsgate, thirty-eight testators left money to one of the several parish fraternities, one to St Botolph Aldgate's Jesus fraternity and one to the guild of Our Lady at St Leonard Eastcheap. Locality was evidently of primary importance in choice of fraternity. Some fraternities may have had a certain cachet to their membership, such as SS Fabian and Sebastian at St Botolph Aldersgate, which was briefly fashionable among gentry and royal officials, while Henry IV convalesced at nearby priories in 1408–9.[33] However, mainly it seems that testators chose fraternities which lay within or close to their own 'patch' of the city. Fraternities of varying levels of status may indeed have been available within a single parish. This was evidently the case at St Lawrence Jewry, where a 'penny brotherhood' was the recipient of a number of bequests alongside the other parish fraternities dedicated to St Ursula and the Holy Cross.

In each parish, locality served as an integrative force within testamentary networks. Fostered by the kinds of institutional involvement recorded by parish, ward and fraternity records as well the less thoroughly recorded although no less important sociability born of proximity to neighbours. The institutions of parish, fraternity and ward were common to all London neighbourhoods, as were prominent local clerical figures such as the parish rector. The local connections forged in these circumstances are precisely the kind of friendships and acquaintances likely to be considered reliable enough to feature in testamentary networks. Locality was therefore a factor in social relations that lowered modularity within testamentary network graphs, albeit that the strength of local ties varied from place to place.

[32] LMA, DL/C/B/004/MS09171/004, fo. 267; TNA, PROB 11/8/34.

[33] 'Introduction', in *Parish Fraternity Register: Fraternity of the Holy Trinity and SS Fabian and Sebastian (Parish of St Botolph without Aldersgate)*, ed. Patricia Basing (London, 1982), pp. vii–xxviii. *British History Online* <http://www.british-history.ac.uk/london-record-soc/vol18/vii-xxviii> [accessed 12 Aug. 2020].

At St Botolph Aldgate, locality appears less important. The parish's networks show the highest average modularity score of any parish. The parish's circumstances seem likely to have fostered fewer shared social connections. First, it was large and had areas of sparse population. By the calculation of the chantry certificates of 1548, it contained 1,100 communicants, 200 more than nearby intramural St Dunstan in the East and yet more than twice St Dunstan's geographical size.[34] As discussed in Chapter One, even its houses seem to have been built in something of a rural style. It may well be that, with a more diffused population, sociability outside the formal structures of the parish and ward was weaker, and people were more likely to rely on other connections to administrate their will. The roads of Aldgate Street, Minories and Houndsditch may have formed their own neighbourhoods, and this may also have been the case with the area around East Smithfield within the Abbot of St Mary Grace's liberty. Indeed, part of the parish was detached and lay outside the jurisdiction of the city. In such a potentially multicentred neighbourhood, parish-level sources have real limitations. The overall modularity score is also closest to the parish of St Lawrence Jewry, where, as will be discussed in the following section, craft and trade connections appear to have played a greater role in the formation of testamentary networks. If craft ties were stronger outside Aldgate, this may have served to reinforce the effects of a less concentrated population. The local population of immigrant aliens showed their own pattern of sociability, which tended to weaken the structure of the testamentary network. The final sample of wills contains six testators who were aliens with few connections within the parish. Migrant identity and background, then, could be a fault line through local society that served to create a kind of cultural disconnection within the neighbourhood, as will be discussed further below. There were other outlying wills in the sample, but this was the only group of outlying testators with a clear trait in common. The impact of cultural disconnection in terms of the experience of sociability will be further explored in Chapter Four. The potential for locality to act as a fulcrum of testamentary networks outside Aldgate may have been lessened by the presence of individuals with close ties to other communities as well as divisions into spatially distinct neighbourhoods.

Bequests tell a different story, one that is more focused on affective ties than high-status social connections. Neighbours were important as friends, and testators often remembered them in their wills. As Table 2.2 indicates, of

[34] 'Chantry certificate, 1548: city of London', in London and Middlesex Chantry Certificates,1548, ed. C. J. Kitching (London, 1980), pp. 1–60, in *British History Online*, <http://www.british-history.ac.uk/london-record-soc/vol16/pp1-60> [accessed 20 Jan. 2017].

more than 400 individuals named in wills (both beneficiaries and officials) who were stated to live within London, the majority lived within the parish of the testator. This was most apparent in Aldgate and Bishopsgate parishes, where 79 per cent and 82 per cent respectively were drawn from the same parish, and at its lowest at Aldersgate, with 69 per cent. This contradicts the higher modularity of St Botolph Aldgate's testamentary networks, suggesting that even if choices of testamentary officials did not overlap, testators still had important local friendships, perhaps made within their patch of the multicentred parish.

Bequests to those outside the testator's own household were only rarely given with a clear description of the relationship between testator and legatee. Among the most popular and easily identified local figures to receive bequests or act as officials were clergy associated with the local parish church. While this was often a formulaic bequest, some testators named specific clergymen, often asking to be remembered in their prayers. For instance, the butcher Richard Hartlepool left twenty pence to Sir Henry Markham, chaplain of the parish of St Botolph Aldersgate, to pray for his soul.[35] Other recipients were evidently lay friends and neighbours, such as Joan Capper, who received twelve pence from the will of her fellow parishioner at Aldersgate, the widow Margaret Morris. Maurice Clerk, a chandler, was left sixteen pence by his neighbour Walter Spencer in 1477.[36] Constance Gates of St Lawrence Jewry left a bequest to an unnamed woman who was described as her 'pewfellow'.[37] At St Katharine and St Lawrence, a considerable minority of individuals were simply described as being 'of London', usually as part of a designation of their citizenship and company membership. This may well indicate the greater importance of citizenship and craft in the parishes within the walls, a factor that is explored more thoroughly in the following section.

In summary, local circumstances produced testamentary networks of different characters. Within this diversity, certain themes can be seen in the factors that affected the connectedness of each network to a greater or lesser degree, as measured in its modularity score. The effect of locality or neighbourly integration served to lower modularity by fostering connections through formal and informal social interaction within the parish. This effect might be reduced where the geography of a parish meant that it could contain smaller, more 'natural' neighbourhoods. Cultural disconnection could also balance the impact of local integration, as social groups with a differing identity to their neighbours sought out other networks.

[35] LMA, DL/C/B/004/MS09171/004, fos. 270–270v.

[36] LMA, DL/C/B/004/MS09171/003, fo. 495v; LMA, DL/C/B/004/MS09171/006, fo. 201v.

[37] LMA, DL/C/B/004/MS09171/010, fo. 154.

Table 2.2 Parishes of residence for all London individuals named in sampled wills

Named location of residence	Aldersgate	Aldgate	Bishopsgate	Cree	Jewry
St Botolph without Aldersgate	47	1			
St Botolph without Aldgate		85	1		
St Botolph without Bishopsgate			83	2	
St Katharine Cree				73	
St Lawrence Jewry					57
'London'	8	8	8	17	16
London religious houses	3	6	1	8	2
Other London locations (Inns, lanes, etc.)	3		3		
St Alphage			1		
St Andrew Castle Baynard		1			
St Andrew Cornhill				1	
St Antonin	1				
St Benet Fink			2		
St Benet Gracechurch	1				
St Gabriel		1		1	
St Giles Cripplegate	1				1
St Helen (Bishopsgate)	1				
St Katharine (unspecified)				1	
St Katherine by the Tower		2			
St Leonard Shoreditch			1		
St Magnus (Bridge, the Martyr)	1				
St Margaret Bridge Street			1		

St Mary Aldermanbury	1				
St Mary Matfelon (Whitechapel)		1			
St Peter Cornhill		1		1	
St Sepulchre		1			1
St Swithin	1				
Total	*68*	*107*	*101*	*104*	*77*

Cultural disconnections

As has already been alluded to, the wills of immigrants expressed a cultural disconnection to their fellow parishioners. The presence of aliens in the final Aldgate sample increased the modularity of the network. There were six testators in this sample whom circumstantial evidence suggests were Dutch or German immigrants: Jacob Johannes, Tuse Bolybrand, Gerard Sleipen, Henry Johnson, Martin Danswick and John Nicholas.[38] Aside from local curate Richard Bostock, who acted as witness to Bolybrand's will, none of these men's circle of officials overlaps with other testators in the parish (or indeed with one another's). Other immigrant wills echoed this pattern. The most extreme example was that of Genoese merchant Giorgio Spinulla, whose will, proved in 1470, named two executors and two witnesses, all from his home city. Spinulla died in the parish of St Katharine Cree but requested burial at Austin Friars.[39] Giles de Hare, a beer brewer of St Botolph Aldgate whose will was proved in 1442, named three executors: his wife, Eleanor; William Billington, who lived in 'Makkyng'; and Guibert Panser, a goldsmith of Southwark. He also left 3s 4d to the 'Dutch fraternity' of St Crispin.[40] Josh Ravenhill, in his recent study of aliens and their experience

[38] All have been identified as aliens on the basis of their names, as well as those of their officials and the fact that all left a will in Latin in a period when virtually all English wills were in the vernacular. Only Nicholas identified his place of origin, Brabant, in his will. The wills of Johnson, Nicholas and Danswick were all witnessed by members of the order of Crossed Friars, who were particularly popular with Germanic and Dutch immigrants and around whom confraternities for immigrants grew up. See J. Colson, 'Alien communities and alien fraternities in later medieval London', *London Journal*, xxxv (2010), 111–43, doi:org/10.1179/174963210X12729493038298.

[39] LMA, DL/C/B/004/MS09171/006 fo. 68v.

[40] LMA, DL/C/B/004/MS09171/004 fo. 121v.

of belonging in late medieval London, argued that immigrants made a range of social connections with other city dwellers, many of whom were neighbours.[41] In the light of his analysis, the cultural disconnection seen in testamentary networks is perhaps best understood as primarily a function of how aliens might gather social capital differently. When it came to making a will, their most trusted and highest status connections were often outside the parish or, where they were within the parish, with local clergy rather than neighbours.

The connections made by aliens outside their parish were fostered by socializing with those who shared their language and origins. That they did so in both informal and institutional settings can be seen in cases heard at the consistory court. For instance, a 1514 marriage contract made in French between two Normans at a house in St Martin le Grand was witnessed by Stephen Sawner, a sheath maker born at Saint-Lô who had come from his home in Southwark to see the contract made.[42] St Martin le Grand was home to a large community of alien craftsmen, and other well-known locations acted as 'hubs' to draw together immigrants resident across the city. The city's friaries served this purpose, particularly in acting as the venues for alien religious fraternities such as the fraternity of St Crispin named in Giles de Hare's will (although the will does not mention the venue of that fraternity). The friaries were popular meeting places for alien fraternities because they often provided religious services and confession in immigrants' native tongues, being able to do so because many friars were migrants themselves.[43] We shall see later in this chapter that English parish fraternities attracted a highly localized membership, but the pattern among alien fraternities was very different. A 1523–4 consistory case concerned the alien fraternity of St Barbara, based at the house of Dominican friars known as Blackfriars: the fraternity's membership were natives of Brabant and Lorraine.[44] The case was brought by the fraternity wardens, who sued two former members apparently for refusing to pay their fraternity dues, with six members appearing as witnesses. The parishes of residence given by the members were spread across the city with no two witnesses originating in the same parish, from St Andrew Castle Baynard in the west to St Dunstan in the East by the Tower. Blackfriars did not form a geographic centre point for the fraternity members; they probably chose it based more on their origins than on proximity to their homes. It is also notable

[41] J. Ravenhill, 'The experiences of aliens in later medieval London and the negotiation of belonging, 1400–1540' (unpublished University of York PhD thesis, 2019), pp. 211–13.

[42] LMA, DL/C/206, fos. 269–69v.

[43] Colson, 'Alien communities and alien fraternities in later medieval London', pp. 113–14.

[44] LMA, DL/C/0207, fos. 198v-199v, 218, 251v–255v.

that the only English witness who spoke in one of the members' defence was a barber surgeon who treated the defendant's wife's chronic illness, suggesting that when a rupture occurred within the alien community reliable character witnesses might be those known in a professional capacity rather than English neighbours. While aliens may have had affective relationships with neighbours, they gathered the kinds of social connection that manifested in testamentary networks in a manner which minimized the role of fellow parishioners.

The most elite testators showed a similar lack of connection to their neighbours or even to those of their own rank. Esquires John Newport and John Aystow and the gentlemen John Rous, Nicholas Bailey and John Taverham were unconnected to other testators in their respective parish networks. Although gentry and aristocratic men still cited artisans (probably Londoners) such as tailors, shearmen, a pinner and a brewer as their officials, their officials were rarely shared with fellow parishioners. In these cases, their elevated social status, as well as their probable mobility between London and other residences, probably meant that the social circle and networks formed by these men were largely external to their final parishes of residence. These cases are similar to that of William Marow, alderman of Bishopsgate, whose will was discussed above; while for Marow his success in city politics meant that his circle of testamentary officials was disconnected from locality, for the gentry and aristocracy it was their position in a national elite which divided them from neighbours. The greater presence of such individuals at St Botolph Aldersgate and St Katharine Cree, as shown in Chapter One, may well be a determining factor in the apparently greater modularity of testamentary network in those parishes and the reason for a low average in-degree among officials in Aldersgate.

Those classed as nobility or gentry cited more textile manufacturers (tailors, shearmen, etc.) as officials than they did those of their own rank. This probably reflects the importance of London as a centre for the production of clothing for the wealthy and fashionable and their trust in men of business in practical matters of handling money. When the gentleman Nicholas Bailey named William Browning, tailor, as his executor and left him a gown and doublet in 1486, it was perhaps because he had been a frequent patron of Browning in life.[45] Those with high status and immigrants had different patterns of will-making to their neighbours, and this was perhaps connected with their not having anticipated death in a city far from their home country or estate.

45 LMA, DL/C/B/004/MS09171/007, fos. 49–49v.

Occupational ties

Chapter One showed that marginal areas attracted particular occupations, especially those which were unwanted within the city walls or which benefited from lower rents for large premises. The kind of occupations found in a neighbourhood affected not just its economy but also the character of its social relations. Occupations could act as the 'central ties' of the city, the key networks supported by the social activities of the craft guilds that connected people from across London and assisted social mobility. Ties based on craft are one of the more easily identifiable kinds of network displayed within the testamentary sample, since occupation is one of the few pieces of information given about many officials and legatees.

There was also a clear tendency to name officials with a similar or shared craft. Table 2.3 indicates the proportion of officials with each occupation type for testators falling into each occupation category. This was most dramatic among the mercantile testators, for whom 31 per cent of their officials were drawn from those with the same kind of occupation. As will be discussed, these testators were mainly mercers living in the parish of St Lawrence Jewry. Among metal workers, too, there was common citation of those with similar occupations. For metal workers, cooperation between allied trades was evidently important in fostering social connections that featured in testamentary networks. The bellfounder William Powtrell named a brazier, Geoffrey Bride, as an executor, and John Robertson, a coppersmith, named Richard Hill, a founder, his executor.[46] Such trades required similar equipment and, especially in the case of bellfounding, a staff of founders and braziers to shape the metal and stoke the furnaces. Metalworkers might have come to know and trust each other as much through working together in the same workshops as through the formal organization of a craft guild.

A notable exception was those who provided services, who evidently gathered wide social connections, which they reflected in their wills. The barber William atte Hill was evidently a wealthy and well-connected man, as he left more than £1 in forgotten tithes and had a girdler and two drapers among the officials to his will. At the more modest end of the scale, John Ingham the minstrel (who left twenty pence in tithes) named a brewer as supervisor to his will, a lute player as one of his witnesses and two barbers among his friends receiving bequests, one of whom was given a small lute.[47] In general, outside of these exceptions, shared and similar occupations played an important role in the formation of testamentary networks.

[46] LMA, DL/C/B/004/MS09171/003, fo.379; DL/C/B/004/MS09171/004, fo. 32.

[47] LMA, DL/C/B/004/MS09171/007, fo. 7.

Shared occupations sometimes reinforced the strength of local testamentary networks. In several of the parishes under discussion here, clusters can be seen to have been formed by those with shared occupations, both in central St Lawrence Jewry and in extramural parishes. For instance, in the third Aldgate sample the butchers William Stallon, Robert Nore, John Roke junior and Thomas Russell were all closely connected. Roke's will was witnessed by both Nore and Stallon, and Nore acted as supervisor for Stallon and executor for Russell.[48] Stallon and Nore appear to have been men of some personal standing in the parish even outside the community of butchers. They were two of the men most commonly chosen as officials in the sample, named by non-butchers and people with unknown occupations. Likewise, at St Lawrence Jewry the sizeable group of mercers often cited those who shared their occupation and, occasionally, they also seem to have shared a connection to the parish. Mercers Geoffrey Fielding and Philip Agmondesham both named Richard Fielding, Geoffrey's son and a fellow company member, as an official.

However, while in some cases shared occupation strengthened local ties, on the whole it appears that it served to create testamentary networks that extended outside the neighbourhood. Fielding and Agmondesham were unusual in sharing an official, in spite of the fact that mercers formed the largest occupational grouping among the St Lawrence Jewry testators. While 31 per cent of the officials chosen by mercers and other mercantile occupations shared their occupation, only two of the fifteen fellow mercers they chose were also cited by another resident of the same parish. Testators here seem to have chosen officials they knew through the Mercers' Company rather than the parish, the company hall being located a short distance away on Poultry. In St Lawrence Jewry, then, the modularity of the network was increased by the existence of a sizeable minority who had close occupational ties which caused their testamentary network to face outwards from the parish. By contrast, for the members of the Fishmongers' Company who lived in the Bridgehead neighbourhood institutional affiliation reinforced and created local testamentary ties.[49] Unlike the Fishmongers, members of the Mercers' Company were residing in increasingly dispersed locations across the city in the late fifteenth and early sixteenth centuries.[50] This was the usual pattern for London guildsmen in the period, and the evidence of the Mercers' wills suggests that declining craft clustering may have made

[48] LMA, DL/C/B/004/MS09171/007 fo. 19v; LMA, DL/C/B/004/MS09171/006 fos. 118, 172.

[49] Colson, 'London's forgotten company?'

[50] J. Colson, 'Commerce, clusters and community', p. 115.

Table 2.3 Proportions (%) of officials with each category of occupation by occupation category of testator. Co-citations in bold.

Official occupation type	Testator occupation type															
	Food distribution	Textile distribution	Mercantile	Other distribution	Metalworking	Food preparation	Textile manufacture	Weaponry manufacture	Other manufacture	Building trades	Clerical	Services	Nobility/Gentry	Other	Civic and household officers	Unknown
Food distribution	**9**	5	0	0	3	3	1	8	3	3	0	5	4	0	4	1
Textile distribution	7	**6**	0	0	0	2	5	8	3	3	0	4	0	0	8	2
Mercantile	3	5	**31**	0	0	0	0	0	0	0	0	2	0	0	8	1
Other distribution	0	0	0	**0**	0	2	1	0	1	2	0	0	0	0	0	0
Metalworking	0	0	4	50	**17**	2	3	0	1	2	3	4	0	0	4	2
Food preparation	7	9	0	0	0	**8**	5	8	4	6	3	7	4	0	4	5
Textile manufacture	7	5	4	0	2	4	**8**	0	3	2	5	2	7	50	0	3
Weaponry manufacture	0	0	0	0	0	0	2	**8**	1	0	0	1	0	0	0	0
Other manufacture	3	2	2	0	2	4	6	0	**10**	2	3	4	4	0	4	2
Assistant	1	0	0	0	0	1	1	0	0	2	0	1	0	0	8	1
Building trades	0	0	0	0	3	2	2	0	1	**9**	0	0	0	0	0	1
Clerical	12	15	16	0	11	9	13	0	9	9	**42**	9	18	0	12	14
Services	7	5	4	0	6	4	3	0	3	0	8	**5**	0	0	4	1
Nobility/Gentry	1	2	2	0	2	1	0	0	2	0	0	1	**14**	0	0	1
Other	0	0	0	0	0	0	0	0	0	3	0	0	0	**0**	0	1
Civic and household officers	1	3	0	0	0	1	0	0	0	0	0	0	4	0	**12**	1
Unknown	39	45	37	50	55	61	51	67	57	59	37	54	46	50	35	**65**
Total of officials (n)	*67*	*65*	*51*	*2*	*64*	*200*	*111*	*12*	*90*	*66*	*38*	*81*	*28*	*4*	*26*	*744*

London guild members increasingly likely to choose their testamentary officials from across the city.

Unfortunately, outside St Lawrence Jewry the identification of occupations was less consistent. This makes it difficult to identify with certainty the extent to which this effect impacted upon networks among craftsmen of humbler status. Nonetheless, there are some revealing contrasts between members of the same parish who had different occupations. Comparing the number of times individuals were named as officials (their in-degree) is very suggestive. The higher the in-degree of named officials, the more frequently they feature in the wills of neighbours and thus the higher the likelihood that those ties were based on locality rather than craft or some other factor peculiar to the circumstances of individual testators. St Botolph Aldgate had the same average in-degree to St Lawrence Jewry: officials, excluding widows of the testator, were named 1.12 times, on average. However, there were significant differences by occupation. A good example of this are those working in food preparation, the most common occupation type in extramural parishes. Butchers (sixteen) named as officials by Aldgate testators had an average in-degree of 1.6, while others who prepared food for a living (brewers: three; and bakers: four) had an average of 1. When butchers are excluded, the average in-degree for all Aldgate officials was 1.09, suggesting that they were much more likely to be chosen as officials. Living near East Smithfield market, butchers such as Stallon and Nore seem to have been part of a densely connected local occupational community, unlike brewers and bakers. These are, admittedly, very small subsets of the wills sampled, and the results could simply be down to chance, but they are suggestive when combined with the evidence from St Lawrence Jewry. Some trades, such as the mercers, encouraged the building of connections across the city, while others, such as the butchers and fishmongers, built densely connected craft clusters. The effects of occupation on local testamentary networks were complex and varied from trade to trade. The evidence presented here is suggestive of patterns which might well have been replicated across the city wherever parishes were not so dominated by one trade as to become the social centre for that occupation in themselves. Occupational connections were a factor influencing the structure of parish testamentary networks, which seem, in general, to have increased modularity. It is likely that the structure and nature of different trades and the presence of local infrastructure (such as markets or company halls) determined the degree to which this was the case.

In some cases, occupation could marginalize people from parish networks. Thomas Kent of St Botolph Aldgate, for instance, is described in his 1432 will as a mariner, and neither his two witnesses nor his executors feature in any of the wills of his neighbours.[51] While proximity to the Thames might have determined his residence at the time of his death, the practicalities of his occupation presumably necessitated long periods of absence and thus a lack of participation in neighbourhood life. Despite the gulf in social status between the mariner Kent and the esquire Newport, both chose officials for their wills in comparable ways. It can be inferred that each held a position which made them part of a group similar to the 'portable communities' described by Erik Spindler who did not depend on a fixed locality for their sociability and networks.[52] Therefore, their impact on modularity can be considered similar to that seen among the aliens of Aldgate parish as a factor of cultural disconnection from their neighbours.

Economic connections were often also social connections in fifteenth-century London, both at the margins and elsewhere. However, unlike among the highly clustered fishmongers, the structures of neighbourhood, parish and craft did not always serve to reinforce one another where occupations were more spread across the city. Those with access to wider economic networks might prefer to use such connections when choosing men of status to carry out or bear witness to their final will. Given that access to financial credit and social status were heavily intertwined, the most respectable executors were also likely to be those with the greatest resources and experience in handling money. These networks would for some at least provide access to men of greater social standing than they might meet as neighbours and fellow parishioners. This raises an important question for the peripheral areas of the city, which, as discussed in Chapter One, were generally poorer and whose populations had fewer ties to the structures of craft and citizenship which drove such economic ties. In the absence of access to these city-wide networks, those at the margins developed alternative networks of support, which will be discussed in Chapter Four.

City-wide ties

Craft connections represent one kind of centralizing network in the fifteenth-century city, but attachment to London was not just expressed in terms of guild allegiances. Bequests were markers of testators' own sense of urban space. By grouping bequests together, a footprint of each parish cohort of testators' understanding of city space can be mapped. This both sheds light on the role of centralizing networks and builds a more nuanced

[51] LMA, DL/C/B/004/MS09171/003, fos. 311–311v.

[52] E. Spindler, 'Between sea and city: portable communities in late medieval London and Bruges', in *London and Beyond: Essays in Honour of Derek Keene*, ed. M. P. Davies, J. A. Galloway and D. Keene (London, 2012), pp. 181–200, at pp. 181–3.

understanding of the meaning of locality beyond the parish. Experiences of urban space were markedly localized, even if they did not always respect institutional boundaries. Nonetheless, Londoners also moved around the city during their lifetime and retained connections to previous neighbourhoods.

When making their wills, testators selected locations with which they had a particular connection as focuses for bequests. Scholars have sometimes assumed, in the absence of other information about testators' lives, that bequests located outside the testator's place of residence indicate prior residence or places of origin.[53] However, analyses of spiritual bequests to religious foundations have revealed more complex patterns of giving, based both on proximity to the testator's residence as well as to their conceptions of space, such as Sheila Sweetinburgh's work on bequests to medieval English hospitals and Anne Lester's on testators in Champagne.[54] Lester wrote that a testator's 'description reflects her own frame of reference, her experience of the urban environment'.[55] Testamentary records cannot be read as unmediated documents of an individual's situation. However, even if not complete, wills are one of the few documents that do partially express a spatial frame of reference for ordinary medieval people, even if greater wealth meant greater freedom for that expression. For example, not all bequests to St Paul's Cathedral can be directly assumed to suggest regular attendance at masses there, since some such gifts could be aspirational statements about how and where the testator wished to be remembered after their death, related to both the perceived status of the object of the bequest, its location and the testator's self-image.[56] The discussion here follows this conception of the will by reading it as a partial record of a testator's spatial frame of reference. In this interpretation, gifts left outside the parish of residence express connections which may well indicate prior residence and migration but also other kinds of personal connection and suggest the prominence of institutions as elements of the urban landscape.

[53] See eg R. A. Wood, 'Life and death: a study of the wills and testaments of men and women in London and Bury St. Edmunds in the late fourteenth and early fifteenth centuries' (unpublished Royal Holloway, University of London PhD thesis, 2013), pp. 125–6.

[54] S. Sweetinburgh, *The Role of the Hospital in Medieval England: Gift-Giving and the Spiritual Economy* (Dublin, 2004), pp. 118–19; A. E. Lester, 'Crafting a charitable landscape: urban topographies in charters and testaments from medieval champagne', in *Cities, Texts and Social Networks 400–1500: Experiences and Perceptions of Medieval Urban Space*, ed. C. Goodson, A. E. Lester and C. Symes (Farnham, 2010), pp. 125–48.

[55] Lester, 'Crafting a charitable landscape', p. 136.

[56] A similar approach, with a prosopographical aim, is taken in J. M. Bennett and C. Whittick, 'Philippa Russell and the wills of London's late medieval singlewomen', *London Journal*, xxxii (2007), 251–69, at pp. 251–2.

Choosing where to be buried was the most common way in which testators showed attachment to places in the city. The parish church or churchyard was the most common choice, with 75 per cent or more making this choice in most parishes.[57] The strength of social ties to neighbours also meant a strong spiritual connection; people wanted to be buried and remembered in the community which had meant the most to them in life. St Lawrence Jewry testators were the most likely to ask for burial in the parish; in fact, of those who made a request for their burial place, only one chose to be buried at any distance from the parish (in Waltham, Essex), while another asked for burial at the Guildhall Chapel, which lay very close to the northern boundary of the parish. The picture was quite different at St Katharine Cree, where the lowest proportion (69 per cent) of testators chose burial in the parish church or churchyard. Sites at neighbouring Holy Trinity Priory were requested by 13 per cent of testators. St Katharine Cree had an unusual arrangement in that its parish church lay in the grounds of Holy Trinity Priory, which was also a major landowner in the parish. It was not just in burial choice that testators showed attachment to the priory. Trusting relationships between the clergy and laity are suggested in the testamentary networks: clergy and staff of the priory were named by local parishioners including rent collector John Fulbourne (seven times), prior Thomas Pomeroy (twice) and canon John Upton (once). The priory was very much knitted into parishioners' experiences of their neighbourhood.

Although to a slightly lesser degree, similar attachment to local religious institutions within or close to the parish was evident in wills from all the extramural parishes. At St Botolph Aldgate, after the parish church, the Abbey of St Mary Graces at Tower Hill was the most popular location for burial, and at St Botolph Bishopsgate 6 per cent of testators chose the hospital of St Mary. At St Botolph Aldersgate, St Paul's Cathedral was the next most popular, and the cathedral was also a significant beneficiary of bequests. Neighbouring parishes and other close institutions also garnered a handful of burial requests, such as the house of Franciscan nuns known as the Minoresses and St Mary Matfelon at Aldgate, St Bartholomew's Hospital and St Giles Cripplegate at St Botolph Aldersgate and the Austin Friars at St Katharine.

Burial locations expressed attachment mainly to places within the testators' neighbourhood, perhaps reinforcing connections with those institutions built in life or expressing ambitions of status through the prestige of being so permanently associated with high-profile religious

[57] I have not distinguished between requests for burial in the body of the church and for burial in the churchyard.

institutions. Some demonstrated a detailed knowledge of their places of burial, such as the widow Margaret Butler of St Katharine Cree parish, who asked to be buried 'in the church of [the Priory of] Holy Trinity London in front of the cross between the high altar and the chapel of Holy Mary'.[58] The religious houses and hospitals of London would have been especially visible to the inhabitants of London's margins in their daily lives, acting as physical reminders of Christian duties of piety and charity, and perhaps it was this constant presence that inspired testators here to request burial within their grounds.

The popularity of local religious houses as recipients of bequests as well as burial locations may also reflect familiarity built through their role as landlords. For instance, among the Bishopsgate testators the hospital of St Mary was more popular than St Mary Bethlehem, both of which lay along Bishopsgate Street.[59] Perhaps the extensive landholdings of the former in the parish meant it was more familiar to local residents. The prominence of a rent collector for Holy Trinity Priory in the wills of St Katharine Cree parishioners has already been mentioned. Generally, the proximity of many burial requests to the resident parish of the testator indicates the importance of locality and community in their lives; even when choosing burial in apparently more prestigious locations, testators still made a choice based on their own experience of urban space.

People also demonstrated this close sense of neighbourhood in their bequests to institutions outside their own parish. Figures 3.4–7 represent such bequests made by testators in each sample parish overlaid on to the parish map of London. Using Geographic Information Systems (GIS) mapping, bequests have been grouped by quantity on to a map of the parishes and liberties of London, with any institutions not attached to a parish church or liberty subsumed into their surrounding parishes. Although bequests to the testator's own parish church have been excluded, it can be seen that, in each, parish institutions located in the immediate environs still dominated the largesse of testators. These included parish fraternities and local religious houses such as the hospital of St Mary at Bishopsgate and the Minoresses at Aldgate. As we have seen, testators were often fraternity members at their own or a neighbouring parish church. There were several institutions which garnered bequests from all parishes, in particular the friaries, prisons and St Paul's Cathedral. However, even here proximity seems to have guided Londoners' choices. The white (Carmelite), black (Dominican) and grey

[58] LMA, DL/C/B/004/MS09171/002, fo. 117v.

[59] Nine testators left bequests to the hospital of St Mary compared to three to the hospital of St Mary Bethlehem.

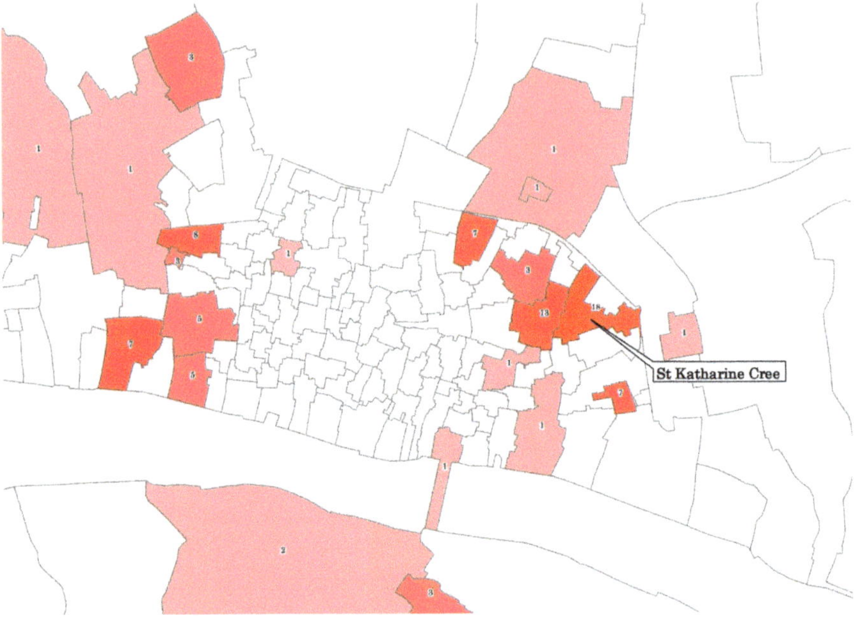

Figure 2.4 Map of bequests to fraternities, religious (and other) institutions and parishes (excluding the testator's parish church); St Katharine Cree testators

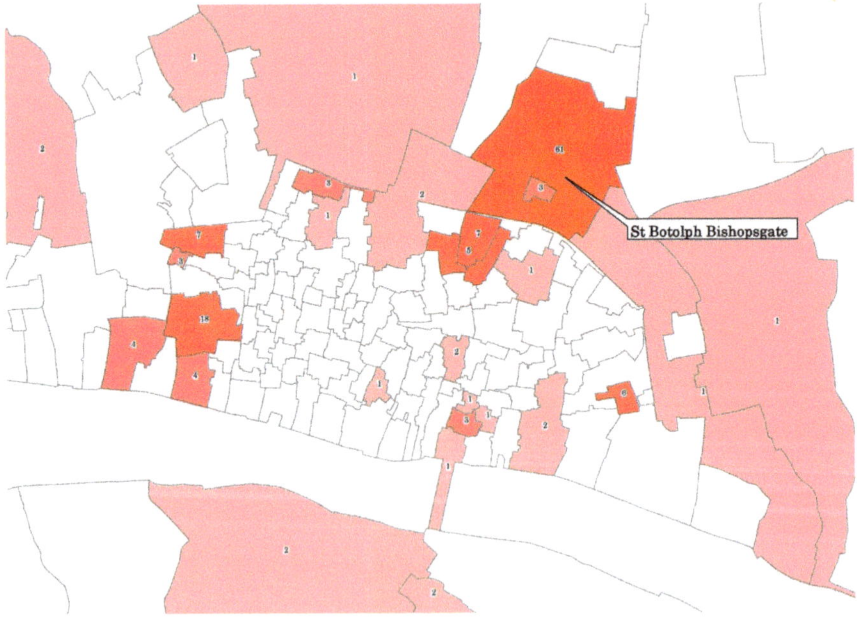

Figure 2.5 Map of bequests to fraternities, religious (and other) institutions and parishes (excluding the testator's parish church); St Botolph Bishopsgate testators

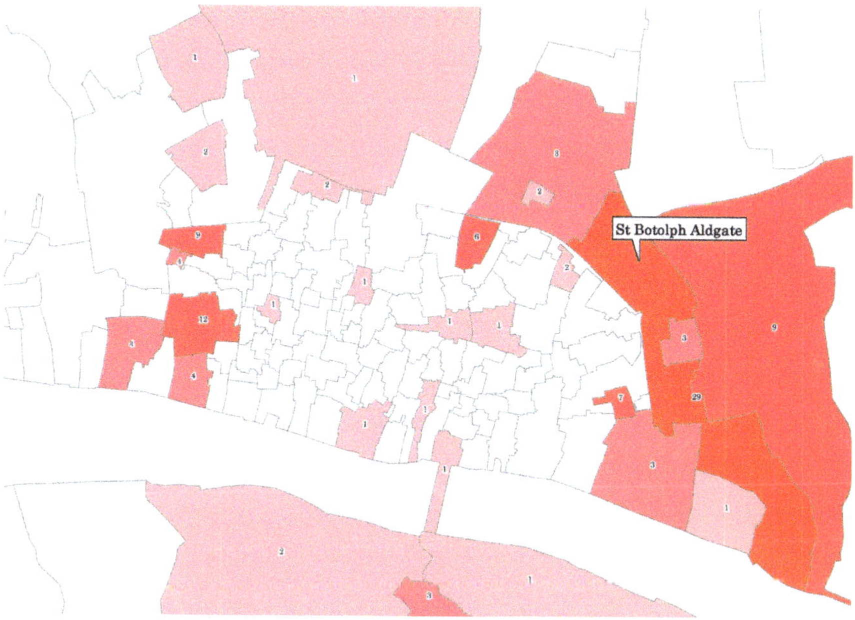

Figure 2.6 Map of bequests to fraternities, religious (and other) institutions and parishes (excluding the testator's parish church); St Botolph Aldgate testators

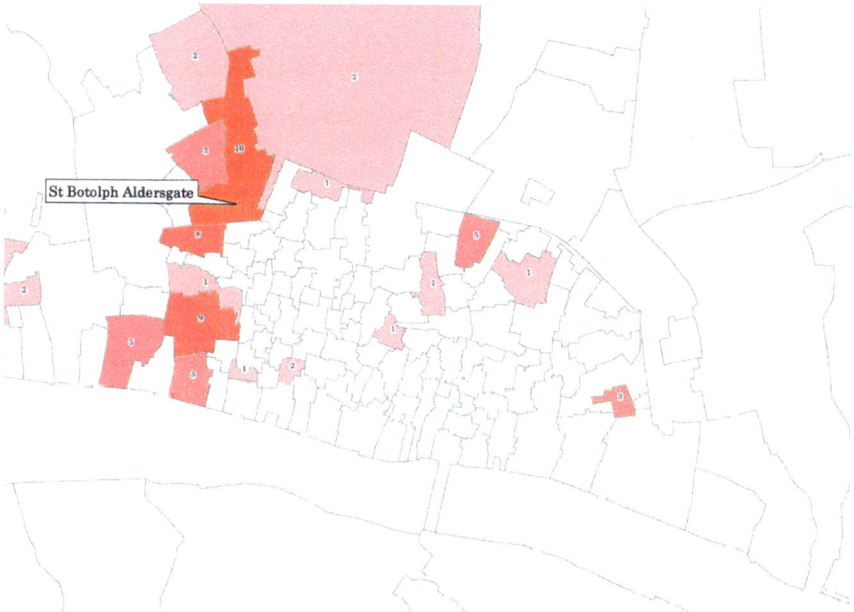

Figure 2.7 Map of bequests to fraternities, religious (and other) institutions and parishes (excluding the testator's parish church); St Botolph Aldersgate testators

(Franciscan) friars were all located in the west of the city, as was St Pauls', and at Aldersgate these institutions were all prominent recipients of bequests. By contrast, at Bishopsgate, the crossed friars, located in the east near Tower Hill, and the Augustinian friars, located within the walls close to Bishopsgate itself, were each equally as popular as the grey friars. Since the friaries, prisons and cathedral were popular in all parishes, including St Lawrence Jewry, they can be thought of as institutions which were central for London testators as common touchpoints for testamentary charity. Testators who left money to central institutions typically left larger than average sums for forgotten tithes to their own parish churches; among this group, the median tithe left was eighty pence, well above the normal range discussed in Chapter One. Such bequests may thus have been aspirational expressions of identity by association with high-status targets for pious giving.

In line with its wealthier local social networks, central locations for charity were somewhat more important for Aldgate parishioners and local institutions less dominant. The grey friars, St Paul's and the prisons of Ludgate and Newgate were relatively popular among testators despite their distance from the parish. A closer look at the evidence suggests that these bequests were not spread equally amongst all testators from St Botolph Aldgate. It was a small group who showed a preference in their charity for those institutions which identified them more clearly with London as a whole than with their immediate neighbourhood. This group was a wealthy subset of parishioners who spread their charity not just across London but also the wider region. Some of these testators, such as the widow Elizabeth Wells, left large bequests to extramural and London institutions while ignoring the parish completely. Wells bequeathed money for prayers and masses for her soul at three religious houses outside London as well as the five London friaries. She did not mention her parish church.[60] Another widow, Joan Nore, showed closer connections to the parish with bequests both to the church and the parish fraternity of Jesus. Nore also demonstrated extra-urban connections, with a torch to St Mary Matfelon and 6s 8d to the repairs of St Dunstan, Stepney. She also left a torch to the grey friars and twelve pence in bread to prisoners incarcerated in four city jails.[61] Wealthy residents of fringe parishes often expressed an urban identity encompassing more than their immediate neighbourhood. Their charity

[60] LMA, DL/C/B/004/MS09171/009, fos. 175–175v. Elizabeth Wells's will suggests that she may have been a lay resident of the Minoresses precinct, explaining her apparent lack of connections to the parish. She requested to be buried in the church of Minoresses 'in the little chapel before the middle of the altar there by my pew wherein I was wont to kneel and hear divine service'.

[61] LMA, DL/C/B/004/MS09171/010, fo. 32.

thus projected a self-image as wealthy Londoners served by a common set of urban institutions but also attached to the city's wider region.

Examining evidence from London-wide bequests indicates that, in general, testators expressed the greatest attachment to institutions that had a physical presence in their neighbourhood. Burial patterns, too, suggest a close attachment to the parish church and its churchyard. Testators' experience of the city as expressed in their bequests appears to have consisted primarily of their immediate environment, and their bequests usually reinforced commitments to their local community. 'Central' institutions that were symbolic of London, such as the Guildhall, the friaries or St Paul's, or civic targets for charity such as the prisons and London Bridge, were popular with a wealthier minority whose wills suggest a broader identification with London as a whole.

The pattern of bequests to parish churches excluding a testator's own varied from neighbourhood to neighbourhood. In general, people left bequests to churches close to their home parish. Bishopsgate residents were the most likely to leave bequests to parishes outside their own, with bequests to fourteen London parishes. The parishes close to the walls inside Bishopsgate were well represented, although parishes close to the river also feature. Two Bishopsgate chandlers, William Bateman and William Blackman, left bequests to the church of St Ethelburga just within the gate; Blackman was explicit that he was a former parishioner, since he left 3s 4d for tithes there.[62] There was a similar, local pattern of giving amongst Aldersgate parishioners. The widow Sibyl Bret left bequests to both mural St Anne Aldersgate and St Thomas the Apostle on Knightrider Street between Cheapside and the Thames.[63] Among both the Aldgate and Bishopsgate testators, most of the recipient parishes lay in the eastern half of the city, while in the Aldersgate sample they all lay west of the bridge. In general, the spatial pattern is similar to that demonstrated in Figures 3.4–7, reflecting bequests across all London institutions.

Bequests to external parish churches were often a result of the fact that people moved around London over the course of their lives, gathering connections to individuals and institutions across the city. This is especially apparent where sums were left for forgotten tithes outside the parish testators resided in at the point of making their will, which are reflected in the maps above. Such bequests were notably more popular in the extramural parishes. One in six testators chose to leave money to London parishes churches other than their own at Aldersgate and Bishopsgate, compared to less than one in twenty within the walls. Most bequests to parish churches around

62 LMA, DL/C/B/004/MS09171/010, fo. 77v; TNA, PROB 11/6/404.

63 LMA, DL/C/B/004/MS09171/010, fo. 77v; TNA, PROB 11/6/404.

the city probably indicated a prior residence of the testator. Occasionally individuals were explicit about their movement. For instance, Margaret Waldern, a widow, left tithes both to St Katharine Cree and to St Andrew Baynard's Castle, 'where I was formerly a parishioner'.[64] Likewise, John Ording, citizen and pasteler (pasty maker) of St Botolph Bishopsgate, left 'to the high altar of St. Leonard in Eastcheap for my tithes when I was a parishioner there twenty pence'. Ording appears to have maintained his connections at St Leonard despite moving, as he also left twenty pence to the fraternity of Our Lady there for prayers for his soul.[65] The butcher Richard Hartlepool of St Botolph Aldersgate, who wished to be buried within the church of St Nicholas Shambles, also left torches for the church and money to the fraternity of St Lucy there.[66] Given that St Nicholas was home to one of the city meat markets and many butchers, it is very likely that Hartlepool was a former parishioner.

The remembrance of former parish churches was a noticeably gendered pattern of giving. Women, almost all of them widows, were most likely to show such evidence that they had moved; of the forty-one wills that include bequests to city parishes outside the testator's own, 34 per cent were made by women (29 per cent were explicitly by widows), despite women having made just 19 per cent of wills overall. The circumstances of such women were apparently quite diverse, and thus a number of different motivations for their movement can be inferred. In some cases, such as the widow Margery Boyden, it appears that reduced circumstances in widowhood may have driven the move; Margery wished to be buried next to her late husband, Robert, in St Leonard Eastcheap and, although she left sums to clergy and the church fabric in her parish of residence (St Botolph Bishopsgate), she left no sum for forgotten tithes at Bishopsgate, and her bequests to St Leonard's were of similar value.[67] She most likely moved to the parish after Robert's death, perhaps to take advantage of the lower cost of housing here. We ought to be cautious in ascribing poverty to this group of women, however. The average tithe left by those who made such bequests is high, at seventy-two pence for men and forty-eight pence for women;[68] Margery herself left forty pence to the rector of St Botolph. More properly, we ought to think of them as perhaps a better-off sort looking to maintain their standard of living by a move outwards. As with the artisans who moved

[64] LMA, DL/C/B/004/MS09171/006, fos. 59v–60.

[65] LMA, DL/C/B/004/MS09171/006, fo. 291v.

[66] LMA, DL/C/B/004/MS09171/004, fos. 270–270v.

[67] LMA, DL/C/B/004/MS09171/002, fo. 47v.

[68] See Chapter One, p. 14 for a discussion of average tithe levels.

there seeking commercial premises, moving to a cheaper extramural parish could be a strategic choice for women.

Some widows seem to have moved beyond the walls because it explicitly suited the needs of their business. For example, the widow Joan Wymark of St Botolph Aldersgate left a brass pot to the parish church of Holy Trinity the Less in her will. She also passed on two cows and a bullock as well as land in Islington which lay a couple of miles out along the main approach road to Aldersgate. For her, easy access to her extramural property, which might have been used for agricultural purposes, perhaps made Aldersgate a good option when she moved from Holy Trinity.[69] In the case of the bellmaker Joan Hill, her bequest to St Mary Axe can be quite closely tied to her craft since this parish lay very close to Founders Hall and there is archaeological evidence of metalworking in the area in this period.[70] Although a widow, it seems likely that Hill's move came during the lifetime of her husband, Richard, since they operated a large foundry, many of whose staff received bequests.[71] A move outside the walls for the Hills would probably have enabled them to run a larger premises and expand their business.[72] There were thus a variety of life-cycle and economic reasons for moves to the extramural areas reflected in bequests. The over-representation of women leaving such bequests, however, suggests that such movement, or at least a wish to reflect it in charitable giving, was particular to women's experiences.

The movement of Londoners around the city has been little considered, and it is difficult to generalize based on the apparently diverse circumstances of testators who left such bequests. What is definite, however, is the degree to which such bequests were more frequent in extramural parishes. Since movement outwards was probably motivated by the practicalities of living costs in one way or another, the new parish does not seem to have wholly provided a substitute for the friendships and spiritual community of the old. At St Botolph Aldgate, the popularity of institutions in nearby Whitechapel and Stepney reflects connections in the immediate area of London that crossed the city's line of jurisdiction into its commercializing hinterland. As will be seen in Chapter Three, everyday movement around the neighbourhoods on the city fringe paid little heed to formal boundaries.

69 LMA, DL/C/B/004/MS09171/006, fo. 340.

70 E. Howe, *Roman Defences and Medieval Industry: Excavations at Baltic House, City of London*, MoLAS Monograph, 7 (London, 2002), pp. 51–2.

71 LMA, DL/C/B/004/MS09171/004, fo. 62.

72 For more on the Hills and their business see C. M. Barron, 'Johanna Hill (d.1441) and Johanna Sturdy (d.*c.*1460), Bell-Founders', in *Medieval London Widows, 1300–1500*, ed. C. M. Barron and A. F. Sutton (London, 1994), pp. 99–112.

Extra-urban ties

Londoners did not, however, confine themselves to the city. In their wills, they remembered family, friendships and economic interests that extended beyond London itself. These connections were formed both by migration and by London's central role in the economy of England in the fifteenth century. For those living on the margins of the city, routes of transport outwards dominated their local environment and also, as will be demonstrated, their lives. Figures 3.8 and 3.9 map the bequests to individuals and institutions outside the city, along with any extra-urban land bequeathed by testators. Bequests to parishes, religious foundations and other establishments outside London formed 12–23 per cent of all institutional bequests in each parish, and there were some striking differences in the geographical spread of the destinations in each which suggest parish communities had strong ties to particular hinterlands.

St Botolph Bishopsgate showed the most distinctive and well-defined geographical spread of extra-urban connections, as indicated in Figure 2.9. The spread of landholding, bequests to institutions and individuals lay mainly to the north-east of London, within the valley of the River Lea on the border between Essex and Hertfordshire and along Ermine Street, the main approach road to the city at Bishopsgate (marked in purple on the map). The bequests to these areas cover the full chronological span of the sample of testators, from John Shoreditch senior, who left a missal book and other goods to the parish church of Hackney in 1410, to Henry Adam, salter, who left money to the churches of Bengeo and Cheshunt in Hertfordshire in 1522.[73] Three testators expressly bequeathed money for the repair of sections of the highway at settlements on or near Ermine Street; the same Henry Adam left a similar bequest, also at Cheshunt, as did John Wilcox, brewer, at Stamford Hill, Middlesex, and John Mortimer, another brewer, for two sections of road near Stanbridge, Bedfordshire, and Enfield, Middlesex. The familiarity with the route and its present condition that these gifts imply are strongly suggestive of individuals who made frequent use of Ermine Street. John Mortimer requested burial at Enfield, 'where my father and mother are buried', and one of his executors, John Bristow, was from that town.[74] Mortimer's family had evidently lived along the immediate route to Bishopsgate. However, the fact that he named an executor from Enfield and that he and other Bishopsgate testators showed knowledge of the present state of the roadway indicated that testators did not simply remember old family ties in the locations of their bequests but affirmed connections which

[73] TNA, PROB 11/21/72.

[74] LMA, DL/C/B/004/MS09171/004, fo. 101v.

had been maintained or created in their adult lives. Thus, business and migration went hand in hand among those living outside Bishopsgate.

At St Botolph Aldgate, too, extra-urban bequests left by testators show attachments to particular areas of London's hinterland. In this case, it is specifically to parts of the county of Essex and eastern Middlesex. Some of these were very close to the Aldgate neighbourhood itself, with six testators leaving bequests in Whitechapel and three in Stepney. Londoners played an important role in developing the city's eastern hinterland during the fifteenth century, investing in pasture and crop-growing lands in Essex, Hertfordshire and eastern Middlesex.[75] These economic connections are also suggested by their bequests. Butchers especially indicated strong ties to the east in their wills. One, Nicholas Long, requested burial at St Peter's church, Hornchurch, Essex, and John Roke junior was to be buried at St Mary Matfelon in Whitechapel.[76] John Edward and Thomas Russell left torches or cash to parish churches east of Aldgate in Middlesex and Essex.[77] Extra-urban giving was indeed motivated by links forged through business concerns rather than migration alone, particularly in a trade which relied on Essex pastureland.[78]

Other Aldgate parishioners also made bequests in the immediate hinterland that suggest connections maintained or built in adulthood. Four testators left sums to the parish fraternities of St Mary Matfelon in Whitechapel, and John Vardon left money for the repair of the highway at Stratford.[79] These were all within five miles of the parish, lying along the old Roman route from Aldgate to Colchester (again marked in purple on the map). The remaining bequests in Essex spread along the south of the county close to the Thames at West and East Ham, the marshy areas around Tilbury and in the areas between the rivers Lea and Roding in the west, suggesting the importance of river as well as road transport in London's eastern region. Once again, it is only occasionally that an explicit familial link can be identified. John Gardener, tallow chandler, pardoned

[75] L. R. Poos, *A Rural Society after the Black Death: Essex 1350–1525* (Cambridge, 1991); M. K. McIntosh, 'Money lending on the periphery of London, 1300–1600', *Albion*, xx (1988), 557–71, at pp. 564–5.

[76] LMA, DL/C/B/004/MS09171/001, fos. 319v–320; LMA, DL/C/B/004/MS09171/006, fo. 172.

[77] LMA, DL/C/B/004/MS09171/004, fos. 104–104v; LMA, DL/C/B/004/MS09171/006, fo. 118.

[78] M. K. McIntosh, *A Community Transformed: the Manor and Liberty of Havering, 1500–1620*, Cambridge Studies in Population, Economy and Society in Past Time, 16 (Cambridge, 1991), pp. 124–5; K. G. T. McDonnell, *Medieval London Suburbs* (London, 1978), pp. 59–61.

[79] LMA, DL/C/B/004/MS09171/004, fos. 82–82v; LMA, DL/C/B/004/MS09171/006, fo. 172; LMA, DL/C/B/004/MS09171/009, fos. 45v, 104v; PROB 11/8/169.

his brother (also named John) who lived at East Ham all the debts he was owed and left to his brother, niece and nephew lands in Essex (at East Ham and Rainham) described as formerly belonging to John's grandfather Roger Gardener.[80] Gardener was evidently a migrant to London with family in southern Essex, as well as landholding concerns which probably drew him to travel home at least occasionally. Gardener's situation indicates that imposing hard-and-fast boundaries between bequests indicative of migration and of business ties is impossible. The economic connections that Londoners cultivated with the hinterland, including landholding, debt and purchase of raw materials, must often have relied on family or, as in Gardener's case, on inherited family property.

That parishioners living outside both Bishopsgate and Aldgate displayed close links to particular areas suggests that these parishes provided the kinds of personal and economic connections which have been observed to structure apprenticeship migration.[81] The patterns raise the possibility that these parishes may have been deliberately sought as destinations by newcomers from those hinterlands. The contrast to other parish samples suggests that this was somewhat unusual within London, and perhaps not general to all extramural parishes, given the lack of such a strong pattern within the Aldersgate sample. Justin Colson has noted the importance of Fishmongers' trade links with east- and south-coast ports in driving migration to parishes where that craft dominated.[82] Similarly, studies of London's migration field have tended to view its size in relation to the status of different crafts. In general, the more prestigious companies had the widest migration fields, while lesser crafts were more reliant on the south-east for new apprentices.[83] The fact that these artisan crafts were more prevalent in the Aldgate and Bishopsgate sample of testators suggests a complex relationship between locality, craft and migration in which the connection between certain trades and the extramural areas may have been reinforced by the economic bonds between a neighbourhood and its hinterland.

Testamentary evidence suggests that at Aldgate and Bishopsgate parishes the hinterland of the parish and its routes of transit were more dominant in the lives of inhabitants than elsewhere. When testators in these parishes

[80] LMA, DL/C/B/004/MS09171/006, fo. 225.

[81] S. R. Hovland, 'Apprenticeship in later medieval London (*c.*1300–*c.*1530)' (unpublished Royal Holloway, University of London PhD thesis, 2006), pp. 48–50.

[82] Colson, 'London's forgotten company?', pp. 25, 27.

[83] J. Wareing, 'Changes in the geographical distribution of the recruitment of apprentices to the London companies, 1486–1750', *Journal of Historical Geography*, vi (1980), 241–9, at p. 247; Hovland, 'Apprenticeship in later medieval London (*c.*1300–*c.*1530)', pp. 62–4.

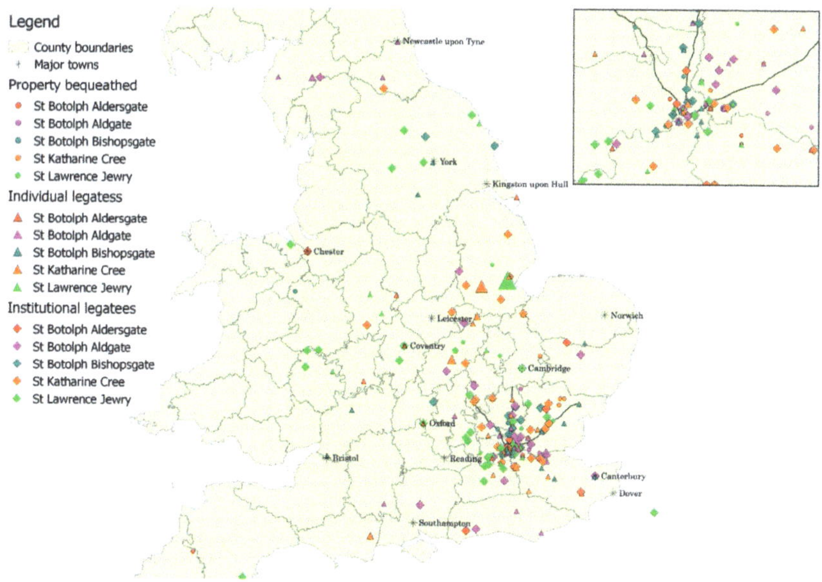

Figure 2.8 Bequests and landholding in England as a whole

remembered people and institutions outside the city, they demonstrated a field of activity and connections which focused closely on the immediate territory. The strength of those connections and the potential for them to form routes of migration will be considered further in Chapter Three. As with bequests to 'central' London institutions, the wealthiest testators had the widest horizons, but the close focus of bequests from the Aldgate and Bishopsgate samples suggests not poverty but parishes with a defined hinterland in which residents conducted their business, held property and most likely migrated.

The remaining parishes showed far less distinctive patterns of bequests; inhabitants had connections all over England. Many of these were made in very different ways to the kinship ties of those who had been economic migrants. Single wealthy individuals might demonstrate a widespread range of connections, such as the mercer Philip Agmondesham from St Lawrence Jewry who left sums to eight churches outside London, four in Buckinghamshire (including the parish from which his surname originates, Amersham) and four in Surrey.[84] John Geryn, a minor royal official from St Botolph Aldersgate, demonstrated an even wider reach in his bequests, leaving seven bequests for highway repairs, the poor of the parish and repairs

[84] TNA, PROB 11/8/340.

a)

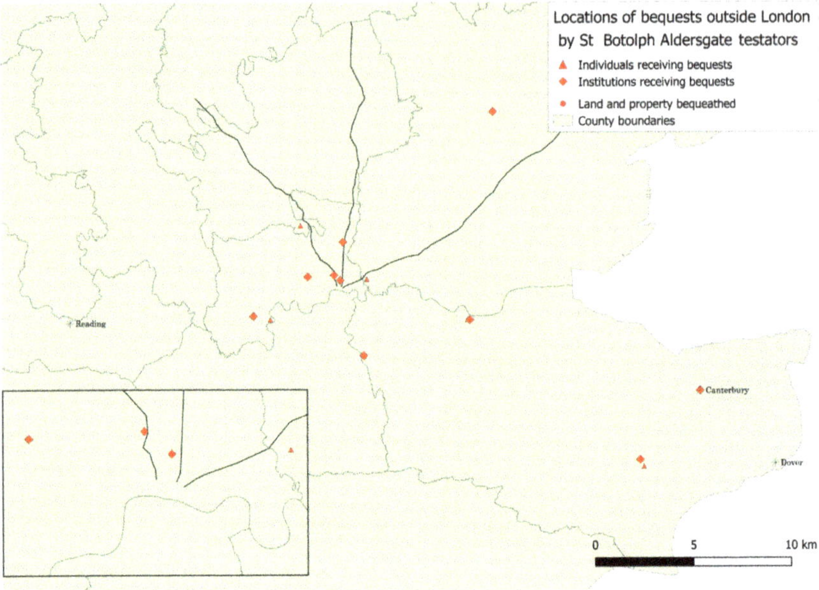
Locations of bequests outside London
by St Botolph Aldersgate testators
Individuals receiving bequests
Institutions receiving bequests
Land and property bequeathed
County boundaries
Reading
Canterbury
Dover
0
5
10 km

b)

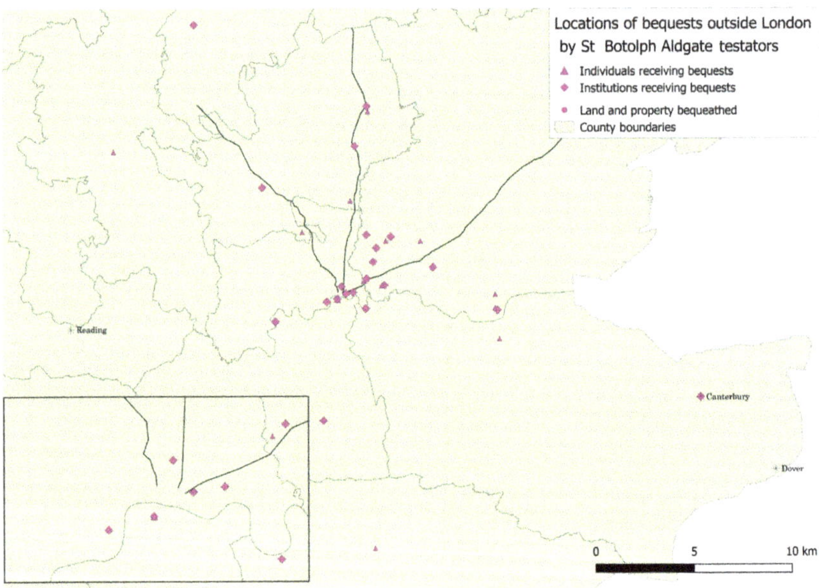
Locations of bequests outside London
by St Botolph Aldgate testators
Individuals receiving bequests
Institutions receiving bequests
Land and property bequeathed
County boundaries
Reading
Canterbury
Dover
0
5
10 km

c)

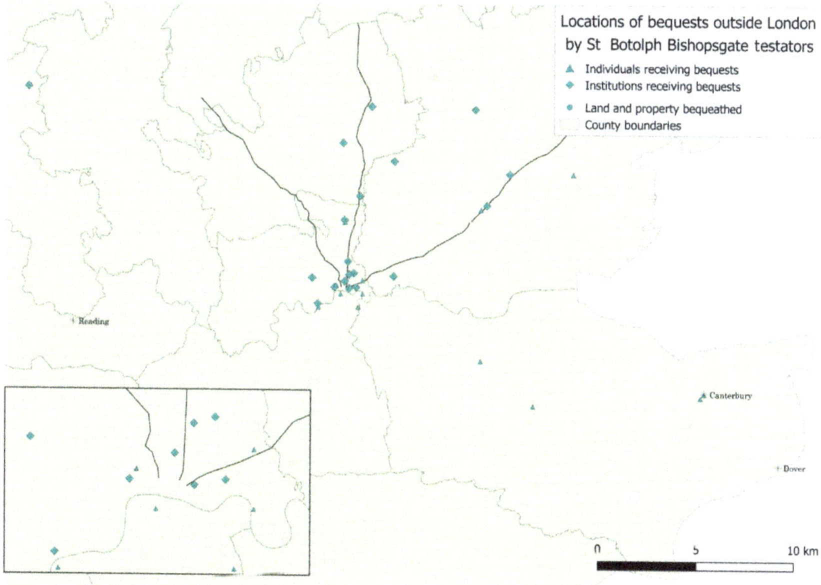

d)

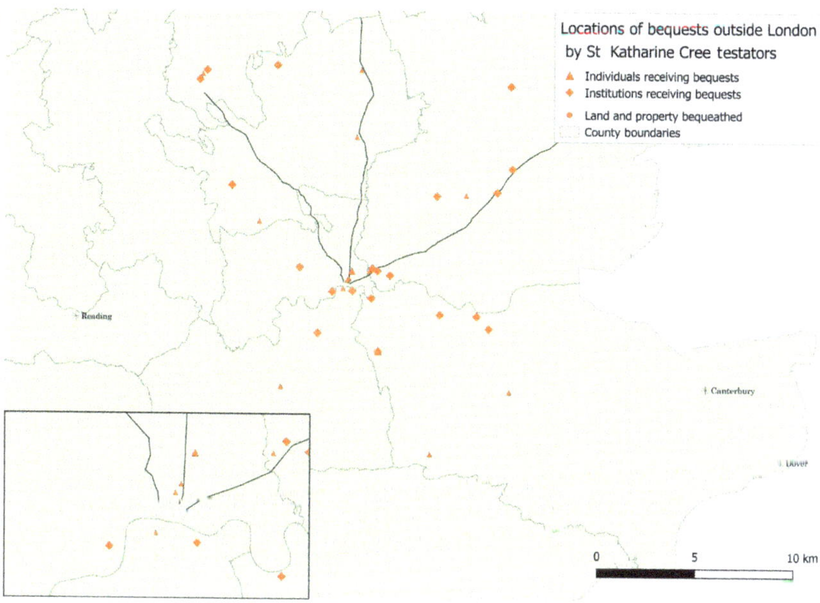

Figure 2.9 Extramural bequests in each sample parish (south-eastern England):
a) St Katharine Cree b) St Botolph Aldgate
c) St Botolph Bishopsgate d) St Botolph Aldersgate

to the church at Ashford in Kent as well as bequests to each order of friars at Chester as well as Canterbury.[85] Geryn had been an auditor of Chester for the crown, which explains his bequests to the friaries and chaplain of the castle there.[86] Aside from the distinctive patterns in St Botolph Aldgate and Bishopsgate, extra-urban bequests reflected wealthy Londoners' wide reach across country as a whole. As demonstrated within testamentary social networks, exceptionally wealthy figures such as Agmondesham and Geryn developed wide-ranging social connections during their lifetimes which extended far beyond their neighbourhood of final residence. In making their wills they remembered places they had accumulated estates and held office.

Conclusions

Being a spatially marginal neighbourhood in London did not have a single, defining effect on the social and spatial networks of residents. Instead, living at the fringe of the city had multiple effects which varied from parish to parish and between groups within the neighbourhood itself. Take, for instance, the citizens who lived in extramural parishes. A butcher living in St Botolph Aldgate resided and sold his wares at East Smithfield market alongside men with whom he travelled to the company hall on the other side of the city for shared guild feasts, elections and funerals. He joined those same butchers when they worshipped together in St Botolph's parish church, participated in the parish fraternity of the name of Jesus or held office together, either in that fraternity or as jurors of the wardmote. He was part of a city-wide institution but one in which many of his interactions with fellow members were local and took place in a range of social settings. He was, however, unusual among citizens living outside the city walls. A tailor or a brewer living in an extramural parish might well live near a few of his fellow company members. However, if he spent his adult years dutifully attending his company hall and building alliances and giving service there, then by the time he came to make his will it was to fellow guildsmen across the city that he likely entrusted his affairs. As we shall see in Chapter Four, all these forms of institutional participation might overlap in advancing a man's career. This kind of citizen network was more common by 1500 than it had been in 1400, due to the waning of traditional craft clusters, and was not exclusive to the extramural neighbourhoods but present throughout the city.

For less well-connected citizens and non-citizens who nonetheless had an estate to bequeath at their death, local connections were more important.

85 TNA, PROB 11/3/426.

86 See T. Thornton, *Cheshire and the Tudor State, 1480–1560* (Woodbridge, 2000), pp. 87–8.

Through their lives, these women and men joined fraternities, assisted their neighbours, got to know their clergy and served on juries and, in their last wishes, relied on those trusted connections made within their patch of the city. Circumstances differed in every neighbourhood. Because the parish outside Bishopsgate was generally poorer than elsewhere, its will-makers tended to be less integrated in guild networks. A carpenter or barber living here had many neighbours of a similar status who participated in the same local institutions and, naturally, chatted in the street over the years too. At the end of their lives, their trusted connections were peculiarly local. A widow living in St Katharine Cree worshipped in a parish church almost within the precinct of a priory, the same priory that probably owned the house in which she lived. In making her will, her choice of canons or lay staff such as the priory rent collector as witnesses or executors reflected the respect she had developed for them through her life and the multiple ways she interacted with them in her neighbourhood.

Yet others found their trusted connections across the city due to a disconnection of culture or status from their immediate neighbours. An immigrant Dutch speaker might wish to make his final wishes in his native language and so call for a friar from a religious house to whom he had given confession in Dutch during his life. He would have other trusting relationships with people from his country of origin living in London, not just in his part of the city, and may well have been a member of a Dutch-speaking confraternity which bolstered those bonds. For members of the gentry with London houses, their geographically closest trusting relationships were unlikely to be with their immediate neighbours but might be with Londoners of lower status than themselves with whom they had business dealings.

People who lived on the fringes of the city had personal and economic connections with London's immediate region. The reasons for this are likely to be manifold; economic ties may have reinforced routes of migration and settlement in the city and the economic interests of particular crafts fuelled investment in easily accessible rural areas. These connections were not the result of a single event, the movement from city to country, but of repeated visits and the mutual interconnection of London with its region. This is a point where testamentary networks on the city's spatial fringe overlapped with processes of social marginality. The mobility which these connections caused drew newcomers into the city, people outside its social networks and unfamiliar to the people of the neighbourhoods which they passed through or settled in. Although, as we have seen in this chapter, many began their lives in London as migrants before setting down roots and building a place for themselves in the community, that did not mean urban society was always welcoming to the newcomer. By contrast, there were social barriers to inclusion of the newly arrived which people overcame with more or less ease depending on their gender, wealth, status and reputation. The following three chapters show the ways that mobility shaped extramural neighbourhoods and the instruments of inclusion and exclusion that operated in London.

3. Mobility

The theme of mobility is one that unites the margins of society with the margins of the city. Neighbourhoods beyond city walls were criss-crossed by routes into the surrounding countryside. People and goods were able to move with ease between spaces jurisdictionally defined as London and those in surrounding counties. Chapter Two was, out of necessity, tied to the unit of the parish and the impression of settled community given by wills. However, as evidence from bequests indicated, mobile life was a characteristic of communities beyond the walls. While migration and movement were essential drivers of urban life, they were also a source of potential suspicion in a society that prized reputation among neighbours as an arbiter of character. In this chapter, we will see in greater detail the extent of that mobility, its impact on the lives of Londoners and on the sense of neighbourhood beyond the walls of the city. This is a new way of looking at mobility in London, which embraces movement around the city as well as long-distance migration and moves beyond the focus of previous scholarship on the city's apprentices.

There was a complicated relationship between mobility and marginality in an urban society that prized stability yet relied on movement for its prosperity. The settled household was held up by wealthy burgesses as the ideal form of familial organization, enabling proper oversight of dependents and commitment to the community through frankpledge, a system whereby neighbours swore oaths to uphold the law.[1] Historians writing on the late medieval household have shown that there was a culture of idealized domesticity and settledness which could be a compensation for the natal villages left behind by socially mobile town-dwellers or even an act of differentiation from the itinerant lives of the poor.[2] Indeed, while

[1] S. Rees Jones, 'Household, work and the problem of mobile labour: the regulation of labour in medieval English towns', in *The Problem of Labour in Fourteenth-Century England*, ed. P. J. P. Goldberg, W. M. Ormrod and J. Bothwell (York, 2000), pp. 133–53.

[2] F. Riddy, 'Looking closely: authority and intimacy in the late medieval urban home', in *Gendering the Master Narrative: Women and Power in the Middle Ages*, ed. M. Kowaleski and M. C. Erler (Ithaca and London, 2003), pp. 212–28; F. Riddy, '"Burgeis" domesticity in late medieval England', in *Medieval Domesticity: Home, Housing and Household in Medieval England.*, ed. P. J. P. Goldberg and M. Kowaleski (Cambridge, 2008), pp. 14–36, at pp. 29–31; Rees Jones, 'Household, work and the problem of mobile labour'.

migration was an experience that united rich and poor in the late medieval town, the movement of the poor was problematized. In the post-Black Death period, attitudes to the wandering poor hardened and royal statutes attempted to limit mobility and curb begging.[3] The late fifteenth and early sixteenth centuries saw a revival of interest in the issue, perhaps connected to the increasing population in London and its region;[4] between the 1460s and 1530s, parliamentary statutes and royal proclamations repeated an insistence that the poor should seek alms where they were born or 'best known'.[5] The decades around 1500 were thus a time when the figure of the vagrant, which was to loom large in early modern concerns over poverty, was being conceptualized. London's civic authorities were very active in this period in defining what kinds of movement required censure.[6] In 1473, ward juries were ordered to make special enquiry into 'all nightwalkers, vagabonds, faytors [rogues] and mighty beggars as well men [and] women the which may get their living by labour and will not labour, coming or repairing into your said wards'.[7] Sometimes mobility, particularly that of women, was associated with prostitution and sexual immorality. On 14 April 1482 the city issued two proclamations referring to vagrancy; one complained of 'strumpets, misguided and idle women daily vagrant and walking about by the streets and lanes' inducing people to lechery, the other of 'vagabonds, idle persons and great beggars daily vagrant and going about within the city of London being of might and power for to get their living by the labour of their bodies or other lawful occupation'.[8] In 1516, the city rounded up thirteen men described as vagabonds. Yellow patches in the shape of a letter V were stitched on to their clothes and they were sent 'unto their country where they were born or to other places in the country where they may get their living in harvest or making hay'.[9] The following year, the city responded to a royal proclamation by devising a system of badges to be issued to a thousand settled paupers so as to distinguish them from 'mighty beggars'; three citizens were also appointed to survey the beggars in

[3] M. K. McIntosh, *Poor Relief in England, 1350–1600* (Cambridge, 2012), p. 43.

[4] V. Harding, 'Families in later medieval London: sex, marriage and mortality', in *Medieval Londoners: Essays to Mark the Eightieth Birthday of Caroline M. Barron*, ed. E. A. New and C. Steer (London, 2019), pp. 11–36, at pp. 13–14.

[5] McIntosh, *Poor Relief in England*, pp. 43–4, 121.

[6] M. Ingram, *Carnal Knowledge: Regulating Sex in England, 1470–1600* (Cambridge and New York, 2017), pp. 286–8.

[7] LMA, Jor. 8, fos. 49–49v.

[8] LMA, Jor. 9, fos. 14–14v.

[9] LMA, Jor. 11, fo. 305.

the city and report on those entering the city to the aldermen.[10] As David Hitchcock has observed of a later period, the attribution of poor migrants as vagrants was highly arbitrary and dependent on local communities or even individual officers executing the law as they saw fit.[11] The movement of goods and people were completely necessary for the continuance of urban life, but the decades around the turn of the sixteenth century saw increasing attempts to categorize the mobility of paupers as unlawful and suspicious.

The terms of such complaints show concern with mobility both as a casual, everyday activity ('vagrant and walking about') and as a more permanent removal from other places in the country to the city. Both are important for understanding the role of movement in communities outside the city walls. Historians working on urban migration have tended to focus most on migrants who made one large journey to London, particularly of apprentices and non-English ('alien') migrants.[12] Immigration from the continent will be discussed in due course within this chapter. Apprentice migration is important since it is easily the best-recorded form of mobility by English people to the capital, and careful examination of guild records has shown that London drew apprentices from a far wider field than any other English city.[13] Yet apprentices were a very specific group: young, overwhelmingly male and, by virtue of their apprenticeship, with some kind of social connection to the city's central institutions. As has been demonstrated, the extramural neighbourhoods had less connection to the guilds and lower levels of citizenship than areas within the walls, so apprentice migration is particularly unlikely to give the full picture of how people arrived in those communities.

[10] LMA, Jor. 11, fos. 337–38v.

[11] D. Hitchcock, *Vagrancy in English Culture and Society, 1650–1750* (London and New York, 2016), p. 93.

[12] On London's alien population see J. J. Lutkin, 'Settled or fleeting?: London's medieval immigrant community revisited', in *Medieval Merchants and Money: Essays in Honour of James L. Bolton*, ed. M. Allen and M. Davies (2016), pp. 137–56'; J. L. Bolton, 'The alien population of London in the fifteenth century: a reappraisal', in *The Alien Communities of London in the Fifteenth Century: the Subsidy Rolls of 1440 and 1483–4* (Stamford, 1998), pp. 1–40; W. M. Ormrod, B. Lambert and J. Mackman, *Immigrant England, 1300–1550* (Manchester, 2019), pp. 59–61 et passim; M. Davies, 'Aliens, crafts and guilds in late medieval London', in *Medieval Londoners: Essays to Mark the Eightieth Birthday of Caroline M. Barron*, ed. E. A. New and C. Steer (London, 2019), pp. 119–48.

[13] J. Wareing, 'Changes in the geographical distribution of the recruitment of apprentices to the London companies, 1486–1750', *Journal of Historical Geography*, vi (1980), 241–9; D. Keene, 'Metropolitan values: migration, mobility and cultural norms, 1300–1700', in *The Development of Standard English, 1300–1800*, ed. L. Wright (Cambridge, 2000), pp. 93–114; S. R. Hovland, 'Apprenticeship in the records of the Goldsmiths' Company of London, 1444–1500', *Medieval Prosopography*, xxii (2001), 89–114.

To account for the crucial importance of mobility to the town, we need a far broader conception which takes account of the experiences of the poor as well as those on the path to citizenship. Although far less consistently recorded, daily movement and intra-city moves do leave traces in legal material. This chapter will show that urban mobility cannot be characterized by a single move, undertaken in youth, after which a person remained in the city more or less their whole life. The picture is far more complex. It is now accepted that London apprenticeships had very high dropout rates, with numbers completing their terms consistently below 50 per cent from the fourteenth to the sixteenth centuries across a range of trades, and apprentices often leaving London before the end of their training.[14] Adding nuance to our understanding of mobility is very important since it was the vital force that sustained and grew the city. The extramural neighbourhoods are the perfect window through which to achieve a broader view.

The economic and social patterns shown by the suburbs thus far could be sustained only by daily mobility: of customers, workers and those with goods to sell. The servants we saw living as tenants outside Bishopsgate in Chapter One would have needed to travel to their places of work, and many goods stored or produced outside the walls needed to be taken to central markets for sale. The location of alehouses and other recreational facilities outside the walls would have encouraged people from the centre to visit. The social profile of extramural neighbourhoods would also have encouraged mobility. Jeremy Boulton's analysis of neighbourhood migration in early seventeenth-century Southwark found that poorer residents were less likely to persist in the same neighbourhood from year to year than those eligible to pay poor rates.[15] Aliens tended to cluster close to points of entry to the city and were often temporary residents of the city who expected to return to their places of origin.[16] Mobility of both permanent and temporary kinds shaped life at the margins of the city. Since stability was privileged as a social ideal, there were results for the overall social character of extramural neighbourhoods as well as implications for how mobile individuals negotiated their social position within London.

[14] C. Minns and P. Wallis, 'Rules and reality: quantifying the practice of apprenticeship in early modern England', *Economic History Review*, lxv (2012), 556–79, at p. 570; Hovland, 'Apprenticeship in the records of the Goldsmiths' Company', p. 233.

[15] J. Boulton, 'Neighbourhood migration in early modern London', in *Migration and Society in Early Modern England*, ed. P. Clark and D. Souden (London, 1987), pp. 107–49, at p. 120.

[16] J. L. Bolton, 'La Répartition spatiale de la population étrangère á Londres au XVe siècle', in *Les Étrangers dans la ville: minorités et espace urbain du bas moyen âge à l'époque moderne*, ed. J. Bottin and D. Calabi (Paris, 1999), pp. 425–52, at p. 427.

Church court depositions and mobility

This chapter will address issues around mobility mainly using evidence drawn from the bishop of London's consistory court. It is worth pausing here to explain the processes of the court, since depositions from this court form the main evidence base for the remainder of this book and the legal strategy of parties and witnesses are of real importance when interpreting the court's records. The consistory was the highest of the church courts within London which heard suits relating to canon law: disputes over tithes, marriages, marital separation and defamation were among the most common matters. Unlike lower ecclesiastical courts, most suits were brought by a named aggrieved party, although cases could also be brought ex officio by order of the court itself.[17] Each party presented a series of witnesses (deponents) who made witness statements (depositions) regarding the disputed events surrounding a case. Depositions were made in response to a series of articles and interrogatories. The articles and interrogatories set out the facts of the case as they were seen by the plaintiff and opposing party respectively. Each was designed by canon lawyers to draw out information that gave credence to either party's narrative.[18] Both articles and interrogatories often asked witnesses questions not just about the material of the case but also about their knowledge of the opposing party's witnesses, their places of residence and reputation within the community. Unlike in a modern court, local gossip about a person or a series of events, often termed their 'fame', was materially important in the consistory and other canon and Roman law courts.[19] All that survives of the London consistory court in this period are its deposition books, meaning that we know neither the outcome of the cases nor the precise arguments of either party, other than what can be inferred from the witness statements. However, the depositions, with their myriad incidental detail about daily life, personal history and social relations, are a rich seam of material for social historians.

As records of individual voices, depositions are problematic, being mediated through both the requirements of the court and the anticipatory

[17] On the process of the consistory and its difference to other ecclesiastical courts see R. M. Wunderli, *London Church Courts and Society on the Eve of the Reformation* (Cambridge, Mass., 1981), pp. 7–15; on the distinction between ex officio and instance suits, see R. H. Helmholz, *The Canon Law and Ecclesiastical Jurisdiction from 597 to the 1640s*, Oxford History of the Laws of England (Oxford and New York, 2003), i, p. 316.

[18] Helmholz, *The Canon Law and Ecclesiastical Jurisdiction from 597 to the 1640s*, i, pp. 338–9.

[19] T. S. Fenster and D. L. Smail, 'Introduction', in *Fama: the Politics of Talk and Reputation in Medieval Europe* (Ithaca, NY, 2003), pp. 1–11; S. A. McDonough, *Witnesses, Neighbors and Community in Late Medieval Marseille* (New York, 2013), pp. 49–50.

'pre-construction' of witnesses themselves.[20] Moreover, as Shannon McSheffrey has argued, they offer no direct window into the events described but instead a series of narratives calculated to appear plausible in court.[21] Nonetheless, ecclesiastical court depositions are very useful records for mobility and migration in England owing to the fact that, unlike in secular courts, witnesses were regularly required to provide details of their age and places of past and present residence. Such sources have been well used by early modern historians and to a lesser degree by late medievalists to study mobility but are yet to be widely exploited for this theme by urban historians or those studying London before the late sixteenth century.[22] Deposition evidence has recently been deployed as a good substitute for random time-use survey data in looking at the gendering of early modern work tasks, and it is for many of the same reasons that it is valuable evidence for day-to-day mobility.[23] Moreover, there was a wide social range of witnesses called by the court, meaning that depositions contain personal residential mobilities for those beyond the boundaries of the groups typically most accessible to historians. Under canon law, the testimony of paupers was supposed to be ineligible.[24] Nonetheless, in London, as has been noted in similar records at Marseille, parties seem to have made their own judgements about who was a suitable witness.[25] Choice of witnesses and determination of who was

[20] T. Johnson, 'The preconstruction of witness testimony: law and social discourse in England before the Reformation', *Law and History Review*, xxxii (2014), 127–47, doi:org/10.1017/S0738248013000618.

[21] S. McSheffrey, *Marriage, Sex and Civic Culture in Late Medieval London* (Philadelphia, 2006), p. 12.

[22] P. Clark, 'Migration in England during the late seventeenth and early eighteenth centuries', in *Migration and Society in Early Modern England*, ed. P. Clark and D. Souden (London, 1987), pp. 213–52; L. R. Poos, *A Rural Society after the Black Death: Essex 1350–1525* (Cambridge, 1991), pp. 164–5; J. Whittle, 'Population mobility in rural Norfolk among landholders and others *c.*1440–*c.*1600', in *The Self-Contained Village? The Social History of Rural Communities, 1250–1900*, ed. C. Dyer, Explorations in Local and Regional History, 2 (Hatfield, 2006), pp. 28–45; P. J. P. Goldberg, *Women, Work and Life Cycle in a Medieval Economy: Women in York and Yorkshire c.1300–1520* (Oxford and New York, 1992), pp. 217–63; L. B. Smith, 'A view from an ecclesiastical court – mobility and marriage in a border society at the end of the Middle Ages', in *From Medieval to Modern Wales: Historical Essays in Honour of Kenneth O. Morgan and Ralph A. Griffiths*, ed. R. R. Davies and G. H. Jenkins (Cardiff, 2004), pp. 64–80.

[23] J. Whittle and M. Hailwood, 'The gender division of labour in early modern England', *Economic History Review*, lxxiii (2020), 3–32, doi:org/10.1111/ehr.12821.

[24] McDonough, *Witnesses, Neighbors and Community*, p. 52; A. Shepard, *Accounting for Oneself: Worth, Status, and the Social Order in Early Modern England* (Oxford and New York, 2015), pp. 133–4.

[25] McDonough, *Witnesses, Neighbors and Community*, pp. 52–4.

Table 3.1 Proportion of deponents with place of birth recorded

Deposition book	**Period covered**	**Total witnesses in selected cases (n)**	**Deponents naming place of birth (n)**	**Proportion with place of birth given (%)**
DL/C/205	1467–76	60	4	6.7
DL/C/A/001/ MS09065, MS09065B	1487–96	51	3	5.9
DL/C/206	1510–16	84	15	18.1
DL/C/207	1520–24	97	71	73.2
DL/C/208	1529–33	109	51	46.8
Total	-	*401*	*144*	*36*

sufficient to depose can tell us much about local social standing, a point which will be returned to in Chapter Five.[26]

As Table 3.1 indicates, the depth of detail recorded for the residence history of witnesses varied considerably over time as well as from one case to another. In the late fifteenth-century books and first sixteenth-century book, residence information is usually limited to present parish of residence, accompanied sometimes by one or two previous residences.[27] Occasionally, these records note a deponent's place of birth, although, interestingly, this appears to have been more common for aliens than for English witnesses. For instance, in the case of Agnes Lyddon *contra* (hereafter c.) Alice Harrys all three witnesses were of a similar humble status, being watermen. However, only Irishman Patrick Mandew was apparently asked to give a place of birth.[28] On one occasion, it appears that the alien status of witnesses was raised as an issue by a defendant to be put to witnesses in the interrogatories, as if it might undermine their suitability to depose. In the case of Larke c. Banester the witnesses on the party of Banester all responded to the first interrogatory with their place of birth, a question perhaps intended to discredit Warren Fanbooke, a goldsmith's journeyman born in Gelderland.[29]

[26] See p. 185ff.

[27] For example, 'Johanna Salman, alias Bernard, of the parish of the hospital of St. Thomas the Martyr in Southwark where she has lived for seven years and before that time in the parish of St. Sepulchre for 20 years', LMA, DL/C/205, fo. 245.

[28] LMA, DL/C/205, fos. 420–21.

[29] LMA, DL/C/206, fos. 324v–327v.

In the deposition books of the 1520s and 1530s, the recording of places of birth (either a specific settlement or a county of birth) became more frequent, alongside information about present and previous residences. This was perhaps under the influence of Cardinal Wolsey's drive against immorality in London and its surroundings, which included a crackdown on vagrancy.[30] In cases where both residence and long memory of local practice were crucial to the outcome, particularly disputes between rectors of neighbouring parishes over their boundaries, depositions might include residence histories that covered the entire lifetime of a deponent.[31] In most cases, however, the purpose of residence histories seems to have been part of vetting the individual's identity and suitability to depose; as will be discussed further in this chapter, instability of residence was often used by parties as a means to discredit opponents.[32]

The evidence used here is drawn from the deposition books for the court in the late fifteenth and early sixteenth centuries. Depositions were largely recorded in Latin, although sections of reported speech were often in English; where the records have been quoted, Latin has been translated but English has been left in the original spelling. Unfortunately, no deposition books survive before the 1460s, but in the context of rising population from the later fifteenth century onwards, experiences of mobility are probably better represented than they would have been earlier. The cases selected for research were chosen based on either their location within extramural parishes or for the insight they gave into other aspects of social marginality. In total, seventy-eight cases featuring 401 deponents were chosen for analysis. The selection of neighbourhoods considered was wider than in the previous two chapters and extended into the settlements and parishes in the immediate hinterland of London, where they were illustrative of the relationship between the city and its environs.

This chapter considers mobility from a number of different angles. In the next section, London's wide migration field is explored and the different ways in which people, whether young apprentices or elderly servants, found themselves in the city are introduced. Then the chapter moves on to neighbourhood migration within and around the city and the reasons why

30 Ingram, *Carnal Knowledge*, pp. 56–60.

31 The long-running case of More c. Evan, heard between 1521 and 1523, is an example of this practice. Lewis More and John Evan were the incumbent rectors of All Hallows on the Wall and St Mary Axe respectively. They were in dispute over which of them was entitled to the tithes from the residents of a new building on the border between the parishes. Thomas Norris, currier (a kind of leather worker) and deponent for More, gave a residence history extending five parishes back to his birth in Hertford around 1460. John Rygate, carpenter and deponent for Evan, had a residence history of six parishes from his birth in Bexley, Kent, in about 1473. LMA, DC/L/207, fos. 35v, 141v.

32 See below, p. 123ff.

Londoners moved around. In a society in which personal reputation was highly valued, mobility carried some risk, and the potential reputational damage caused by movement is the next topic of discussion. Finally, the chapter returns to a specific focus on London's extramural areas and the way in which everyday movement around the city rendered them spaces defined by mobility and a particularly wide sense of neighbourhood.

Migration to London

Migrants to London came from far and wide in the late fifteenth and early sixteenth centuries. Figure 3.1 maps the origins of 109 English and Welsh consistory witnesses who named a specific birthplace, and Figure 3.2 shows the origins of these witnesses alongside those who identified only a county of origin. Thirteen witnesses were born within the city and Middlesex, the largest number in any county. However, those who came from outside the south-east tended to come from northern England, from Yorkshire, Lancashire and Northumberland, or from the west midlands. London had an extraordinarily wide migration field and people travelled from far outside its immediate economic hinterland to live in the city.

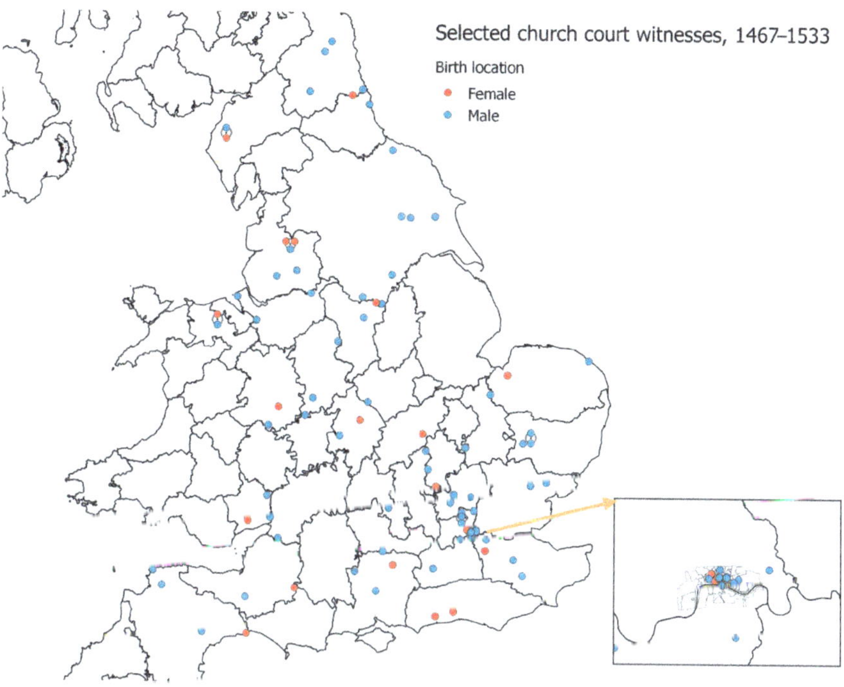

Figure 3.1 Consistory witnesses who gave a specific place of birth in England. N = 109.

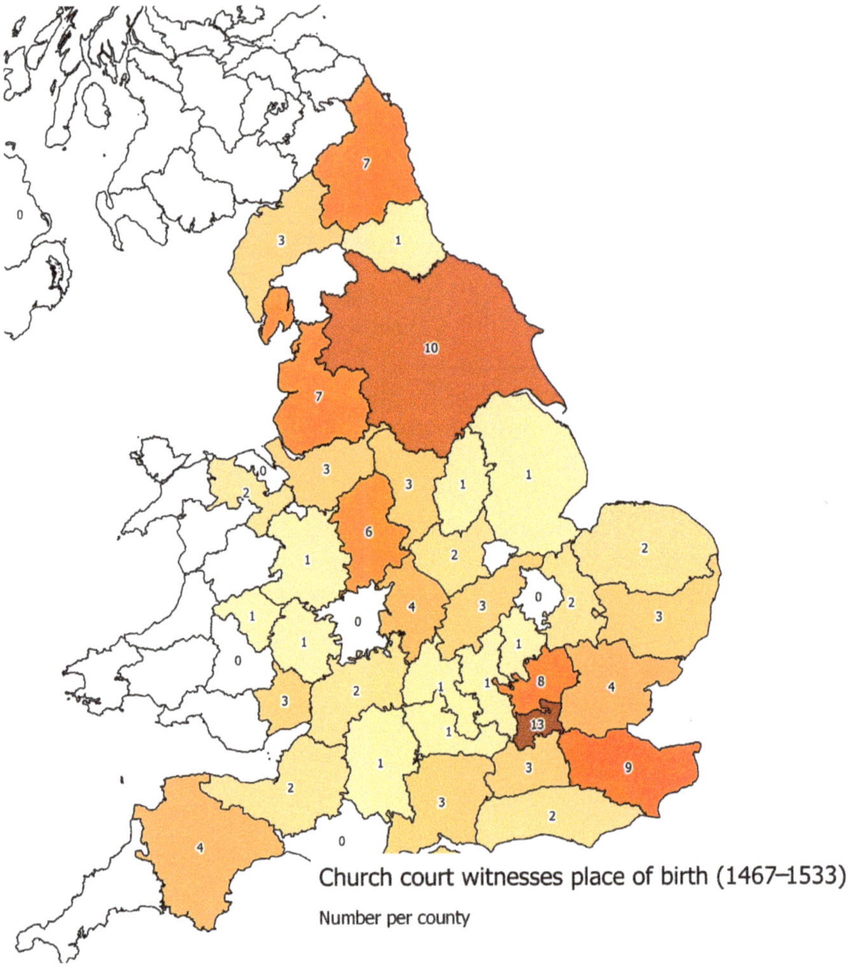

Figure 3.2 Consistory deponents giving place of birth including county. N = 121.

This pattern of origins tallies to an extent with the existing literature on London's migration field in the period, where it has been argued that London at the end of the fifteenth century had an expansive draw within England.[33] Stephanie Hovland noted that the field from which apprentices came widened over the fifteenth century.[34] She argued that the widest fields of migration were found among the most prestigious London crafts. However,

[33] Wareing, 'Changes in the geographical distribution of the recruitment of apprentices', pp. 241–3.

[34] Hovland, 'Apprenticeship in the records of the Goldsmiths' Company', pp. 60–64.

the circumstances of consistory witnesses with northern origins suggests that this was not necessarily the case in the wider pool of London inhabitants. Among the witnesses from Yorkshire were people of solid artisan occupations such as William Wylson, grey tawyer (a kind of leather worker); Richard Smyth, brewer; John Frethe, poulterer; and Joan Fytt, a carpenter's wife.[35] Servant deponents had come from as far afield as Newcastle upon Tyne, Exeter and Newport in Wales.[36] Indeed, one of the main advantages of the consistory deposition evidence is that previous studies in this area have relied upon data from apprenticeship records of particular companies, making it difficult to distinguish between craft-specific patterns and change over time.[37] The evidence presented here suggests that the wide field detected in apprentice origins from greater crafts at the end of the fifteenth century may well be representative of London's population as a whole. Matthew Davies has demonstrated the essential role of the labour of the city's non-citizen population in the many smaller crafts and occupations without a guild, a population who were highly mobile.[38] The city's economy was driven by migrants and mobility at every level, from the regulated trade of citizens to the informally or unorganized trades of non-citizens and, as Davies stresses, the important grey area in between where migrants and failed apprentices worked on the fringes of regulated trades. At all levels, people travelled long distances to take advantage of the city's prosperity in an era when many other English towns' fortunes were faltering.

In Chapter Two, we saw how certain extramural parishes had distinctive fields of migration and mobility. Consistory deposition evidence for cases centred on the parish of St Sepulchre without Newgate, to the north-west of the city walls, shows a similar pattern visualized in Figure 3.3. This map includes both those who lived in the parish at the time of their deposition and those who came from elsewhere to witness events in the parish; for the moment, I will concentrate on the twenty-one resident deponents. These men and women tended to have come from the midlands; eight deponents (of the eleven with a named place of birth) were born within the counties of Staffordshire, Worcestershire, Leicestershire and Derbyshire. As with the relationship between Essex and St Botolph Aldgate, the butchery

[35] LMA, DL/C/207, fos. 40, 144v, 225v.

[36] LMA, DL/C/207, fos. 159, 236.

[37] Wareing, 'Changes in the geographical distribution of the recruitment of apprentices', p. 247.

[38] M. Davies, 'Citizens and "foreyns": crafts, guilds and regulation in late medieval London', in *Between Regulation and Freedom: Work and Manufactures in European Cities, 14th–18th Centuries*, ed. A. Caracausi, L. Mocarelli and M. Davies (Newcastle upon Tyne, 2018), 1–21, at pp. 7–10.

trade appears to be the driving force in this trend. Six deponents from St Sepulchre were either butchers or butchers' servants, all of them working or living on St John's Street close to the West Smithfield cattle and flesh market. St John's Street was in fact a liberty of the priory of St John of Jerusalem, about which more will be said shortly. This pattern reflects that seen in later sixteenth-century apprenticeship evidence for London's butchers, where the droving routes to the midlands dominated the pattern of recruitment.[39] This was, it seems, part of a wider extramural pattern of migration driven by the economic connections of certain neighbourhoods to a specific hinterland.

As this suggests, it is important not simply to consider migration in isolation. Mobility, far from a one-time movement from country to city, was life-long for many of those who lived in fifteenth-century London and especially for those living in the extramural neighbourhoods. Although less consistently given than the information about places of birth, some witnesses described fuller residence histories that give a sense of mobility over their life course. Figures 4.3 and 4.4, using cases based in St Sepulchre and All Hallows London Wall parishes, show deponents' previous parishes of residence, termed as epochs between their place of birth and present place of residence. The All Hallows deponents were a particularly well-documented cohort because of a case based on a tithe dispute between the rectors of that parish and neighbouring St Mary Axe, whose witnesses needed to prove the length of their memory of the parish boundaries. No deponents described having been born in their present parish of residence, with their origins scattered across England. All those who described a second movement 'epoch' (that is, a first residence after their birthplace and before moving to their present home) had moved to the city or its suburbs. Most of these moves were to All Hallows itself or its neighbouring parishes, apart from Richard Williams, who had lived at Bermondsey. Most subsequent movements were closer to the parish, although Thomas Norris moved from All Hallows to Stepney, Middlesex, before returning to the city, and William Wylson spent some time in Sussex. Four witnesses had been apprenticed in All Hallows parish, two of whom had moved there for their apprenticeships and never left. One of the former apprentices, William Wylson, related that he had been apprenticed in the parish, moved elsewhere and returned about ten years later to occupy his former master's house. The map of residences from All Hallows suggests a similar sense of neighbourhood to that in the testamentary evidence, with witnesses demonstrating ties to a part of the city which could extend across a lifetime. Nevertheless, it also suggests that

[39] Keene, 'Metropolitan values', p. 109.

movement between parishes was common, albeit that the witnesses had gravitated towards particular neighbourhoods of the city. The results of this pattern of movement were seen in Chapter Two, in terms of the bequests to fraternities and institutions made at the end of individuals' lives, which, although ranging outside the parish, were usually within distinct 'quarters' of London. Late medieval Londoners primarily encountered urban space through quite small areas which were bound up with sociability and economic activity.

As this suggests, migration was usually not a single journey to a London parish but might consist of several steps. Such a process is well attested among migrants from continental Europe, particularly craftsmen, for whom London was one stop on a wider *wanderjahr* training route across Europe.[40] It seems likely that for some of the apprentices who never completed their terms in London, they may have done something similar by moving within the towns of England, or even the parishes in and around the city itself, working for different masters and developing their skills. In her work on London's seventeenth-century Dutch community, Catherine Wright stresses that for many migrants, and particularly women, family connections facilitated their move to the city.[41] Well-worn routes where family, friends and fellow craftsmen had been before were undoubtedly also important facilitators of mobility in the fifteenth century. In some consistory cases, the sharing of unusual surnames among servants in the same household suggests families sent siblings or cousins to London together. Witnesses Agnes and Thomas Rawlyns were both servants in the household of Agnes Corbe, and Stephen and John Felix were both members of Margaret Harvey's household.[42] In these examples, young men and women had been sent perhaps to the house of a relative or friend, or simply had gone together so that they could provide support for one another. Londoners' wide economic interests and social connections outside the city would have given them a foot in both camps, allowing them to remain in contact with family and using their position to support those who followed them to the city.

[40] C. Berry, 'Guilds, immigration and immigrant economic organization: alien goldsmiths in London, 1480–1540', pp. 545–46; C. Wright, 'The Dutch in London: connections and identities, *c.*1660–*c.*1720' (unpublished University of London PhD thesis, 2015), pp. 120–28; L. Luu, *Immigrants and the Industries of London, 1500–1700* (Aldershot, Hants, 2005). On the wanderjahr more generally see R. Reith, 'Circulation of skilled labour in late medieval and early modern Central Europe', in *Guilds, Innovation and the European Economy, 1400–1800*, ed. S. R. Epstein and M. Prak (Cambridge, 2008), pp. 114–42.

[41] Wright, 'The Dutch in London', pp. 130–31.

[42] LMA, DL/C/206, fos. 153v, 466.

However, it is important to note that this type of support network relied on economic connections which were probably not available to the poorest migrants to London. These men and women may have been migrating in response to a sudden worsening in their circumstances, rather than for a service position prearranged through family. The poor may also have been moving when they were older than the typical servant or apprentice. For instance, thirty-five-year-old widow Helen Elys lived in St Dunstan in the East at the time of her deposition in 1529 as a servant to Edmund Wright, having moved from the village of Stone in Kent only at the previous Christmas.[43] She had lived at Stone for four years. Helen responded to one of the interrogatories 'that she is poor but honest and would value in goods a little above ten shillings', and it may have been her impoverished widowhood that prompted her move to London in search of a service position when in her mid-thirties.[44] Ages given in depositions should be treated as useful approximations, given the propensity of medieval court witnesses to give ages in round decades and the suspiciously high number of alleged octogenarians and even older witnesses.[45] The examples of John Waldron and William Fryday, to be discussed in greater detail below, also indicate men who moved from southern counties into London who were of particularly low status and who moved when they were older than the typical apprentice. Both had lived elsewhere well into adulthood before moving to London; Waldron lived in Berkshire until his mid-twenties and Fryday lived at Great Gransden in Huntingdonshire until he was about thirty-four.[46] Alongside those who set out on the well-worn path of service or apprenticeship and failed, we can also locate among London's poor those who found themselves in the city later in life compelled by economic necessity rather than through familial networks. London's centrality to the south-east's economic network would have made it a very likely destination for chain migrants.[47] The social networks that supported such migrants and helped them find places to work and live were almost certainly so informal as to be unrecoverable in the archives. The gossip of alehouses and inns and

[43] LMA, DL/C/208, fo. 64v.

[44] LMA, DL/C/208, fo. 65v.

[45] Poos, *A Rural Society after the Black Death*, p. 173.

[46] Fryday's residence history in London totals around fifty-four years and he was said to be ninety at the time of his deposition. LMA, DL/C/207, fo. 141v. Waldron was noted by Reginald a Redemayn as living at Wantage in Berkshire five or six years before he moved to the Precinct of St Katharine in about 1490. Waldron claimed to be '30 years old and more' in his deposition. 'Elizabeth Brown, Marion Lauson c. Laurence Gilis', *Consistory Database*, <http://consistory.ca/obj.php?p=973> [accessed 11 Oct. 2017].

[47] Keene, 'Metropolitan values', pp. 100–101.

chance meetings with old acquaintances may have played a part. Perhaps knowledge of a London religious house through its role as a rural landowner may also have helped, as it did for rural migrants elsewhere in the country.[48] Among those who were poorer, London's economic connections with its region were probably less used for arranging secure employment in advance but still shaped their mobility. For poor migrants arriving in pre-modern and modern cities, exploiting social connections and gathering knowledge about the urban environment are crucial to finding a place in the city without formal access to citizenship.[49]

Causes of movement around the city

Mobility could be enforced, a response to poverty or other forms of social difficulty or a positive and expected step in the course of an individual's life. The diversity of reasons why people moved around London, and particularly why the poor found themselves on the move, are demonstrated in many consistory cases. Cases highlight a range of issues related to mobility, including the portability (or otherwise) of reputation around the city, mobility's relationship to poverty, mobility as a survival strategy and the practicalities of finding new accommodation.

Widowhood

Widows, as was suggested in Chapter Two, had a life-cycle reason for mobility. Alice Bayly was a sixty-nine-year-old widow at the time of her deposition and had lived in the parish of St Michael Bassingshaw just inside the northern city wall for two months.[50] Bayly was a witness in the case of Cockerel c. Beckett, which is explored below. Previously, she had lived in the central parish of St Mary Woolnoth for twenty-seven years, and a close reading of her testimony and relationship to another witness is highly suggestive of the cause of the move. Bayly appeared as a witness alongside her former apprentice Richard Holand. The twenty-nine-year-old Holand testified that at the time of the events described, around two months previously, he was still in Bayly's service in St Mary Woolchurch, but for the past month he had lived at St Giles Cripplegate. He gave his occupation

[48] D. Postles, 'Migration and mobility in a less mature economy: English internal migration, *c.*1200–1350', *Social History*, xxv (2000), 285–99, at pp. 290–92, doi:o rg/10.1080/03071020050143329.

[49] E. Canepari and E. Rosa, 'A quiet claim to citizenship: mobility, urban spaces and city practices over time', *Citizenship Studies*, xxi (2017), 657–74, doi:o rg/10.1080/13621025.2017.1341654.

[50] LMA, DL/C/207, fo. 102.

as tailor.[51] The reason for Bayly's involvement in the case was that she had agreed to let a house in St Mary Woolnoth to a woman of questionable character.[52] It seems feasible that this was Bayly's former dwelling house, and a series of events can be plausibly constructed that may have been similar to those which surrounded the widows living beyond the walls discussed in Chapter Two. Bayly was of quite advanced years, and without Holand's labour as her apprentice it would have been difficult for her to continue her business; perhaps failing eyesight made tailoring particularly difficult in her old age. Therefore, once Holand had completed his term, Bayly retired and no longer needed a house in a central parish or the shop which may have been attached to it. She sought to sublet her house at St Mary Woolnoth for the remainder of the lease and move somewhere more affordable without, or with reduced, income from her craft. Moreover, Bayly was anxious to protect her reputation; as will be discussed below, she showed considerable diligence in seeking to establish the character of her prospective tenant, apparently keen to protect herself from being tainted by association with nefarious activity. Alice Bayly's case is therefore a good example both of the socio-economic circumstances that caused widows to be mobile and the fact that widows could remain highly involved in the protection of their status during mobility. Nonetheless, her anxiety about her reputation was perhaps related to the fact that she was a recent arrival at St Giles. She may also, like the widows leaving bequests to their former parishes of residence discussed in Chapter Two, have wanted to maintain good connections with her old home.

Leaving service or apprenticeship

Like widows, men in their mid- to late twenties were especially mobile across city parish boundaries. This kind of mobility was not suspicious: it formed part of the ideal career path in the city. This was the age at which prosperous late medieval men generally married and, if they could, began to be masters of their own household. William Grene was a twenty-eight-year-old butcher at the time of his deposition in 1521; two years previously, he had moved from St Nicholas Shambles, where he had lived 'as a jorney man', to St Sepulchre. His move involved becoming a householder and his deposition included mention that he was respectfully addressed as 'neybor Grene' in conversation with a fellow butcher.[53] Henry Bathe, a skinner of the parish of St Antolin, was also twenty-eight at the time of his deposition

[51] LMA, DL/C/207, fo. 100v.

[52] LMA, DL/C/207, fo. 102.

[53] LMA, DL/C/207, fo. 33v.

in 1522 and had also lived in his parish for only two years or so.[54] Likewise, William Goldsmyth, a haberdasher, was twenty-eight and had also lived in his parish of St Nicholas Lombard Street for two years.[55] All these men were most likely citizens and all moved between parishes at around the same point in their life. Grene, Bathe and Goldsmyth all testified to having been busily working at the time of the events they described; Bathe even added that 'at the time he was busy in his shop and did not pay much attention to the [defamatory] words'.[56] The overall impression is of successful, industrious young men who had recently become masters of their own households, a process facilitated by a move to a new parish. In their cases, neighbourhood migration was very much a process through which they accrued social capital or, at least, the furnishings of a respectable life.

Most who began an apprenticeship never completed it and, even for those who did, they might enter a precarious period of mobile service rather than immediately find the capital to set up their own workshop.[57] The tailor John Edmound was about thirty years old at the time of his deposition in July 1529 and was described as 'staying in a certain chamber within the parish of St. Botolph without Bishopsgate' for the previous two years. Tellingly, in a deleted phrase, the clerk had written 'having no fixed abode' (*nulla habens certa mansionem*) before the description of Edmound's residential status.[58] Edmound had apparently moved to the cheaper periphery of the city after his apprenticeship ended, and his inability to establish a permanent household even here is suggestive of meagre resources. In another case from 1493, John Maliber, a glover's apprentice, was said to have renounced his dead master's bequest of forty shillings in return for deliverance by the widow from the remaining six years of his apprenticeship. Maliber implored his mistress 'that if he were freed from the terms of his service he considered that he could gain much more than the bequest in a year'.[59] He moved to St Botolph Bishopsgate to set himself up,[60] but the plan evidently went awry and nine

54 LMA, DL/C/207, fo. 132v.

55 LMA, DL/C/207, fo. 229v.

56 LMA, DL/C/207, fo. 132v.

57 Minns and Wallis, 'Rules and reality'; S. R. Hovland, 'Apprenticeship in later medieval London (*c*.1300–*c*.1530)' (unpublished Royal Holloway, University of London PhD thesis, 2006)', pp. 216–17, 233–4.

58 LMA, DL/C/208, fo. 39v.

59 'Testimony of William Bale', *Consistory Database* <http://consistory.ca/obj.php?p=1415.> [accessed 14 Feb. 2017].

60 This is inferred from the fact that this parish church formed the venue where he subsequently demanded the bequest, according to the widow. 'Testimony of Agnes Dalston, alias Boste', *Consistory Database* <http://consistory.ca/obj.php?p=1379> [accessed 14 Feb. 2017].

years later Maliber sued the widow for the bequest he had so blithely given up. Whether they were left to fend for themselves after dutifully completing or prematurely curtailing an apprenticeship, young men who could not afford to immediately establish a stable household faced a period of mobility and uncertainty in which a move to the suburbs might be an affordable option.

During the terms of their contracts, apprentices and live-in servants were vulnerable to any instability in their masters and mistresses' lives that disrupted the household and might find themselves on the move sooner than expected. This is particularly apparent in consistory suits for marital separation involving spousal abuse, where servants were often key witnesses whose own lives had been disrupted as a result. In the suit for separation of Agnes Corbe from her husband, John, a butcher, all the deponents on behalf of Agnes were current or former servants within her household. The violent beatings they described John Corbe inflicting on his wife were committed in the presence of 'diverse servants'.[61] William Williams, Thomas Rawlyns and Agnes Rawlyns, the deponents, had all been servants of Agnes Corbe during her earlier marriage to James Baram. Conspicuously, none of them was still in John Corbe's employment by February 1516, when the case was heard (eighteen months after the events described); twenty-one-year-old Agnes Rawlyns served Agnes Corbe in her new household in St Giles without Cripplegate, and twenty-one-year-old Thomas Rawlyns and twenty-nine-year-old William Williams had both found employment with new masters.[62] Thomas and William had remained within the parish of St Nicholas Shambles where John Corbe lived, and both served other butchers. The case of Corbe c. Corbe suggests that the close-quarter relationships involved in late medieval service were potential sources of economic instability; instead of stable and lasting employment, proximity to such a distressing domestic situation evidently encouraged servants to seek employment elsewhere. Living at the heart of the city's butchery trade, William Williams and Thomas Rawlyns did not have to look far for alternative employers, although in another trade it may well have been that young men in their situation would have needed to leave their parish.

There were many other servants in less fortunate positions. The Irish smith Dennis Grey was living in the parish of St Olave Silver Street when he was called to depose in a testamentary case in January 1512. However, Grey had been resident here for only two months. While usually such a recent

61 LMA, DL/C/206, fos. 466–69.

62 William Williams lived with Andrew Mason, butcher, in St Nicholas Shambles at the time of his deposition and Thomas Rawlyns with Thomas Cobham of the same parish. LMA, DL/C/206, fos. 267, 268.

incomer would give a previous residence history of about two years, Grey is simply recorded as having been resident before that 'in several parishes of the city of London for fourteen years'.[63] This suggests either that Grey was not sufficiently familiar with everywhere he had lived to give a full account, or that he had lived in too many places for the clerks to bother recording; either way, Grey evidently needed to move frequently and did not have the resources to establish himself more permanently. The circumstances of the case further underline Grey's apparent low status. Grey was witness to an attempt to write a fraudulent will for a priest who had already died. A man named William Wodwarde had asked Grey's master to bear witness. The master refused but apparently sent Grey in his place to the chamber where the priest's corpse lay, where Wodwarde asked him 'to say and depose that Sir John gave instruction to him in his chamber' to witness a will which made Wodwarde an executor.[64] Wodwarde offered him the furred coat in which the priest had died as a bribe.[65] Grey was evidently perceived as a poor enough man that he might perjure himself for the sake of a coat. His master's manipulation was perhaps the cause of the end of his service, and Grey had moved parish by the time of his deposition.[66] Like the servants in the Corbe household, Grey moved employer following an incident that strained the master–servant relationship. Unlike John Corbe's servants, however, Grey was required to uproot himself and find a new master in a new neighbourhood.

Poverty and vagrancy

For the very poorest in society, their need to move for work left them open to both personal suspicion and classification as part of a social problem perceived to be on the increase in the late fifteenth and early sixteenth centuries: vagrancy. The labourer John Fuller was called to bear witness in a disputed marriage case in June 1474. Fuller described himself as living in the parish of Coggeshall, Essex, although his testimony concerned a marriage contract that took place in the parish of St Mary Axe in the city. Fuller was no chance visitor, since two witnesses from St Mary attested to having

[63] LMA, DL/C/206, fo. 94v.

[64] Grey's master, John Warkman, deposed that Wodwarde had asked him to give false testimony that he was executor of Mores' will, which he refused to do. LMA, DL/C/206, fo. 94.

[65] LMA, DL/C/206, fo. 94v.

[66] The master, John Warkman, lived in the hospital of St Mary Bethlehem and Grey deposed that he had moved to St Olave Silver Street within the last two months. LMA, DL/C/206, fos. 94–94v.

known him since the previous Christmas, while another reported on his character according to the 'public voice and fame' in the parish.[67] Fuller's testimony reveals that he had been in service to the family of another witness, William Oldale, 'and William his father for six years. And before that time this witness kept a family of his own.'[68] The younger Oldale had moved to London at the most recent Easter, having served previously with a London girdler.[69] Fuller perhaps acted as a go-between for the Oldale family, moving between Coggeshall and London to bring messages for their son and run errands.[70] However, the impression of him among the parishioners of St Mary Axe was entirely disreputable, according to counter-witnesses in the suit. Fuller was described as very poor, a vagabond and lacking a fixed place to live. He was 'always drunk and … is called by many names that he does not always use'.[71] The picture painted is, of course, an attempt to discredit Fuller and the party he spoke for; nonetheless, it is notable how his mobility between London and Essex could be interpreted as homelessness. Further, his mention of previously having 'kept his own family' before taking up service is suggestive of a man whose fortunes had faltered somewhat. Fuller's appearance and possessions may indeed have suggested poverty to the residents of St Mary Axe as it was common for counter-witnesses to make reference to material culture in describing the poverty of fellow deponents.[72] John Fuller appeared at the consistory the year after Edward IV's 1473 proclamation against rootless vagabonds, which was probably influential in the casting of his characters by counter-witnesses.[73] The connections between mobility, poverty and suspicion were intricate; lacking a full knowledge of Fuller and his circumstances, the 'public voice' in the parish cast him in the classic image of the vagabond whose suitability as a witness could easily be undermined.

The language of vagrancy legislation and proclamations also seeped into the description of witnesses with plenty of other aspects of dubious

[67] LMA, DL/C/205, fos. 236, 236v.

[68] LMA, DL/C/205, fo. 225.

[69] LMA, DL/C/205, fo. 222v.

[70] The case concerned a disputed marriage contract between Agnes Rogers and James Whitington. The statements of a number of witnesses suggest that Oldale attempted to bribe Agnes Rogers with £40 to agree to the marriage and that Whitington called on distant relatives as his witnesses. The use of Fuller as a witness is perhaps another example of the exploitative use of low-status servants as deponents, for example Dennis Grey above. LMA, DL/C/205, fos. 236, 238v–240.

[71] LMA, DL/C/205, fo. 236.

[72] Shepard, *Accounting for Oneself*, pp. 120–21.

[73] See below, p. 139; Wunderli, *London Church Courts and Society*, p. 27

character. One counter-witness in a 1491 case described William Alston as 'a man of ill fame, a vagabond, and an adulterer' and John Waldron as having 'consorted with prostitutes and thieves … he is commonly said, held and reputed as a vagabond and an adulterer and a thief'.[74] These examples offer insight into the means by which rhetoric around the social underworld of London, as theorized by Frank Rexroth, interacted with the treatment of real poor people in the judgements that others made about their lives.[75] Thus, mobility attracted suspicion particularly by compelling individuals into new places where their reputation was unknown and their circumstances could be reinterpreted to their detriment. Mobility was both a marker of poverty and undermined an individual's character.

Those on a downward social trajectory might nonetheless turn mobility to their advantage. The opportunities afforded by movement for those at the very fringes of London society are well exemplified by a series of witnesses from a complex marriage case heard at the consistory court in 1491 and 1492. The two competing marriage contracts that formed the subject of the case are not the focus here but instead the proliferation of apparently disreputable deponents (and resulting counter-witnesses) who claimed to have witnessed one of the contracts. Their shady activities would suggest that they occupied Frank Rexroth's 'underworld' of London life and they were notably mobile around the city's fringes. Margaret Morgan alias Smyth, who lived within St Helen's Priory at the time of her deposition, was alleged by a counter-witness to have been expelled from both Langbourn and Billingsgate wards as well as from the precinct of St Katharine's during an attempt to clear it of 'infamous people and prostitutes'.[76] Other witnesses who had not been expelled were nonetheless mobile, particularly around the city's liberties. John Waldron had held three different bawdy houses in turn within the Stews at Southwark and frequently came to the attention of the court held at the Clink and the constable of St Margaret's parish, before moving to the precinct of St Katharine. William Alston had left the home he shared with his wife in Southwark to run a bawdy house there before moving to St Katharine's.[77] Interestingly, in their own testimonies both men claimed that some ten years

[74] 'Testimony of Ralph Boste', *Consistory Database* <http://consistory.ca/obj.php?p=1163> [accessed 30 March 2020].

[75] F. Rexroth, *Deviance and Power in Late Medieval London*, pp. 221–3.

[76] 'Elizabeth Brown, Marion Lauson c. Laurence Gilis', *Consistory Database* <http://consistory.ca/obj.php?p=973> [accessed 14 Feb. 2017].

[77] Shannon McSheffrey has discussed this case in her 'Liberties of London: social networks, sexual disorder and independent jurisdiction in the late medieval English metropolis', in *Crossing Borders: Boundaries and Margins in Medieval and Early Modern Britain*, ed. K. J. Kesselring and S. Butler (Leiden, 2018), pp. 216–36.

before they had been heads of their own houses, Waldron at Newbury in Berkshire and Alston at the parish of St Peter by the Tower. It seems likely that these were men who, like John Fuller, had experienced a downturn in their fortunes that had precipitated a mobile life. These witnesses appear to have had a strategy to their movement, choosing to move around the precincts and areas outside the city's jurisdiction. Transitory life was not just caused by economic necessity; mobility was also a means through which individuals exercised agency in responding to their circumstances and mitigating them.

Domestic abuse

Like those experiencing poverty, women who were subject to domestic abuse engaged in forms of mobility that stood somewhere between compulsion and strategy. As David Hitchcock argued for a later period, personal crisis is an often underappreciated reason why those defined by society as 'vagrant' started out on the road.[78] The people undergoing personal crisis most commonly found in the records are those who had been abused by their spouse. These cases were usually brought either by husbands who sued their wives for breaking marriage vows by leaving the marital home or were suits for dissolution of the marriage.[79] Legally, it was difficult for wives to leave and find a new home with relatives or friends, because those who took in another man's wife left themselves open to suits of trespass or even abduction and ravishment.[80] Setting up on their own would also have been challenging, given social anxiety about ungoverned women and formal barriers to participation in a trade. While this is just one kind of personal crisis that caused people to move, the tactics employed by women trying to escape their marriages may well be indicative of how other vulnerable people in medieval society coped with their circumstances.

In the case of Corbe c. Corbe discussed above, two servants of the household escaped their violent master John Corbe by finding other masters within the same parish. For many women, their first support network when experiencing abuse was probably within the parish itself, as Tim Reinke-Williams has noted for early modern London.[81] However, as Reinke-Williams makes clear, this depended upon standing in good

[78] Hitchcock, *Vagrancy in English Culture and Society, 1650–1750*, p. 118.

[79] S. Butler, 'Runaway wives: husband desertion in medieval England', *Journal of Social History*, xl (2006), 337–59, at pp. 338–9, doi:org/10.1353/jsh.2007.0007.

[80] McSheffrey, *Marriage, Sex and Civic Culture*, pp. 140–41; Butler, 'Runaway wives', pp. 341–44, 350.

[81] T. Reinke-Williams, *Women, Work and Sociability in Early Modern London* (Basingstoke, Hampshire, and New York, 2014), pp. 130–31.

stead with the community; where a woman lacked a good local reputation, mobility may have been the only option available. Prolonged violence may also have driven some women away, even when they had local friends, simply to avoid discovery; a number of cases show that neighbours were willing to intercede on the part of women who subsequently moved.[82] The degree to which women were able to establish a new household once they left their husbands varied. Agnes Corbe, for instance, moved to St Giles Cripplegate outside the city walls and took her servant Agnes Rawlyns with her, suggesting that she could support herself independently. It seems likely that she would have continued in the trade of butchery, given the continuity of that trade in her household between her two marriages.[83] Elizabeth Spenser, who also suffered cruel treatment at the hands of her husband, Edmund, appears to have moved in the opposite direction, from an extramural parish into the city centre, to escape. The two witnesses in the separation case she brought against Edmund recall their separate dwelling places, Edmund at St Clement without the Bars to the west of the city and Elizabeth at London Stone (probably the parish of St Swithin) in the eastern city centre.[84] Unfortunately for Elizabeth, this tactic seems not to have worked, as the witnesses recalled Edmund drawing his dagger to threaten her at each house. Nonetheless, it is notable that in both cases, women chose to cross the city walls to find new accommodation and in doing so appear to have been attempting to evade public fame in some way. They seem to have calculated that the social distance between city centre and periphery offered them some protection.

Expulsion

Expulsion from a city ward by its alderman was the most socially damaging form of mobility in fifteenth-century London. It was a standard punishment for those who persistently flouted civic authority, more serious than imprisonment and far more common than exemplary trials before the mayor.[85] Decisions over who to expel appear to have been made by the

[82] See eg Spenser c. Spenser, LMA, DL/C/208, fos. 16v–17, 39v.

[83] The probability of Agnes' proficiency in this trade is suggested by the stability of association with butchery among her servants after leaving her employment as well as their continuity in her household between her two marriages. One of Agnes Corbe's servants (William Williams) noted having been with her during the lifetime of her previous husband, John Baram, and he went on to work for another butcher. Both her male servants remained in St Nicholas Shambles after leaving the Corbe household. LMA, DL/C/206, fos. 467–68.

[84] LMA, DL/C/208, fos. 16v, 39v.

[85] Ingram, *Carnal Knowledge*, pp. 223–4.

ward's alderman rather than by local officers or wardmote juries, although, as we shall see in this chapter and in Chapter Four, it was probably their knowledge and advice which identified potential targets. It is quite striking that throughout the late medieval period the routine means of dealing with offenders remained within the ward itself and generally did not require the expelled to abjure the city totally, other than during concerted morality drives by the civic government and crown.[86] Even if cases were referred on to the church courts, the most severe punishment available was excommunication, a threat that does not seem to have been especially effective among those whose reputation was already poor.[87] This suggests that the primary nuisance caused by persistent offenders was perceived to be that to neighbours, a problem that could be solved by moving people along.

One particularly detailed case indicates the effects of expulsion on personal reputation and the practical difficulties faced by the expelled. Agnes Cockerel appeared as the plaintiff of a defamation case heard in the consistory court in November 1521. Cockerel had brought the case against John Beckett, capper, and his wife, Elizabeth, of the parish of St Sepulchre without Newgate. Witnesses were questioned about a series of events which began with an argument witnessed by John Gruege, a fletcher. While working in his shop opposite John Beckett's house in late June 1521, Gruege saw a passionate dispute between Agnes, John and Elizabeth. Standing in the door of John's shop, Agnes 'said openly and in an audible voice and an evil and angry manner' to John:

> thow pyllery knave and papyr face knave I shall make the to were a papyr[88] and make the over dere of a grote and to shytt in thy wyndowes and I have done with the

In response, John told her to 'gete the hens dame, I pray the hens or ells wyll I', and his wife added, 'I defye the dame. I sett not by thy malesse thow art known well, I nowe what though arte.'[89] Allusions to 'knowing' someone's character were a common way to suggest the publicity of their poor reputation.[90] The knowledge Elizabeth Beckett alluded to was the local

[86] Ingram, *Carnal Knowledge*, pp. 231–7.

[87] Wunderli, *London Church Courts and Society*, p. 53.

[88] Wearing a paper was synonymous with wearing a badge of conviction of a crime. 'paper, n. and adj.: 8', *OED online* <http://0-www.oed.com.catalogue.libraries.london.ac.uk/view/Entry/137122?rskey=5wfEbI&result=1&isAdvanced=false> [accessed 14 March 2017].

[89] LMA, DL/C/207, fo. 99.

[90] T. Johnson, *Law in Common: Legal Cultures in Late medieval England* (Oxford and New York, 2020), p. 192.

belief that Agnes Cockerel had some kind of sexual relationship with her servant Robert Dyngley; around this time, Agnes was arrested, imprisoned and expelled from her house in St Sepulchre parish.[91]

Two weeks later, the sixty-nine-year-old widow Alice Bayly, introduced above, arrived at the Becketts' house, accompanied by her apprentice.[92] Bayly approached John Beckett as he worked in his shop and asked him whether he knew 'Maystres Cockerel the midwyff' who had recently lived in that neighbourhood. Beckett replied in the affirmative, but according to Holand he evaded Bayly's next question about her character, instead inviting her to 'come nere and drynke'.[93] In the Becketts' house there followed a conversation about Agnes Cockerel's character. Bayly explained, 'I have letten her a howse off myn and I wolde be glade to knowe off what conversation she wer.'[94] She had taken a penny from Agnes as surety for her rent but had been concerned by rumours of her new tenant's ill fame. The house that Bayly had intended to lease to Agnes lay on Lombard Street in the parish of St Mary Woolnoth, from which one would pass through fourteen parishes to reach St Sepulchre; evidently, the rumours of Agnes' ill fame were remarkably widespread. John Beckett was initially evasive, telling Bayly to go and speak to Agnes' previous neighbours at Holborn Cross. Implicitly, Agnes had left more than one neighbourhood in disgrace;[95] she had perhaps chosen St Mary Woolnoth in the hope that its centrality surpassed the reach of networks of knowledge about her reputation. Although Ingram cites this case as an example of the pervasive surveillance in late medieval London society,[96] it was in fact anxiety about a lack of proper surveillance of a mobile individual that motivated Bayly's visit. Agnes Cockerel's movement around London exposed the difficulty of knowing the character of a stranger in a city with around 50,000 inhabitants and thus the flaws in a social system reliant on personal reputation for everyday transactions such as the letting of a house.

At length, the Becketts were persuaded to speak. They told Bayly that she had been deceived in letting to Agnes, since 'Dyngley her servaunt kepyth her', implying that he was her pimp[97] and Agnes 'a brothel of hyr taylle'.

[91] LMA, DL/C/207, fos. 99, 101, 102.

[92] LMA, DL/C/207, fos. 99v, 102.

[93] LMA, DL/C/207, fo.100v.

[94] LMA, DL/C/207, fo. 102.

[95] Holborn Cross lay within St Sepulchre parish.

[96] Ingram, *Carnal Knowledge*, pp. 221–4.

[97] LMA, DL/C/207, fo. 102.

This probably meant that she sold sex.[98] They recalled that Agnes had been 'warnyed ought of the howse she dwelt in for hyr yll name', following a search of her house made at night.[99] The Becketts also warned Bayly about Agnes' reliability as a tenant, and that Bayly ought to be wary 'that she do not pute yow clene ought of your howse for ye shall fynde hyr a crafty dame'.[100] The hesitancy of the Becketts is suggestive of the distance between the suburbs and the city centre. Reputation in the city was fundamentally made at neighbourhood level and, once Agnes moved to a distant neighbourhood, it was awkward for the Becketts to take the risk of a defamation charge by acting as linchpins between the two parish networks of knowledge about reputation. In moving to a city-centre parish, Agnes perhaps calculated that not just geographic distance but also social distance would insulate her from the consequences of a chequered reputation. She seems to have taken up her case at the consistory court as an attempt to portray this transfer of knowledge outside St Sepulchre as defamation. Knowledge that in one social space was treated as commonly known fact became potentially defamatory when removed from the social context which legitimated it.

Other cases give more insight into how expulsion worked and the role of local lobbying in determining who was to be expelled. Fulk Pygott, of St Andrew Undershaft, deposed that the wives of three other witnesses were biased against the party he appeared in favour of Katharine Mett. Pygott deposed that a witness's wife had said, 'we [came] to se her ride in a carte one day or ells we wyll dryve her […] owt of the parishe or she shall dryve us out' and subsequently made a suit to the wardmote for Mett's expulsion which the jury judged to be malicious.[101] In this case, the failure of the attempt was what, Pygott alleged, had motivated the defamation case against Mett in the consistory court, suggesting that expulsion was a preferred method through which to disgrace a neighbour. If reputation was made at the neighbourhood level, then expulsion represented a failure to successfully establish a good character. However, as we have seen, expulsion was just one of the kinds of mobility undertaken by those Londoners with

[98] According to the *OED*, in this period the word 'taylle' could refer to a person's posterior or genitalia. 'tail, n.1', *OED online* <http://0-www.oed.com.catalogue.libraries.london.ac.uk/view/Entry/197067?rskey=7mDRuz&result=1&isAdvanced=false> [accessed March 14, 2017].

[99] LMA, DL/C/207, fos. 99v, 101.

[100] LMA, DL/C/207, fos. 99v, 101.

[101] The phrase 'to ride in a cart' was a reference to a form of punishment enacted in many medieval towns where the offender was drawn through the streets on a cart holding a symbol of their misdemeanour. LMA, DL/C/208, unnumbered folio, deposition of Fulk Pygott, 21 Jan. 1533.

precarious lives. Those subject to expulsion might just try their luck and drift back to the city.[102] It was one of a range of motivations for moving neighbourhood and may have been ineffective at deterring those engaged in illicit activity because mobility was simply a fact of life for them anyway. Where expulsion made a difference was when individuals were determined to find a place to live within the city wards. It was a punishment designed and carried out by the section of urban society that prized stability and had the means to secure it.

Finding a new home

All those who moved around London faced the issue of where to go next and how to secure a new home. The circumstances which surrounded an individual's movement would have had a significant impact on their ability to secure a new home. Finding new accommodation for those who had been expelled would have been a considerable challenge. Agnes Cockerel had apparently told her new landlady that she was a midwife, a legitimate way in which a woman might provide herself with the income to live independently. Certainly by the later part of the sixteenth century, midwives could be highly respected figures with clients across the city and suburbs and a good reputation that extended outside their own parish.[103] Nonetheless, as the subsequent journey made by Alice Bayly to discover Agnes' reputation suggests, the character of lessees was of keen interest to landlords or tenants who sublet. A poor reputation and suspicious behaviour by occupying tenants posed an embarrassing risk to the reputation of the property owner.[104] Mobility outside the social space in which one's reputation was established thus presented difficulties in finding a place to live. Although Agnes seems to have attempted to use this 'knowledge gap' between neighbourhoods to her advantage, this presumably would have been a difficulty for everyone who was mobile around the city and speaks, at a basic level, to the importance of personal connections in finding accommodation.

Women who suffered domestic abuse may have faced many of the same issues as Agnes Cockerel in setting up on their own. Their ability to establish a new household was probably in part determined by their economic

[102] Five men of the parish of St Botolph Aldersgate were indicted at the Aldersgate wardmote 'for vacabonds and were put owte of the citie afore'. Aldersgate Wardmote presentment, undated (c.1510–20), LMA, CLC/W/FA/007/MS01501.

[103] D. E. Harkness, 'A view from the streets: women and medical work in Elizabethan London', *Bulletin of the History of Medicine*, lxxxii (2008), 52–85, doi:org/10.1353/bhm.2008.0001.

[104] R. H. Helmholz, 'Harboring sexual offenders: ecclesiastical courts and controlling misbehavior', *Journal of British Studies*, xxxvii (1998), 258–68, at p. 260.

resources. Agnes Corbe, the butcher's wife whose servants bore witness to her abuse at the hands of a new husband, was evidently successful in taking one of her female servants with her to a new household, and perhaps her skill in butchery, like Agnes Cockerel's claims to be a midwife, was enough to convince a landlord that she could support herself respectably. For yet others in desperate circumstances, the establishment of their own separate household appears not to have been a possibility, and yet the periphery was still an important route of escape. Eleanor Brownynge ran to the house of the sisters within the precinct of St Bartholomew's Hospital in spring 1463 when her husband, Alexander, chased her with a drawn dagger. The hospital sisters admitted her and closed the door against Alexander, an action which, in the judgement of a brother of the hospital, saved her life.[105] As we shall see in Chapter Five, religious houses were used by lay Londoners to evade the attention of others and conceal morally or legally questionable behaviour. As well as social distance from the city, religious houses had a practical layer of protection in the form of walls and gates, although evidently the presence of lay tenants within the precinct made it possible for Alexander to enter and continue to terrorize his wife.

Other women looking to escape their husbands sought out kin in the environs of London. Joan Yngolsby alias Wryther was involved in a complicated case of disputed marriage after she left her husband, John Wryther. John and Joan's marriage had been solemnized in St Botolph Bishopsgate, where John continued to live, but Joan now lived at Waltham Cross, one of the towns along Ermine Street, which featured in the testamentary hinterland of Bishopsgate.[106] Joan claimed she had made a pre-contract with a man in her sister's house at Waltham six years before the case was heard which invalidated her marriage to John, suggesting this was either the place of her birth or at least a place in which she had relatives.[107] Either way, when she sought to leave Wryther it was to relatives that she turned to offer support. This same tactic was used by Joan Wood. The sole surviving witness statement in Joan's 1519 case against her husband, William Wood, is by Thomas West, beadle of the parish of St Olave Southwark.[108] Joan approached West in the house of a grocer in the parish of St Magnus the Martyr near London Bridge and implored him to help her, saying 'yonder ys my husband in the church and I dare not goo home for he

[105] LMA, DL/C/205, fos. 203–203v

[106] LMA, DL/C/206, fos. 314–14v, 316.

[107] LMA, DL/C/206, fo. 316.

[108] This deposition occurs at the very start of DL/C/207 and thus the other depositions were presumably contained in an earlier book which is now lost.

wel kyll me'.[109] She asked West to escort her to her daughter's house at the village of Bermondsey, south-east of Southwark. After an altercation with her husband, they proceeded to Bermondsey, where West heard from Joan's daughter's neighbours about his cruelty.

In both Wood's and Yngolsby's case, the maintenance of family connections outside the city was crucial to their ability to support themselves outside the marital household. The fact that neighbours at Bermondsey could attest to William Wood's treatment of his wife suggests that Joan visited her daughter with some frequency. Moving between city and hinterland to maintain social connections was not just a matter of overseeing economic interests but also cultivated support networks that might be turned to in times of need. For women who could not establish their own household in the city, moving in with relatives beyond the walls was a pragmatic defence against homelessness.

Those in trouble with the law could also draw on social connections and the connectivity of London's region to find a safe place to stay. This was evident in the story of John Curlews, whose background came under the scrutiny of counter-witnesses when he was a deponent in a disputed marriage case in 1533. Two years before, the carcasses of two stolen sheep were found in the chamber Curlews rented at Totteridge, Middlesex. Fearing prosecution for theft, he took sanctuary at the churchyard in Totteridge before fleeing to the sanctuary of St Martin le Grand in London.[110] Witnesses' descriptions suggested that Curlews was a poor man; 'being then unmarried', he held a chamber in Totteridge and, at the age of about forty[111] he was no young chamber-holding servant but perhaps a man who had never been able to afford to set up his own household.[112] In two depositions, 'alias Cornyshe' was appended to his surname, which may well indicate his distant origins.[113] When faced with a charge of theft, Curlews knew that fleeing to St Martin le Grand would enable him to escape prosecution, knowledge that would have been common in the community in which he lived owing to the frequency of movement to and from the north-west of the city occasioned by the midlands droving route. Moreover, Curlews's strategy worked, as two London butchers interceded with the shepherd he had stolen from and visited Curlews in

[109] LMA, DL/C/207, fo. 2.

[110] LMA, DL/C/208, unnumbered folios, deposition of John Hayward, 10 March 1533.

[111] LMA, DL/C/208, unnumbered folio, deposition of William Hayward, 10 March 1533; unnumbered folio, deposition of John Curlews, 17 Jan. 1533.

[112] LMA, DL/C/208, unnumbered folio, deposition of William Hayward, 10 March 1533; unnumbered folio, deposition of John Curlews, 17 Jan. 1533.

[113] LMA, DL/C/0208, unnumbered folios, depositions of William Hayward and William Holmes, 1 March 1533.

sanctuary to negotiate an amicable settlement.[114] This was an especially mobile community with knowledge of London and its topography and connections to its tradesmen which enabled Curlews to evade prosecution, using mobility to his advantage and exploiting the jurisdictional topography of the city.

Mobility was often enforced through unforeseen or unfortunate circumstances. Where an element of strategy is most discernible in the mobility of the marginalized, however, is in the choice of where to go next. Some, such as several of the women faced with spousal abuse, used family connections to escape. For most others it seems that their own knowledge of London's social topography was key, whether that was Eleanor Brownynge fleeing to a hospital, Agnes Cockerel moving to the city centre or John Waldron going to St Katharine's. Although mobility could not always be anticipated, a knowledge of where cheaper rents could be found or where prostitution was only periodically punished was useful when movement became necessary.

Mobility and reputation

Securing somewhere new to live did not mean automatic acceptance among new neighbours. Mobility could be interpreted as a suspicious activity and used to cast aspersions on an individual's character. One case suggests that this might even happen to someone who otherwise was well placed in London's social hierarchy. In May 1532 a meeting of the head parishioners of St Clement Eastcheap descended into acrimony when James Pott grumbled about being imposed with a greater assessment than usual, after everyone else had agreed to the new charges for the parish clerk's wages.[115] His fellow parishioner John Hooke became so frustrated with Pott's complaints that he angrily proposed paying Pott's increase himself and removing Pott's wife from her accustomed pew in church 'rather then we wyll have all this brablyng'.[116] Hooke went on to exclaim:

> 'ye made a brablyng her as ye have in other parishes as ye have com from'. Pott asking '[what] parishes be that' [and] Hooke saying 'from St. Marten Orgor and St. [Christopher] at Stockes for ther men wer glad that they wer ryd of yow'[117]

In Pott's own testimony he countered accusations that he had called Hooke a knave and wretch by saying he did so only after Hooke had accused him of being 'dryven owt of dyvers parishes'. This seems an exaggeration of Hooke's

[114] LMA, DL/C/0208, unnumbered folios, depositions of Thomas Marten and Thomas Arrett, 4 March 1533.

[115] LMA, DL/C/208, unnumbered folio, deposition of Benedict Jackson, 8 July 1532.

[116] LMA, DL/C/208, unnumbered folio, deposition of John Knyll, 8 July 1532.

[117] LMA, DL/C/208, unnumbered folio, deposition of John Knyll, 8 July 1532.

words but one that shows the insult caused by accusations of expulsion.[118] Thus, it was to Pott's mobility that Hooke turned as a weak point, an aspect of his life that could be reinterpreted as potentially suspicious. Mobility for Pott was a kind of liminal state, open to insinuation. As will be discussed further below, neighbourly oversight was crucial in the establishment of reputation.

An important implication for the relationship between mobility and reputation is the necessity of local context to legitimate movement. Movement which one's neighbours could ascribe to a clear life-cycle stage was less likely to arouse suspicion. As we have seen, the move from a master's house to leading a household was one anticipated to accrue wealth and respect for young men. For men and women in later life, age and infirmity may have been a contingency which limited the impact of mobility on reputation, as suggested by the movement of widows into marginal parishes. For all movement, it was the perception of purpose or purposelessness that tipped the balance of acceptance or suspicion. Just as civic authorities stressed that disruptive 'nightwalkers' had no good reason for their nocturnal wanderings,[119] so could more permanent kinds of mobility be judged in relation to purpose, and thus perceptions of personal status and circumstances by neighbours were important.

Indeed, throughout the consistory court records the reporting of residence histories seems to have partly been a method of establishing suitability to depose. Impressions of residential stability offered by individuals in their own depositions were challenged by counter-witnesses; mobility seems to have been one of the ways that reliability as a witness was judged. The suspected thief John Curlews, a poor chamberholder, claimed in his own deposition to have lived in Totteridge, Middlesex, for twelve years, making no mention of his spell in sanctuary at St Martin le Grand well attested by counter-witnesses.[120] John Waldron deposed that he had lived in St Katharine's Hospital for just over a year and before that time at Newbury, Berkshire, although the constable of Southwark deposed that he had held brothels there for the previous four years. William Alston claimed to have lived in St Katharine's for seven years, despite counter-witnesses connecting

[118] LMA, DL/C/208, unnumbered folio, deposition of James Pott, 15 Nov. 1532.

[119] M. K. McIntosh, 'Finding language for misconduct: jurors in fifteenth-century local courts', in *Bodies and Disciplines: Intersections of Literature and History in Fifteenth-Century England*, ed. B. Hanawalt and D. Wallace (Minneapolis, 1996), pp. 87–122, at p. 92.

[120] LMA, DL/C/208, unnumbered folio, deposition of John Curlews, 17 Jan. 1533. See above, p. 121ff for further discussion of this case.

him with Southwark for the past four or five years.[121] This process of vetting and contesting residence histories is highly suggestive of their importance to status, since presumably the court was interested in this material only in as far as it shored up or cast doubt upon the reliability of a witness's testimony. Occasionally, witnesses were compelled (or felt compelled) to justify periods of movement. Elizabeth Weston's deposition begins thus:

> Elizabeth Weston of the parish of St. Martin in the Fields where she has lived for eight years and more with her mother, born in the town of Cockermouth in northern parts. Except that for a time she lived with a certain man named Newton, now deceased, in the parish of St. Dunstan in the West of the city of London for nine months. And she says that consequently she departed from the parish of St. Martin to the said parish of St. Dunstan to fulfil her position in the service of a good man [*boni viri*]. And she says that she left for nine months, the reason of her return to the parish of St. Martin being mutually agreed [by] she and her master.[122]

The fact that both Weston's short period of service and the reason for its conclusion were recorded implies either that the court was interested to know the reason for the breaking of her contract or that Elizabeth was anxious to pre-empt any assumptions. Perhaps she thought it might be assumed that she had been expelled from her master's house, or that the nine months' service was in fact time spent lying in for a pre-marital pregnancy.[123] In either case, the example speaks to the importance of witnesses being able to demonstrate stability (or the potential for stability) in their residence. Residential stability was being used in the consistory court as one of the means through which character and reliability was assessed. Witnesses felt compelled to edit their own residence histories to appear more stable, which speaks to an acknowledgement that mobility was a mark against their character that required mitigation. As Tom Johnson wrote of the late medieval English legal system, 'the learned law and the law of the street interacted in such routine ways that it is hardly surprising that they were mutually influential',[124] and it seems likely that consistory court witnesses reflected judgements that were commonly made about mobility

[121] Both witnesses' histories were described by various deponents in 'Elizabeth Brown, Marion Lauson c. Laurence Gilis', *Consistory Database* <http://consistory.ca/obj.php?p=973> [accessed 11 Oct. 2017].

[122] LMA, DL/C/206, fo. 168.

[123] Poor unmarried women could give birth in some of London's hospitals discretely. C. Rawcliffe, *Urban Bodies: Communal Health in Late Medieval English Towns and Cities* (Woodbridge, 2013), pp. 334, 346.

[124] Johnson, *Law in Common*, pp. 192–3.

in London. Poor witnesses anticipated mobility as a factor that could cause their exclusion from the proceedings of the court just as it could cause their marginalization from neighbourhood society.

The connection between mobility and exclusion is also seen in the treatment of immigrant aliens. William Hilton, a skinner's journeymen, impregnated a Dutch woman called Alice Fantell after promising to marry her.[125] When he subsequently became engaged to his master's daughter, Alice challenged him over the contract they had made together. William responded, 'what wenyst thow that I will for sake this inglisse maide that I am sewer too […] and mary the a doche hore, nay'.[126] The implication that Alice was expendable when he had a far more advantageous wife in prospect was firmly associated with her alien status and drew on tropes about Dutch women's engagement in prostitution.[127] There was also, perhaps, a sense that slighting aliens had fewer repercussions for one's character because of their less permanent position within London society. Indeed, one of the witnesses to this exchange between Hilton and Fantell was a servant called Barbara Frees, who, by the time the case was heard at the consistory, was 'living in the country beyond the Rhine'.[128] There were high levels of transience among alien Londoners; many eventually returned to their countries of birth and even those who stayed several years lived in anticipation of an eventual return.[129] For aliens, then, their unsettled status probably made them vulnerable to suspicion and mistreatment. Although, as we have seen, English witnesses were also mainly migrants, it was linguistic identity that continued to be the key marker of 'otherness' for aliens.[130] Aside from one reference to a drunk youth calling an elderly man an 'old peasant' (*senem rusticum*), there is little evidence in the church courts for abuse of English migrants based on their place of origin alone.[131] Although aliens found belonging in London in many ways, when they fell out with their neighbours, insults such as 'horson owtlandyssshe knave' or 'Lumberd knave' were used to mark their difference.[132]

[125] LMA, DL/C/206, fo. 457v.

[126] LMA, DL/C/206, fo. 458v.

[127] J. Ravenhill, 'The experiences of aliens in later medieval London and the negotiation of belonging, 1400–1540' (unpublished University of York PhD thesis, 2019), p. 158.

[128] LMA, DL/C/206, fo. 458.

[129] Lutkin, 'Settled or fleeting?', pp. 137–56; Bolton, 'The alien population of London', pp. 25–7; Ravenhill, 'The experience of aliens in later medieval London', pp. 60–64.

[130] Ormrod, Lambert and Mackman, *Immigrant England*, pp. 213–16.

[131] LMA, DL/C/206, fo. 258v.

[132] LMA, DL/C/207, fos. 227v, 229v.

The concern over stability in residences for witnesses also ought to be related to the mitigating circumstances considered for the mobility of 'respectable' witnesses. In particular, status and wealth were important elements of the judgements made about the problematic or unproblematic status of witnesses' mobility. As well as implying stable relationships with one's neighbours, stability also suggested access to the financial and social resources needed to weather difficult times, a motive that has been suggested for displays of wealth by burgesses.[133] Wealth and a profitable craft were bulwarks against uncertainty. The relationship between social marginality and mobility formed an exclusionary circle; on the one hand, maintaining a stable residence necessitated a good local reputation, and on the other, good reputation provided access to the credit and support networks that enabled stability.

Mobility and the extramural neighbourhoods

The final part of this chapter is focused on the ways in which mobility had an impact upon London's extramural neighbourhoods. In Chapter Two it was argued that people's personal frame of reference for urban space, created by their patterns of movement around the city, had an impact on their testamentary bequests. This spatial footprint would have been created not just by neighbourhood migration but also by day-to-day movement in urban space. Consistory court depositions provide a wealth of detail about the circumstances surrounding the events of cases, often detailing who was in a certain place, who they were with and why they were there. The depositions thus provide an important insight into day-to-day mobility within and around the city. Through everyday mobility for work and socializing as well as neighbourhood migration, there was a sense of a differentiated and sprawling social space beyond the walls. A sense of social and spatial separation of extramural areas from the central city is evident in the language used by their residents to describe where they lived. In a case from St Botolph Aldersgate, one witness described how she happened to see local women arguing as they washed clothes when she 'returned from the city of London to her dwelling house'.[134] Similarly, John Edmound of St Botolph Bishopsgate explained that before living in a chamber outside Bishopsgate he had lived 'in the city of London with a certain Walter Wright with whom he was apprenticed'.[135] Both these examples suggest a sense of difference between the extramural neighbourhoods and the city

[133] Riddy, '"Burgeis" domesticity in late medieval England', pp. 29–31.

[134] LMA, DL/C/208, fo. 71v.

[135] LMA, DL/C/208, fo. 39v.

centre. Jurisdictionally, both Conquest and Edmound were residents of the city of London itself, but the sense these depositions give of moving into a differentiated space beyond the walls is borne out elsewhere.

Sociability and other forms of everyday movement evidenced in cases are good indicators of how mobility shaped extramural neighbourhoods. Using GIS, it is possible to map the spread of individuals and events which were associated with cases. In this section, analysis will be based on the mapping of two different kinds of data associated with consistory cases. One is the residence history of deponents, including the present parish of residence provided by witnesses when they gave a deposition. In a few cases, the gap in time between the disputed events of the case and the suit appearing at the consistory might mean that individuals had moved, although this was unusual. The other data mapped, in Figure 3.5, are incidents pertinent to the case. These are usually specific events, such as the witnessing of a contract, that can be placed within an identifiable parish, precinct or street. Occasionally, a more nebulous kind of event is mapped, such as the 'public fame' in a parish of an incident or person. All mapping has been undertaken at parish level, although, as we shall see, neighbourhood could sometimes mean smaller or larger social spaces. Figures 4.3–4.5 collate information from all the cases with at least one event in a given parish. This method produces maps that focus on the parties and witnesses who can be sited within that location for at least some of the events associated with a case. Although a few cases had incidents spread over several parishes, as seen in Figure 3.5 (which maps the events themselves for cases associated with St Botolph Bishopsgate), these were usually few. Such cases can tell us something about the movement of people coming to a given parish. Some more complicated cases could involve multiple counter-witnesses who had little to depose about the main events at issue and so the mapping focuses on case studies where this is not a factor distorting the visualization.

There was a clear tendency for people to be mobile around the fringes of the city. This is particularly noticeable in cases that centred on St Botolph Bishopsgate, represented in Figure 3.5. The immediate 'neighbourhood' of Bishopsgate drawing in witnesses included Norton Folgate liberty, the precincts of St Mary of Bethlehem and the hospital of St Mary and Shoreditch, all of which acted as settings for events disputed in cases as well as providing witnesses to events in Bishopsgate. The case of the hospital of St Mary Bishopsgate c. Pellet is particularly illustrative of the way that the Bishopsgate neighbourhood crossed jurisdictional boundaries. Robert and Joan Pellet were sued by the hospital for repeated defamation.[136] The Pellets

[136] LMA, DL/C/0206, fos. 60v–63v, 107v–109v, 167–170v.

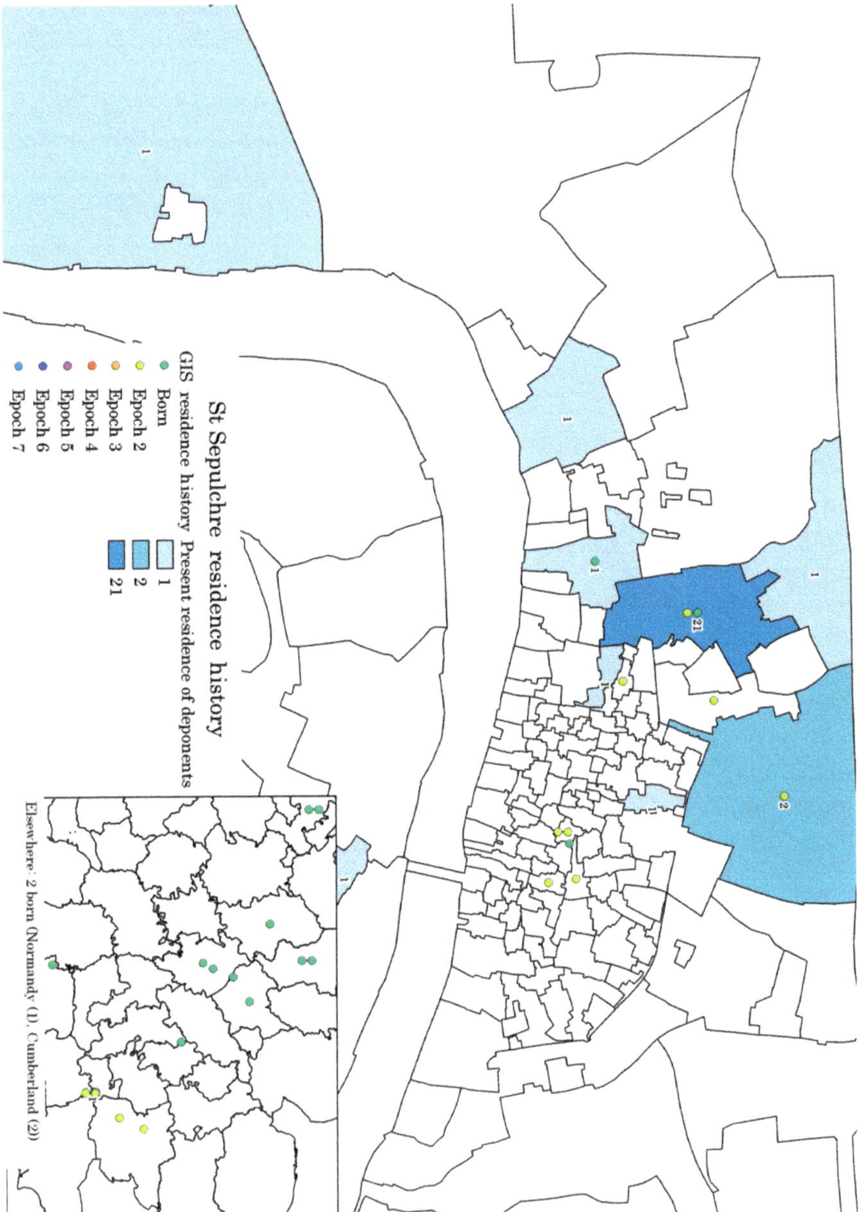

Figure 3.3 Residence history map for deponents in cases with events in St Sepulchre without Newgate

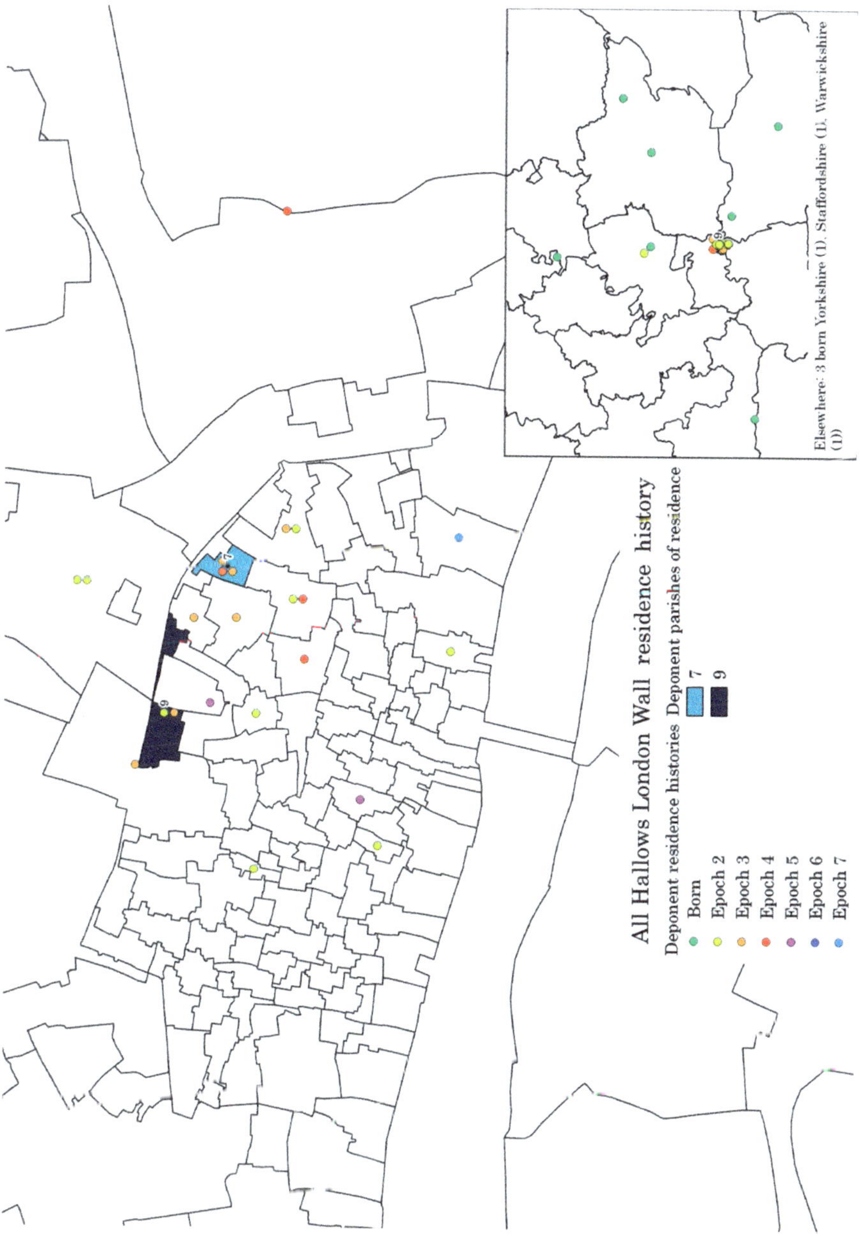

Figure 3.4 Residence history map for deponents in cases with events in All Hallows London Wall

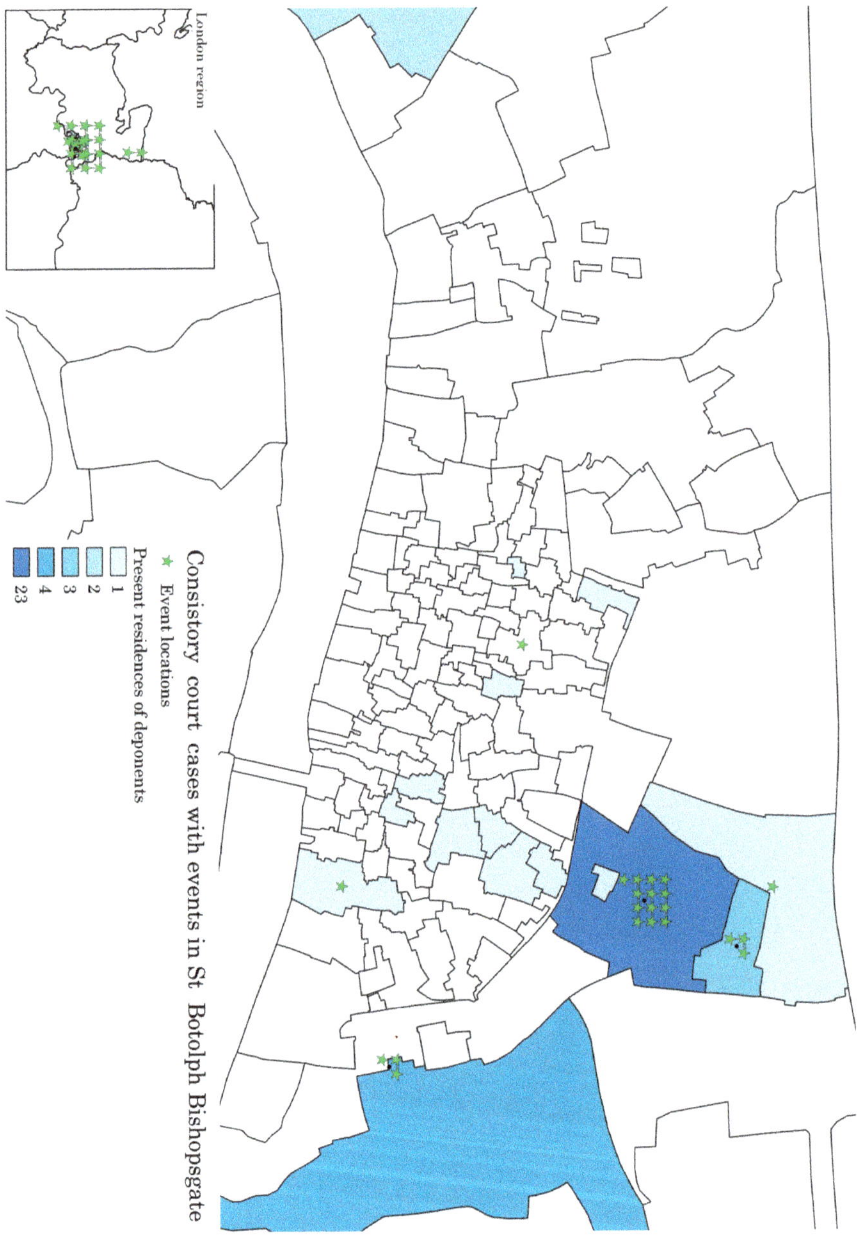

Figure 3.5 Map of events and present residences for deponents in cases with events in St Botolph Bishopsgate

allegedly called the prior 'pilled [wretched] prior and knave prior and that he is a mayntener of bawddes and harlottes' within his precinct and in the surrounding area.[137] Witnesses recounted that they did so repeatedly and in different places: before the hospital gates in Bishopsgate Street, within the precinct of the hospital, in a nearby garden, outside Bishopsgate itself and in the hospital churchyard. Robert also repeated the accusations in a legal case at the guildhall.[138] Robert was a former servant of the hospital who was sued for debts incurred while in the prior's and canons' employment.[139] The witnesses called upon to testify against them were nearly all drawn from Bishopsgate, both in Bishopsgate Street as well as residents of the hospital of St Mary and the liberty of Norton Folgate: thirteen in total, the largest set for a single party among the chosen cases. The reasons for this large witness group appear to be twofold. Firstly, the Pellets had annoyed a remarkable number of their neighbours: Joan Pellet was said to have proclaimed many times:

> in the king's highway in the street called Bishopsgate Street that there is no good woman of good and honest conversation in the whole street 'but hores and bawdes'[140]

Such behaviour was bound to have been unpopular, and the Pellets' accusations against the hospital similarly implicated their neighbours by suggesting that they were the 'bawddes and harlotts' that the prior and canons maintained. The case demonstrates how the neighbourhood could be an extended area at the margins of the city, overspilling jurisdictional boundaries. A related aspect is that two witnesses who appeared for the prior were tenants of the hospital's Bishopsgate properties, as a contemporary rental from their estate reveals.[141] This is suggestive of the role that a landlord such as the hospital could play in controlling the neighbourhood where they owned large amounts of property around their precincts.

The services of both suburbs and city centre drove everyday movement between the neighbourhood outside Bishopsgate and intramural London. The parishes that lay along the road within the walls from the gate to London

[137] LMA DL/C/0206, fo. 60v.

[138] LMA, DL/C/206, fos. 60v–62.

[139] LMA, DL/C/206, fos. 108–108v.

[140] LMA, DL/C/206, fo. 62.

[141] Henry Adams, salter, was a witness for the hospital on 18 July 1511 and appears as a tenant of theirs in a rental dated 1505: LMA, DL/C/206, fo. 62v; TNA SC 11/975. Richard Wylkenson gave a deposition on 28 Feb. 1512 and appears as a tenant of two properties owned by the hospital in the same 1505 rental: LMA, DL/C/206, fo. 108v, TNA SC 11/975.

Bridge (via Bishopsgate Street and Gracechurch Street) were home to several witnesses to events here. Hugh Wellys, who was drinking in the White Hert without Bishopsgate when Richard Bek publicly attacked his wife, Anne, there, had travelled to drink from the parish of St Ethelburga just within the gate.[142] John Sawnder, a scrivener of St Edmund Lumbard Street close to Gracechurch Street, was called to Bishopsgate by Richard Ely, who wished Sawnder to witness his marriage contract.[143] John Nores, a glazier of the parish of St Olave Jewry, was witness to the Pellet case. Interestingly, despite living at the centre of the city, Nores held a shop at Norton Folgate.[144] Movement between centre and periphery for economic reasons can also be seen working in the other direction. The tailor Thomas Wylletts and capper John Brown, both of St., Botolph Bishopsgate, went to Eastcheap market on an autumn morning in 1529 to buy victuals, where they became witnesses to an alleged defamation.[145] In these cases, the economic relationship between centre and periphery served to pull people into networks of knowledge outside their own neighbourhood. Bishopsgate residents who needed scriveners or food markets used the services of the city centre, while residents within the walls looking for affordable industrial property or simply a good time might go to Bishopsgate. Unsurprisingly, this kind of movement was still governed by proximity: just as most of the deponents who saw events in Bishopsgate were from parishes along the main road to that area, so most of the witnesses to St Sepulchre cases (mapped in Figure 3.3) had come from the surrounding extramural parishes. In the case of Austyn c. Hill, two men from outside St Sepulchre happened to witness an incident of defamation because they were having a shave in the shop of barber William Austyn.[146] When one was asked in court to testify to the local 'fame' of the incident, he replied that he had nothing to depose 'because he is unknown in that area'.[147] Nonetheless, both claimed to have known the barber's wife for four or five years, suggesting that heading to Austyn's shop for a shave might have been a regular occurrence. Day-to-day movement might be casual with regard to the whole local community but it was still rooted in personal relationships.

Permanent residential moves echoed the pattern of everyday mobility. In several cases, couples whose marriages became subject to a consistory case had moved from the parish where it had been solemnized. Thomas Wulley

[142] LMA, DL/C/207, fo. 236v.

[143] LMA, DL/C/207, fo. 146v.

[144] LMA, DL/C/206, fo. 61.

[145] LMA, DL/C/208, fos. 108, 110.

[146] LMA, DL/C/208, fos. 105v–06.

[147] LMA, DL/C/208, fo. 105v.

and Margaret Isot had banns issued for their wedding in their home parish of St Sepulchre and then lived together in St Giles Cripplegate for three years.[148] The marriage of William and Isabel Newport was solemnized in St Botolph Aldgate, from where they subsequently moved to Bishopsgate, where their violent rows became well known.[149] These examples are suggestive of a trend visible elsewhere for witnesses living at the margins of the city to move around in the orbit of London. Richard Bysshopp, who lived in Westminster in January 1524 when he gave a deposition, had been born in the parish of St Mary Whitechapel.[150] John Jervys, who was sued to fulfil a marriage contract he had made in the precinct of St Katharine, was said by one witness to have lived at Rotherhithe at the time of the contract but now to live at Stepney; it seems likely that Jervys was a mariner from his movement around the port.[151] Katharine and Thomas Atkynson lived at St James Clerkenwell for twelve or thirteen years, where they ran an alehouse, but by the time of their depositions they had moved to St Giles Cripplegate.[152] Also moving between these two northern suburbs was William Hosyer, a butcher who lived at Clerkenwell at the time of his deposition having previously been resident of St Giles; additionally, Hosyer seems to have travelled to his employment since he described working in the shop of Robert Dunne, his master, in St John Street.[153]

For these men and women, all of apparently low status, moving around in the extramural zone of London presumably enabled them to stay in contact with friends and take advantage of the demand for services and labour in the city and its region, as well as the cheaper accommodation available outside its walls. Given how the Bishopsgate neighbourhood extended across jurisdictional boundaries, for those moving between adjoining parishes such as St Giles Cripplegate and Clerkenwell, the move may not have been very far. As Jeremy Boulton noted for seventeenth-century Southwark, short-range movement was very common, especially for poorer residents, meaning that parish boundaries were often crossed by those who were nonetheless

[148] 'Thomas Wulley c. Margaret Isot John Heth', Consistory Database < http://consistory.ca/obj.php?object=case&action=view&id=41&expand=cases&case_results_format=full> [accessed 14 Feb. 2017].

[149] Deposition of William Roger, *Consistory Database* <http://consistory.ca/obj.php?p=1182> [accessed 4 Aug. 2020].

[150] LMA, DL/C/207, fo. 259v.

[151] LMA, DL/C/207, fo. 87v. More about this case below, p. 190ff.

[152] LMA, DL/C/207, fos. 83, 96.

[153] LMA, DL/C/207, fo. 34v. The deposition of Robert Dunne, his master, which gives the site of the shop in St John's Street, is at f.20v.

remaining within the same area.[154] A very similar pattern seems to have been in place in the late fifteenth and early sixteenth centuries, suggesting that this was a long-term continuity in London's suburbs across the period of the city's expansion. Mobility around extramural space connected together suburban settlements decades before urban development did.

Migration connected the extramural parishes to the city's wider region. The kinds of mobility that created the distinctive hinterlands of Bishopsgate and Aldgate seen in Chapter Two were in evidence in witness depositions. Migration between Bishopsgate and the settlements of the Lea Valley is suggested in the 1514 case of Wryther c. Wryther. John and Joan Wryther had married at St Botolph Bishopsgate but, after learning of an impediment to their marriage, Joan separated from her husband and returned to her family at Waltham Cross.[155] The inset map in Figure 3.5 shows the events of this case in Waltham Cross, in the same area so prominently featured in Bishopsgate wills. At St Botolph Aldgate, more casual forms of movement are recorded eastwards into the area which dominated extramural bequests. Peter at Pele, a butcher of St Mary Magdalene Milk Street, was passing the churchyard at Aldgate on his way to Stepney when he overheard Juliana Bylby's defamation of her neighbour.[156] John Clyff, who had lived at St Botolph Aldgate for twenty years, evidently maintained social contacts in Stepney, since he was invited by Alice Godard to dinner there on Easter Sunday in 1531, where he witnessed her marriage contract.[157]

The complex interconnections of suburbs and their wider region, often just hinted at in wills, are demonstrated clearly in one case from the 1470s which reveals just how interwoven social and economic connections were between St Botolph Aldgate and its hinterland. An action of debt made between Joan Plummere and John Olyve involved two witnesses from the eastern periphery; John Wavery from St Botolph Aldgate and John Godbolt from St Mary Matfelon. They testified to having been present in the town of Stapleford Abbotts in Essex in 1474 when Plummere paid ten shillings to Olyve in satisfaction of a debt owed to him by her father.[158] Wavery and Godbolt were both smiths, and it seems likely that they had some involvement in the business related to the debt since Godbolt was questioned in court as to whether he and Wavery were fellow pledges to the debt. Godbolt denied

[154] Boulton, 'Neighbourhood migration in early modern London', pp. 123–5.

[155] LMA, DL/C/206, fo. 316. More on this case below.

[156] LMA, DL/C/208, unnumbered folio, deposition of Peter at Pele dated 1 March 1533.

[157] LMA, DL/C/208, fos. 224v–25.

[158] LMA, DL/C/205, fos. 261–262v.

this.[159] Wavery had known Plummere for six years, the same amount of time that he had lived in St Botolph Aldgate.[160] Taken together, this suggests a group with ties of occupation and friendship based in the east of the city and using the routes of transport there to conduct business. Connections outwards from the city were not simply created by one-time migration events but were cultivated through regular economic and sociable contact. Furthermore, the final example suggests the close intertwining of London neighbours, their occupations and the wider region.

Mobility was central to the function of the city. London was a city of migrants, and the meaning of mobility became contested as everyone sought to establish their place in urban society. Individual crafts and extramural neighbourhoods had their own hinterlands, within which intertwined social and economic connections drove migration. Mobility was thus not a marginal process, but it profoundly shaped London's spatial margins as sites of transit and transition between city and country. The effect of mobility in the extramural parishes was a key aspect of what made them 'marginal'. The sense of neighbourhood outside the walls, meaning the locality in which people were known and conducted their lives, was very broad and crossed parochial and jurisdictional boundaries. The situation was similar within the walls, with neighbourhood migration taking place around parishes in a particular part of the city, but the key difference at the fringes of the city was both that such migration occurred in parishes that were far larger than those within the walls and that the precincts of religious houses and neighbouring settlements appear to have been included in residents' field of movement. The lower levels of citizenship among those who lived beyond the walls, discussed in Chapter Two, corresponds to not just the economic status of these neighbourhoods but also their ambiguous social space with connections across jurisdictional lines. This understanding of extramural space also explains the tendency for individuals to move around the urban fringe with little regard for the formal boundaries of London. Already in the fifteenth and early sixteenth centuries the geographical space of London was diffused beyond the walls by the mobility of its inhabitants before the built environment reflected its sprawl.

As the experience of the extramural parishes shows, migration from country to city was not the only meaningful way that mobility shaped urban life. Neighbourhood migration within London, as well as even more transient kinds of movement, were important for shaping senses of social space as well as carrying social meaning for the individual. Those with only

[159] LMA, DL/C/205, fo. 262.

[160] LMA, DL/C/205, fo. 261.

fleeting connections to a locality might be interpreted as vagrants. Instability was relatively common among the poor; mobility was a habitual risk born of lack of resources and compounded by the practices of expulsion and illicit trades such as prostitution. Neighbourhood migration around London was undertaken utilizing knowledge of the socio-economic topography of the city and what was advantageous for the trade or life stage of an individual. Such knowledge would undoubtedly have been gained through local social networks and connections to institutions.

Despite the pervasiveness of mobility, for many it was a reputational risk. The greatest risks came for those whose circumstances of wealth, status, age and life-cycle stage meant that neighbours might associate their movement with vagrancy, expulsion or a suspiciously unstable lifestyle. This is crucial to understanding social marginality more generally: while anyone might find themselves at risk of exclusion, the less social capital someone had, the more serious the consequences might be. Neighbourhood was a crucial venue for making and substantiating reputation, a process mobility challenged by enabling individuals to detach themselves from the social context in which they were known and their character was established. The following two chapters will demonstrate the systems of marginalization that Londoners navigated and argue that the pervasive mobility we have seen could be exploited to make use of marginal urban space in defence or management of reputation.

4. Controlling inclusion and exclusion

Finding your place in London meant navigating a complex system of social control that scrutinized behaviour in pursuit of peaceful community.[1] As we saw in Chapter Three, neighbours could and did force people to leave a city ward if their behaviour or reputation was deemed unacceptable. This chapter demonstrates the wider system of marginalization that expulsion sat within as one of the most severe punishments. It sets out what behaviour was unacceptable and the means by which that unacceptability was decided within urban neighbourhoods. Collective determination of who was to be excluded or punished was socially significant. It developed a sense of community as well as allowing certain individuals to assert their moral worth and right to exert authority.[2] My focus here is not exclusively on the extramural areas of the city, because it is necessary to see how the system functioned as a whole in order to understand how some people became marginalized from local society.

Determining who to exclude and punish also involved the constant negotiation of status and authority in the community. This encompassed both the definition of who was respectable and, for those who aspired to the local elite, who was worthy to hold office and pass judgement on others. This chapter establishes these dual processes of marginalization and inclusion as they played out in London neighbourhoods. Local officers, jurors and neighbours without an official role had a considerable degree of flexibility in determining who to marginalize. Drawing on records of ward courts alongside wills, I will show the beneficial effects that participation in the jury could have for the few men who succeeded in becoming regular members of their local wardmotes.

This negotiation was carried out in a complex legal landscape where royal, civic and ecclesiastical jurisdictions overlapped and combined with

1 See p. xxxii for discussion of the definition of community as used here.

2 R. W. Scribner, 'Wie wird man Außenseiter? Ein- und Ausgrenzung im frühneuzeitlichen Deutschland', in *Aussenseiter zwischen Mittelalter und Neuzeit: Festschrift für Hans-Jürgen Goertz zum 60. Geburtstag*, ed. N. Fischer and M. Kobelt-Groch (Leiden, 1997), pp. 21–46, at pp. 23–4; S. Bardsley, *Venomous Tongues: Speech and Gender in Late Medieval England* (Philadelphia, 2011), pp. 147–9; K. Simon-Muscheid, 'Randgruppen, Bürgerschaft und Obrigkeit: der basler Kohlenburg, 14.–16. Jahrhundert', p. 211.

informal modes of community regulation. Royal and civic jurisdictions in London intertwined: felonies and trespasses were reserved to the king's courts, but the city held the right to nominate the local royal officers, the sheriffs of London and Middlesex, who were usually already aldermen of the city or set to become one soon after. Offences which in other parts of England were heard in leet courts, such as the regulation of standards of bread and ale, environmental 'nuisances' and behavioural misdemeanours such as scolding, fell under the jurisdiction of the mayor and aldermen. The scope of civic regulation also overlapped with the ecclesiastical courts. The church handled matters pertaining to the soul and the clergy, such as marital disputes, defamation and tithes, but also sexual misdemeanours, which were also counted as nuisances in civic jurisdiction. Indeed, cases were sometimes referred by ward officers to the church's commissary court, effectively meaning that offenders faced punishment in two systems for the same incident.[3] The boundaries between all these jurisdictions were contested, in legal and spatial terms. This contestation was not a peculiar product of London's population density but a marked feature of law in all late medieval English towns and cities.[4]

This chapter makes use of the court records which give the greatest direct insight into local dynamics of marginalization. The lowest level of civic courts – the ward courts, or wardmotes – are thus central because presentations were made by juries of neighbours. I also make extensive use of records from the consistory court, London's highest ecclesiastical court, because witnesses and parties in this court often articulated otherwise unspoken aspects of community regulation by pointing to failures of alternative legal avenues or unsuccessful neighbourly mediation in their explanations of how a dispute had escalated to its present state. In this chapter and Chapter Five the records of the lower ecclesiastical court – the commissary – are also occasionally touched upon. This court, like the wardmotes, brought cases largely based on local suspicion and information rather than the party-and-party suits typical of the consistory. I do not dwell on the commissary records, however, as they are usually very brief in their description of offences and have been dealt with extensively by other historians, particularly in the work of Martin Ingram, Richard Wunderli

3 S. McSheffrey, *Marriage, Sex and Civic Culture in Late Medieval London* (Philadelphia, 2006), pp. 155–6; M. Ingram, *Carnal Knowledge: Regulating Sex in England, 1470–1600* (Cambridge and New York, 2017), pp. 218–20.

4 T. Johnson, *Law in Common: Legal Cultures in Late medieval England* (Oxford and New York, 2020).

and Shannon McSheffrey.[5] The offences with which this chapter concerns itself largely exclude felonies and trespasses such as theft, homicide and violent assaults, which fell into royal jurisdiction, although a token of the intertwining of royal and civic jurisdiction in London is the fact that trespasses were heard in both the mayor's and the sheriff's courts.[6] The records for these more serious offences survive only patchily, though it should be borne in mind that local disputes might result in suits in several courts under multiple categories of offence. The only area where more serious offences are considered is in liberties where jurors cited nuisances alongside felonies and trespasses, represented here by the records of Norton Folgate. This small area of Bishopsgate Street was both a manor held by St Paul's Cathedral and a liberty, with surviving records of its annual view of frankpledge, which are used here to show the particular circumstances and challenges of regulating behaviour in a liberty.

The practice of community regulation in London was often highly localized. In 1473, in the midst of a morality drive that saw the unusual copying of wardmote presentments into the journals of the city's common council, ward jurors were sworn to make presentment of a wide range of offenders. These included 'all manner [of] persons by whom any manner of treason, murder, felony or robbery in your wards hath been now late committed or done', alongside vagrants, tellers of 'false or feigned' seditious tales, adulterers and keepers of 'petty hostry' (unregistered lodging houses).[7] The offences cited were covered by a mixture of civic and royal jurisdiction (and, in the case of adultery, could have fallen into the church courts' purview), indicating the fuzzy boundaries between jurisdictions in the initial local detection of misdemeanours. While more serious offences under royal jurisdiction would be referred to higher courts, in a normal year the punishment of vagrants, keepers of petty hostry and other minor civic offences seems to have remained within the ward itself – or, to the chagrin of jurors, not punished formally at all beyond indictment.[8] Referral to higher courts of these misdemeanours appears to have been sporadic; while there are occasional records of such offenders being prosecuted by central civic courts, these are relatively few compared to the number of citations in wardmotes, which could extend to over a hundred

[5] See, in particular, Ingram, *Carnal Knowledge*; McSheffrey, *Marriage, Sex and Civic Culture*; R. M. Wunderli, *London Church Courts and Society on the Eve of the Reformation* (Cambridge, Mass., 1981).

[6] P. Tucker, *Law Courts and Lawyers in the City of London, 1300–1550* (Cambridge, 2007), pp. 149–54.

[7] LMA, Jor. 8, fos. 49–49v.

[8] Tucker, *Law Courts and Lawyers*, p. 88.

presentments in a single ward in a year.[9] This is comparable to the situation across England, where what Marjorie McIntosh calls 'social misbehaviour' was largely dealt with locally rather than troubling the travelling assize justices or royal courts at Westminster.[10] The procedures and scope of London's higher courts have been brilliantly set out by Penny Tucker. Tucker largely excluded wardmotes from her account because they 'formed at most the preliminary stage of legal proceedings'.[11] While this is absolutely true, the purpose here is similar to McIntosh's approach to local courts elsewhere in England, in framing wardmotes as embedded in processes of community management in which they could be a preliminary legal tool for escalating local disputes and concerns. As shall be shown, their flexibility and broad scope was crucial to that function.

Apprehending the culprits of all kinds of offences relied on the watchfulness and knowledge of neighbours. Building on the work of scholars who have looked in particular at sexual regulation, this chapter makes a novel contribution by demonstrating the importance of local power dynamics in determining who was to be included and who was to be excluded in London society. These dynamics operated in the context of the social networks described in Chapter Two. The testamentary relationships discussed there were often rooted in joint participation in the instruments of local regulation, and the social capital evidenced by citation as a testamentary official was accrued through years of demonstrating local authority. There was, however, no immutable set of individuals who exercised local authority but a constant negotiation of position in which the odds were stacked in favour of some over others.

Defining anti-social behaviour

As both Marjorie McIntosh and Sandy Bardsley argued, the definition of problematic behaviour in fifteenth-century England was variable according to location and social context. Both stressed that presentations in local courts were highly influenced by local circumstance and concerns, although Bardsley argued that they were even more specific in being driven by individuals.[12] Ian

9 Offences were translated to higher courts during periods when the civic government carried out drives on immorality, such as in 1473, when extracts from wardmotes relating to sexual offences were copied into the Journals of the Common Council. LMA, Jor. 8, fos. 45v–48v; Ingram, *Carnal Knowledge*, p. 229.

10 M. K. McIntosh, *Controlling Misbehavior in England, 1370–1600* (Cambridge, 1998), p. 26.

11 Tucker, *Law Courts and Lawyers*, p. 88.

12 McIntosh, *Controlling Misbehavior in England*, pp. 33–6; S. Bardsley, *Venomous Tongues: Speech and Gender in Late Medieval England* (Philadelphia, 2011), pp. 115–19.

Forrest has argued that the trustworthy men who reported on local affairs to bishops walked a difficult line between the 'self-interest or the perspective of the parish elite' and 'the will of "the parishioners"' in their choice of offences to report.[13] The London wardmotes operated in a similar way to the local courts elsewhere in relying on a jury of twelve men to report local misdemeanours. Although the civic precepts or 'articles' of the wardmote broadly shaped what was to be presented, jurors also exercised quite a degree of autonomy in their choices. Jurors might, during periods of civic or royal anxiety about particular issues, have been encouraged to focus on particular types of offence.[14] However, it is probable that juries responded to neighbourhood politics to a significant degree, just as they did in other English towns and villages.

The local issues indicted at the wardmote fell within a very wide range, and they have been categorized for the purposes of considering trends, as in Table 4.1 and Figure 4.1. Common environmental nuisances included blockages in the highway and unsafe buildings as well as gates left open overnight. Unruly behaviour included disruptive speech such as scolding or being a 'noyer' of one's neighbours, and sexual offences included adultery, bawdry or 'misgovernment' of the body. Failures to uphold proper household order fell under unruly behaviour and included accusations of 'keeping ill rule', 'receiving suspicious persons' or being a 'maintainer' of those who were poorly behaved. Such misgovernment was occasionally difficult to distinguish from those who were accused of bawdry (which fell under sexual offences) or of keeping foreigners in their houses. Economic offences were mainly indictments for breaching the statutes of ale and bread, which featured little after the 1420s. Not all offences were considered equally damaging to personal reputation. As Christine Winter noted in her analysis of the Portsoken presentments, indictments for environmental nuisances appear not to have affected one's opportunity to join the jury, whereas few who were accused of immoral behaviour or selling without the freedom of the city were ever jurors.[15] Nonetheless, as we shall see, membership of the jury was an important means of defining the 'respectable' group in neighbourhood society, and jurors could mitigate the impact of previous indictments on their reputation in order to serve.

What behaviour caused most concern shifted over time and varied between neighbourhoods. Figure 4.1 and Table 4.1 demonstrate how the

[13] I. Forrest, *Trustworthy Men: How Inequality and Faith Made the Medieval Church* (Princeton and Oxford, 2018), p. 194.

[14] Ingram, *Carnal Knowledge*, pp. 233–7.

[15] C. L. Winter, 'The Portsoken presentments: an analysis of a London ward in the 15th century', *Transactions of the London and Middlesex Archaeology Society*, lvi (2005), 97–162, at p. 101.

proportions of different types of presentment at the ward courts varied over time. These have been categorized into economic, environmental and sexual offences and those related to unruly behaviour and foreigners living or trading in the city without either citizenship or frankpledge.[16] The chart prioritizes trends over time, so some years include returns from many parts of the city and some from single wards. Where there are returns only from a single ward, it is evident in the Portsoken (1466–1507) and Aldersgate (1510, *c.*1512–24 and 1528) presentments that even juries in the same place varied year to year in the balance between the different offences they presented. There were also considerable differences between wards; the presentment for Broad Street in 1528 contained no indictments for sexual offences, compared with between 13 per cent and 25 per cent in other sixteenth-century presentments from Aldersgate and Portsoken. Sometimes intensely local issues might dominate a presentment for just a single year, as in the undated Aldersgate wardmote where forty-nine stranger craftsmen living in St Martin le Grand were indicted. While the wardmote was undoubtedly part of a wider civic justice system, jurors often responded to local concerns rather than simply exercising the will of the mayor and aldermen.

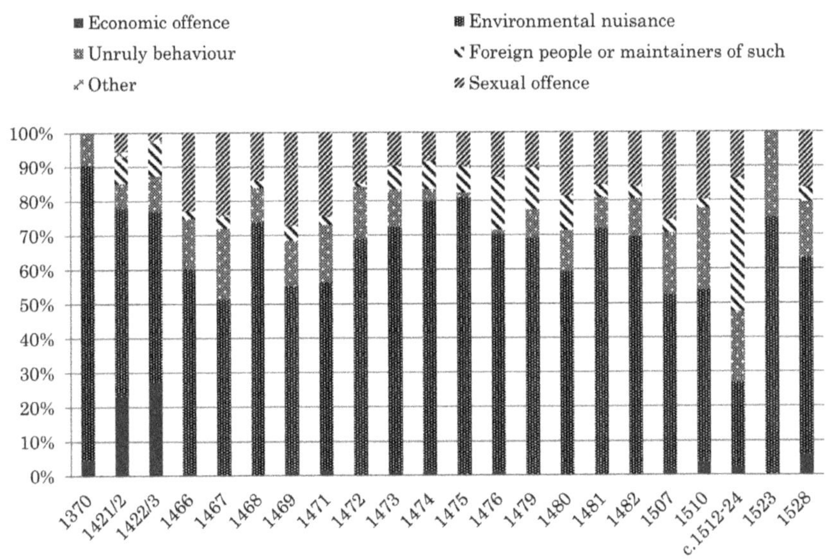

Figure 4.1 Proportions of wardmote indictment categories. Data for 1370, 1421/22 and 1522/23 represents presentments from multiple wards. The years 1466–1507 represent single returns from Portsoken. Undated (c.1512–24), 1510 and 1523 returns represent Aldersgate ward. The 1528 presentment was from Broad Street ward.

16 On frankpledge, see above, p. 93.

Table 4.1 Numbers of offences reported by year of presentment

	Economic offence	Environmental nuisance	Sexual offence	Unruly behaviour	Foreign people or maintainers of such	Other	**Total**
1370	1	18	0	2	0	0	**21**
1421/2	101	239	24	31	34	7	**436**
1422/3	45	81	3	17	16	2	**164**
1466	1	78	30	19	3	0	**131**
1467	0	77	36	31	5	1	**150**
1468	0	73	14	10	2	0	**99**
1469	1	62	31	15	5	0	**114**
1471	2	69	31	21	3	0	**126**
1472	0	69	15	15	1	0	**100**
1473	1	72	10	11	7	0	**101**
1474	1	66	7	3	7	0	**84**
1475	0	64	8	1	6	0	**79**
1476	1	63	12	1	14	0	**91**
1479	0	67	10	8	12	0	**97**
1480	0	35	11	7	6	0	**59**
1481	0	56	12	7	3	0	**78**
1482	0	57	13	9	3	0	**82**
1507	1	40	20	14	3	0	**78**
1510	3	38	15	18	2	0	**76**
***c.*1512–24**	3	31	17	26	49	0	**126**
1523	0	30	0	10	0	0	**40**
1528	4	39	11	11	3	0	**68**

There were also broader changes over time. For instance, Caroline Barron has pointed out that regulation of wages, which featured in wardmote precepts in the 1370s and the *Liber Albus* of the 1420s despite no indictments in the surviving presentments, was removed from precepts produced in the 1470s.[17] Likewise, the indictments for breaking the assize of bread and ale that were dominant in the earlier surviving presentments are absent in the Portsoken, Aldersgate and Broad Street presentments in the later fifteenth and early sixteenth centuries. This was despite a restatement of this precept by the common council in 1508.[18] Behavioural concerns also shifted somewhat across the period; sexual immorality was indicted in every surviving presentment bar 1373, but in the early presentments unruly behaviour indictments outnumbered sexual offences, a ratio reversed from the 1460s onwards. On the whole, these behavioural offences became more dominant over time. In the early presentments recorded in the Plea and Memoranda Rolls, an average of just 11 per cent of indictments were for sexual offences or unruly behaviour, compared to 27 per cent in the mid- to late fifteenth-century Portsoken presentments and 36 per cent in the early sixteenth-century documents. However, there were some important continuities across the long fifteenth century. Concern with foreigners and evading the city's jurisdiction, which Barron notes were novelties in the wardmote precepts in the 1470s,[19] were already apparent in the presentments from the 1420s (see Figure 4.1), suggesting the degree to which juries could make indictments which did not conform to the precepts put to them by the civic government.

Consistory court depositions reveal definitions of marginal and antisocial behaviour in other ways, many of which were similar to the categories in wardmote indictments. The deposition of George Barretson, who gave testimony against the characters of an opposing party's witnesses in 1523, has a revealing depth in its description of why they were unfit to depose:

> ... he says that John Pruddon is accustomed to be drunk and spreads gossip amongst his neighbours and is very poor and needy and has little or nothing in goods in as much as this witness can tell. Further he says that Richard Trussyngton was indicted at the 'warmolquest' this last year for a quarrelsome person and also is a pauper as he believes. And he says that Thomas Plowghe is a pauper as he says that [deleted: he is 'le water man' travelling the sea] save that he is an honest

[17] C. M. Barron, 'Lay solidarities: the wards of medieval London', in *Law, Laity and Solidarities: Essays in Honour of Susan Reynolds.*, ed. J. Martindale, P. Stafford and J. L. Nelson (Manchester, 2001), pp. 218–33, at pp. 223–4.

[18] LMA, Jor. 11, fo. 93v.

[19] Barron, 'Lay solidarities', pp. 223–4.

> pauper. And moreover he says that William Rede is quarrelsome and also violent with his neighbours and he says that around the feast of Christmas last passed this witness saw him fighting with some of his neighbours.[20]

Barretson gave a wide range of descriptors indicating that the opposing witnesses were not respectable: drunkenness, quarrelling, gossiping, violence, itinerant occupation and poverty. The reference to indictment at the wardmote served as proof of his description of Trussyngton's character. It is interesting that, even though he stated that Plowghe was an 'honest pauper', his poverty and that of Pruddon and Trussyngton was still relevant to assessment of their suitability as witnesses. In canon and Roman law courts such as the consistory, the word of a pauper could be discounted, although there is ample evidence that parties nonetheless presented pauper witnesses and defended their right to depose.[21]

This raises the question of how far the characteristics that were held to make an unreliable witness can be used as proxies for marginalization outside the court. Was it simply that counter-witnesses were using objections based on advice from canon lawyers, or did such characteristics truly mean exclusion from neighbourhood society on a day-to-day basis? Similarly, did a wardmote indictment for keeping foreigners or adultery really mean one had become a social pariah? This is a difficult issue, as in some sense court records shape and define our sense of exclusion and inclusion because they are the closest we can get to the lived experiences of these complex social processes. A plausible answer is offered in Erik Spindler's framework for marginality, in which he proposes no binary mainstream/marginal divide but instead that marginality is a condition of being between social groups caused by a combination of jeopardy and instability.[22] As we saw in Chapter Three, an individual who was an outsider to the local community could find their position and behaviour portrayed as suspicious. Mobility was particularly associated with the poor and also jeopardized reputation. Sandy Bardsley argues that prosecutions for scolding were dependent on varying local priorities and officers: while gossiping and chiding were common and would no doubt have been considered unpleasant by their object, prosecution relied upon local circumstance.[23] Exclusion and inclusion were thus constantly being

[20] LMA, DL/C/207, fo. 268v.

[21] S. A. McDonough, *Witnesses, Neighbors and Community in Late Medieval Marseille* (New York, 2013), p. 52; A. Shepard, *Accounting for Oneself: Worth, Status, and the Social Order in Early Modern England* (Oxford and New York, 2015), pp. 118–19.

[22] E. Spindler, 'Marginality and social relations in London and the Bruges area, 1370–1440' (unpublished University of Oxford DPhil thesis, 2008), pp. 8–15.

[23] Bardsley, *Venomous Tongues*, pp. 105–8.

negotiated, rather than every neighbourhood having a fixed social 'margin', and the indictment of problematic behaviours was a part of that process. They brought local knowledge about reputation into the court, a fame which itself might have contradictory or contested aspects, and used it to define their opponent as an unfit witness or a person who should be punished. This constant negotiation is a process to which I will return over the course of this chapter and in Chapter Five, as it was central to the management of community. Maintaining a good reputation for the poor would have been an important but challenging task, given that they were both vulnerable to the changes of fortune which engendered mobility (and thus suspicion) and ineligible for the leadership roles which could cement good reputation.

The wardmote

The wardmote was the primary formal means of raising concerns about those who broke civic regulations or 'the king's peace' in London. It was also, as an institution reliant on local knowledge, embedded within neighbourhood society. Wardmotes were flexible institutions, responsive to local concerns. This meant they could accommodate political dissent, usually sidelined from civic government.[24] Their responsiveness was rooted, as Sarah Rees Jones argued, in the elastic discourse of 'nuisance' which entrusted all kinds of environmental hazards and moral misdemeanours to the judgement of ordinary people.[25] This flexibility meant that the wardmote itself was arranged to reinforce local social hierarchies. Surviving presentments from many wards list nuisances by their separate parish of location, suggesting that the presentation of complaints was organized along parish lines, a unit which in most of the city was probably closer to the neighbourhood in which knowledge of issues circulated than the whole ward.[26] Over the course of the sixteenth century, wards were divided into small precincts, presumably for similar reasons.[27] Furthermore, it was common practice to repeat annually indictments for persistent environmental nuisances or individuals who continued to misbehave, a process that reinforced such local networks of

[24] Barron, 'Lay solidarities', pp. 230–32.

[25] S. Rees Jones, 'The regulation of "nuisance": civic government and the built environment in the medieval city', in *Evolução da Paisagem Urbana: Sociedade e Economia*, ed. M. do C. F. Ribeiro and A. S. Melo (Braga, 2012), pp. 283–94.

[26] This is the case in the surviving Aldersgate returns, LMA, CLC/W/FA/005/MS01499, CLC/W/FA/006/MS01500 and CLC/W/FA/007/MS01501. It is also the case within Bishopsgate, Farringdon Without and Within, Aldersgate, Vintry, Broad Street and Bread Street in the returns in 1421–2. *P&M Rolls*, vol. 4, pp. 116–41.

[27] V. Pearl, 'Change and stability in 17th century London', *London Journal*, v (1979), 3–34, at pp. 16–17.

knowledge. Although Richard Wunderli argued that this repetition shows that the wardmote was an ineffective means of policing the neighbourhood, depositions made at the consistory in fact suggest this repetition served a useful purpose in defining marginal individuals.[28] Martin Ingram argued that the very act of recording offenders on parchment was a valuable part of wider communal policing which might result in harsher punishment down the line.[29] While this may have been a valuable aspect of wardmotes from the view of the alderman, for those who were indicted it was probably not the written record of the event that mattered so much as the popular local memory of their indictment. Counter-witnesses often used memory of indictments at the wardmote as a means to discredit individuals and their testimony. For instance, when a counter-witness accused Henry Fyt of being 'a man of ill fame' in 1529 he substantiated this claim by reference to Fyt's indictment for quarrelling with his neighbours at the wardmote four years previously.[30] Likewise, in 1512, John Saunderson's reliability as a witness was undermined by a counter-witness who recalled that he had been 'compelled to appear before the wardmote inquest' for abusing his wife and turning her out of their house.[31] Fyt and Saunderson's misgovernment of themselves and their households was apparently felt to be material evidence of their unreliability as witnesses, and the memory of their indictment was proof of this. By repeating indictments each year, the wardmote thus attempted to fix this knowledge of character within local networks of knowledge, an appearance before the jury being itself a reputational punishment. Ingram argued that the wardmote and church courts, through referrals from one to the other, were mutually reinforcing.[32] The importance of the memory of indictment further suggests that the wardmote had a significance for punishment within the local community itself, serving as a verification of reputation and in the process legitimating what would otherwise be gossip or rumour about an individual.

The use of repeated indictments also reflected the mutability of reputation. Looking at the various interactions an individual might have with the wardmote shows just how far local reputation was constantly renegotiated. Although Henry Fyt had been indicted for quarrelling with his neighbours

[28] Wunderli, *London Church Courts and Society*, pp. 34–45.

[29] M. Ingram, 'Regulating sex in pre-Reformation London', in *Authority and Consent in Tudor England: Essays Presented to C. S. L. Davies*, ed. G. W. Bernard and S. J. Gunn (Aldershot, 2002), pp. 79–95, at p. 89.

[30] LMA, DL/C/208, fo. 10.

[31] LMA, DL/C/206, fo. 170.

[32] Ingram, 'Regulating sex in pre-Reformation London', pp. 89–90.

in 1525, he also served as a member of the jury in 1528 and 1529, suggesting a degree of rehabilitation before the time of the consistory court case.[33] In this instance, utilization of a previous indictment by a counter-witness sought to fix his character based on an earlier point in time, ignoring the fact that he had apparently (and unusually) overcome the reputational damage of an indictment in the intervening period. Repeating indictments year after year may thus have sought to avoid this kind of use of old judgements, making it clear that there were some individuals who continued to disrupt the neighbourhood while implying that others had amended their ways or left. Nonetheless, a single indictment seems to have had a powerful enough effect in local memory to be useful in the description of reputation a number of years later; it is difficult to imagine how a person without Fyt's long parish residence and householder status, which enabled him to participate positively in the wardmote as a juror, would have recovered their reputation from an indictment.[34] The question of rehabilitation is one which will be returned to in Chapter Five.

The profile of those indicted at the wardmote for their behaviour suggests that those most vulnerable were women. Four of the five most common categories of behavioural indictment were dominated by women: strumpet (eighty-three indictments for women; none for men), scold (fifty-three women; three men), bawd (fifty-two women; twenty-five men) and harlot (thirty-nine women; seven men). Moreover, it is notable that both apparently single women and wives were mentioned in the second most common category of indictment, receiving suspicious people (fifty-nine indictments), even where a husband's legal identity ought to have covered the whole household. Women were thus commonly complained about for a failure to maintain proper control over others and their households. The wardmote was used to express jurors' discomfort about women with power to 'keep ill rule' in their house, no great surprise in the context of an institution that was an expression of masculine moral authority.[35] Women never participated in the jury, were barred from office-holding and, as Shannon McSheffrey has argued, respectable women were defined by their total absence from the wardmote.[36] The only capacity in which women

[33] LMA, Aldersgate Wardmote Book, CLC/W/FA/001/MS02050/001fo. 8v.

[34] See below, p. 151, for the use of the wardmote as a venue for the positive creation of reputation.

[35] S. McSheffrey, 'Jurors, respectable masculinity and Christian morality: a comment on Marjorie McIntosh's "Controlling Misbehavior"', *Journal of British Studies*, xxxvii (1998), 269–78, pp. 270–73.

[36] McSheffrey, 'Jurors, respectable masculinity and Christian morality', p. 272.

legitimately participated in ward procedures was as appointed 'tipplers' (testers) of ale and beer. At Aldersgate in an undated early sixteenth-century presentment, Annes Sawnderson, 'Fereby's wife', 'the good wife Alyn' and Mother Dolbye were among the named tipplers.[37] Most were men but, since brewing could be a domestic activity, tippling was evidently seen as a legitimate extension of female expertise. Male behaviour that attracted wardmote complaints was most likely to centre on a man's failure to govern himself by acting as a baratour, nightwalker or a non-specific 'noyer of neighbours', a trend that fits with contemporary expectations of male behaviour in which, for instance, abusive husbands had to be proved to be incapable of governing themselves (let alone their wives) for a separation to be granted.[38] The wardmote presentments thus indicate gendered patterns of indictment in which women's ability to govern themselves and their households was frequently challenged.

Alongside women, immigrants were another group who dominated indictments. There are indications that many of those who were cited for being a 'foreigner occupying as a freeman' were continental aliens, despite the fact that technically a 'foreigner' was meant to distinguish English non-citizens resident in the city, with 'alien' being the correct term for the legal status of migrants from outside the kingdom. At Portsoken names such as Sote Dutchwoman, John Leflaimder and Michell Milpekkar among the indicted suggest this was the case.[39] The German and Dutch population at Portsoken, which grew across the fifteenth century, was discussed in Chapter One. Conveniently coinciding with the dating of the surviving Portsoken presentments, the mixed reception of this community is suggested by the wardmote records. As well as being indicted for breaching the privileges of the freedom, Portsoken's immigrants seem to have been commonly indicted for disruptive behaviour, although most have to be identified by their Germanic, French or Dutch-sounding names rather than any greater affirmation of their status. Trewde Stutfold and her husband, Thomas, were indicted as common bawds, Margaret Olasson was named a common bawd, Reynold Fremet was a common strumpetmonger and four women given the surname 'Dutchwoman' were indicted for being a leper, a harlot, a strumpet and a bawd.[40] The association between aliens and sexual immorality or disruptive behaviour is borne out in other presentments. Guyse and Willyman Pawnser of Broad Street were

[37] LMA, CLC/W/FA/007/MS01501, dorse.

[38] McSheffrey, *Marriage, Sex and Civic Culture*, pp. 140–42.

[39] Winter, 'Portsoken presentments', pp. 150–55.

[40] Winter, 'Portsoken presentments', pp. 150–55.

accused of keeping a stew in Broad Street at the 1421 wardmote, and in 1422 Gerard Clayson and his wife from Cripplegate Without were accused of an extensive list of offences including being 'evildoers' who received and maintained harlots, bawds, strumpets and 'an evil coven'.[41] Indeed, it may be that prostitutes were often alien immigrants, as was the case in Bruges, where English and other foreign women commonly worked in brothels.[42] In a legal context, where prostitution and other forms of fornication were not distinguished, and where the epithet 'whore' often implied general loose sexual mores rather than definite engagement in prostitution,[43] it is also likely that many of these presentments simply reflect women who were believed to have sex outside marriage or people whose control of dependents' sexuality was lax. Thus, there was considerable room for xenophobia and misogyny, as much as any real connection to the sex trade, to lead to presentation of immigrants.

Nonetheless, what is perhaps surprising about the Portsoken presentments is that, despite a growing community of immigrants, indictments of foreigners trading without the freedom formed only 2–8 per cent of indictments most years, except in 1476, 1479 and 1480, when they were 10–15 per cent, as Figure 4.1 indicates. This suggests that concern tended to fluctuate year on year, independent of sheer immigrant population size; alongside the economic adaptation of the area to serve the alien community demonstrated in Chapter One, it seems that relations were in general cordial though punctuated by occasional concern. In 1508, a new clause was added to the wardmote precepts that no 'stranger born' (another term for alien which became more common in the sixteenth century), even those granted letters of denization, was to be elected to any ward office or wardmote jury.[44] While undoubtedly an example of civic xenophobia, it is striking that it took so long for such a precept to be added; it also suggests that some aliens had actually been elected jurors by their neighbours. At Aldersgate in an early sixteenth-century wardmote presentment there was a mass indictment of aliens, residents in the neighbouring precinct of St Martin le Grand. This was highly unusual for the ward: the other surviving wardmote presentations in this period from Aldersgate contain just two indictments each of foreigners

[41] *P&M Rolls*, vol. 4, p. 154.

[42] E. Spindler, 'Were medieval prostitutes marginals? Evidence from Sluis, 1387–1440', *Revue Belge de philologie et d'histoire*, lxxxvii (2009), 239–72, doi:org/10.3406/rbph.2009.7673, p. 253.

[43] P. J. P. Goldberg, 'Pigs and prostitutes: streetwalking in comparative perspective', in *Young Medieval Women*, ed. K. J. Lewis, N. Menuge and K. M. Philips (Stroud, 1999), pp. 172–93, at pp. 174–5; Bardsley, *Venomous Tongues*, pp. 111–12.

[44] LMA, Jor. 11, fo. 93.

infringing on the freedom: 3–4 per cent of total complaints. The indictment in which multiple aliens are named unfortunately lacks its dating preamble and jury list, which would allow it to be precisely dated, but by chance a presentment mentions the alderman as 'Master [Robert] Fenrother', who held this office from 1512 to 1524. During this period the city was making efforts to challenge the legal basis for the sanctuary at St Martin le Grand, the precinct in which the indicted aliens probably lived, and tensions spilled over when alien-owned shops in St Martin's were attacked on Evil May Day in 1517.[45] The precinct was a long-standing thorn in the side of the city, but local jurors indicted its immigrant residents only in a climate of acute tension in the city over alien craftsmen. Chapter Five considers in more detail the jurisdictional implications of the indictment. Wardmotes were venues where local social priorities were negotiated, influenced by the concerns of individual jurors as well as the social issues subject to civic and royal proclamations at any given time.

The wardmote records thus suggest that those vulnerable to indictment were most often people who challenged gendered conventions of behaviour or whose identity or circumstances made them vulnerable to the present concerns of the jury. As Shannon McSheffrey has argued, the wardmote was a process through which the community defined 'which men were respectable, worthy, and of a certain stature' to the exclusion of those who appeared indicted.[46] This aspect of the wardmote has significant implications for understanding the inquest within the broader context of social marginalization in London neighbourhoods. She noted how the wardmotes allowed middling households to control misbehaviour and impose their own model of respectability on others.[47] As well as determining who was excluded from the community, the inquest was also a public demonstration of the jurors' right and ability to govern, and thus who was included within the 'respectable middle' of local society.

A comparison of the jury lists from Aldersgate and Portsoken wards with the testamentary social networks in Chapter Two suggests the role that the wardmote played in the definition of the respectable portion of a local community. Figures 5.2 and 5.3 show these networks in the periods which coincide with jury lists with those who featured as jurors (or as officers where this information survives at Portsoken) circled in red. Both graphs indicate that those who had served as ward jurors were very likely to be mentioned

[45] S. McSheffrey, 'Stranger artisans and the London sanctuary of St Martin Le Grand in the Reign of Henry VIII', *Journal of Medieval and Early Modern Studies*, xliii (2013), 545–71.

[46] McSheffrey, 'Jurors, respectable masculinity and Christian morality', pp. 271–2.

[47] McSheffrey, 'Jurors, respectable masculinity and Christian morality', pp. 270–71.

by others; all jurors in the Aldersgate network bar one had an in-degree of one or more, as did sixteen out of twenty-four jurors and officials in the Aldgate parish network. Within these limited samples, there is thus a sense that ward jurors were somewhat more likely to be the kind of men trusted by their neighbours to take on important testamentary roles.

Participation in institutions was part of London's *cursus honorum*, the hierarchy of city offices. Both Marjorie McIntosh and Dana Durkee have shown that such participation was a route to the accrual of social capital, the gathering of contacts and the development of cooperative government and financial management skills, the same men often taking on roles in several institutional contexts.[48] Tracing the careers of a number of jurors who also feature in testamentary networks suggests that the wardmote played a specific, early role in the process of accruing social capital. The wealthy bladesmith Richard Stotfold (juror, constable and probable second-generation immigrant) held office or was a ward juror four times between 1474 and 1481. Stotfold's will, dated 1493, named two adult children and one son, John, who was still a minor.[49] It seems reasonable to conjecture that the date of Stotfold's initial involvement in the ward some nineteen years before his death had thus come while his children were still young, within a few years of marrying and becoming a householder. One of the men who named him as witness to their will was Thomas Dalston, a glover, who had served as ward constable in the late 1460s and then as one of the ward's representatives on the city common council ten times from 1470 to 1483, when he died. Another of the men who named Stotfold as witness to their will was John Mansfield, who served on the jury three times in the late 1460s and was then five times constable of the ward in the 1470s. Office-holding within the ward was, as Christine Winter noted in her analysis of the Portsoken presentments, often preceded by a period of jury service.[50] The evidence from Portsoken suggests that participation in a jury could thus be a route to advancement through the holding of local positions of responsibility within the ward itself. All three men would probably have become well known among their neighbours as constables, responsible for the apprehension of local offenders as well as raising the hue and cry

[48] M. K. McIntosh, 'The diversity of social capital in English communities, 1300–1640 (with a Glance at Modern Nigeria)', in *Patterns of Social Capital: Stability and Change in Historical Perspective*, ed. R. I. Rotberg (Cambridge and New York, 2001), pp. 121–52, at pp. 123–8; D. Durkee, 'A cursus for craftsmen? Career cycles of the worsted weavers of late medieval Norwich', in *Cities and Solidarities: Urban Communities in Pre-Modern Europe*, ed. J. Colson and A. van Steensel (Abingdon, 2017), pp. 151–68.

[49] TNA, PROB 11/12/81.

[50] Winter, 'Portsoken presentments', p. 100.

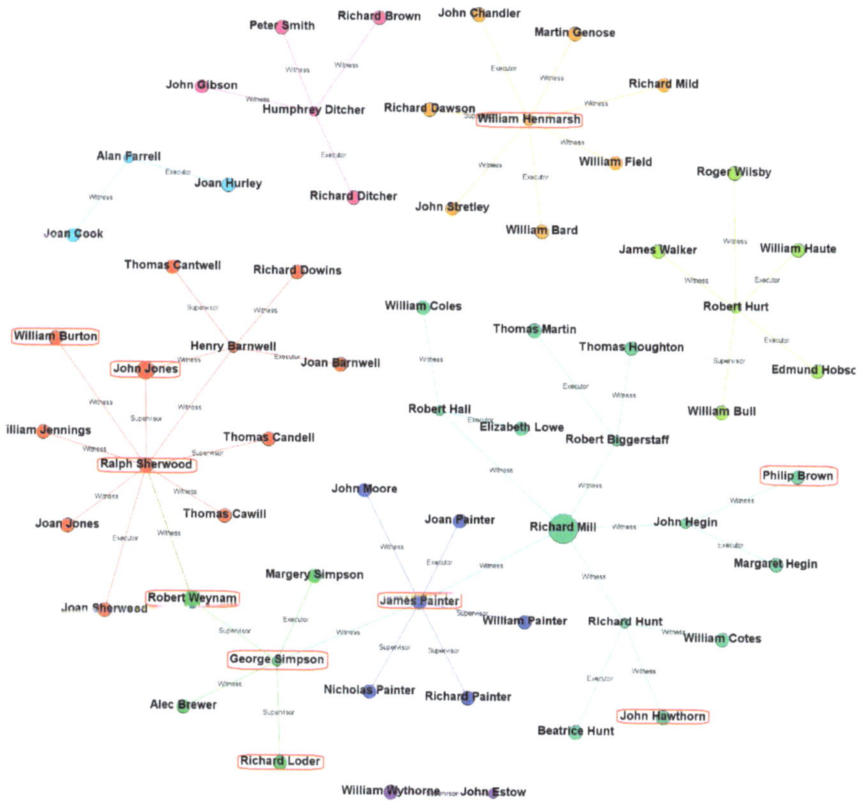

Figure 4.2 St Botolph Aldersgate testamentary network 1515–40 with Aldersgate wardmote jurors highlighted

and organizing juries.[51] The benefits accrued to one's creditworthiness as a result of participation in the jury thus derived both from the opportunity to become acquainted with wealthy and influential men like Stotfold as well as, in the longer term, through progression to greater positions of local respect and responsibility.

Wardmote jury service seems to have been an early rung in the ladder of local office holding, associated with the first few years of householding. Two more constables of Portsoken ward, Philip Thomson, a brewer, and William Pywale, a barber, who also held office in the 1460s and 1470s are shown connected in Figure 4.3. Thomson named Dalston and Pywale as supervisors to his will. Thomson's will was proved in December 1471, just

[51] C. M. Barron, *London in the Later Middle Ages: Government and People, 1200–1500* (Oxford, 2004), pp. 124–5.

Figure 4.3 St Botolph Aldgate testamentary network 1465–95 with Portsoken wardmote jurors highlighted

after his first year as constable of the ward following three stints on the jury in 1466–8. He left an apparently modest estate with just twelve pence set aside to the parish church for forgotten tithes.[52] His will mentions his surviving wife, Hawys, but no children were explicitly named. Comparison between Thomson and Pywale's wills as contemporaries suggests that Thomson died relatively young before having the opportunity to amass much wealth; by contrast, Pywale's will, proved seventeen years later in May 1488, includes twenty shillings for forgotten tithes and detailed requirements for memorial masses and doles to the poor.[53] Thomson thus appears to have died young, before his emerging office-holding career could afford him the success that his testamentary supervisors Dalston and Pywale went on to

52 LMA, DL/C/B/004/MS9171/006, fo. 93.

53 TNA, PROB 11/8/169.

Table 4.2 Aldersgate jury participation, 1467–1540[54]

No. times named as jury member	Total jury members (n)	Proportion of jury members (%)
5+	48	11.9
3–4	50	12.4
2	66	16.4
1	238	59.2
Total	*402*	*100*

achieve. Likewise, Thomas Warren appeared on the jury for the first time in 1479, a year after he married Marion Roke and received her portion of inheritance held as a bond by three prominent Portsoken ward officials, Dalston, Stotfold and Andrew Todd.[55]

While these are all examples of men who successfully navigated wardmote service and accrued social capital, it is important to remember that there was no guarantee that early service led smoothly to higher office. A list of ordinances regulating the behaviour of jurors drawn up by the Aldersgate inquest in 1540 demonstrates that participation in the jury was a test of masculine virtues rather than its proof. The ordinances ranged from not speaking up in favour of offenders while they were being examined to the fines paid if jurors violently confronted one another 'either with weapon or withoute as smyting with hand or fist, violent plucking, wrastling, hurlyng, tearing or punching'.[56] The regulations suggest that, while disagreement was to be expected within the inquest, calm self-government was prized among jurors.[57] This accords well with both McSheffrey's and McIntosh's conceptions of the jury as a space in which social capital was accrued through the demonstration of proper masculine authority. It was not simply through the distinction between those indicted and those who were

[54] Calculated from lists of Aldersgate jurors in LMA, CLC/W/FA/001/MS02050/001, fos. 2–15v.

[55] Marion Roke was the daughter of John Roke, junior, who had served twice as a common councillor for Portsoken. Andrew Todd served as juror, constable and common councillor in the 1470s and 80s. 'Folios 131–140: Nov. 1477', in *Calendar of Letter Books of the City of London: L, Edward IV–Henry VII*, ed. Reginald R. Sharpe (London, 1912), pp. 153–62, *British History Online*, <http://www.british-history.ac.uk/london-letter-books/voll/pp153-162> [accessed 14 July 2016].

[56] LMA, CLC/W/FA/001/MS02050/001, fos. 54v–55.

[57] C. Berry, '"To avoide all envye, malys, grudge and displeasure": sociability and social networking at the London Wardmote Inquest, *c*.1470–1540', *London Journal*, xlii (2017), 201–17, doi:org/10.1080/03058034.2017.1378058, pp. 210–11.

called to jury service that the wardmote shaped inclusion and exclusion but also through the testing of jurors themselves. As Table 4.2 shows, 59.2 per cent of Aldersgate jurors appeared only once during the period 1467–1540, while those who did appear again were more likely to serve three or more times than to remain at just two appearances. At any one time the disparity between the pool of those who served and the number asked back could be more dramatic: of the eighty-seven jurors who served at Aldersgate in 1486–96, sixty-one appeared only once and eleven twice, leaving just fifteen regular members of the inquest in a decade. In this decade, between two and four members of each year's jury reappeared in the next, perhaps to ensure some continuity and memory of the previous year's indictments, as well as oversee the behaviour of more inexperienced jurors.[58] The majority who appeared perhaps failed to meet the required standards of behaviour to be trusted a second time. By governing themselves properly, jurors demonstrated their adherence to dominant values of masculine behaviour, standards which were transgressed by those indicted as offenders.

If a man was successful, wardmote jury service could be a doorway to other kinds of local office-holding and institutional involvement. The parish of St Botolph Aldersgate, which made up most of the geographical extent of Aldersgate ward, left considerable surviving records of both its churchwardens' accounts and the parish fraternity. Between 1468 and 1540, 52.7 per cent of those who featured in the churchwardens' accounts (either as wardens or as parishioners who were expected to sign off the accounts) were also Aldersgate wardmote jurors.[59] The timelines of involvement for many of these men suggest that acting as a juror was a precursor to parochial office. Robert Woodhouse served five times as a member of the ward inquest between 1490 and 1501 and was then churchwarden four times between 1501 and his death in office sometime in 1504 or 1505. Similarly, Roger Russell served twice on the jury in the 1470s and went on to be churchwarden in 1483–4 and another four times in the early 1500s, including serving as deputy for Woodhouse in the year of the latter's death. When Russell died around 1513 he was a wealthy enough man to be commemorated in one of the windows in St Botolph Aldersgate's parish church.[60]

[58] LMA, CLC/W/FA/001/MS02050/001, fos. 2–2v.

[59] Drawn from St Botolph Aldersgate churchwardens accounts, 1468–1506, LMA, P69/BOT1/B/013/MS01454/002-025.

[60] Patricia Basing, 'Introduction', in *Parish Fraternity Register: Fraternity of the Holy Trinity and SS Fabian and Sebastian (Parish of St Botolph without Aldersgate)*, ed. Patricia Basing (London, 1982), pp. vii–xxviii, *British History Online*, <http://www.british-history.ac.uk/london-record-soc/vol18/vii-xxviii> [accessed 17 Aug. 2016].

In joining the jury a new householder might expect to meet men who formed part of the parish elite that steered local decision-making. Wardmote service thus served as a route for making connections with the respectable men of the neighbourhood. For the successful, this could result in building the social capital necessary to progress to a prominent local role as churchwarden or, indeed, to take on greater responsibility in the ward as an officer and perhaps eventually a common councilman. Even for the many who do not appear to have been involved in other institutions, participation in the wardmote may have been socially useful. Just as Dana Durkee has shown juries to be essential venues for young Norwich weavers looking to establish their businesses, so too would the London wardmote have provided young men with important connections.[61] As well as economic benefits, these men could prove to be important allies and witnesses in the event of an individual becoming subject to accusations in the church or civic courts, or be sureties to debts, and so access to them in itself could have positive social and economic benefits. In the act of judgement of their neighbours, jurors could display their sound governance and adherence to conventional morality in the presence of an influential group of men. Ultimately, the successful juror might expect to earn his own place among the worthy of the neighbourhood. In London's *cursus honorum*, wardmote jury service was a small step, less time-consuming than full office-holding, and yet participation formed part of one of the routes to advancement.

It was not just participation in the wardmote which made the difference to a man's career, but how he conducted himself within it. As discussed below, the right of an individual to participate in the jury could be challenged, and the wardmote was an early opportunity for men to demonstrate their capacity to exercise authority, a venue in which they often seem not to have succeeded. The wardmote was therefore a very active part of processes of marginalization and social capital formation, where both the jury and the offenders presented were subject to assessment of their reputation. For the jurors, the good governance they demonstrated at the wardmote might transfer into informal authority in policing the neighbourhood throughout the year, as the following section will discuss. Becoming 'central' to the neighbourhood group was no linear process but a negotiation involving the accrual of social capital in which there was no hard-and-fast boundary between the local elite and the rest. This is a theme to which Chapter Five returns because, as it implies, marginality itself was negotiated rather than fixed

[61] Durkee, 'A cursus for craftsmen?', pp. 158–9.

'Wo worth them that gave me towncell first to go to the law': informal mediation

On a day-to-day level, the punishment of disruptive behaviour in the neighbourhood fell to a combination of ward officers and informal attempts to ostracize individuals and mediate between neighbours. Control of behaviour operated through ongoing, local exertions of power of which formal punishment through the courts might just be a part or endpoint. The detailed depositions of the consistory court are excellent sources for these forms of local control which might otherwise easily slip under the historians' radar. Deponents recounted the investigations of constables and the interventions of concerned friends as ways to substantiate their narratives or assessments of character. The depositions reveal that ward officers and jurors brought their accrued social capital to bear on informal modes of reconciliation and that legal redress might be the result of the failure of such informal processes.

The role of the officials appointed by the ward – the constables and beadles – were formally defined and yet relied on informal interpersonal relationships to carry out their duties. The 1488 deposition of John Calton recalled an incident seventeen years earlier when he, the constable of the liberty of St John, was asked by a local man named Wulley to apprehend the Wulleys' son Thomas, who was fornicating with a local girl in a neighbour's house.[62] By calling the constable on his own son, perhaps the intended result was for Wulley to preserve the family's reputation by publicly expressing his disapproval of his son's actions and demonstrating his own continued adherence to communally expected standards of behaviour. Collecting a party of neighbours into a 'watch' to assist a constable in an arrest was normal process,[63] a further indication of the blurred line between formal and informal exercise of authority.

Women had no formal access to local authority but occasionally they were able to influence its exercise, despite contemporary norms of gender and governance. At the parish of St Andrew Hubbard in 1533, two women were alleged to have said they were determined to see their neighbour, Katharine Mett, expelled from the parish and together with their husbands set about petitioning their alderman.[64] In the consistory case against Mett, it was female rivalries that drove her marginalization, despite the plaintiff and his witnesses all being male. Deponent Henry Rolf told the consistory that

[62] 'Deposition of John Calton', *Consistory Database* <http://consistory.ca/obj.php?p=796>, [accessed 3 March 2017].

[63] Ingram, *Carnal Knowledge*, p. 222.

[64] LMA, DL/C/208 unnumbered folio, deposition of Fulk Pygott, 21 Jan. 1533.

'the wives of those witnesses [for the plaintiff] and Katharine are enemies'.[65] Although women were excluded from the wardmote, female social networks nonetheless could appeal to men with formal and informal policing power to ostracize individuals. This is one of the ways in which authority could be exercised by households rather than just male householders, thus giving women a stake in the operation of formal authority, which was notionally masculine. What we see in consistory depositions is perhaps just a glimpse of the extent of women's informal local power to make or break the reputations of their neighbours.

Even when exercised by men, informal attempts to admonish neighbours could be highly divisive. One case reveals that the activities of ward officers could be both partisan in their execution and contentious in their outcomes. In 1529 Thomas Hoskyns, constable of Aldersgate ward, was encouraged to raid the alehouse of Henry Fyt by the carpenter William Bowser.[66] Sixty-year-old Bowser had sat on the Aldersgate wardmote jury six times during the 1510s and 1520s, including in the year before the case was heard.[67] It was claimed by Fyt that Bowser harboured grudges against a number of the men and women who had been drinking together in Fyt's house that evening, including the target of his arrest and eventual consistory plaintiff Dorothy Swyndon.[68] In this example we see the potentially blurred line between formal and informal management of the community, with Bowser apparently exploiting his seniority and connections to encourage punishment of those he personally deemed disruptive. As shall be discussed further, this case had a complex history in both the consistory court and local attempts at arbitration. The consistory case emerged from a situation where neighbours, friends and fellow jurors were at odds, and the act of witnessing itself engendered further divisions. The line between formal and informal control was not fixed, it had to be contested, and both forms of managing community might fail to produce concord.

William Bowser was by no means extraordinary in expecting to manage local concerns beyond the formal setting of a court. Certain senior individuals within a community expected to take a leading role in mediating relationships between their neighbours. Thomas Wornegey, a mercer of St Katharine Cree, deposed at the consistory in a case which concerned defamatory accusations of fornication in 1475. Wornegey stated that he had warned a young man named Thomas Hay 'not to resort to the house of

65 LMA, DL/C/208, unnumbered folio, deposition of Henry Rolf, 22 Jan. 1533.

66 LMA, DL/C/208, fos. 36v–37, 38–38v.

67 LMA, CLC/W/FA/001/MS02050/001, fos. 7–8v.

68 LMA, DL/C/208, fos. 36v–37.

Agnes Howell because of the suspicion that many men had against him due to the manner of his evening visits'.[69] Although Hay angrily rejected his advice, Wornegey evidently felt a responsibility for advising Hay to watch his behaviour. Similarly, the grocer Robert Haskyn deposed in 1474 that Agnes Roger, who he stood as witness for, could not have contracted a marriage as the plaintiff alleged 'because … if the said Agnes had intended that [marriage] then Agnes would have spoken to this witness'.[70] Personal status probably played a role in both men's sense of responsibility. Both Wornegey and Haskyn were older men (Wornegey described himself as over forty at the time of his deposition, and Haskyn was forty-eight) with prestigious mercantile occupations. Their age and status were very similar to those of the 'trustworthy men' described by Forrest who were relied upon by bishops as local administrators, arbitrators and agents of church business.[71] These men expected their advice to be respected and sought by their neighbours. In these examples, we can see something of the boundary between the formal and informal exertion of authority within the neighbourhood. The same kind of men who offered this personal advice were those who joined wardmote juries to judge their neighbours.

Local, informal networks of arbitration allowed such men to exercise their personal judgement in a way which enhanced their own power. This kind of solution to disputes might well have been preferable to the processes of a deposition court such as the consistory in which counter-witnesses called into question the status of each party's deponents. Returning to the case of Swyndon c. Hoskyns provides evidence of both the damage depositions could do and local attempts at arbitration. During the original testimonies, Henry Fyt had recounted his neighbour William Bowser's affair with a servant as evidence of Bowser's poor character. He knew the story because Bowser had asked him to be godfather to the child born as a result, suggesting a past friendship between the two men which his deposition can only have damaged.[72] Fyt himself found his reputation challenged by counter-witnesses through reference to a previous wardmote indictment, as discussed above. The rehearsal of embarrassing histories was very likely damaging to local relationships, especially when the reputation of a prominent man such as Bowser was called into question. As we saw in Chapter Three, the process of giving counter-testimony often exploited local forms of knowledge about reputation, particularly of those who were known to be highly mobile. However, as the case in question shows,

[69] LMA, DL/C/205, fo. 308v.

[70] LMA, DL/C/205, fo. 239.

[71] Forrest, *Trustworthy Men*, pp. 133–6.

[72] LMA, DL/C/208, fo. 14v.

counter-testimony at the consistory might also undermine the basis on which individuals claimed to be respectable among their neighbours. In January 1531, nearly two years after the original depositions, the case returned to the consistory. The witnesses who appeared this time attested to a local mediation process which they thought had resolved the dispute. In October 1530 several local men called a meeting with Dorothy Swyndon and 'warned Dorothy for her to cause an amicable conclusion' to the case.[73] With the intercession of the parish curate, an agreement was drawn up that she would be paid ten shillings to withdraw her suit.[74] Swyndon was said to have exclaimed 'wo worth them that gave me cowncell first to go to the law'.[75] This exclamation, whether real reported speech or a legal fiction, seems to express a communal regret at the damage a messy consistory case could wreak to social relations. By contrast, informal resolutions avoided both expense to the parties and the potential embarrassment to the whole community which could be brought about by a consistory case. Such a case posed a threat to those who exerted local decision-making power, unlike informal resolutions, in which they could demonstrate and extend that authority.

Ecclesiastical courts and the failure of informal mediation

If a consistory case risked undermining the basis on which local respectable men asserted informal power, why did they resort to them at all? Litigants in the consistory had to pay for advocates and, in marriage cases at least, were most likely to have a comfortable standard of living[76] – that is, precisely the group that had the most to lose through exposure of their behaviour to counter-witnessing and the most to gain by resort to informal policing or their formalized roles within the wardmote. An answer seems to be offered by cases such as Swyndon c. Hoskyns, where more localized mechanisms of mediation and marginalization had failed. Although eventually Dorothy Swyndon was called to resolve her dispute by mutual agreement, the complex history of the case and its counter-testimonies suggests that it was originally born out of a situation of considerable communal discord in which even the local trustworthy men were at odds. Likewise, in the defamation case of Kyrkham c. Mett, a witness argued that the suit was brought because the plaintiff was persuaded by a neighbour:

[73] LMA, DL/C/208, fo. 179v.

[74] LMA, DL/C/208, fo. 186v.

[75] LMA, DL/C/208, fo. 183.

[76] P. J. P. Goldberg, 'Fiction in the archives: the York Cause papers as a source for later medieval social history', *Continuity and Change*, xii (1997), 425–45, at pp. 427–9.

> rather thene the mater should stope thus (menyng by way of entreatie) he wold complain hier [the consistory] and make all that ever he cowld rather then she shuld skape unpunyshed.[77]

The case came after a number of appeals to the alderman for the same woman to be expelled were ignored.[78] The vagaries of informal resolutions, reliant as they were on the personal exercise of authority and unspoken overlaps between ward and parish administration, meant that they were likely to be partial and influenced by local factions. The wardmote's non-specific indictments against those who were 'noyers of their neighbours' may also have driven victims to become consistory plaintiffs. Similarly, those who felt troublesome neighbours were getting off lightly from ex officio cases at the commissary court could escalate to a personal suit to the consistory.[79] Those who felt aggrieved by or dissatisfied with informal policing or communal accusations at the wardmote or commissary court could instead turn to the consistory as a legal mechanism that bypassed local networks, albeit at some personal risk of reputation through the process of counter-witnessing. Most suits in the consistory were party-and-party, enabling the pursuit of personal animosities. Even the lower commissary court was shifting towards a far larger number of party-and-party suits in the early sixteenth century, suggesting the increasing popularity of this kind of redress.[80] In Hoskyns c. Swyndon, key witnesses switched sides away from Dorothy Swyndon when she attempted to revive her case two years later, suggesting that in the end the power of local informal authority was reasserted and few wanted to risk their reputation with a repeat of the mud-slinging of the earlier depositions.

Divisions within the group who exerted informal power thus necessitated the removal of disputes from the neighbourhood, and the consistory provided a useful (if risky) outlet. For instance, in 1523 there was dissension over the choice of jurors for the wardmote in Farringdon Within. At the selection of grocer Roger Wryght as a juror, several witnesses claimed that Roger Newesse called 'nay he ys nott worthy to have yt' and, when asked why, Newesse said, 'ye shall knowe ferder here after for there ys a padde yn the strawe', meaning a lurking danger.[81] Newesse resolutely refused to

[77] LMA, DL/C/208, unnumbered folio, deposition of Henry Rolf, 22 Jan. 1533.

[78] LMA, DL/C/208 unnumbered folio, deposition of Fulk Pygott, 21 Jan. 1533.

[79] Wunderli, *London Church Courts and Society*, p. 41.

[80] Ingram, *Carnal Knowledge*, pp. 194–5.

[81] LMA, DL/C/207, fo. 270v; 'pad, n.1.', *OED online* <www.oed.com/view/Entry/135885> [accessed 22 Nov. 2017].

clarify what he meant by this,[82] but nonetheless rumours spread about Wryght's wife.[83] Wryght launched a defamation suit against Newesse in the consistory court in an attempt to defend his wife's reputation, dispel the doubt which Newesse had sowed about his character and, implicitly, regain his potential future status as a wardmote juror. Unusually, it is possible to evidence the causes of Newesse's accusations. Wryght and his wife, Constance, had reputations for illicit sexual behaviour: Constance successfully sued for defamation a women who called her a priest's whore in 1516, and Roger was indicted at the Queenhithe wardmote in 1520 for keeping a stew in that ward.[84] At the time of his consistory case, Wright would have been about thirty years old, just the age when men seeking an office-holding career would expect to sit as wardmote jurors and thus want to guard their reputations against these past incidents.[85] A consistory court case could result from either a failure of informal local arbitration or from a division among those who would normally exert local power, or both. Furthermore, the intertwining of personal standing, informal and formal policing power meant that the choice of venue to pursue grievances might be differentiated by status: Wryght needed to protect his position as a juror and chose a defamation suit as a route to achieve that aim. As Chapter Five will discuss further, defence of reputation was necessary for most Londoners in order to maintain stable home and friendships but could be achieved by very different means for those who did not expect to exert local power.

Alternative authorities outside the walls

So far this chapter has been concerned with the mechanisms of policing that prevailed throughout London. As we have seen, the neighbourhood was central and the ward court allowed neighbours to set local priorities, suggesting at least a degree of differentiation across the city. There were also alternative authorities in the extramural neighbourhoods of London which complicated the range of actors exerting social power and the apprehension and punishment of those deemed to have violated acceptable standards. The manner in which urban space beyond the walls offered opportunities for

[82] LMA, DL/C/207, fo. 271.

[83] LMA, DL/C/207, fo. 271v.

[84] LMA, COL/CA/01/01/005, Repertory of the Court of Aldermen, 1519–1522, fo. 100v; Westminster Abbey Muniments, MS 13294. I am grateful to Shannon McSheffrey for these references.

[85] His age is estimated from a later deposition given in 1537, when he said, at an inquest into the boundaries of sanctuary at St Martin le Grand, that he was forty-five. TNA, STAC 2/20/323, mm. 6–9.

evading the consequences of illicit behaviour is a topic for Chapter Five, but these alternative poles of authority and understandings of neighbourhood have an important bearing on how the formal and informal modes of authority set out here operated in extramural areas.

Space was a meaningful dimension to the definition of community and so to the exercise of exclusion. In a 1521 defamation case, Thomas Hodgson was said to have exclaimed to Margaret Fyfeld 'thow skotts drab I will bere never a shert to my back but I will have thy husband owte of this strete'.[86] Hodgson's insistence that it was the street that he wanted to see the Fyfelds leave suggests that senses of community, and thus instances of marginalization, could be highly localized. St John Street, where the parties lived, was the centre of an occupational community (the butchery trade, attached to nearby Smithfield market) as well as a liberty.[87] However, senses of community and jurisdictional boundaries might not always overlap. Sometimes witnesses spoke of expelling people from their parish even though, technically, expulsion was enacted at the ward level.[88] The physical proximity of fellow parishioners and the collective experience of worship probably meant that the parish was closer to a sense of neighbourhood in most parts of the city than a ward, although, as discussed in Chapter Three, senses of community in extramural space might be very flexible. Therefore, the legal inaccuracy of statements about expulsion 'from the parish' probably reflects a perception of the spatial bounds of the community from which an individual was to be removed rather than a strict technical understanding of local jurisdiction.

Beyond the walls, the presence of religious houses and particularly their attendant liberties provided alternative poles of formal authority and complications to the bounds of communal control. As we saw in Chapter Three, in the neighbourhood outside Bishopsgate people from a wide area encompassing Bishopsgate Street, the liberty of Norton Folgate and the precinct of the hospital of St Mary all seem to have been aware of one

[86] LMA, DL/C/207, fo. 58.

[87] St John Street was one of the exempt places named by the city in a 1455 proclamation against those citizens who lived in liberties. LMA, Jor. 5, fo. 260. It also occasionally operated as sanctuary, deriving this status from its ownership by the Knights Hospitaller. S. McSheffrey, *Seeking Sanctuary: Crime, Mercy and Politics in English Courts, 1400–1550* (Oxford and New York, 2017), pp. 99–102.

[88] See the case of Katherine Mett, discussed above at p. 118, and Cockerel c. Bennett, as discussed in C. Berry, '"Go to hyr neybors wher she dwelte before": reputation and mobility at the London consistory court in the early sixteenth century', in *Medieval Londoners: Essays to Mark the Eightieth Birthday of Caroline M. Barron*, ed. E. A. New and C. Steer (London, 2019), pp. 95–116, doi:org/10.2307/j.ctvc16qcm.14.

another's comings and goings. The formal boundaries between the three are somewhat hazy in the records and were perhaps ambiguous on the ground. The legal basis and boundaries of Norton Folgate's liberty are obscure; while the manor itself dated to at least the eleventh century, the area considered a liberty was smaller and seems to have consisted only of the parts within the precinct of the hospital of St Mary east of Bishopsgate Street, established in the late twelfth century.[89] The legal situation was ambiguous even to contemporaries. In 1501, a terrible incident involving the rape and murder of two young girls was presented by the Norton Folgate view of frankpledge jury to the court of the king's bench in Southwark. However, the defendants (who included the prior of St Mary's Hospital alongside the men accused of direct involvement) claimed that the case could not be heard because 'there is no such town, hamlet, or other place called Seyntmaryspetyll where the aforesaid felony was said to have been committed'.[90] This is a curious defence which suggests that there was an unclear relationship between the manor and liberty known as Norton Folgate and the status of the hospital within it.

It was a busy place, and the manor's officials were kept occupied with the misdeeds of incomers at least as much if not more than those of its hundred or so residents. As part of his duties the constable arrested suspected felons for offences committed outside Norton Folgate. In 1445 an unnamed man was arrested by the manor's constable on suspicion of theft because he was carrying 300 smoked eels worth 16d. The suspected thief was subsequently taken to jail at Finsbury, Middlesex.[91] In 1455, constables apprehended a London apprentice wanted within the city for theft from his master.[92] These wanted men may have simply been passing through on their escape from the city, but many others cited in the court rolls deliberately came to Norton Folgate for recreation. The small manor housed numerous alehouses and bowling alleys which brought in people from the city and surrounding areas to drink, socialize and occasionally get into trouble. In 1448, three people all

[89] 'The manor and liberty of Norton Folgate', in *Survey of London: Volume 27, Spitalfields and Mile End New Town*, ed. F. H. W. Sheppard (London, 1957), 15–20. British History online <http://www.british-history.ac.uk/survey-london/vol27/pp15-20> [accessed 16 Feb. 2021].

[90] TNA, KB 27/0960, m. 14. *Anglo-American Legal Tradition* <http://aalt.law.uh.edu/AALT5/H7/KB27no960/aKB27no960fronts/IMG_0226.htm> [accessed 16 Feb. 2021].

[91] Manor court and view of frankpledge of Norton Folgate held 29 June 1445, LMA, CLC/313/A/047/MS25287, rot. 3.

[92] William Tanner, apprentice to Richard Clerk, joiner, of St Sepulchre, was apprehended by the constable of Norton Folgate with three gold nobles stolen from his master. Manor court and view of frankpledge held 29 June 1455, CLC/313/A/047/MS25287, rot. 4 dorse.

described as living in Shoreditch were fined for affray in Norton Folgate, and there were repeated indictments for keeping 'closhbanes', alleys for a Dutch form of bowling, and for brewing.[93] Norton Folgate's residents used the manor court to name the troublemakers who came from its surroundings, like John Deraunt of Golding Lane, Middlesex, who attacked a man with a bill hook, and John Gebon, gentleman, of London, who made affray against William Drayton of Tottenham, another gentleman, all in incidents within Norton Folgate in 1461.[94] The manor court records do not appear to make distinctions between parts of the manor deemed a liberty and those not, and it seems that Norton Folgate was no clearly segregated liberty but a space moved to and through by outsiders with freedom.

Aside from the officers of liberties, in extramural neighbourhoods the religious houses could exert power over social relations. In part this came from their extensive local landholding: we have already seen in Chapter One how religious houses might be the landlords for significant parts of their neighbourhood. This authority went even further in Portsoken ward, where the prior of Holy Trinity acted as alderman, but religious houses and their officers could also exert informal power over local laity. For example, the marriage of Joan Floraunce of St Botolph Aldgate to Robert Partridge appears to have been mediated by the abbot of St Mary Graces at Tower Hill. Henry Chamberley, servant of the abbot, presided over the creation of the contract in Joan's yard, asking her, 'how say ye Johan, ar ye the same woman that ye wer an as ye promised my lord abbot of Towr Hill?'[95] The contract appears unusual in the profile of its witnesses as well as in the apparent resistance of Joan's friends. Most witnesses were outsiders to the parish; one of them was apparently a cleric as he lived within the city's Whittington college. The witnesses in favour of the marriage to Partridge revealed that a servant girl who objected was detained in another room while Joan swore to the contract in the yard.[96] The servant was not the only one of Joan's acquaintances hostile to the match, and three local witnesses appeared in favour of a rival suitor who claimed pre-contract with Joan.[97] A contemporary rental of the abbey's

[93] In 1448, three people all described as living in Shoreditch were fined for affray in Norton Folgate. Manor court and view of frankpledge held 29 June 1485, LMA, CLC/313/A/047/MS25287, rot. 3 dorse. See eg the indictment of Herman Yonker for playing of closh in his yard and his indictment the same year for brewing against the assize. Manor court and view of frankpledge held 29 June 1458, LMA, CLC/313/A/047/MS25287, rot. 5.

[94] Manor court and view of frankpledge held 29 June 1461, LMA, CLC/313/A/047/MS25287, rot. 5 dorse.

[95] LMA, DL/C/208, fos. 81v–82, 85.

[96] LMA, DL/C/208, fos. 81v–86.

[97] LMA, DL/C/208, fos. 63v–65v, 69v–70.

London estates shows that Robert Partridge, the bridegroom, was a tenant of the abbey of St Mary Graces in East Smithfield and thus of the aforesaid 'lord abbot of Towr Hill'. Other probable tenants of the abbey's estate, John Colfox and Henry Chamberley, witnessed the contract.[98] The marriage contract thus seems to have been arranged under the influence of the abbot, using the mediation of at least one wealthy tenant to bring pressure on the couple to contract and bear witness. This kind of authority is comparable to that of respectable local laymen, like the mercer mentioned above who expected a local widow would consult him about her remarriage, suggesting that through their role as landowners and employers the heads of religious houses could exert some pressure on those in their localities.

For Joan Floraunce, this relationship with a religious house may have been rather one-sided. However, more prominent tenants could turn this role to their own advantage. As has been argued of Westminster Abbey, the relationship between a religious house and a wealthy tenant could be mutually beneficial, and so the abbot viewed tenants as potentially influential friends in the laity.[99] It was perhaps this kind of relationship which led to the prior of Holy Trinity Aldgate evicting William Smyth and his family from a substantial property in St Botolph Aldgate in August 1510 in favour of William Culverden, a wealthy bellfounder and wardmote jurist whom the prior would have known through his role as Portsoken alderman.[100] Smyth refused to leave the house and launched a campaign of abuse against Culverden, which resulted in a defamation case at the consistory, where many witnesses recounted Smyth's dramatic eviction.[101] Culverden was presumably able to pay higher rents than Smyth and exploited the connections he had with the prior to get a property that he wanted. In this case, the ability of a religious house to favour certain residents over others was a source of disharmony. In Chapter Three, a case where the prior of St Mary's hospital, Bishopsgate, sued a former employee named Robert Pellet was discussed. The case shows another example of religious houses' local

[98] Rental of the estates of the abbey of St Mary Graces, 1523–9, TNA SC 12/11/43. Robert Partridge was a tenant in East Smithfield in 1528. John Colfax was a tenant in the parish of All Hallows Staining 1524–9. Henry Chamberley, servant to the abbot, may be the Henry Chamber or Chambers who appears as a tenant in East Smithfield 1524–9.

[99] B. F. Harvey, 'Westminster abbey and Londoners, 1440–1540', in *London and the Kingdom: Essays in Honour of Caroline M. Barron*, ed. M. P. Davies and A. Prescott, Harlaxton Medieval Studies, 16 (Donington, 2008), pp. 12–37, at pp. 20–21.

[100] William Culverden featured as a witness in another consistory case deposing about incidents that happened when he was on the Portsoken ward jury. LMA, DL/C/206, fo. 20v.

[101] LMA, DL/C/206, fos. 37v–39, 44–6.

power as landowners in that thirteen Bishopsgate residents, including two tenants of the hospital, were lined up to testify against Pellet. The close economic ties between religious houses and their local neighbourhoods, discussed in Chapter One, fed into local power dynamics in complex ways.

It would be reductive, however, to say that religious houses played a purely coercive role in the lives of individuals on the fringes of the city. The local laity were able to contest the local authority of religious houses and even royal liberties. The wardmote, with its malleable agenda, was an opportunity to do so. The wardmote jurors of Portsoken were particularly vociferous in their opposition to the neighbouring abbey of St Mary Graces, hospital of St Katherine and the royal Tower liberty. Their complaints centred on access to the river Thames by the ward's inhabitants: disputes over river access were recurrent features of Portsoken wardmote presentment from 1370 until the 1470s. Complaints were raised against the constable of the Tower for charging Londoners for access to the river stairs and against the master of St Katharine's hospital for similarly charging wharfage or for blocking the highway to the hospital's water mill.[102] These presentments suggest resistance to religious and royal precincts' liberties and that, alongside their power as landowners, came a degree of local resentment. In addition to the tensions inherent in the exercise of informal power in the neighbourhood, the religious houses were another source of authority in marginal neighbourhoods. While this secular power might be contested, we should not underestimate the deep spiritual relationships expressed between laity and extramural houses which were present in the wills discussed in Chapter Two. It was a complex relationship and, as we shall see in Chapter Five, the laity were able to make use of religious houses' precincts as spaces for evading sanction of their behaviour.

In a face-to-face society, detection of unwanted behaviour relied on the eyes and ears of neighbours as well as on their judgement of what constituted antisocial activity. As a result, the process of identifying offenders could in fact boost the reputations of those whom it involved, in turn enhancing their ability to participate in the informal exercise of authority over neighbours that would have suffused community life. The bounds of acceptable behaviour were set, and continually adapted, by neighbours. Chapter Five turns to the reverse of this process: the ways in which those who found themselves marginalized responded to authority and managed

[102] 'Roll A 18: 1372-73', in *Calendar of the Plea and Memoranda Rolls of the City of London: Volume 2, 1364–1381*, ed. A. H. Thomas (London, 1929), pp. 150–62, in *British History Online* <http://www.british-history.ac.uk/plea-memoranda-rolls/vol2/pp150-162> [accessed 15 Aug. 2017]; Winter, 'Portsoken presentments', p. 125.

their reputation as a means to either avoid the consequences of their marginalization or achieve rehabilitation.

These were processes which affected everybody, not just those whom we might consider to be classic marginal groups. Marginalization happened along a sliding scale, but the experience of the disadvantage of personal status was situational and fluctuating. As was demonstrated in Chapter Three, gender, status and place of origin all factored into judgements of individual character. As we shall see Chapter Five, they also influenced the possible extent of rehabilitation. People who aspired to inclusion in the office-holding section of local society could find themselves excluded because their reputation and behaviour were subject to just as much scrutiny as others, particularly when they sat on the wardmote jury. All were engaged in negotiating their position in society, improvising in response to the situations that faced them. Social marginality was therefore not a status that was simply assigned based solely on membership of a group, with everyone else automatically included in the local community by default. Marginality was contingent on individual behaviour, status, gender and background, as well as on the social resources which an individual could bring to bear when faced with a challenge to their behaviour or their right to live in a neighbourhood.

The relationship that individuals had with institutions of social control also had a significant impact on how likely they were to find themselves effectively marginalized. For men of sufficient social status, participation in local ward juries reinforced their reputation. For others, their relationship to institutions was more complicated. Women were formally excluded and yet they could evidently have influence on community management, although this would greatly depend on their social connections to the men who participated formally. For others, exclusion from institutions meant having to negotiate their inclusion in local society through alternative means, as we shall see in Chapter Five. In liberties and extramural neighbourhoods with powerful local religious houses a different set of institutions affected people's lives and could exert personal and coercive power in a manner similar to the ward officers whose power also rested on a mix of the institutional and the informal.

5. Reputation, marginalization and space

Underlying all forms of punishment in late medieval London was an understanding that those who had transgressed communal norms would and should be publicly recognized and known. The denunciation of offenders at the wardmote inquest or ritual penances before a Sunday congregation required by the church courts aimed both to warn the offender against further transgressions and to fix knowledge of their wrongdoing among neighbours. We have already seen in Chapter Three how, in the most extreme cases, a poor reputation could make it difficult for a Londoner to maintain a stable home, as they might face expulsion from their ward. This chapter demonstrates how people engaged in the defence or rehabilitation of their reputations: in effect, how those who faced civic punishment or neighbourly approbation could reintegrate themselves into local society. Central to the argument is that strategies of reintegration depended on the subtleties of social and spatial difference in the city. Gradations of social status determined how people mitigated or avoided loss of reputation. Spatial difference was also important to the defence of reputation: illicit rubbish-dumping and the running of brothels could be undertaken on the jurisdictional and geographic peripheries of London with less risk of punishment. The consequences of embarrassing moral transgressions such as illicit pregnancies and coerced marriages could be confined to religious houses and hospitals as a way to evade the local rumour mill. The workings of marginalization thus had a direct impact on the uses of London's spatial periphery.

Gossip, fama *and marginality*

In a largely oral society, gossip was an important means through which reputations were made; a person's local fame (or *fama*, in the Latin of court records) was frequently used in court to substantiate or undermine them. We saw in Chapter Three how histories of mobility could be used in the consistory court to undermine parties or witnesses.[1] Knowledge about past behaviour and character was spread through gossip, which, according to anthropologists, flourishes best in 'close-knit, highly connected social

[1] See above, p. 113.

networks' with shared notions of proper behaviour.[2] Gossip has been considered by sociologists as primarily a concern of those in the middle of the social hierarchy competing for social capital.[3] However, Sandy Bardsley's study of scolding accusations in late medieval England suggests that participation in speech that aimed to marginalize was widespread across the social hierarchy.[4] Gossip needs to be understood in the broader context of late medieval cities, which were, as Christian Liddy argues, 'surveillance societies, in which townspeople habitually watched each other and reported their activities for the benefit of government'.[5] That reporting was horizontal, that is, among neighbours, as much as vertical: speech about, for example, sexual reputation was used to crystallize public opinion about those with a poor reputation which could then form the basis for further action.[6] Within an area of dense population such as London and its region, the knowledge created by gossip would have circulated in small local areas rather than across the whole city.[7] It was within the neighbourhood that character was best known and people could exploit local mechanisms of knowledge sharing and publicity to shame others or negotiate their own reputations.[8] As we have seen in previous chapters, the formal mechanisms for exclusion and marginalization in London largely centred on local units such as the ward and the parish and relied on the knowledge that circulated within them to identify and punish offenders.

The importance of neighbourhood in developing and defending reputation was a key social continuity from the medieval to the early modern city, crucial as it is to Tim Reinke-Williams's analysis of how women cultivated good reputation, and thus support networks, in the latter

[2] S. Engle Merry, 'Rethinking gossip and scandal', in *Reputation: Studies in the Voluntary Elicitation of Good Conduct*, ed. D. B. Klein (Ann Arbor, Mich., 1997), pp. 47–74, at pp. 52–3.

[3] Engle Merry, 'Rethinking gossip and scandal', p. 48.

[4] S. Bardsley, *Venomous Tongues: Speech and Gender in Late Medieval England* (Philadelphia, 2011), pp. 133–7.

[5] C. Liddy, 'Cultures of surveillance in late medieval English towns: the monitoring of speech and the fear of revolt', in *The Routledge History Handbook of Medieval Revolt*, ed. J. Firnhaber-Baker and D. Schoenaers (London, 2019).

[6] M. Ingram, *Carnal Knowledge: Regulating Sex in England, 1470–1600* (Cambridge and New York, 2017), pp. 69–74.

[7] T. Johnson, *Law in Common: Legal Cultures in Late medieval England* (Oxford and New York, 2020), pp. 188–9.

[8] E. Spindler, 'Marginality and social relations in London and the Bruges area, 1370–1440' (unpublished University of Oxford DPhil thesis, 2008), pp. 217–18.

period.[9] Participation in marginalization was itself part of the making of reputation in both late medieval and early modern communities, as we saw in the careers of wardmote jurors in Chapter Four.[10] All Londoners were engaged in negotiating their own reputation through interactions with formal and informal authority. This is a theme that has recently been taken up by Ingram, who argued the importance of the late medieval wardmote and church courts in asserting the wishes of local householders keen to enforce moral standards.[11] However, Ingram followed Frank Rexroth in viewing the wardmote as assigning a 'persistent identity' to malefactors, stating that 'from such imposed identities, there was no escape'.[12] Ingram's focus on the instruments of sexual regulation tends, as this statement suggests, to downplay the extent to which individuals who stood accused of misdemeanours were also engaged in negotiating their reputation as much as any householder who accused them. As will be demonstrated, both 'respectable' householders and their poor neighbours participated in processes of marginalization and differences of status were important in how reputation was negotiated.

This chapter is primarily concerned with those on the receiving end of surveillance and marginalizing speech. Marginality, as set out in the introduction to this book, was a state of jeopardy in which an individual's accrued social capital was insufficient to prevent something bad happening to them. The previous chapters have discussed many people in such situations, whether they were imprisoned, suffered local humiliation or became homeless. In stark contrast to Rexroth and Ingram's characterization of such individuals as assigned persistent stigmatizing labels, Erik Spindler's work on marginalization argued that 'even in situations of marginality, individuals had agency'.[13] For Spindler, those who were marginalized were able to draw on their own social networks to mitigate the effects of prosecution or punishment.[14] Indeed, while many people did not possess social capital gained through participation in urban institutions and juries,

9 T. Reinke-Williams, *Women, Work and Sociability in Early Modern London* (Basingstoke, Hampshire, and New York, 2014), pp. 127–33.

10 S. McSheffrey, 'Jurors, respectable masculinity and Christian morality: a comment on Marjorie McIntosh's "Controlling Misbehavior"', *Journal of British Studies*, xxxvii (1998), 269–78, pp. 271–72; L. Gowing, *Domestic Dangers: Women, Words and Sex in Early Modern London* (Oxford, 1996), pp. 70–72; Ingram, *Carnal Knowledge*, pp. 74–75, 220.

11 Ingram, *Carnal Knowledge*, pp. 165–6, 172, 179–87, 194, 212–22.

12 Ingram, *Carnal Knowledge*, p. 224.

13 Spindler, 'Marginality and social relations', pp. 122–3, 242.

14 Spindler, 'Marginality and social relations', pp. 102–23.

they might, as Marjorie McIntosh suggests of women's credit networks, have separate webs of connections through which they could draw social and economic resources.[15] Those of low social status given the opportunity to bear witness in court might use this opportunity to enhance their own social capital and demonstrate their own good fame.[16] Avoiding punishment could also involve the deployment of something closer to what Bourdieu termed cultural capital, in the form of knowledge about how to navigate and manipulate the requirements of the court.[17] Decisions about marginalization rested on the negotiation of *fama* and, while it was a negotiation in which juries and trustworthy men undoubtedly held many of the cards, individuals were able to adapt their own behaviour and use their social capital to influence the outcome.[18]

This chapter explores the possibilities and limits of strategy for those whose reputations were sullied by local gossip. In doing so, much of the discussion centres on defamation cases at the consistory court which shine a light on how reputations were made and broken. Defamation cases required some measure of legal fiction in their testimonies, since to be effective witnesses had to claim they no longer respected the plaintiff as a result of the defamatory words (which, if it were true, would have made them unlikely to be willing to bear witness). They needed to prove that a defendant had used certain actionable words that damaged the plaintiff's local standing and shaped testimonies to fit the required legal narrative. Nonetheless, careful reading of depositions can yield significant insight into whose speech was cast as defamatory and whose as legitimate criticism of a neighbour.

The significance of the neighbourhood as the venue for making and disseminating *fama* highlights the connection between space and reputation in the urban environment. In the introduction to this book, we saw how medieval culture drew strong associations between the fringes of the city

[15] M. K. McIntosh, 'The diversity of social capital in English communities, 1300–1640 (with a Glance at Modern Nigeria)', in *Patterns of Social Capital: Stability and Change in Historical Perspective*, ed. R. I. Rotberg (Cambridge and New York, 2001), pp. 121–52, AT pp. 130, 133–4.

[16] S. A. McDonough, *Witnesses, Neighbors and Community in Late Medieval Marseille* (New York, 2013), p. 38; Johnson, *Law in Common*, pp. 202–3.

[17] P. Bourdieu, 'The forms of capital', in *The Sociology of Economic Life*, ed. M. Granovetter and R. Swedberg, 3rd edn (Boulder, Colo., 2011), pp. 78–92, at pp. 17–20.

[18] R. W. Scribner, 'Wie wird man Außenseiter? Ein- und Ausgrenzung im frühneuzeitlichen Deutschland', in *Aussenseiter zwischen Mittelalter und Neuzeit: Festschrift für Hans-Jürgen Goertz zum 60. Geburtstag*, ed. N. Fischer and M. Kobelt-Groch (Leiden, 1997), pp. 21–46, at pp. 40–42.

and physical and moral pollution. More than a rhetorical connection, there were also more nuanced understandings of space among urban dwellers which they might exploit in the defence of their reputations. Spatial agency – that is, the ability of people to produce and use space – is at the heart of geographers' contributions to subaltern studies, an approach with great relevance here for its centring of those marginalized from urban society. The city margin is, according to Ananya Roy, a space in which there are multiple possibilities for adaptation and innovation by residents.[19] This chapter shares the approach of Roy and of historians such as Shannon McSheffrey and Tom Johnson, who have stressed the ability of medieval people to make astute use of urban space in navigating the legal system. As we shall see, there was considerable scope for the use of suburban space in negotiating reputation and evading *fama*.

Managing and renegotiating reputation

The business of negotiating reputation was, as has been suggested in previous chapters, a constant concern and intersected with the various methods of policing that prevailed in London. I now want to explicitly turn to how individuals went about this negotiation. They did so in the manner of their interaction with their neighbours and with the legal system and in their day-to-day conduct. How could people ensure they had a good reputation and, if their *fama* was poor, how did they attempt rehabilitation? The answer to both questions was highly dependent on status, both in terms of socio-economic position and aspects of personal identity.

There were some for whom maintaining a good reputation was difficult because disorderly behaviour was to an extent expected of them. We saw in Chapter Four how immigrant aliens were frequently indicted at the wardmote for sexual misdemeanours, due to either a real association with the sex trade or xenophobic stereotypes. Another group who faced frequent wardmote indictments were those who operated alehouses and other venues for the sale and consumption of food and drink. About 9 per cent of all the surviving wardmote indictments were for huckstry of ale or beer or for selling ale contrary to the stipulations of the assize.[20] As has been argued by Helen Carrel, food retailers were viewed with particular suspicion by civic authorities, who often identified them as disruptive and even morally corrupting influences, and alehouses were often ordered to close early during

[19] A. Roy, 'Slumdog cities: rethinking subaltern urbanism', *International Journal of Urban and Regional Research*, xxxv (2011), 223–38, doi.org/10.1111/j.1468-2427.2011.01051.x., at p. 232.

[20] Ninety indictments out of the 984 analysed, as discussed above at p. 143.

major festivals as a matter of public order.[21] While, as Barbara Hanawalt argues, more substantial taverners and innkeepers who lodged guests were expected to police their guests' behaviour, her work also shows a general fear among authorities of the disorder drinking houses encouraged and a mistrust of women inhabiting or running such establishments.[22] Keepers of drinking establishments were held responsible for unruly behaviour in their houses and would have particularly feared presentation at the wardmote, their precarious position in relation to authority making them vulnerable to the spread of rumour and scandal, which could damage their business.[23] Not only was food retailing itself considered morally suspicious, but also the acceptance of customers into the home could easily be construed as misgovernance of the household, given their mix of domestic and commercial space.[24] The lines between drinking houses and illicit lodgings outside major inns could be blurred, and we saw in Chapter One that such businesses were liable to complaints at the wardmote. At this lower end of the scale, food and drink retailers were a group whose precarious position in society fits well within Erik Spindler's definition of the marginalized.

In response, the food and drink retailers who appear within consistory court cases acted in ways which seem designed to mitigate the impact of their trade upon their reputations, particularly when their premises had been the settings for disorder. In 1510 Robert Gustard, a brewer of St Botolph Aldersgate, was said to have intervened to prevent one of the customers at his bowling alley angrily throwing a bowling ball at a priest's head.[25] In Robert's own testimony about the incident, however, he was evasive: 'as to the blow or violence specified in the article [of interrogation] he has nothing to depose'.[26] It was wholly within Gustard's interests to publicly downplay the violence of the dispute within his premises, as disorderly guests could have caused him an embarrassing wardmote indictment. Just the year before

[21] H. Carrel, 'Food, drink and public order in the London liber albus', *Urban History*, xxxiii (2006), 176–94, at pp. 185–8; S. Lindenbaum, 'Ceremony and oligarchy: the London midsummer watch', in *City and Spectacle in Medieval Europe*, ed. K. L. Reyerson and B. A. Hanawalt (Minneapolis, Minn., and London, 1994), pp. 171–88, at p. 173.

[22] B. A. Hanawalt, 'The host, the law and the ambiguous space of medieval London taverns', in *Medieval Crime and Social Control*, ed. B. A. Hanawalt and D. Wallace (Minneapolis and London, 1999), pp. 204–23.

[23] Carrel, 'Food, drink and public order in the London liber albus', pp. 192–3; Hanawalt, 'The host, the law and the ambiguous space of medieval London taverns', p. 214.

[24] Hanawalt, 'The host, the law and the ambiguous space of medieval London taverns', p. 205.

[25] LMA, DL/C/206, fo. 75.

[26] LMA, DL/C/206, fo. 75.

the fight at his own bowling alley, Gustard had been part of the Aldersgate wardmote jury which indicted one of his neighbours 'for resorting of yll dyspossed pepull to hys howse and on Seint Stephens day laste passed ii suspessyowse persons lyke to make murder in her [sic] howse'.[27] Gustard managed his reputation both in the heat of the moment by attempting to control the behaviour of his customers and in his deposition, where, in minimizing the violence of the incident, he perhaps sought to avoid creating further public fame about his establishment. This strategy appears to have worked for Gustard, as he continued to be selected for service on the wardmote jury, participating a total of four times in 1503–13.[28] Gustard was probably running the kind of large establishment which Hanawalt saw as integrated into structures of policing, and his actions suggest he took his role as *paterfamilias* to his guests seriously and as such was careful to maintain his good reputation.

However, it was not just those with respected local positions as jurors who were concerned to defend their reputations. Another case suggests that rather humbler food and drink retailers tried to prevent the behaviour of disorderly customers from tarnishing the reputation of their establishments. Thomas and Katharine Atkynson, who appeared as deponents at the consistory in 1521, seem from many of the details of the case to have lived a somewhat precarious existence. It was Katharine Atkynson who, in the words of her deposition, 'kepyd a vytylyng howse' in the extramural parish of St Giles Cripplegate, while her husband was described as a wheelwright.[29] This was a mixed household economy where the Atkynsons brought in income from a variety of sources to support themselves. Their 'vytylyng howse' – perhaps just a front room – was also apparently quite small, with neighbours in both chambers above and next door disturbed by a commotion within it.[30] Evidently, this was not the kind of permanent establishment run by a male citizen who the civic authorities trusted to control their guests.[31] The commotion in question was caused by a man called John Wright, who entered the house shouting, 'how many hoorys [whores] have we here,' before beating and stripping his wife, Elizabeth, who had come there to eat. The responses of the Atkynsons and their testimonies speak to a concern with their own reputations. Thomas Atkynson replied, 'none withoute

[27] LMA, CLC/W/FA/005/MS01499.

[28] LMA, CLC/W/FA/001/MS02050/001, fos. 5v–7.

[29] LMA, DL/C/207, fos. 83, 96.

[30] LMA, DL/C/207, fo. 97v.

[31] Hanawalt, 'The host, the law and the ambiguous space of medieval London taverns', p. 215.

thow bryng hem [i.e. whores] with the' to Wryght's provocative statement and, when Thomas learned that Elizabeth was John's wife, urged John to 'take her and get the owt off my howse'.[32] By rejecting Wryght's description of his customers as whores and telling Wryght to take his abuse of his wife elsewhere, Thomas Atkynson perhaps sought to avoid a potentially damaging escalation of disorder in his home. In his conspicuous failure to intervene in John's abuse of Elizabeth, Atkynson may also have sought to avoid suggestions that the Atkynsons had assisted Elizabeth in leaving her abusive husband, which could invite their own prosecution.[33]

John also challenged Thomas's suitability to keep a house, saying, 'yf thow were withowt thy howse as thow art withyn thow shuld never come withyn agayn': that is, if he acted publicly as he did privately he would be expelled from the neighbourhood.[34] This direct challenge to Thomas's authority is very suggestive of how vulnerable poor victuallers such as the Atkynsons were to slanders against their reputation. Indeed, by the time the case came to the consistory, Thomas and Katharine had left the parish where their victualling house had been, St James Clerkenwell, moving to St Giles Cripplegate. There is nothing to explicitly link the case to their movement, but it can be imagined that this sort of incident, cast as misgovernment of the household, could have damaged their local reputation. Margaret Margetson, an alehouse keeper who acted as plaintiff in another case, was said to have 'made expenses and labours in the prosecution' of Ralph Trerise, who drunkenly claimed, 'this howse is common for hors, theves and bawds' when she threw him out for falling asleep before the fire.[35] As one of Margaret's witnesses sagely reflected, 'such people good and evil, honest and dishonest are received in such a house';[36] alehouse keepers could not be too choosy about their customers, making them vulnerable to aspersions on their governance which even a sympathetic witness was cautious to portray as defamation. Margaret's use of the consistory court to pursue Ralph is interesting, as it suggests the lengths to which she was prepared to go to defend the reputation of her business. The church courts were a useful venue for a plaintiff such as Margaret, whose defamer used tropes about alehouses that civic justice reinforced and whose rehabilitation thus relied on exoneration from another source. As we shall see, the potential for the

[32] LMA, DL/C/207, fo. 96.

[33] S. McSheffrey, *Marriage, Sex and Civic Culture in Late Medieval London* (Philadelphia, 2006), pp. 140–41.

[34] LMA, DL/C/207, fo. 96.

[35] LMA, DL/C/206, fos. 257v–59.

[36] LMA, DL/C/207, fo. 257v.

church court cases to challenge judgements made elsewhere made them useful for those trying to redefine their poor local *fama*.

While Robert Gustard successfully defended the reputation of his brewhouse and retained his local position of influence, the examples of the Atkynsons and Margaret Margetson demonstrate the difficulties that food and drink retailers faced. It is likely that gender was an important factor here. Margaret Margetson and Katharine Atkynson were women held responsible for their customers despite dominant gender norms that defined proper governance as a masculine role. Women's presence within the 'permeable domestic space' of the inn or tavern was problematic, implying 'tainted womanhood'.[37] Female retail of food and drink, particularly huckstery, was a persistent target of civic complaint.[38] Households which retailed food and drink were thus at the nexus of anxieties about gender, governance, public order and moral standards, which forced their owners to work hard in the negotiation of their reputations, a struggle that was easily lost.

The definition of governance as a masculine activity meant that women who engaged in the kinds of informal policing which, as we saw in Chapter Four, could bolster men's status were vulnerable to having their actions cast as defamation.[39] In 1520, a woman called Edith Stocker rushed to the defence of her husband's and her employer's reputations against the ill spoken of them by a neighbour. As reported by a deponent, she framed her criticism of her neighbour's harsh words in terms of the prestige placed on residential stability, which, as we saw in Chapter Three, was a common value in late medieval urban society. Edith reportedly told her husband that:

> 'Roydon [her neighbour] hathe callyd the and Masterr Rowland knave and he hathe been her in this parishe 21 yeres' referring to Rowland 'and the tother haithe not been her 4 yeres' referring to Roydon.[40]

Despite couching her criticism of him in terms of social norms, Roydon reacted aggressively, having overheard the conversation from his chamber above the Stockers' house. He called Edith a whore and accused her husband of not being lawfully wed to her. The Stockers subsequently brought a case

[37] Hanawalt, 'The host, the law and the ambiguous space of medieval London taverns', pp. 206–8.

[38] B. A. Hanawalt, *The Wealth of Wives: Women, Law and Economy in Late Medieval London* (Oxford, 2007), pp. 198–201.

[39] On defamation as a form of policing, see Ingram, *Carnal Knowledge*, pp. 70–75; L. Gowing, *Domestic Dangers: Women, Words and Sex in Early Modern London* (Oxford, 1996), pp. 70–72.

[40] LMA, DL/C/207, fo. 19.

of defamation at the consistory court against Roydon to protect Edith's reputation. One of their witnesses claimed that Edith's husband took Roydon's insult so seriously that he refused to share a bed with his wife for a week,[41] though this seems likely to be a legal fiction calculated to stress the deleterious impact of Roydon's words. The gendered nature of the abuse she received in return is typical of the defamatory language used against women, but in this context also challenged her right to pass judgement on a neighbour.

Even operating within the framework of accepted social conventions, women's speech or attempts to curtail the behaviour of others could be unwelcome. In 1529, Elizabeth Philpott of the parish of St Sepulchre without Newgate found herself accused of defamation when she admonished her neighbour, William Stevenson, for not tackling local antisocial behaviour. She told Stevenson 'he was as good as culpable because he allowed certain persons to keep bawdry so near to him'.[42] Perhaps ill advisedly, she went on to add, 'Mary, ther be curtiers [courtiers] and harlotts resorting to Raff Long house at unlawfull seasons of the nyght and about iiii of the clock in the morning the harlotts be conveyed away in spanyshe clokes'.[43] It is not clear precisely why she felt Stevenson was responsible for policing Long's behaviour: perhaps he was Long's landlord or perhaps, being forty years old and having been resident in the parish for six years, Stevenson was the kind of local man expected to take a role in formal and informal policing of the neighbourhood. In any case, an accusation that could well have formed the basis of a wardmote indictment when made by a man instead resulted in Elizabeth being accused at the consistory court of defamation by the alleged bawd Ralph Long. The problematization of women's speech in a legal context was not new. In the fourteenth century, women were increasingly excluded from raising the hue and cry about crimes at the same time as a discourse of scolding, which problematized women's voices in legal and social contexts, was on the rise.[44] Defamation accusations such as scolding could be a response to women's attempts to engage in processes of marginalization that were considered more properly conducted by men. While men accrued social capital from institutional participation, female social capital was gained through sociability and reciprocity.[45] As a result,

[41] LMA, DL/C/207, fo. 19v.

[42] LMA, DL/C/208, fo. 9v.

[43] LMA, DL/C/208, fo. 9.

[44] Bardsley, *Venomous Tongues*, pp. 75–7.

[45] I. Forrest, *Trustworthy Men: How Inequality and Faith Made the Medieval Church* (Princeton and Oxford, 2018), pp. 190, 198–200; McIntosh, 'The diversity of social capital in English communities, 1300–1640', pp. 129–34.

even women considered reliable could find that their standing did not translate easily into the arena of community regulation.

However, it is possible that the alternative venues in which women gained their social capital also insulated them to a degree from the consequences of institutional marginalization. Women who had faced official censure for their behaviour could still maintain local female friendships. For instance, Margaret Thompson was a witness to a 1530 defamation case in the parish of St Anne and St Agnes against whom the defendant brought a counter-witness. The counter-witness was Thomas Adyson, a man who served on the Aldersgate wardmote jury seven times from 1514 onwards. He testified that Margaret had committed adultery in George and Agnes Browne's house in the previous year, for which she had been imprisoned in the counter by order of the alderman of Aldersgate.[46] The circumstances of the case in which Thompson was a witness, however, suggest she was not marginalized from female social networks in the parish. At three o'clock in the afternoon she had been chatting in the doorway of the Browne's house together with Agnes Browne, the wife of Dean, the goldsmith, and 'a number of others living in that place' when they all witnessed a quarrel on the other side of the street.[47] This case suggests that a woman such as Margaret Thompson, who had been not just publicly indicted but also punished by institutional structures, might still have a social network among the women of her neighbourhood. As we saw in Chapter Three, women fleeing violent relationships employed their social resources in a range of ways both to evade the social networks of their husbands and to build themselves new lives. Although the social lives of women in late medieval London are hard to reconstruct, less intertwined as they were with the formal and thus recorded world of institutions and office-holding, it seems that their social capital might not always have been destroyed by formal mechanisms of marginalization. This is an important reminder that we cannot always read formal indictments of individuals as proof that they were totally ostracized from their communities; there would have been multiple social groups within a neighbourhood with their own dynamics of inclusion and exclusion.

For those male householders who held local office and expected to be able to exert some informal power, the management of reputation could involve a skilful negotiation of the line between defence of one's own character and defamation of another. In the previous chapter, we encountered Roger Newesse, who was evasive when, in 1523, he objected to the selection of Roger Wryght to the wardmote of Farringdon Within, saying that there

[46] LMA, DL/C/208, fo. 180.

[47] LMA, DL/C/208, fos. 158v–59.

was 'a pad in the straw' (a toad in the haystack, that is, an unknown danger) which disqualified Wryght.[48] Newesse's subsequent refusal to clarify his statement or make any more specific accusation was probably motivated by the desire to avoid becoming accused of defamation himself. When confronted at his house by Wryght and the alderman, Newesse was alleged to have said, 'I sayde soo or as ylle and ye may saye that I am a good fellowe for I sayd no thing be hynde your backe but I saye yt to your face.'[49] His careful avoidance of any specific accusation while at the same time bragging of his honest dealings in the matter, can be interpreted as a targeted attempt to lower Wryght's status without any damage to himself. Although judgement of others was a way for men to demonstrate their authority and status, when directly confronted with a threat a wise strategy was to avoid direct criticism of others' behaviour. Tom Johnson has argued that consistory court depositions show witnesses both employing social discourses and moulding them to fit what the court required. This was both in the crafting of depositions and in their own actions leading up to a case, which might be engineered with an eye to building a successful court case.[50] The ability to 'pre-construct' testimony, and to know the line between defamation and legitimate exercise of authority, would have been learned through participation in legal processes as jurors and witnesses. It was thus a resource that, arguably, was more available to those wealthier people who most commonly occupied such positions. We can perhaps get a sense of this balancing act in the words of Marion Chylderly, who, when accused of being a leper by her neighbour Agnes Wylkyns in 1523, allegedly replied:

> 'that there was never good woman that callyd me soo'. To which Wylkyns said 'Callyst thow me harlott', Chylderley replying 'nay, as trewe ys the oone as the other'.[51]

Whether this is what Chylderly really said, or a later construction by her witnesses to avoid a countersuit, it suggests an awareness and a clever avoidance of actionable words. Crafting plausible legal stories in the church courts and having access to the witnesses who provided plausibility were important elements of the social and cultural capital that householders could bring to bear in maintaining their reputation and authority.

[48] LMA, DL/C/207, fo. 270v; 'pad, n.1.', *OED online* < www.oed.com/view/Entry/135885> [accessed 22 Nov. 2017].

[49] LMA, DL/C/207, fo. 271.

[50] T. Johnson, 'The preconstruction of witness testimony: law and social discourse in England before the Reformation', *Law and History Review*, xxxii (2014), 127–47, pp. 142–44.

[51] LMA, DL/C/207, fo. 197v.

In this context, vocalizing judgement of others when one's position exercising informal power was not assured could be a reputationally risky activity, as Guy Dobyns of St Botolph Aldgate found. He appears to have launched a campaign against his neighbour Elizabeth Goodfeld to damage her local fame. He claimed, among other accusations, that she had acted as a bawd between a gentleman and a tailor's wife, she accepted sex as repayment for debts and that she had conceived a child with a priest.[52] Dobyns made these accusations to the Portsoken wardmote jury sitting at the Three Kings inn in June 1510 and again before the alderman, the prior of Holy Trinity Aldgate, in July. He claimed as proof that when her husband was a wardmote juror he had signed an indictment against her. Guy Dobyns apparently failed in these attempts: the wardmote jury refused to indict Elizabeth, which presumably explains why he took his complaints to the alderman directly, and by December he himself was a defendant in the consistory court, accused of defamation.[53] The case suggests the risks associated with calling out others' behaviour when, even as a man, you were not apparently considered of sufficient authority to do so. It also suggests some of the legal skill and knowledge required in demonstrating one's own authority. Although jurors probably had specific incidents in mind when they indicted individuals which the general terms of wardmote indictments disguise, Dobyns was not a member of the jury and, in appearing before them and the alderman with such specific accusations, he seems to have miscalculated. Two long-standing wardmote jurors appeared against him in the consistory defamation case, serving to distinguish between their legitimate authority, in the words of one, 'to inquire as to diverse gross excesses and those men and priests suspected of ill rule' and Dobyns's illegitimate attempt to marginalize a neighbour.[54] For Dobyns, his inability to convince the jury and marshal persuasive witnesses for his own case suggests lesser social resources, and thus the importance of both social networks and legal knowledge to negotiating reputation. In a society where so much community management was done informally, it was important for the institutional basis of judgement to be reaffirmed in a case such as this, avoiding the possibility that the wardmote could itself be associated with defamation. For Dobyns, what could have been an attempt to gain respect among his neighbours for his exposure of Elizabeth's alleged behaviour probably damaged his reputation, given the jurors' depositions against him.

52 LMA, DL/C/207, fo. 16.

53 LMA, DL/C/207, fos. 19v–20v.

54 LMA, DL/C/207, fos. 19v–20v. These were John Hygyns and William Culverden, who also featured within the Aldgate testamentary network discussed in Chapter Two.

As these examples suggest, the pressures of managing reputation worked horizontally as well as vertically; that is, householders who aspired to authority still had to negotiate their right to exert it through management of their own reputations. Ian Forrest's close examination of who made up local elites notes that fortunes could rise and fall and, even where they were of equal socio-economic status, men needed to prove themselves to other local trustworthy men before taking on the role.[55] Reputationally, the high dropout rates for wardmote jurors discussed in Chapter Four and the need to take up defamation cases suggests that such status was mutable and contested rather than there being a fixed social centre of neighbourhood life. The shaming of neighbours was not just used to exert pressure downwards on the poor but also to shape and reshape the pecking order among the relative elite.

However, while all might have faced the pressure to maintain or defend their reputation, the means by which they did so varied. We have already seen that food and drink retailers who were likely to receive short shrift in civic courts might turn to the consistory court instead to defend their reputations. Roger Wright (the 'pad in the straw') aspired to be a wardmote juror himself and, according to one witness, was 'vexed by many expenses in this case' to restore his wife's lost reputation.[56] But for those without the cash for such expenses and without the expectation of gaining a respected position as an officeholder through a renegotiated reputation, there were other options. Richard Trussyngton, a waterman (plier of small taxi boats on the Thames) of the parish of St Michael Queenhithe, appeared as a deponent in a defamation suit in 1523.[57] The plaintiff called several opposing witnesses who said Trussyngton was not a trustworthy character: that he was a pauper who got into drunken brawls, provoked arguments among his neighbours and was likely to have been paid for his deposition.[58] Unsurprisingly, he had come to the attention of the wardmote inquest and had, according to the counter-witnesses (two of whom were wardmote jurors), been indicted seven years in a row as a quarrelsome man and once for failing to chasten his scolding wife.[59] One of the counter-witnesses gave an insight into why Trussyngton could be indicted so many times without being expelled from

55 Forrest, *Trustworthy Men*, pp. 188–9.

56 LMA, DL/C/207, fo. 271v.

57 LMA, DL/C/207, fo. 207v.

58 LMA, DL/C/207, fos. 268v–69v.

59 LMA, DL/C/207, fo. 269. William Florence, shipwright, and Thomas Swyndon, dyer, were both deponents who said they had been part of wardmote juries which indicted Trussyngton.

the ward: Trussyngton had found people to provide surety to the alderman that he would keep better rule in future.[60] That he could find sureties for his behaviour suggests that, despite the repeated judgements against him, he had not lost all local credit and may indeed have endeavoured by better behaviour to regain reputation. Yet, as demonstrated by the attitude of the counter-witness against him, the admission of guilt involved in such a process was nonetheless considered deeply damaging by those who aspired to exercise authority themselves. For those such as Trussyngton without the means to defend themselves through defamation suits, showing deference to the authorities of the ward and contrition through use of sureties was enough to protect themselves against expulsion. Similarly, in the church courts, the lower commissary court offered those indicted the option of compurgation, which allowed the accused to present a certain number of sureties who declared their innocence. While this may have made church courts ineffective as a deterrent against misdemeanours in an urban environment where witnesses were easy to come by,[61] from the perspective of poorer Londoners it allowed them to avoid either the expense of pursuing accusers through defamation suits in the consistory court or the shame of excommunication. Martin Ingram contrasted the harsh, arbitrary nature of civic justice with the reintegration offered by church courts.[62] In fact, both systems allowed leeway for those without great financial resources to avoid harsh punishment or legal expense so long as they showed deference and had enough friends to vouch for them.

In the ecclesiastical legal system, the higher and lower courts dealt with offenders of differing status. As a result, different neighbourhoods tended to send cases to different courts. In Ingram's analysis of over a thousand late fifteenth-century commissary records, the most common parishes of origin for cases were nearly all extramural: St Botolph Aldgate, St Botolph Bishopsgate, St Mary Matfelon, St Botolph Aldersgate, St Bride and St Sepulchre.[63] In 1515, 13 per cent of all commissary cases with a recorded outcome were generated from St Botolph Aldgate alone.[64] As discussed, the commissary court largely heard cases on the accusations of neighbours, some of which were brought after wardmote indictments, and the accused could evade punishment by finding

[60] LMA, DL/C/207, fo. 268v.

[61] R. M. Wunderli, *London Church Courts and Society on the Eve of the Reformation* (Cambridge, Mass., 1981), pp. 29, 41.

[62] Ingram, *Carnal Knowledge*, p. 223.

[63] Ingram, *Carnal Knowledge*, p. 180.

[64] Based on analysis of 104 cases in the Commissary *Acta* which recorded outcomes of actions heard in 1515. LMA, DL/C/B/043/MS09064/011, fos. 224v–246.

compurgators who swore that the accusations were not true. The situation at the higher consistory court – which heard personal suits – was very different. Even with careful selection it was possible to find only seventeen consistory suits that originated in St Botolph Aldgate, St Botolph Aldersgate and St Botolph Bishopsgate combined in the deposition books surviving from 1467 to 1533.[65] This pattern makes sense if we understand the consistory court as a venue in which the better-off could launch civil suits to defend their reputations against those who had specifically defamed them, often (but not always) their householding neighbours. In extramural neighbourhoods where the wealthy constituted a smaller portion of the population, the consistory simply had less of a constituency of potential users. The poorer population of extramural neighbourhoods was more likely to be indicted to the lower commissary court or wardmote for bad behaviour and to accept its authority by submitting themselves to compurgation or finding sureties. In doing so, they might affirm social ties with those who were willing to vouch for them. This was probably enough to rehabilitate their reputations among their peers, negating the need to dispute the accusations and launch a counter-suit for defamation in the consistory. As a result, the occasions where the extramural poor felt the need to defend themselves with suits in the consistory were comparatively rare. An unusual example was that of alleged prostitute Agnes Cockerel, discussed in Chapter Three, and it seems that her case was unlikely to succeed, given that her neighbours in St Sepulchre without Newgate were apparently certain of her poor reputation.[66] Rehabilitation probably meant different things to different Londoners and the church courts performed different functions for different sections of the community, enabling rehabilitation in different ways.

For the poor, formal mechanisms of marginalization impacted upon their reputation in complex ways that were different to those aspiring to local authority. When called as deponents, respectable men could be lined up as counter-witnesses against them to attest to their low status and unreliability, using wardmote appearances as evidence. Yet the poor were still called on by neighbours to bear witness. Sometimes other aspects of their status, such as great age, might lead to a reliance on their opinion and memory in local

[65] The selection process is explained above at p. 100. 'Originating' is interpreted broadly to mean cases in which one or more events subject to deposition took place, as the consistory deposition books do not ascribe cases to parishes in the same manner as the commissary *Acta*.

[66] For a discussion of why Cockerel might have brought the case see C. Berry, '"Go to hyr neybors wher she dwelte before": reputation and mobility at the London consistory court in the early sixteenth century', in *Medieval Londoners: Essays to Mark the Eightieth Birthday of Caroline M. Barron*, ed. E. A. New and C. Steer (London, 2019), pp. 95–116, doi:org/10.2307/j.ctvc16qcm.14., at pp. 106–8.

disputes: it is hard to imagine that William Fryday, an alleged ninety-year-old who had dug graves for a living, was anything other than poor, and yet his testimony in a parish boundary dispute went undisputed.[67] The value of memory in court meant that great age could overcome what were otherwise legal disabilities, such as gender and poverty.[68] Deponents sometimes tried to distinguish between the general unreliability of the poor as witnesses and the character of individual paupers: several times, counter-witnesses used some combination of the words 'honest pauper' or 'poor yet honest' to describe others.[69] James Lovan in 1524 deposed that 'John Broke is an honest person yet he is poor and has few goods of his own.'[70] The rhetoric of honesty *despite* poverty, also common in the early modern church courts, reinforced the assumed co-dependence of morality and social status.[71] Yet such statements also hint at the limitations of deposition evidence for assessing social relations between the economically marginalized and their better-off neighbours: legalistic categories of who was and was not fit to depose might map unevenly on to social assessments of individuals. Deponents made their own judgements about who of their neighbours could be relied upon as a witness, even if others called them paupers.[72] Given their assumed dishonesty, the best defence of reputation for the poor was perhaps to stay out of trouble, as far as possible. As we have seen in a number of cases, formal judgements against the poor may not have resulted in them being cut off from local social networks. The mobility of the poor, discussed in Chapter Three, perhaps made it possible to maintain a support network around London's suburbs and liberties. Negotiation of reputation may have been far more about staying out of trouble as much as possible and reinforcing friendships which could turn into sureties when faced with legal indictments.

[67] Fryday's expertise in the case in fact derived from his lowly occupation: he deposed regarding graves he had dug for residents of a house sited on the disputed boundary of two parishes. LMA, DL/C/207, fos. 241v–242v.

[68] Johnson, *Law in Common*, pp. 196–7.

[69] John Yaldyche uses this formulation twice to describe other witnesses in a case heard in December 1475: '*reputatur pro paupere, dicit tamen quod honesta est et fidelis*' ('he/she is reputed as a pauper yet he/she says he/she is honest and faithful'). LMA, DL/C/205, fo. 310. George Barretson, also in 1524, deposed that 'Thomas Plowghe is poor … save that he says he is an honest pauper' ('*Thomas Plowghe est paupere … tamen dicit quia est honestus paupere*'). LMA, DL/C/207, fo. 268v.

[70] '*Johannes Broke est honesta persona tamen est paupere et habet pavum in bonis suis.*' LMA, DL/C/207, fo. 252.

[71] A. Shepard, *Accounting for Oneself: Worth, Status, and the Social Order in Early Modern England* (Oxford and New York, 2015), pp. 140–3.

[72] S.A. McDonough, *Witnesses, Neighbors and Community*, pp. 65–6.

Those aspiring to local prominence played a different game with its own risks, where demonstration of authority was both a key marker of success and a potentially defamatory activity. Because these middling individuals relied on those with local authority for their social networks, finding oneself on the wrong end of a wardmote indictment required a robust defence which the consistory could provide. Legal knowledge and access to respectable witnesses were thus social resources that were very useful in the negotiation of respectability and marginality; the middling sort could more easily defend themselves through both a good understanding of how to 'pre-construct' testimony and their social networks, which contained men and women who might be thought reliable witnesses.

In general, those who lived in marginal neighbourhoods had less access to such social resources; authorities here instead expected the poor to rely on one another for support, which they had to do in order to mitigate the impact of wardmote or commissary court indictments. As we saw in Chapters Three and Four, there were also alternative forms of authority on the margins of the city in the form of liberties and religious houses, as well as a jurisdictional complexity that could allow people to evade punishment. This is the point where geographic and social marginality overlapped – not because people were simply pushed to the fringes but because, in marginal spaces, the poor could attempt to defend or renegotiate their reputations. Space was, as the following section shows, a resource which all used in attempting to manage their reputations.

Navigating justice at the margins

Negotiating reputation could mean instrumentalizing spatial as well as legal knowledge of London. It is salient at this point to return to the nuanced spatial and jurisdictional arrangements of extramural neighbourhoods discussed in previous chapters. The presence of religious houses with growing lay communities and legal privileges for their populations, the division of extramural parishes by the city's line of jurisdiction and the less intensive development of land combined to create a distinctive extramural environment. This was underlined by ceremonial uses of civic space, which prioritized the city within the walls as a site of pageantry, and even by the symbolic 'othering' of London beyond the walls as a criminal space by civic proclamations.[73] Prostitution and the convalescence of the sick were activities which seemed

[73] F. Rexroth, 'Grenzen der Stadt, Grenzen der Moral: der urbane Raum im Imaginarium einer vormodernen Stadtgesellschaft', in *Die Stadt und ihr Rand*, ed. P. Johannek (Cologne, 2008), pp. 147–65., at pp. 158–60, 163; S. J. Minson, 'Political culture and urban space in early Tudor London' (unpublished Oxford University DPhil thesis, 2013), at pp. 84, 87–9.

to gravitate outside the city walls, as discussed in Chapter One, sometimes with tacit civic approval.[74] The concept of the 'zone of exception', developed by geographer Ananya Roy, has been used to compare ethnic quarters and religious precincts in medieval cities to modern gated communities and private developments which spatialize urban citizenship, often to the exclusion of particular groups, enabling some behaviours prohibited in the surrounding city while prohibiting others.[75] Recent readings of the concept of sanctuary and jurisdictional privilege in medieval English cities have stressed that people were adept at navigating spatial complexity; the multiplicity of medieval urban jurisdictions was part of a dynamic process whereby individuals and competing authorities negotiated social relationships.[76] Boundaries of sanctuary space were determined 'through social practice, its observation and its recognition'.[77] Londoners with an understanding of the legal topography of the city, and of its 'zones of exceptions', could thus instrumentalize that knowledge in the defence of their reputations. As we saw in relation to mobility in Chapter Three, the fringes of the city afforded opportunities for individuals to escape their reputation and avoid public fame. Consistory court depositions give an insight into how they did that, as well as the way legal processes could themselves be influenced by the utilization of spatial and jurisdictional difference.

Control of behaviour in London depended on close observation, with wards increasingly divided into tiny precincts as population density increased.[78] However, the open character of extramural neighbourhoods and the presence of 'zones of exception' undermined neighbourly watchfulness. As discussed in Chapter Three, the complex consistory cases of Elizabeth Brown and Marion Lauson c. Lawrence Gilis featured an impressive array of disreputable witnesses and revolved around two competing marriage suits. One of the contracts was made within the city centre parish of St Andrew Undershaft and the other in St Botolph Aldgate. The contract made in St Andrew's between Gilis and Lauson bore the hallmarks of legitimate marriages outlined by Shannon McSheffrey; statements of present consent were made in the hall of Lauson's

[74] See above, p. 30.

[75] N. Alsayyad and A. Roy, 'Medieval modernity: on citizenship and urbanism in a global era', *Space & Polity*, x (2006), 1–20, at pp. 10–16.

[76] Johnson, *Law in Common*, ch. 3; T. Johnson, 'The tree and the rod: jurisdiction in late medieval England', *Past & Present*, ccxxxvii (2017), 13–51, at pp. 44–8, doi:org/10.1093/pastj/gtx051.

[77] S. McSheffrey, 'Sanctuary and the legal topography of pre-Reformation London', *Law and History Review*, xxvii (2009), 483–514, at p. 488.

[78] V. Pearl, 'Change and stability in 17th century London', *London Journal*, v (1979), 3–34, at p. 27.

house and were repeated at a neighbour's, witnessed by many, including the parish chaplain, who advised on the proper words of consent.[79] By contrast, the Aldgate contract with Brown took place in the house of a man described as a 'beermaker', so probably a drinking establishment, with just two witnesses. These were William Alston and John Waldron, men whose disreputable characters, association with Stewside brothels and mobile lives have already been noted.[80] The easy mobility of these men and their ilk between the precinct space of their home at St Katharine's, with its port-side character and reputation for licentiousness, and St Botolph Aldgate affected the character of the latter. The ward of Portsoken, which was largely coterminous with St Botolph Aldgate, produced numerous indictments for sexual misdemeanours and soliciting heard at the commissary court.[81] As seen in previous chapters, the boundaries of jurisdiction were freely crossed by the everyday mobility of Londoners. 'Zones of exception' and the deviant behaviour and morality which characterized them, could spill over into areas within the jurisdiction of the city. Laurence Gilis perhaps felt confident of being able to easily break a promise of marriage made in an alehouse outside Aldgate in favour of what was probably a more advantageous match with an 'honest' woman, probably a widow of means, since Marion Lauson had her own house. Through its border with St Katharine's precinct, the neighbourhood outside Aldgate was something of a grey area into which undesirable elements of urban society could drift and within which Londoners from the intramural city might expect their actions to have fewer consequences. The twist in the tale is that Laurence Gilis and Marion Lauson solemnized their marriage, contrary to the injunction of the consistory, in the hospital of St Giles in the Fields, thereby utilizing an extramural religious house to evade sanction.[82] This use of religious precincts to avoid scrutiny is a theme to which will be returned to later in this chapter.

Within the precinct of St Katharine's itself, the highly mobile maritime community could evade neighbourly oversight and social responsibilities. The case of Sutton c. Jervys, regarding a disputed marriage contract made at St Katharine's in May 1521, suggests how the unsettled lives of the sailors who lodged there, taking advantage of its proximity to the river, created a community where standards of behaviour might be difficult to enforce.

79 'Testimony of William Walker', Consistory Database <http://consistory.ca/obj.php?p=1123> [accessed 19 Oct. 2017].

80 'Testimony of William Alston', Consistory Database <http://consistory.ca/obj.php?p=978> [accessed 19 Oct. 2017].

81 See discussion in Ch. One, p. 31.

82 'Testimony of Laurence Gilis', Consistory Database <http://consistory.ca/obj.php?p=1234>

There were only two witnesses to the alleged contract who appeared in the consistory, both the wives of mariners who lived at St Katharine's.[83] Although three men were also said to have been present for the contract, unusually for a marriage case, none appeared as deponents, perhaps because they were sailors not in London at the time the case was heard. The alleged groom (John Jervys) was said to have lived at Rotherhithe at the time of the contract and Stepney at the time of the depositions, places abutting the river's north and south banks to the east of St Katharine's. Such an unsettled living arrangement was shared by a mariner deponent in another case, said to be 'living about the city of London, not having a particular house, staying at St. Katharine's by the Tower', a situation perhaps similar to that of John Jervys.[84] The highly mobile community of mariners living in St Katharine's precinct but moving easily around its neighbouring areas did not conform at all to the ideal model of the stable household. Men here could easily evade responsibilities, and wives who remained on land might be the mainstay of the neighbourhood community.

Precincts could support those whose lives did not fit the urban social ideal. The classic example of this is their association with prostitution, and here the ability of local communities to shape legal indictments, discussed in the previous chapter, was probably a factor. At Norton Folgate, the liberty outside Bishopsgate, a woman named Alice Pounfreyt was indicted every year from 1449 to 1464 as a prostitute and keeper of prostitutes.[85] Although she was regularly fined forty shillings and once, in 1462, asked to expel specific prostitutes named Agnes and Emmota from her property,[86] she was never herself expelled or asked to leave, as other prostitutes and maintainers of malefactors were. She was the widow of long-standing local resident Thomas Pounfreyt and seems to have inherited from him the freehold of her property.[87] As a well-established resident of Norton Folgate who presumably had many friends and acquaintances among her neighbours, Pounfreyt seems

[83] LMA, DL/C/207, fos. 86v–89.

[84] '*Johannes Browne nauta occupans circa civitatem London nulla habens certam mansionem hospitans apud Sanctam Katherinam iuxta Turrum London*'. LMA, DL/C/208, unnumbered folio, deposition of John Browne, 24 April 1532.

[85] LMA, CLC/313/A/047/MS25287, rots. 4–6.

[86] LMA, CLC/313/A/047/MS25287, rot. 5 dorse.

[87] 'London and Middlesex Fines: Edward IV', in *A Calendar to the Feet of Fines for London and Middlesex: Volume 1, Richard I–Richard III*, ed. W. J. Hardy and W. Page (London, 1892), 202–212, *British History Online* <http://www.british-history.ac.uk/feet-of-fines-london-middx/vol1/pp202-212> [accessed 15 Feb. 2020]. Her tenement is noted as 'late of Thomas Pounfreyt' in the 1454 Norton Folgate court roll. LMA, CLC/313/A/047/MS25287, rot. 4 front.

to have been tolerated and fined, admittedly at quite a high level, rather than driven from the neighbourhood. Repeated fines as a kind of licensing system were a common manner of handling prostitution in many of the liberties surrounding London.[88] The status of precincts as 'zones of exception' enabled the determination and enforcement of communal standards which could be at odds with civic and broader social ideals.

The creation of precincts by their residents as spaces in which otherwise frowned-upon activity might be tolerated apparently influenced the manner in which they were understood and used by otherwise 'respectable' Londoners seeking to hide activity which might pose a risk to their reputation. In July 1529, Henry Fyt of St Mary Staining, Aldersgate ward, deposed how two years before his neighbour William Bowser had an adulterous affair with servant Joan Stere, resulting in a pregnancy. Joan was sent to the hospital of St Mary without Bishopsgate to give birth. Her baby son was baptised there and subsequently the boy was raised at Bowser's expense in the village of Havering-atte-Bower in Essex.[89] By the time of the case, Joan lived with a widow in Carter Lane in Castle Baynard ward, where Bowser maintained and continued to visit her.[90] Bowser appears to have arranged the affair and its fallout such that it was kept at a distance from the space of the parish. Both Joan and her child were maintained outside the neighbourhood. Although the ward of Castle Baynard had complained about Joan Stere's adultery and expelled her,[91] Bowser himself avoided consequences and continued to serve on the Aldersgate wardmote jury,[92] suggesting a (depressing) degree of success in his strategy.

Other kinds of activities that could pose a reputational risk within the parish instead took place in the precincts of religious houses. In the following examples, Londoners exploited discourses of urban space in the handling of circumstances around marriage and separation. When the draper Thomas Dudley, a long-standing resident of St Michael Cornhill, discovered in 1525 that his servant Anne Trym was pregnant by his apprentice John Sandock, Dudley took the pair to the conventual church of Austin Friars. While

[88] R. M. Karras, *Common Women: Prostitution and Sexuality in Medieval England* (Oxford, 1998), pp. 22–23.

[89] LMA, DL/C/208, fos. 36–36v. Havering appears to have been a popular place for the nursing of illegitimate children from London. Marjorie McIntosh noted the prevalence of such children in its post-Reformation parish burials in her *A Community Transformed: the Manor and Liberty of Havering, 1500–1620*, Cambridge Studies in Population, Economy and Society in Past Time, 16 (Cambridge, 1991), p. 47.

[90] LMA, DL/C/208, fo. 37.

[91] LMA, DL/C/208, fo. 37v.

[92] LMA, CLC/W/FA/001/MS02050/001, fos. 7–8v.

there, he and his neighbour Thomas Knyght pressured John and Anne to contract marriage, and they returned to Dudley's house to exchange the proper promises, witnessed only by Knyght, Dudley and Dudley's wife.[93] In this example, it is notable that the frank discussions leading up to the marriage were sited within the Austin Friars, while the contract that made the marriage binding was still witnessed in its proper location in the hall of Dudley's house.[94] A contrasting example is provided by the contract of Agnes Wellys and William Rote, which took place under threat of violence in Agnes' father, John Wellys', house; John Wellys drew his knife to threaten Rote, and Rote attempted to escape, instead being returned to the house after Agnes and her mother cried, 'keep the thief!' to passers-by.[95]

It was perhaps to avoid these kinds of dramatic scenes, which could invalidate a marriage by implying coercion, that Thomas Dudley used Austin Friars as a space in which to ensure compliance, using an understanding of the legal requirements about a valid marriage and of urban space. In the friary church, he 'reproached or chastised' John Sandock, who, 'because of fear of being incarcerated by Thomas Knyght' and 'the course of his apprenticeship not expiring for three years … submitted himself to the discipline and arbitration' of Dudley and Knyght.[96] Of course, Sandock's testimony was shaped to emphasize his lack of consent. Nonetheless, Dudley and Knyght broadly corroborated his version of events, stating that Austin Friars was the location in which Sandock 'confessed … that Anne was impregnated and the time and place when he committed the offence'.[97] Disciplining Sandock at Austin Friars and ensuring his compliance in advance of the contract avoided the chaotic scenes described in Wellys c. Rote. It also may have been intended to secure the contract against subsequent challenge. By ensuring the proper creation of a marriage contract within its legitimate space, the hall of the master's house, while keeping discussions that revealed the illegitimate origins of the marriage in a 'zone of exception' such as Austin Friars, Thomas Dudley probably hoped to keep his lapse of governance quiet. In Wellys c. Rote, by contrast, the conjunction of the threats to Rote and the contract itself within the household resulted in witnesses who could attest to the full, embarrassing circumstances. Wellys' witnesses Robert Ryngbell and Richard Hadley were called to the house at three in the afternoon to witness

93 LMA, DL/C/208, fos. 162, 166–66v.

94 On the meaning of space in contracting marriage see S. McSheffrey, 'Place, space and situation: public and private in the making of marriage in late medieval London', *Speculum*, lxxix (2004), 960–90.

95 LMA, DL/C/205, fos. 275–76v.

96 LMA, DL/C/208, fo. 162.

97 LMA, DL/C/208, fo. 166.

the contract, apparently after the incident where Wellys drew a knife, which happened during a meal.[98] The failure of patriarchal control suggested by Anne Trym's pregnancy was spatially disassociated from both the marriage and the Dudley household, which both minimized the risk to Dudley's reputation and upheld the legitimacy of the contract. Austin Friars, at a few parishes' distance from St Michael Cornhill, was perhaps considered just far enough away to be discreet. Once again, the management of events surrounding a case involved the careful use of urban space, separating conventional and disorderly activities into appropriate spaces.

The exceptional space of a religious precinct could also be used in the unmaking of a marriage. While divorce in the modern sense was not possible under canon law, couples could obtain a legal separation from 'bed and board' (although not the freedom to remarry) if they could prove that their spouse was excessively cruel or violent.[99] We saw in Chapter Three how victims of domestic abuse might move around the city, hoping to escape the attentions of their spouse. In a suit for separation from the consistory court in 1532, the extramural hospital of St Bartholomew and its resident clergy seem to have played an important role in the legal strategy of the couple. The suit was brought by John Hawkyns against his wife, Elizabeth, who lived near Red Cross Street outside Aldersgate. John's deponents related incidents where Elizabeth had told her husband, 'if I can not be divorced of yow I will be the cause of your dethe', both at their house and within the hospital of St Bartholomew.[100] Both of these witnesses lived in the hospital: one was Henry Manocke, described as a servant of 'Master Barley, chaplain of our Lord King', and the other was Thomas Carter.[101] Elizabeth's alleged threats of violence if a separation could not be procured were made both in the hall of the hospital and within the Hawkyns's own house, where both deponents said they had been invited. The circumstances suggest that Elizabeth, perhaps with the cooperation of her husband, engineered the context of her threat to give it legal force in procuring a separation. As R. H. Helmholz noted, canon law required concrete evidence of violence rather than simple threats, and other separation cases often include detailed

[98] LMA, DL/C/205, fos. 252v–256.

[99] R. H. Helmholz, *Marriage Litigation in Medieval England* (Cambridge, 2007), pp. 105–6; S. Butler, *Divorce in Medieval England: From One to Two Persons in Law* (New York and Abingdon, Oxon, 2013), pp. 32–3.

[100] LMA, DL/C/208, unnumbered folio, deposition of Thomas Carter, 13 June 1532.

[101] Carter explicitly said that he lived in the hospital and Manocke probably lived there, since he heard threats of violence made by Elizabeth in the hall of the hospital. LMA, DL/C/208, unnumbered folio, deposition of Henry Manocke, 13 June 1532.

descriptions of public violence witnessed by neighbours.[102] By contrast, Thomas Carter simply deposed that Elizabeth Hawkyns made her threat with 'a mischievous mind', but no weapon or assault was mentioned.[103] Instead of acts of reputationally damaging public violence, the Hawkyns's separation case relied upon the residents and space of a hospital precinct in order to procure reliable witnesses.

In this instance, the precinct stood as an alternative space to the neighbourhood; rather than relying on the creation of local scandal to justify the annulment, Hawkyns c. Hawkyns involved hospital spaces in a manner that was presumably less hazardous to reputation. While the testimonies in other separation cases were recollections by neighbours of the disorderly lives of a couple, the deponents in the Hawkyns's case were, notably, outsiders to their parish. Thereby the Hawkynses made their case for a separation without having created a disorderly local fame. The rehearsal of Elizabeth's threat to John before the same witnesses in a semi-private household space and in the 'exceptional' space of the hospital seems part of a performance made in anticipation of a consistory case. Such a performance is analogous to marriage cases, where vows were made and marriage tokens shown to multiple witnesses as part of a conscious demonstration of the legitimacy of the contract.[104] Although we ought to be cautious in ascribing such performance to all cases, particularly given the creation of narrative at work in retrospective testimony, here it is justified by the remarkably careful use of urban space and choice of witnesses.

However, while it sometimes suited Londoners to use the exceptional space of the precinct to bypass the court of neighbourhood opinion, their exceptional status was by no means unchallenged. As discussed in Chapter Four, wardmotes could be used to challenge liberties. In the early sixteenth century, the wardmote jury of Aldersgate targeted residents of St Martin le Grand.[105] In the context of ongoing hostility between the city

[102] Helmholz, *Marriage Litigation in Medieval England*, p. 106. See the examples cited in Ch. Three, p. 114ff. In one comparable case of spousal abuse of a husband by a wife, neighbours described separate incidents where a wife brandished a knife and called her husband a 'whoreson cuckold' before throwing him into Houndsditch. 'Testimony of John Twemlove', Consistory Database <http://consistory.ca/obj.php?p=1186> [accessed 19 Oct. 2017].

[103] LMA, DL/C/208, unnumbered folio, deposition of Thomas Carter, 13 June 1532.

[104] A. Boeles Rowland, 'Material mnemonics and social relationships in the diocese of London, 1467–1524' (unpublished University of Oxford DPhil thesis, 2017), pp. 132–45.

[105] 'Aidryan Betson, shomaker', 'Harry Jonson'. 'Anthony Sanctis, goldsmyth' (Anthony Saynte) and 'Anthony Johnson' indicted as aliens in LMA, CLC/W/FA/007/MS01501: all correspond to known aliens resident in the sanctuary in this period. See Shannon McSheffrey 'Residents of St Martin le Grand *c.*1510–1550', <https://shannonmcsheffrey.wordpress.com/research/> [accessed 9 May 2017].

and St Martin's, this presentment offers a local perspective on the dispute, in which the infringement of the city's jurisdiction was expressed not in terms of legal principle but through recitation of the individual sanctuary dwellers who were known in the neighbourhood.[106] It is quite striking, considering the importance of the boundaries dividing sanctuary, that not only household heads but also servants could be named by the Aldersgate jurors.[107] This further emphasizes how networks of social knowledge did not respect jurisdictional boundaries in areas containing exempt precincts. Indeed, this sense of neighbourhood across the boundaries may explain why such presentments were made; rather than being isolated and external, those in other jurisdictions were the neighbours of Londoners who lacked their privileged status. Therefore, the presence of a sanctuary and liberty meant far more than an abstract legal division between Londoners and privileged liberty-dwellers. It was instead an active source of division within local communities and, as Gervase Rosser argued of similar disputes in Hereford, articulation of complaints appealed to the notion that the urban community ought to be a unified whole.[108] At Norton Folgate, the manor's chief pledges consistently complained of Bishopsgate innkeepers and a gongfarmer (who cleared privies and cesspits for a living) dumping their refuse within the boundaries of the precinct. They knew these men by name because they were their neighbours but could do little to prevent them exploiting Norton Folgate's status.[109]

How could it be possible that precincts could act simultaneously as social space contiguous with the surrounding neighbourhood and as zones of exception providing venues for activity that could escape wider lay notice? These dual uses produced unresolvable tensions inherent in the complex jurisdictional landscape of London and shared in common with many English towns.[110] There are three principal reasons why these tensions developed on the margins of London and why such dual uses could coexist.

[106] For the history of this dispute see S. McSheffrey, 'Sanctuary and the legal topography of pre-Reformation London'.

[107] For example 'Nicolas Deryk goldsmith John and Jone his servants … Greffyn Taylor William and Thomas his servants … Anthony Sanill goldsmith Richard and John his servants'. LMA, CL/W/FA/007/MS01501.

[108] Gervase Rosser, 'Conflict and political community in the medieval town: disputes between clergy and laity in Hereford', in *The Church in the Medieval Town*, ed. T. R. Slater and G. Rosser (Aldershot, and Burlington, Vt., 1998), pp. 20–42, at p. 28.

[109] See eg the indictments of Henry Cole, the innholder of the Swan, and another innholder, all of Bishopsgate Street, in 1489, and George Broun, gongfarmer, in 1492. LMA, CLC/313/A/047/MS25287, rot 16 dorse, 19 front.

[110] Johnson, 'The tree and the rod'.

First, the precincts of religious houses and hospitals maintained a range of spaces which we have seen being used in the examples in this chapter in different ways. The church within the Austin Friars where John Sandock and Anne Trym confessed to fornication or the hall of the hospital of St Bartholomew where Elizabeth Hawkyns threatened to kill her husband were very likely spaces to which the laity had only controlled access and from which, we can therefore assume, it was harder for *fama* to develop. However, the development of extensive lay housing within precincts in the later fifteenth century, discussed in Chapter One, must have had a considerable impact on the accessibility of outer precinct space to the laity and contact with the wider neighbourhood.[111] The extremely crowded nature of the sanctuary at St Martin le Grand in the early sixteenth century brought residents into close contact with outsiders, the precinct boundary running through the Bull's Head tavern, where sanctuary men believed they could drink in a back room in safety.[112] Precincts could hold contradictory purposes because their legal privileges were tied to a space that was under constant contestation and adaptation, existing at close quarters with and sometimes only ambiguously demarcated from surrounding neighbourhoods.

A second and related reason for the contradiction is that most of those who seem to have used extramural space to evade fame chose areas at some distance from their home. Henry Fyt sent his pregnant servant to give birth at a hospital away from his own Aldersgate neighbourhood, and Lawrence Gilis reneged on the marriage contract he made in St Botolph Aldgate, not the one he made close to his city centre home. While social boundaries were porous between precincts and surrounding areas, people who lived within the walls might calculate that *fama* of their misdeeds might not circulate far enough to make it to their own parish. Third, even when it was people from a neighbouring area who misbehaved in precinct space, like the gongfarmer who dumped rubbish in Norton Folgate's bounds or the brawlers from Shoreditch in the same liberty discussed in Chapter Three, the precinct's jurisdictional separation hindered any court presentation or prosecution that might have fixed *fama* of their misdeed in local memory. While, as we saw in Chapter Four, liberty courts reported outsiders who were violent or disruptive, jurisdictional complexity probably made the task of constables in the liberties difficult. This would have been particularly the case when offenders were part of the highly mobile extramural population, discussed

[111] C. Thomas, B. Sloane and C. Phillpotts, *Excavations at the Priory and Hospital of St Mary Spital, London*, MoLAS Monograph (London, 1997), p. 79.

[112] S. McSheffrey, *Seeking Sanctuary: Crime, Mercy and Politics in English Courts, 1400–1550* (Oxford and New York, 2017), pp. 131–2.

in Chapter Three, who might easily move on. There were thus practical barriers to the management of behaviour that perpetuated the ambiguous status of precinct space.

This chapter has shown that reputation was not fixed in late medieval London and that people could reintegrate themselves and renegotiate their reputation with neighbours when rumour or their own behaviour threatened their position in local society. The majority of the local community, getting by as well as they could, maintained their place if they found themselves accused of misdemeanours by submitting themselves to compurgation or finding sureties, so long as they avoided being enough of a nuisance to warrant expulsion. Their social capital might be drawn from informal social networks; friends, fellow workers, gossips and employers who could step in to help in times of need. A smaller elite aspired to office-holding and influence, carefully seeking to gain and preserve social capital that was more closely tied to urban institutions such as guilds and juries. And yet, the constitution of this smaller group was contested and changeable. The wardmote jury acted as a testing ground for inclusion, as we saw in Chapter Four. Personal rivalries within this 'elite' produced consistory cases where authority could be questioned and undermined, albeit that greater social resources, including access to good witnesses and knowledge of how to 'pre-construct' testimony, would have been a considerable advantage. Unlike parish records, which often suggest a narrow, fixed elite who presented their decisions as unanimous and uncontroversial, the perspective I have presented on local society from church court cases is one that contains important nuances. One could be marginalized from the parish elite and yet still have a social network of friendship and support within the neighbourhood and be considered of good character. Even formal punishment appears not to have always broken social ties, given that neighbourhoods themselves contained a multiplicity of groups with their own patterns of sociability. Those friendships could turn into sureties, witnesses or compurgators in times of need.

The extramural areas themselves were spaces in which people could evade reputational damage. Their jurisdictional complexity both permitted some kinds of activity unwanted by respectable citizens elsewhere to continue with relative freedom and allowed citizens themselves to shirk social norms and the watchful eyes of their neighbours. Throughout this book, I have been careful not to simply equate spatial with social marginality, but this is a point where the two coincided and interacted with one another. This relationship was active and produced by the actions of Londoners. Extramural space was instrumentalized as a means to preserve good fame or at least to evade consequences. If, as Frank Rexroth argued, the extramural zone was considered beyond the 'moral boundary' of the city, it was a designation reinforced by the behaviour of citizens themselves. Just as the physical development of the extramural neighbourhoods was heavily influenced by the presence of religious houses, as we saw in Chapter One, so was their social character. These twin legacies of urban development and jurisdictional separation cast a long shadow over early modern London, as many former precincts continued to hold liberty status despite the closure of the institutions from which that status had derived.

Conclusion

This book has roamed widely through the society and space of fifteenth-century London in search of what it meant to be marginal. We have met people from all walks of city life, from those traditionally considered marginal to those with assured positions in urban institutions and society. Being marginal was not simply a fixed aspect of a person's status but was experienced when their social and economic resources were not equal to a position of jeopardy in which they found themselves, a situation far more common for the poor than for others. Marginality connected urban space and society not simply by displacing certain groups to the city fringe but by acting as a set of constraints on the uses of space and the actions of people. For both places and people, the forces, economic or social, that determined their nature were very similar whether at the centre or on the fringe, but the position of marginality shaped their responses. Marginality could be a force for creativity, making people instrumentalize their knowledge of urban space to maintain a home and living and giving extramural spaces a distinctive built environment and pattern of development. This concluding chapter draws together the new picture of the fifteenth-century city that has emerged from placing marginality at the centre of the narrative. It also traces the implications for the transition between the medieval and early modern city which took place at the end of the period this book has considered. Finally, it reflects on how medieval marginality connects to our own time.

The medieval margins

One of the key contentions of this book has been the complex nature of marginality as a quality of urban space. There was no template to which all neighbourhoods outside the city's walls conformed and there were spaces within the walls that could be considered peripheral. Nonetheless, there were a set of social and environmental characteristics which marked the city's fringe, among them lower property values, lower levels of citizenship, open spaces, gardens, noxious trades and a wide field of daily mobility by inhabitants. It is not possible to simply describe the city's fringe as poor or to take lower property values as an indication that well-off citizens avoided such neighbourhoods altogether because, as this book has shown, they were socially mixed areas. In other words, purely economic assessments cannot capture the total character of urban neighbourhoods. To spatialize our understanding of urban history means to look closely at a range of factors which created particular places, economic as well as social. These include aspects of socio-economic structure as traditionally studied by historians, including the gender, occupations and households of inhabitants, but also more intangible aspects of the use of space, the most important of which considered here is mobility. How people moved around urban space, which services they travelled to use and which they could access near their home are essential in understanding not just marginal spaces but also how the city as a whole functioned, with its multiple social networks and institutions all reliant on the movement of people. Marginal spaces were mobile of necessity, partly because people needed to travel to and from them to take advantage of urban amenities but also because their inhabitants moved very freely between the city and its wider region.

Looking at the city as an agglomeration of social spaces in which people conducted their lives encourages a reassessment of social marginality. Social knowledge was central to determining who was marginalized and, because reputation could change, we cannot see marginality as static and permanent. There were certain identities and behaviours which might predispose someone to encountering suspicion: having a foreign accent, being a woman without male governance, appearing to be poor or wandering around in the streets. However, in a neighbourhood in which someone had friends or a good reputation, those markers could be contextualized or overlooked by the people around them. Moving into a place in which they were unknown, however, made an individual vulnerable to marginalization. Throughout this book, marginality has not been seen as a fixed identity into which individuals were locked, nor as defined by membership of a given social group. The city enabled people to make many social connections and, while some identities did mean exclusion from a social elite or a specific institution, marginality was mutable, dependent on context and primarily experienced when an individual's social resources were not able to extricate them from a difficult situation. Women, alien immigrants and prostitutes were all subject to exclusions on the basis of identity in certain contexts but, as this book has shown, far more important to whether they were able to build a stable life in the city were the relationships with others they could rely on in times of adversity. Crucial, too, was their knowledge of London itself, its liberties and the limits of the spread of gossip and rumour, which could be instrumentalized in periods of crisis.

Moreover, the narrow social elite that steered local decision-making was not a fixed group; its membership was being constantly negotiated. Certain people by virtue of wealth and status might expect inclusion, but they nonetheless had to cultivate their social capital, often in the form of a good reputation, in order to assure a local position of respect. In other words, everyone, from the poor day labourer to the prosperous guild master, was concerned with social capital, whether their aim was climbing the *cursus honorum* or simply keeping a roof over their heads. To be sure, wealth was an important bulwark against misfortune, but it could not prevent it totally. Reputation had important social and economic implications for everyone, but while for some it determined their acceptance as a suitable wardmote juror, for others it dictated whether their activity in an unfamiliar parish resulted in an arrest for vagrancy. There was, it should be added, no fundamental change to this model of social inclusion and exclusion as the late medieval period passed into the early modern, although the scale of hardship undoubtedly increased as wages were depressed in the sixteenth century. This description of fifteenth-century society bears much in common with scholarship on the sixteenth and seventeenth centuries. Alexandra Shepherd and David Hitchcock have both stressed that the poor had a strong sense of their own status and that the labels that were applied to them by others were often convenient classifications masking complex realities.[1] While our source material is more limited, medievalists need to be alert to the shifting social realities obscured by the Latin of legal records: *meretrix*, *vagabundus* and *pauper* do not represent immutable categories but labels applied by the judgement of a particular set of people in a particular place to a neighbour or stranger.

This book has in addition sought to flesh out and nuance the picture of life beyond the city walls. Mobility and the close connections between the extramural areas and the wider region have already been alluded to. What has also emerged strongly is the importance of immigrant communities outside the walls. They were a growing presence in the fifteenth century and shaped its society and economy in tangible ways that had a lasting impact on the city. One was in the character of the city's fringe as a space for pleasure and recreation: bowling alleys operated by 'Dutch' immigrants and offering the game of cloche were a distinctive aspect of the entertainment on offer to Londoners to the city's east and north. They often combined games with the opportunity to drink. Such a mix of recreational functions was also characteristic of the precursors of London's theatres, which emerged in Shoreditch in the mid-sixteenth century.[2] Immigrants thus contributed

[1] D. Hitchcock, *Vagrancy in English Culture and Society, 1650–1750* (London and New York, 2016); A. Shepard, *Accounting for Oneself. Worth, Status, and the Social Order in Early Modern England* (Oxford and New York, 2015).

[2] C. Davies, 'Bowling alleys and playhouses in London, 1560–90', *Early Theatre*, xxii (2019), 39–65, doi:org/10.12745/et.22.2.3918.

towards the long-standing role of the city's margins as spaces of play and entertainment, as well as the commercial exploitation of leisure. More generally, the large alien population to the city's east in the fifteenth century is part of a continuity of international migration and settlement of this area stretching from the late medieval period through the Huguenots of seventeenth-century Spitalfields to the Jewish and Bengali immigrants of the nineteenth and twentieth centuries. The proximity of London's port and the persistence of lower rents in the city's east, which underwrote its attraction to Dutch-speaking immigrants in the fifteenth century, were continuities until the very recent past. Fifteenth-century immigrant communities clearly socialized within their linguistic groups and even preferred compatriots to execute their final wishes in wills, but they were generally not a class apart. The predominantly artisan aliens living in the extramural areas had much in common with their English neighbours, often shared their trades and, unlike later Protestant refugees, worshipped in the same parish churches. There was certainly an undercurrent of anti-alien rhetoric and occasional outbursts of violence but, echoing a recent reassessment of immigrants in late medieval English society, this book has primarily found a 'reasonably peaceful co-existence' between natives and incomers.[3]

Women's relationship with the spatial margins of the city is another thread that has weaved through this book. This is part of a conscious decision not to hive gender off as a separate category of analysis into its own chapter, because all urban experience was highly gendered. Women navigated a society in which the formal mechanisms of power were assumed to be masculine. This is not to say that they had no power within the city, but they had to work around those mechanisms. Exploiting their knowledge of urban space was one of the ways to do so. Those who faced domestic abuse and widows who no longer could afford city-centre houses with workshops moved into extramural neighbourhoods as a means to deal with their circumstances. For those escaping their husbands, such a move exploited the disconnect in social knowledge between centre and periphery as well as social networks maintained around the city. For widows and perhaps also single women with a trade, the urban periphery afforded opportunities to maintain a household and livelihood with reduced means. The liberties that dotted the city's fringe represented a mixture of opportunity and limitations for women. They afforded space into which women fleeing poor reputation or looking to work in the sex trade could move and expect less official censure. However, liberties still had their own internal mechanisms of power

[3] W. M. Ormrod, B. Lambert and J. Mackman, *Immigrant England, 1300–1550* (Manchester, 2019), p. 260.

and authority which could still result in women's expulsion. Women might even, as we saw with Dorothy Swyndon's marriage in Chapter Five, find themselves subject to the coercive power of local landowners in their lives. At a broader level, women were engaged in the defence of their reputations and accrual of social capital just as much as men were. However, their exclusion from formal policing meant that their role in marginalization (and indeed in ensuring a good reputation) took alternative forms that touched only occasionally on institutional records.

Underlying much of the discussion in this book has been the extent and limitations of institutions in shaping urban society. While parish and ward office-holding was important, it was a formal expression of policing that contributed to and overlapped with informal exercises of local power. Exclusion from institutions was not synonymous with exclusion from urban society: wardmotes, groups of senior parishioners and guilds were not meant to be representative bodies of Londoners from all walks of life. As much as they did constitute a form of civil society for those who gained access, membership of all came with prerequisites that lay partly in socio-economic status and partly in reputation. For many and even the majority of city-dwellers, maintaining a stable living in the city meant building friendships and resources outside a formal setting. Positive, reputation-building participation in institutions was largely the preserve of those who managed to complete apprenticeships or gain enough credit with their neighbours to be elected to local jury service. However, the poor interacted with institutions as recipients of charity, as employees, in the courts as witnesses or compurgators and, more negatively, as the subject of indictments and complaints. These interactions could well prove socially useful, particularly when institutions could provide support or accommodation. Given the opportunity, people without a formal stake in local government might use the act of witnessing to present themselves as honest and respectable members of the community.

Taking this broad view of the role of institutions in society requires careful reading of their surviving records, often in ways which are 'against the grain' of the record's original purpose. This is an area where the insights of early modern historians could be more readily adopted by medievalists. Court depositions are sources that lend themselves particularly well to this kind of approach, and in this book they have been used to explore experiences of social phenomena such as mobility which were tangential to the purpose of the cases themselves. This is a more common technique among early modernists, who are doing so with increasing sophistication as tools of digital scholarship are more widely adopted.[4] Many late medieval English ecclesiastical courts have extensive surviving deposition material that could be more widely exploited in similar ways, building on the path broken three decades ago by Jeremy Goldberg.[5] Another important aspect of setting the role of institutions and society in context in this book has been the use of multiple institutions' records alongside one another. This is particularly fruitful when looking at the effects of institutional participation on people's lives and future office-holding careers, as was demonstrated in Chapter Four. Of course, across a whole city, such an approach would be a daunting archival undertaking, but with a focus on individual neighbourhoods the volume of records to consult becomes far more manageable. Indeed, doing so is vital as urban historians pay increasing attention to the nuances of space in the city and therefore can answer questions about how the institutions that governed the whole city interacted with the myriad local communities they encompassed.

From medieval to early modern city

By the early sixteenth century, London was in a state of transition. The city in 1540 was in the midst of great change which eventually transformed a modest late medieval city into a metropolis to rival the greatest in Europe. Population growth was accelerating and was to reach a peak within a few decades. Urban development within and without the walls was intensifying, gradually stripping away the open spaces and pastureland in the immediate extramural zone. New religious ideas had been circulating in the city for almost two decades and England's painful process of religious reformation already inflected city politics, as it would for a long time to come.[6] The religious houses that have so dominated the story of the city's margins told in this book had been recently dissolved or were in the process of dissolution, their estates carved up between the nobility and wealthy

[4] For instance the use of quantitative 'verb-oriented' analysis of depositions is demonstrated in J. J. Whittle and M. Hailwood, 'The gender division of labour in early modern England', *Economic History Review*, lxxiii (2020), 3–32, doi:org/10.1111/ehr.12821; C. Mansell, 'The variety of women's experiences as servants in England (1548–1649): evidence from church court depositions', *Continuity and Change*, xxxiii (2018), 315–38, doi:org/10.1017/S0268416018000267.

[5] P. J. P. Goldberg, *Women, Work and Life Cycle in a Medieval Economy: Women in York and Yorkshire c.1300–1520* (Oxford and New York, 1992).

[6] S. Brigden, *London and the Reformation* (Oxford, 1989), pp. 152–61; L. Branch, *Faith and Fraternity: London Livery Companies and the Reformation, 1510–1603* (Leiden, 2017), pp. 43–5.

citizens.[7] Citizenship was becoming a majority status among the male inhabitants of the city's jurisdiction rather than, as it had been in the late medieval period, the preserve of a relative elite.[8] The following decades were to bring a new wave of migrants across the English Channel, Protestants fleeing religious persecution, economically distinct from their late medieval forebears for their skill in crafting luxury items.[9] There was a ready market for such goods among an urban elite growing ever more wealthy on the profits of globalizing trade and joint stock companies.[10]

Amid all of this change, however, there was a considerable degree of continuity. It has long been acknowledged that many of the institutional traditions that adapted to the new realities of the sixteenth and seventeenth centuries had medieval roots.[11] Even the political rhetoric of governance showed remarkable similarities with fifteenth-century rationales for hierarchy.[12] In terms of London's broader social history, however, the scale of late sixteenth-century population growth, the expansion of citizenship and the crises of the 1590s have resulted in an early modern historiography which focuses on the period after 1550 and sometimes assumes novelty in responses to social phenomena.[13] These assumptions have begun to be overturned by scholars such as Marjorie McIntosh and Martin Ingram, whose recent work complicates the boundary between the medieval and the early modern and places important themes such as attitudes to poverty and sexual regulation in a broader chronological content.[14] It is now well recognized, for example, that the concerns about poverty that became an increasingly central part of early modern national policy, culminating in the advent of the Poor Law, were in fact part of a long-term development with roots in the late fifteenth

[7] Brigden, *London and the Reformation*, p. 293.

[8] S. Rappaport, *Worlds within Worlds: Structures of Life in Sixteenth-Century London* (Cambridge, 1989).

[9] L. Luu, *Immigrants and the Industries of London, 1500–1700* (Aldershot, Hants, 2005).

[10] S. Alford, *London's Triumph: Merchant Adventurers and the Tudor City* (London, 2017).

[11] Rappaport, *Worlds within Worlds*, pp. 31–36.

[12] D. Harry, *Constructing a Civic Community in Late Medieval London: the Common Profit, Charity and Commemoration* (Woodbridge, 2019).

[13] See eg L. C. Orlin, 'Temporary lives in London lodgings', *Huntingdon Library Quarterly*, lxxi (2008), 219–42; reference to the 'newly emergent "vagrant" economy' in P. Fumerton, 'London's vagrant economy: making space for "low" subjectivity', in *Material London, c. 1600*, ed. L. C. Orlin, New Cultural Studies (Pittsburgh, Pa., 2000), pp. 206–25, at p. 207.

[14] M. K. McIntosh, *Poor Relief in England, 1350–1600* (Cambridge, 2012); M. Ingram, *Carnal Knowledge: Regulating Sex in England, 1470–1600* (Cambridge and New York, 2017).

century, and harsh treatment of vagrancy really began in the 1530s.[15] In looking to the social and spatial margins of the late medieval city, this book has revealed that many of the great changes wrought in the early modern city had their roots in the late fifteenth century or even earlier.

Neighbourhoods outside the city walls in the fifteenth century were not homogeneously poor. Nonetheless, in the development of cheap alleyway 'rents' in the later fifteenth century lay one of the templates for the overcrowded suburbs of the early modern city. The effects of population growth seem to have been felt first in the extramural neighbourhoods in the late fifteenth century. People lived outside the walls because they could afford to do so, and it gave them access to the city's economy, reasons common to those trying survive on a meagre income as well as those maximizing the premises they could afford to rent. They remained mixed areas well into the early modern era: the wealthier residents of the city's eastern suburbs ebbed away gradually over the late sixteenth and seventeenth centuries.[16] For some, living beyond the walls enabled them to make a living outside the city's guilded trades. Those of slender means operating outside or on the periphery of the institutionally-governed economy moved with ease between the immediate extramural areas and parishes slightly farther afield. The development of rhetoric around poverty and vagrancy in both national and civic policy ought to be seen in this context, as the city and its region increased in population from the late fifteenth century onwards. As Ingram argued, royal policy on vagrancy under Henry VIII was formed in response to the situation in the immediate area of London and Westminster.[17] The mobility of the city fringe allowed the poor to move around to areas in which they had little prior reputation and, since local people made judgements about the deserving and undeserving poor based on what they knew of their character and lives, marginalization was intimately linked to space. There was an association between poverty and the city fringe, but it was one in which the poor were not simply pushed to the edge but actively made use of peripheral space to secure their livelihoods. This interpretation encourages a reassessment of the formation of the early modern suburbs that makes the choices of the poor far more central.

One of the great changes between the medieval and the early modern city was the expansion of citizenship in the 1530s, which Steve Rappaport posited

[15] McIntosh, *Poor Relief in England*, pp. 1–4; C. Dyer, 'Poverty and its relief in late medieval England', *Past & Present*, ccxvi (2012), 41–78, doi:org/10.1093/pastj/gts016.

[16] P. Baker and M. Merry, '"The poore lost a good frend and the parish a good neighbour": the lives of the poor and their supporters in London's eastern suburb, *c.*1583–*c.*1679', in *London and Beyond: Essays in Honour of Derek Keene*, ed. D. Keene, J. A. Galloway and M. Davies (London, 2012), pp. 155–80, at pp. 156–9.

[17] Ingram, *Carnal Knowledge*, pp. 233–7.

more than thirty years ago as the keystone ensuring stability as population grew. Undoubtedly, giving a greater share of the city's population a stake in its institutions was an important shift. However, given that the mechanisms governing inclusion and exclusion in the city remained local, and perhaps became even more intensely so as wards were divided into precincts to cope with greater population density, there remain many unanswered questions about how that stability was produced. Did, for example, an expansion of citizenship broaden the composition of wardmote juries and create a wider pool of those with a stake in governing their neighbourhood? Were the newly enfranchised majority successful in gaining the same kind of social capital and informal policing power that prominent local men had held previously? Within the companies, a broadened base of membership seems to have accompanied an intensification of divisions between privileged 'livery' and company rank and file, with power concentrated at the centre.[18] Another unanswered question is whether the dissolution of the religious houses led to a power vacuum in the extramural neighbourhoods, where they had held so much property, and, if so, how did that affect social relations? These questions are beyond the scope of the present work and it would be unwise to speculate here on potential answers. But what this book has shown is that space was a powerful force in urban society with profound consequences for life in the city which ought to be integrated into the answers to such questions. The neighbourhood was where city-dwellers worked, prayed and socialized. If we want to find answers to questions about change and continuity in urban history, the neighbourhood should therefore be one of the first places we look.

Marginality and the urban experience

The experience of the medieval city was in many ways radically different from that of the modern metropolis. However, marginality is a social phenomenon that recurs through time and space and for which the pre-modern city offers surprising echoes of the present. As Nezar Al Sayyad and Ananya Roy argued, the medieval city offers a model of urban space that is surprisingly similar to that of contemporary cities, particularly in the way that corporate entities were able to co-opt space, leading to a spatialization of urban citizenship.[19] The result was to marginalize certain individuals from urban space, leaving them to improvise their experience in

[18] S. Rappaport, *Worlds within Worlds: Structures of Life in Sixteenth-Century London* (Cambridge, 1989), pp. 250–2.

[19] N. Alsayyad and A. Roy, 'Medieval modernity: on citizenship and urbanism in a global era', *Space & Polity*, x (2006), 1–20.

the city, a conclusion borne out in comparative study of early modern and contemporary Italy.[20]

The comparisons extend beyond the uses of space and into the ways that urban institutions interacted with individuals. Throughout this book, we have seen how far the experience of the majority of medieval Londoners deviated from the standard household form that urban government perceived as the ideal type. Structures of governance assumed that households were headed by a man in charge of his wife and dependents' behaviour, and also assumed that man was himself governed by an incorporated guild and by local trustworthy men in their roles as churchwardens, jurors and fraternity members. This model persisted in spite of its disconnect from the messy reality of urban society and, at the margins of the city, was particularly far removed from a society with high proportions of women living alone, immigrant aliens and households in essential but unregulated economic activities. In other words, the model of society assumed by government was not representative of the life of the majority they governed, with the result that the spatial fringes of their jurisdiction looked radically different from the image of stability they projected. This situation has echoes in British society in the early twenty-first century, where policy is often predicated on an economic and social model – permanent and stable employment with a single employer, majority home-ownership, stable residence – increasingly out of the reach of many in society, particularly the young and those without inherited wealth. It is difficult to trace the effects of this disjuncture in the lives of medieval London's non-citizens, though the difficulties of holding down a stable residence when stability and respectability were so closely linked is perhaps a symptom. In contemporary society, the unequal impact of the COVID-19 pandemic draws from a similar disconnect, particularly in the way that government responses have often assumed stable contracted employment, spacious housing and access to private transport. Eventually, the late medieval government decided that drawing more of the population into the city's institutions was necessary; it did not, of course, end social marginality or economic inequality in London, but it did create a framework for urban society to grow and, theoretically at least, opened up the possibility of economic stability to a wider group. The role of history is not to offer models or lessons for our time, but it is important to understand how a recurring phenomenon such as marginality comes to be and, as this book has demonstrated, how its study can deepen our understanding of urban society as a whole.

[20] E. Canepari and E. Rosa, 'A quiet claim to citizenship: mobility, urban spaces and city practices over time', *Citizenship Studies*, xxi (2017), 657–74, doi:org/10.1080/13621025.2017.1341654.

Bibliography

Unpublished primary sources

British Library, London

Cotton Charter XIII.10 Hospital of St Mary within Cripplegate rental, 1448

Cotton MS Appendix XIX Cartulary of St Botolph without Aldgate, fourth quarter of the fifteenth century

London Metropolitan Archives

CLA/007/FN/02, Bridge House Bridgemaster's annual accounts and rentals, fifteenth century

CLC/313/A/047/MS25287, Court rolls of the liberty of Norton Folgate

CLC/313/L/D/001/MS25125, St Paul's Cathedral account rolls of the collector of rents in London and its suburbs

CLC/313/O/015/MS25153, St Paul's Cathedral agreement with executors of John of Gaunt for establishment of chantry [1408?]

CLC/313/O/018/MS25151, St Paul's Cathedral account rolls of the collector of rents of the chantry of the duke of Lancaster

CLC/L/CC/D/002/MS04326/001, Carpenters' Company wardens' accounts

CLC/L/CL/G/026/MS18889, Cutlers' Company plans and deeds of property in Aldersgate Street

CLC/L/CL/G/027/MS18890, Cutlers' Company deeds, leases, plans and assignments related to 13 Aldersgate Street

CLC/W/FA/001/MS02050, Aldersgate wardmote minute book

CLC/W/FA/005/MS01499–1501, Aldersgate wardmote presentments

COL/CC/01/01, Court of common council journals

DL/C/0205–08, Consistory court of London deposition books

DL/C/B/004/MS09171/001–011, Commissary court of London registers of wills

DL/C/B/043/MS09064/011, Commissary court of London, *Acta quoad correctionem delinquentium*

P69/BOT1/B/013/MS01454, St Botolph Aldersgate churchwardens' accounts

P69/BOT1/D/002/MS06641, St Botolph Aldersgate charities and estates evidence book

P69/MRY4/B/005/MS01239/001, St Mary at Hill churchwardens' accounts.

The National Archives, London

C 47/24/13/18, Writ of certioriari for lands at Calais taken into king's possession, 15 Ric II

E 179/141/113, Ossulstone Hundred (Middlesex) subsidy assessment

E 179/251/15B, Assessment of London wards for a forced loan to the crown

E 303/20/100, 109, 114, Evesham Abbey's leases of London property

E 303/9/183, 187, 197, 200, Minoresses' leases of London property

E 303/10/300, 303, 310, 314, 318–20, 327, 330–31, 335, St Mary Graces by the Tower leases.

PROB 11, Prerogative court of Canterbury will registers

SC 6/HENVII/395, SC 11/955, Minoresses' accounts of possessions

SC 11/971–5, 977–9, Hospital of St Mary Bishopsgate rentals of London and Middlesex estates

SC 12/1/21, Rental of London possessions of William Eynsham

SC 12/11/43, St Mary Graces by the Tower rentals

SC 11/451, 12/25/55, 12/22/77, Charterhouse rentals of possessions

SC 12/26/61, St Katharine Cree rental of the parish

CLA/007/EM/04/003/A, Bridge House small register of deeds

Published and online primary sources

Agas Map of London 1561 ([s.l.]: [s.n.], 1633), *British History Online* <http://www.british-history.ac.uk/no-series/london-map-agas/1561/map> [accessed 2 March 2018]

Basing, Patricia (ed.), *Parish Fraternity Register: Fraternity of the Holy Trinity and SS. Fabian and Sebastian (Parish of St Botolph without Aldersgate)* (London, 1982), *British History Online* <http://www.british-history.ac.uk/london-record-soc/vol18> [accessed 14 Dec. 2017]

Bird, W. H. B., and Ledward, K. H. (ed.), *Calendar of Close Rolls, Edward IV: Volume 1, 1461–1468* (London, 1949), *British History Online* <http://www.british-history.ac.uk/cal-close-rolls/edw4/vol1> [accessed 15 Aug. 2017]

Brewer, J. S. (ed.), *Letters and Papers, Foreign and Domestic, Henry VIII, Volume 3, 1519–1523*, (London, 1867), *British History Online* <http://www.british-history.ac.uk/letters-papers-hen8/vol3> [accessed 18 Dec. 2017]

Carpenter, John, *Liber Albus: the White Book of the City of London*, ed. Henry Thomas Riley (London, 1861)

Chew, Helen M. and Kellaway, William (ed.), *London Assize of Nuisance, 1301-1431: A Calendar* (London, 1973), *British History Online* <http://www.british-history.ac.uk/london-record-soc/vol10> [accessed 14 Dec. 2017].

Kitching, C.L. (ed.), *London and Middlesex Chantry Certificates, 1548* (London, 1980), *British History Online* <http://www.british-history.ac.uk/london-record-soc/vol16> [accessed 14 Dec. 2017].

Lydgate, J., 'Henry VI's triumphal entry into London', in *Mummings and Entertainments*, ed. C. Sponsler, TEAMS Middle English Texts (Kalamazoo, MI, 2010) <https://d.lib.rochester.edu/teams/text/sponsler-lydgate-mummings-and-entertainments-henry-vi-triumphal-entry-into-london> [accessed 8 Jan. 2021]

Marsh, Bower (ed.), *Records of the Worshipful Company of Carpenters. Vol. 2 Warden's Account Book, 1438–1516* (Oxford, 1914)

McSheffrey, Shannon, 'Residents of St Martin le Grand *c.*1510–1550', <https://shannonmcsheffrey.wordpress.com/research/> [accessed 9 May 2017]

—, *Consistory Database* <http://digitalhistory.concordia.ca/consistory/index.php> [accessed 14 Dec. 2017]

Ormrod, William Mark, et al., (ed.), *England's Immigrants*, <https://www.englandsimmigrants.com/> [accessed 17 Sept. 2020]

Senderowitz Loengard, Janet (ed.), *London Viewers and their Certificates, 1508–1558: Certificates of the Sworn Viewers of the City of London* (London, 1989), *British History Online* <http://www.british-history.ac.uk/london-record-soc/vol26> [accessed 14 Dec. 2017]

Sharpe, R. R. (ed.), *Calendar of Letter Books of the City of London*, 11 vols (London, 1899–1912), *British History Online* <http://www.british-history.ac.uk/search/series/london-letter-books> [accessed 14 Dec. 2017]

Stow, John, *A Survey of London. Reprinted from the Text of 1603*, ed. C. L. Kingsford (Oxford, 1908), *British History Online* <http://www.british-history.ac.uk/no-series/survey-of-london-stow/1603> [accessed 14 Dec. 2017]

Thomas, A. H. (ed.), *Calendar of Plea and Memoranda Rolls of the City of London*, 3 vols, (London, 1926–32), *British History Online* <http://www.british-history.ac.uk/search/series/plea-memoranda-rolls> [accessed 12 Dec. 2017].

Thomas, A. H. (ed.), *Calendar of Plea and Memoranda Rolls of the City of London, Vol. 4: 1413–37* (London, 1943)

Welch, Charles (ed.), *The Churchwardens' Accounts of the Parish of Allhallows, London Wall, in the City of London, 33 Henry VI to 27 Henry VIII (ad1455–ad 1536)* (London, 1912)

Secondary works

Alford, S., *London's Triumph: Merchant Adventurers and the Tudor City* (London, 2017)

Alsayyad, N., and A. Roy, 'Medieval modernity: on citizenship and urbanism in a global era', *Space & Polity*, x (2006), 1–20

Anthony, S., *Medieval Settlement to 18th-/19th-Century Rookery: Excavations at Central Saint Giles, London Borough of Camden, 2006–8* (London, 2011)

Archer, I. W., *The Pursuit of Stability: Social Relations in Elizabethan London*, Cambridge Studies in Early Modern British History (Cambridge, 1991)

Arnade, P., M. Howell and W. Simons, 'Fertile spaces: the productivity of urban space in Northern Europe', *Journal of Interdisciplinary History*, xxxii (2002), 515–48

Arnaud, C., 'Mapping urban communities: a comparative topography of neighbourhoods in Bologna and Strasbourg in the late middle ages', in *Cities and Solidarities: Urban Communities in Pre-Modern Europe*, ed. J. Colson and A. van Steensel (London and New York, 2017), pp. 60–78

Baker, P., and M. Merry, '"The poore lost a good frend and the parish a good neighbour": the lives of the poor and their supporters in London's eastern suburb, *c.*1583–*c.*1679', in *London and Beyond: Essays in Honour of Derek Keene*, ed. D. Keene, J. A. Galloway and M. Davies (London, 2012), pp. 155–80

Bardsley, S., *Venomous Tongues: Speech and Gender in Late Medieval England* (Philadelphia, 2011)

Barron, C. M., 'A virtual London parish: the precinct of St Bartholomew's Hospital in the Fifteenth Century' (presented at the Harlaxton Medieval Symposium: Church and City in the Middle Ages, Harlaxton Manor, 2017)

———, 'Johanna Hill (d. 1441) and Johanna Sturdy (d. *c.*1460), Bell-Founders', in *Medieval London Widows, 1300–1500*, ed. C. M. Barron and A. F. Sutton (London, 1994), pp. 99–112

———, 'Lay solidarities: the wards of medieval London', in *Law, Laity and Solidarities: Essays in Honour of Susan Reynolds*, ed. J. Martindale, P. Stafford and J. L. Nelson (Manchester, 2001), pp. 218–33

———, 'London 1300–1540', in *The Cambridge Urban History of Britain, 600–1540*, ed. D. M. Palliser (Cambridge, 2000), i, 395–440

———, *London in the Later Middle Ages: Government and People, 1200–1500* (Oxford, 2004)

———, 'Searching for the "small people" of medieval London', *Local Historian*, xxxviii (2008), 83–94

———, 'The "golden age" of women in medieval London', *Reading Medieval Studies*, xv, 35–58

———, 'The parish fraternities of medieval London', in *The Church in Pre-Reformation Society: Essays in Honour of F. R. H. Du Boulay*, ed. C. Harper-Bill and C. M. Barron (Woodbridge, 1985), pp. 13–37

Bennett, J. M., *Ale, Beer and Brewsters in England: Women's Work in a Changing World, 1300–1600* (New York, 1996)

Bennett, J. M., and C. Whittick, 'Philippa Russell and the wills of London's late medieval singlewomen', *London Journal*, xxxii (2007), 251–69

Berry, C., '"Go to hyr neybors wher she dwelte before": reputation and mobility at the London consistory court in the early sixteenth century', in *Medieval Londoners: Essays to Mark the Eightieth Birthday of Caroline M. Barron*, ed. E. A. New and C. Steer (London, 2019), pp. 95–116, doi:org/10.2307/j.ctvc16qcm.14

———, 'Guilds, immigration and immigrant economic organization: alien goldsmiths in London, 1480–1540', *Journal of British Studies*, lx (2021), 534–62

———, '"To avoide all envye, malys, grudge and displeasure": sociability and social networking at the London wardmote inquest, *c*.1470–1540', *London Journal*, xlii (2017), 201–17, doi:o rg/10.1080/03058034.2017.1378058

Boeles Rowland, A., 'Material mnemonics and social relationships in the diocese of London, 1467–1524' (unpublished University of Oxford DPhil thesis, 2017)

Bolton, J. L., 'La Répartition spatiale de la population étrangère á Londres au XVe siècle', in *Les Étrangers dans la ville: minorités et espace urbain du bas moyen âge à l'époque moderne*, ed. J. Bottin and D. Calabi (Paris, 1999), pp. 425–52

———, 'The alien population of London in the fifteenth century: a reappraisal', in *The Alien Communities of London in the Fifteenth Century: the Subsidy Rolls of 1440 and 1483–4* (Stamford, 1998), pp. 1–40

Boulton, J., 'Neighbourhood migration in early Modern London', in *Migration and Society in Early Modern England*, ed. P. Clark and D. Souden (London, 1987), pp. 107–49

Bourdieu, P., 'The forms of capital', in *The Sociology of Economic Life*, ed. M. Granovetter and R. Swedberg, 3rd edn (Boulder, Co., 2011), pp. 78–92

Bove, B., 'Penser les périphéries: l'apport du concept d'urbain pour Paris au XIVe siècle', in *Subaltern City? Alternative and Peripheral Spaces in the Pre-modern Period* (Turnhout, Belgium, 2019), pp. 67–94

Branch, L., *Faith and Fraternity: London Livery Companies and the Reformation 1510–1603* (Leiden, 2017)

Brigden, S., *London and the Reformation* (Oxford, 1989)

Burgess, C., 'Late medieval wills and pious convention: testamentary evidence reconsidered', in *Profit, Piety and the Professions in Later Medieval England*, ed. M. A. Hicks (Gloucester, 1990), pp. 14–33

———, 'Shaping the parish: St Mary at Hill, London, in the fifteenth century', in *The Cloister and the World: Essays in Medieval History in Honour of Barbara Harvey*, ed. J. Blair and B. Golding (Oxford, 1996), pp. 246–85

Burkhardt, M., 'Networks as social structures in late medieval and early modern towns: a theoretical approach to historical network analysis', in *Commercial Networks and European Cities, 1400–1800*, ed. A. Caracausi and C. Jeggle (London, 2014), pp. 13–43

Butler, S., *Divorce in Medieval England: From One to Two Persons in Law* (New York and Abingdon, Oxon, 2013)

———, 'Runaway wives: husband desertion in medieval England', *Journal of Social History*, xl (2006), 337–59, doi:org/10.1353/jsh.2007.0007

Canepari, E., 'An unsettled space: the suburban parish of San Giovanni in Laterano and its inhabitants (1630–1655)', *Quaderni Storici*, mmxvi (2016), 113–35, doi:org/10.1408/84143

Canepari, E., and E. Rosa, 'A quiet claim to citizenship: mobility, urban spaces and city practices over time', *Citizenship Studies*, xxi (2017), 657–74, doi:org/10.1080/13621025.2017.1341654

Carlin, M., *Medieval Southwark* (London, 1996)

———, *St Botolph Aldgate Gazetteer* (London, 1987)

Carrel, H., 'Food, drink and public order in the London liber albus', *Urban History*, xxxiii (2006), 176–94

Casson, C., and M. Casson, 'Property rents in medieval English towns: Hull in the fourteenth century', *Urban History*, xlvi (2019), 374–97

Cerutti, S., *Étrangers: étude d'une condition d'incertitude dans une société d'Ancien Régime* (Montrouge, 2012)

Clark, P., *European Cities and Towns: 400–2000*, Repr. edn (Oxford and New York, 2009)

———, 'Migration in England during the late seventeenth and early eighteenth centuries', in *Migration and Society in Early Modern England*, ed. P. Clark and D. Souden (London, 1987), pp. 213–52

Clark, P., and D. Menjot, 'Introduction', in *Subaltern City? Alternative and Peripheral Spaces in the Pre-Modern Period* (Turnhout, Belgium, 2019), pp. 9–22

Colson, J., 'Alien communities and alien fraternities in later medieval London', *London Journal*, xxxv (2010), 111–43, doi:org/10.1179/174963210X12729493038298

———, 'Commerce, clusters and community: a re-evaluation of the occupational geography of London, *c.*1400–*c.*1550', *Economic History Review*, lxix (2016), 104–30, doi:org/10.1111/ehr.12104

———, 'Local communities in fifteenth century London: craft, parish and neighbourhood' (unpublished Royal Holloway, University of London PhD thesis, 2011)

———, 'London's forgotten company? Fishmongers: their trade and their networks in later medieval London', in *The Medieval Merchant: Proceedings of the 2012 Harlaxton Symposium*, ed. C. M. Barron and A. F. Sutton (Donington, 2014), pp. 20–40

———, 'Reinterpreting space: mapping people and relationships in late medieval and early modern English cities using GIS', *Urban History*, xlvii (2020), 1–17, doi:org/10.1017/S0963926820000164

Colson, J., and A. van Steensel, 'Introduction', in *Cities and Solidarities: Urban Communities in Pre-Modern Europe* (London and New York, 2017), pp. 1–24

Craven, P., and B. Wellman, 'The network city', *Sociological Inquiry*, xliii (1973), 57–88, doi:org/10.1111/j.1475-682X.1973.tb00003.x

Creighton, C., *A History of Epidemics in Britain*, 2nd edn, 2 vols (London, 1965), i

Davies, C., 'Bowling alleys and playhouses in London, 1560–90', *Early Theatre*, xxii (2019), 39–65, doi:org/10.12745/et.22.2.3918

Davies, M., 'Aliens, crafts and guilds in late medieval London', in *Medieval Londoners: Essays to Mark the Eightieth Birthday of Caroline M. Barron*, ed. E. A. New and C. Steer (London, 2019), pp. 119–48

———, 'Citizens and "foreyns": crafts, guilds and regulation in late medieval London', in *Between Regulation and Freedom: Work and Manufactures in European Cities, 14th–18th Centuries*, ed. A. Caracausi, L. Mocarelli and M. Davies (Newcastle upon Tyne, 2018), pp. 1–21

Davies, M. P., and A. Prescott, ed., *London and the Kingdom: Essays in Honour of Caroline M. Barron: Proceedings of the 2004 Harlaxton Symposium* (Donington, 2008)

Dinn, R. B., 'Popular religion in late medieval Bury St Edmunds' (unpublished University of Manchester PhD, 1990)

Dobson, R. B., 'Urban decline in late medieval England', *Transactions of the Royal Historical Society*, xxvii (1977), 1–22, doi:org/10.2307/3679185

Duncan, D., 'Margins and minorities: contemporary concerns?', in *At the Margins: Minority Groups in Premodern Italy*, ed. S. J. Milner (Minneapolis, 2005), pp. 21–35

Düring, M., and U. Eumann, 'Historische Netzwerkforschung: ein neuer Ansatz in den Geschichtswissenschaften', *Geschichte und Gesellschaft*, xxxix (2013), 369–90

Durkee, D., 'A cursus for craftsmen? Career cycles of the worsted weavers of late medieval Norwich', in *Cities and Solidarities: Urban Communities in Pre-Modern Europe*, ed. J. Colson and A. van Steensel (Abingdon, 2017), pp. 151–68

Dyer, A., '"Urban decline" in England, 1377–1525', in *Towns in Decline, ad 100–1600*, ed. T. R. Slater (Aldershot, 2000), pp. 266–88

Dyer, C., *A Country Merchant, 1495–1520: Trading and Farming at the End of the Middle Ages* (Oxford, 2012)

———, 'Poverty and its relief in late medieval England', *Past & Present*, ccxvi (2012), 41–78, doi:org/10.1093/pastj/gts016

Engle Merry, S., 'Rethinking gossip and scandal', in *Reputation: Studies in the Voluntary Elicitation of Good Conduct*, ed. D. B. Klein (Ann Arbor, Mich., 1997), pp. 47–74

Fenster, T. S., and D. L. Smail, 'Introduction', in *Fama: the Politics of Talk and Reputation in Medieval Europe* (Ithaca, NY, 2003), pp. 1–11

Forrest, I., *Trustworthy Men: How Inequality and Faith Made the Medieval Church* (Princeton and Oxford, 2018)

Forrest, M., 'Patterns of economic change in the south-west during the fifteenth century: evidence from the reductions to the fifteenths and tenths', *Economic History Review*, lxx (2017), 423–51, doi:org/10.1111/ehr.12373

Fortini Brown, P., 'Not one but many cities: housing diversity in sixteenth-century Venice', in *Home and Homelessness in the Medieval and Renaissance World*, ed. N. Howe (Notre Dame, Ind., 2004), pp. 13–44

French, K. L., 'Loving friends: surviving widowhood in late medieval Westminster', *Gender & History*, xxii (2010), 21–37, doi:org/10.1111/j.1468-0424.2010.01576.x

———, 'Rebuilding St Margaret's: parish involvement and community action in late medieval Westminster', *Journal of Social History*, xlv (2011), 148–71, doi:org/10.1093/jsh/shr017

———, 'Women in the late medieval English parish', in *Gendering the Master Narrative: Women and Power in the Middle Ages*, ed. M. C. Erler and M. Kowaleski (Ithaca, NY, 2003), pp. 156–73

Fumerton, P., 'London's vagrant economy: making space for "low" subjectivity', in *Material London, c.1600*, ed. L. C. Orlin, New Cultural Studies (Pittsburgh, Pa., 2000), pp. 206–25

———, *Unsettled: the Culture of Mobility and the Working Poor in Early Modern England* (Chicago, Ill., 2006)

Geremek, B., *The Margins of Society in Late Medieval Paris* (Cambridge, 1987)

Goddard, R., 'Medieval business networks: St Mary's guild and the borough court in later medieval Nottingham', *Urban History*, xl (2013), 3–27, doi:org/10.1017/S0963926812000600

Goldberg, P. J. P., 'Fiction in the archives: the York cause papers as a source for later medieval social history', *Continuity and Change*, xii (1997), 425–45

———, 'Pigs and prostitutes: streetwalking in comparative perspective', in *Young Medieval Women*, ed. K. J. Lewis, N. Menuge and K. M. Philips (Stroud, 1999), pp. 172–93

———, 'Space and gender in the later medieval English house', *Viator*, xlii (2011), 205–32, doi:org/10.1484/J.VIATOR.1.102250

———, *Women, Work and Life Cycle in a Medieval Economy: Women in York and Yorkshire c.1300–1520* (Oxford and New York, 1992)

Gowing, L., *Domestic Dangers: Women, Words and Sex in Early Modern London* (Oxford, 1996)

Grainger, I., and C. Phillpotts, *The Cistercian Abbey of St Mary Graces, East Smithfield, London*, MoLA Monograph, 44 (London, 2011)

Hanawalt, B. A., *Ceremony and Civility: Civic Culture in Late Medieval London* (Oxford and New York, 2017)

———, 'Introduction', in *Living Dangerously: On the Margins in Medieval and Early Modern Europe*, ed. B. A. Hanawalt and A. A. Grotans (Notre Dame, Ind., 2005), pp. 1–7

———, 'The host, the law and the ambiguous space of medieval London taverns', in *Medieval Crime and Social Control*, ed. B. A. Hanawalt and D. Wallace (Minneapolis and London, 1999), pp. 204–23

———, *The Wealth of Wives: Women, Law, and Economy in Late Medieval London* (Oxford, 2007)

Harding, V., 'Families in later medieval London: Sex, Marriage and Mortality', in *Medieval Londoners: Essays to Mark the Eightieth Birthday of Caroline M. Barron*, ed. E. A. New and C. Steer (London, 2019), pp. 11–36

———, 'Houses and households in Cheapside *c.*1500–1550', in *London and Beyond: Essays in Honour of Derek Keene.*, ed. M. P. Davies, J. A. Galloway, and D. Keene (London, 2012), pp. 135–54

———, 'The population of London, 1550–1700: a review of the published evidence', *London Journal*, xv (1990), 111–28, doi:org/10.1179/ldn.1990.15.2.111

Hare, J., 'Inns, innkeepers and the society of later medieval England, 1350–1600', *Journal of Medieval History*, xxxix (2013), 477–97, do i:org/10.1080/03044181.2013.833132

Harkness, D. E., 'A view from the streets: Women and medical work in Elizabethan London', *Bulletin of the History of Medicine*, lxxxii (2008), 52–85, doi:org/10.1353/bhm.2008.0001

Harry, D., *Constructing a Civic Community in Late Medieval London: the Common Profit, Charity and Commemoration* (Woodbridge, 2019)

Harvey, B. F., 'Westminster abbey and Londoners, 1440–1540', in *London and the Kingdom: Essays in Honour of Caroline M. Barron*, ed. M. P. Davies and A. Prescott, Harlaxton Medieval Studies, 16 (Donington, 2008), pp. 12–37

Harvey, J. H., 'Four 15th century London plans', *London Topographical Record*, xx (1952), 1–8

Helmholz, R. H., 'Harboring sexual offenders: ecclesiastical courts and controlling misbehavior', *Journal of British Studies*, xxxvii (1998), 258–68

———, *Marriage Litigation in Medieval England* (Cambridge, 2007)

———, *The Canon Law and Ecclesiastical Jurisdiction from 597 to the 1640s*, The Oxford History of the Laws of England (Oxford and New York, 2003), i

Hill, T., 'Die Stadt und ihr Rand im Mittelalter: das Beispiel Bremen', in *Die Stadt und ihr Rand*, ed. P. Johannek (Cologne, 2008), pp. 167–90

Hitchcock, D., *Vagrancy in English Culture and Society, 1650–1750* (London and New York, 2016)

Holder, N., *The Friaries of Medieval London: From Foundation to Dissolution* (Woodbridge, 2017)

———, 'The medieval Friaries of London: a topographic and archaeological history, before and after the Dissolution' (University of London, 2011)

Hovland, S. R., 'Apprenticeship in later medieval London, (*c*.1300–*c*.1530)' (unpublished Royal Holloway, University of London PhD thesis, 2006)

———, 'Apprenticeship in the records of the Goldsmiths' Company of London, 1444–1500', *Medieval Prosopography*, xxii (2001), 89–114

Howe, E., *Roman Defences and Medieval Industry: Excavations at Baltic House, City of London*, MoLAS Monograph, 7 (London, 2002)

Humphries, J., and J. Weisdorf, 'The wages of women in England, 1260–1850', *Journal of Economic History*, lxxv (2015), 405–47, doi:org/10.1017/S0022050715000662

Ingram, M., *Carnal Knowledge: Regulating Sex in England, 1470–1600* (Cambridge and New York, 2017)

———, 'Regulating sex in pre-Reformation London', in *Authority and Consent in Tudor England: Essays Presented to C. S. L. Davies*, ed. G. W. Bernard and S. J. Gunn (Aldershot, 2002), pp. 79–95

Innes, J., '"Networks" in British history', *East Asian Journal of British History*, v (2016), 51–72

Jervis, B., 'Decline or transformation? Archaeology and the late medieval "urban decline" in southern England', *Archaeological Journal*, clxxiv (2017), 211–43, doi:org/10.1080/00665983.2017.1229895

Johnson, T., *Law in Common: Legal Cultures in Late medieval England* (Oxford and New York, 2020)

———, 'The preconstruction of witness testimony: law and social discourse in England before the Reformation', *Law and History Review*, xxxii (2014), 127–47, doi:org/10.1017/S0738248013000618

———, 'The tree and the rod: jurisdiction in late medieval England', *Past & Present*, ccxxxvii (2017), 13–51, doi:org/10.1093/pastj/gtx051

Jullien, E., 'Netzwerkanalyse in der Mediävistik: Probleme und Perspektiven im Umgang mit mittelalterlichen Quellen', *Vierteljahrschrift für Sozial- und Wirtschaftsgeschichte*, c.(2013), 135–53

Karras, R. M., *Common Women: Prostitution and Sexuality in Medieval England* (Oxford, 1998)

———, 'The regulation of brothels in later medieval England', *Signs: Journal of Women in Culture & Society*, xiv (1988), 399–433

Kaufman, A. L., 'Jack Cade's rebellion of 1450 and the London midsummer watch', *Nottingham Medieval Studies*, li (2007), 143–66, doi:org/10.1484/J.NMS.3.411

Keene, D., 'A new study of London before the Great Fire', *Urban History*, xi (1984), 11–21

———, 'Introduction: segregation, zoning and assimilation in medieval towns', in *Segregation – Integration – Assimilation: Religious and Ethnic Groups in the Medieval Towns of Central and Eastern Europe*, ed. D. Keene, B. Nagy and K. Szende (Farnham, Surrey, 2009), pp. 1–14

———, 'Issues of water in medieval London to *c.*1300', *Urban History*, xxviii (2001), 161–79

———, 'Landlords, the property market and urban development in medieval England', in *Power, Profit and Urban Land: Landownership in Medieval and Early Modern Northern European Towns*, ed. F.-E. Eliassen and G. A. Ersland (Aldershot, Surrey, 1996), pp. 93–109

———, 'Metropolitan values: migration, mobility and cultural norms, 1300–1700', in *The Development of Standard English 1300–1800*, ed. L. Wright (Cambridge, 2000), pp. 93–114

———, 'The medieval urban environment in written records', *Archives*, xvi (1983), 137–44

———, 'The medieval urban landscape, ad 900–1540', in *The English Urban Landscape* (Oxford, 2000)

Keene, D. J., and V. Harding, ed., *Historical Gazetteer of London before the Great Fire* (Cambridge, 1987)

Kellett, J. R., 'The breakdown of guild and corporation control over the handicraft and retail trade in London', *Economic History Review*, x (1958), 381–94

Kowaleski, M., and P. J. P. Goldberg, 'Introduction', in *Medieval Domesticity: Home, Housing and Household in Medieval England*, ed. M. Kowaleski and P. J. P. Goldberg (Cambridge and New York, 2008), pp. 1–13

Kümin, B. A., *The Shaping of a Community: the Rise and Reformation of the English Parish, c.1400–1560*, trans. D. Nicholson-Smith (Brookfield, 1996)

Lefebvre, H., *The Production of Space* (Oxford, 1991)

Lemercier, C., 'Formal network methods in history: why and how?', in *Social Networks, Political Institution, and Rural Societies*, ed. G. Fertig (Turnhout, 2015), pp. 281–310

Lester, A. E., 'Crafting a charitable landscape: urban topographies in charters and testaments from medieval Champagne', in *Cities, Texts and Social Networks 400–1500: Experiences and Perceptions of Medieval Urban Space*, ed. C. Goodson, A. E. Lester and C. Symes (Farnham, 2010), pp. 125–48

Liddy, C., *Contesting the City: the Politics of Citizenship in English Towns, 1250–1530* (Oxford and New York, 2017)

———, 'Cultures of surveillance in late medieval English towns: the Monitoring of speech and the fear of revolt', in *The Routledge History Handbook of Medieval Revolt*, ed. J. Firnhaber-Baker and D. Schoenaers (London, 2019)

Lilley, K. D., *City and Cosmos: the Medieval World in Urban Form* (London, 2009)

———, 'Urban planning after the Black Death: townscape transformation in later medieval England (1350–1530)', *Urban History*, xlii (2014), 1–21, doi:org/10.1017/S0963926814000492

Lindenbaum, S., 'Ceremony and oligarchy: the London midsummer watch', in *City and Spectacle in Medieval Europe*, ed. K. L. Reyerson and B. A. Hanawalt (Minneapolis, Minn., and London, 1994), pp. 171–88

Lobel, M. D., *The City of London from Prehistoric Times to c.1520*, The British Atlas of Historic Towns (Oxford, 1989), iii

Lutkin, J., 'Settled or fleeting?: London's medieval immigrant community revisited', in *Medieval Merchants and Money*, ed. M. Allen and M. Davies, Essays in Honour of James L. Bolton (2016), pp. 137–56

Luu, L., *Immigrants and the Industries of London, 1500–1700* (Aldershot, Hants, 2005)

Lyon, J., *Within these Walls: Roman and Medieval Defences North of Newgate at the Merrill Lynch Financial Centre, City of London*, MoLAS Monograph, 33 (London, 2007)

Mansell, C., 'The variety of women's experiences as servants in England (1548–1649): evidence from church court depositions', *Continuity and Change*, xxxiii (2018), 315–38, doi:org/10.1017/S0268416018000267

Marsh, D. J. E., 'The gardens and gardeners of later Stuart London' (unpublished Birkbeck, University of London PhD, 2005)

Martin, C. A., 'Transport for London, 1250–1550' (unpublished Royal Holloway, University of London PhD, 2008)

McDonnell, K. G. T., *Medieval London Suburbs* (London, 1978)

McDonough, S. A., *Witnesses, Neighbors and Community in Late Medieval Marseille* (New York, 2013)

McIntosh, M. K., *A Community Transformed: the Manor and Liberty of Havering, 1500–1620*, Cambridge Studies in Population, Economy and Society in Past Time, 16 (Cambridge, 1991)

———, *Controlling Misbehavior in England, 1370–1600* (Cambridge, 1998)

———, 'Finding language for misconduct: jurors in fifteenth-century local courts', in *Bodies and Disciplines: Intersections of Literature and History in Fifteenth-Century England*, ed. B. Hanawalt and D. Wallace (Minneapolis, 1996), pp. 87–122

———, 'Money Lending on the Periphery of London, 1300–1600', *Albion*, xx (1988), 557–71

———, *Poor Relief in England, 1350–1600* (Cambridge, 2012)

———, 'The diversity of social capital in English communities, 1300–1640 (with a Glance at Modern Nigeria)', in *Patterns of Social Capital: Stability and Change in Historical Perspective*, ed. R. I. Rotberg (Cambridge and New York, 2001), pp. 121–52

McSheffrey, S., 'Jurors, respectable masculinity and Christian morality: a comment on Marjorie McIntosh's "Controlling Misbehavior"', *Journal of British Studies*, xxxvii (1998), 269–78

———, 'Liberties of London: social networks, sexual disorder and independent jurisdiction in the late medieval English metropolis', in *Crossing Borders: Boundaries and Margins in Medieval and Early Modern Britain*, ed. K. J. Kesselring and S. Butler (Leiden, 2018), pp. 216–36

———, 'Man and masculinity in late medieval London civic culture: governance, patriarchy and reputation', in *Conflicted Identities and Multiple Masculinities: Men in the Medieval West*, ed. J. Murray (New York, 1999), pp. 243–78

———, *Marriage, Sex and Civic Culture in Late Medieval London* (Philadelphia, 2006)

———, 'Place, space and situation: public and private in the making of marriage in late medieval London', *Speculum*, lxxix (2004), 960–90

———, 'Sanctuary and the legal topography of pre-Reformation London', *Law and History Review*, xxvii (2009), 483–514

———, *Seeking Sanctuary: Crime, Mercy and Politics in English Courts, 1400–1550* (Oxford and New York, 2017)

———, 'Stranger artisans and the London sanctuary of St Martin Le Grand in the reign of Henry VIII', *Journal of Medieval and Early Modern Studies*, xliii (2013), 545–71

Mercer, M., 'A forgotten Kentish rebellion, September–October 1470', *Archaeologia Cantiana: Being Contributions to the History and Archaeology of Kent*, cxxii (2002), 143–51

Minns, C., and P. Wallis, 'Rules and reality: quantifying the practice of apprenticeship in early modern England', *Economic History Review*, lxv (2012), 556–79, doi:org/10.1111/j.1468-0289.2010.00591.x

Minson, S. J., 'Political culture and urban space in early Tudor London' (unpublished Oxford University DPhil thesis, 2013)

Munck, B. D., 'Re-assembling actor–network theory and urban history', *Urban History*, xliv (2017), 111–22, doi:org/10.1017/S0963926816000298

Nightingale, P., 'Some new evidence of crises and trends of mortality in late medieval England', *Past & Present*, clxxxvii (2005), 33–68

Ogilvie, S., *Institutions and European Trade: Merchant Guilds, 1000–1800* (Cambridge, 2011)

Orlin, L. C., 'Temporary lives in London lodgings', *Huntingdon Library Quarterly*, lxxi (2008), 219–42

Ormrod, W. M., B. Lambert and J. Mackman, *Immigrant England, 1300–1550* (Manchester, 2019)

Padgett, J. F., and C. K. Ansell, 'Robust action and the rise of the Medici, 1400–1434', *American Journal of Sociology*, xcviii (1993), 1259–1319, doi:org/10.1086/230190

Palliser, D. M., 'Urban decay revisited', in *Towns and Townspeople in the Fifteenth Century*, ed. J. A. F. Thomson (Gloucester, 1988), pp. 1–21

Pearl, V., 'Change and stability in 17th century London', *London Journal*, v (1979), 3–34

Pfizenmaier, S., *Charterhouse Square: Black Death Cemetery and Carthusian Monastery, Meat Market and Suburb* (London, 2016)

Phythian-Adams, C., *Desolation of a City: Coventry and the Urban Crisis of the Later Middle Ages* (Cambridge, 1979)

Poos, L. R., *A Rural Society after the Black Death: Essex 1350–1525* (Cambridge, 1991)

Postles, D., 'Migration and mobility in a less mature economy: English internal Migration, *c.*1200–1350', *Social History*, xxv (2000), 285–99, doi:org/10.1080/030710200050143329

Rappaport, S., *Worlds within Worlds: Structures of Life in Sixteenth-Century London* (Cambridge, 1989)

Ravenhill, J., 'The experiences of aliens in later medieval London and the negotiation of belonging, 1400–1540' (unpublished University of York PhD thesis, 2019)

Rawcliffe, C., 'A marginal occupation? The medieval laundress and her work', *Gender & History*, xxi (2009), 147–69, doi:org/10.1111/j.1468-0424.2009.01539.x

———, *Urban Bodies: Communal Health in Late Medieval English Towns and Cities* (Woodbridge, 2013)

Rees Jones, S., 'Household, work and the problem of mobile labour: the regulation of labour in medieval English towns', in *The Problem of Labour in Fourteenth-Century England*, ed. P. J. P. Goldberg, W. M. Ormrod and J. Bothwell (York, 2000), pp. 133–53

———, 'The regulation of "nuisance": civic government and the built environment in the medieval city', in *Evolução da Paisagem Urbana: Sociedade e Economia*, ed. M. do C. F. Ribeiro and A. S. Melo (Braga, 2012), pp. 283–94

———, 'Women and citizenship in later medieval York: a case study', in *The Routledge History Handbook of Gender and the Urban Experience*, ed. D. Simonton (Abingdon, Oxon and New York, 2017), p. 169

———, *York: The Making of a City, 1068–1350* (Oxford and New York, 2013)

Reinke-Williams, T., *Women, Work and Sociability in Early Modern London* (Basingstoke, Hampshire, and New York, 2014)

Reith, R., 'Circulation of skilled labour in late medieval and early modern central Europe', in *Guilds, Innovation and the European Economy, 1400–1800*, ed. S. R. Epstein and M. Prak (Cambridge, 2008), pp. 114–42

Rexroth, F., *Deviance and Power in Late Medieval London*, Past and Present Publications (Cambridge, 2007)

———, 'Grenzen der Stadt, Grenzen der Moral: der urbane Raum im Imaginarium einer vormodernen Stadtgesellschaft', in *Die Stadt und ihr Rand*, ed. P. Johannek (Cologne, 2008), pp. 147–65

Riddy, F., '"Burgeis" domesticity in late medieval England', in *Medieval Domesticity: Home, Housing and Household in Medieval England*, ed. P. J. P. Goldberg and M. Kowaleski (Cambridge, 2008), pp. 14–36

———, 'Looking closely: authority and intimacy in the late medieval urban home', in *Gendering the Master Narrative: Women and Power in the Middle Ages*, ed. M. Kowaleski and M. C. Erler (Ithaca and London, 2003), pp. 212–28

Rigby, S. H., and E. Ewan, 'Government, power and authority, 1300–1540', in *The Cambridge Urban History of Britain*, ed. D. M. Palliser (Cambridge, 2000), i, 291–312, doi:org/10.1017/CHOL9780521444613.014

Roger, E. C., 'Blakberd's treasure: a study in fifteenth-century administration at St Bartholomew's Hospital, London', in *Exploring the Evidence: Commemoration, Administration and the Economy*, ed. L. Clark, The Fifteenth Century, 13 (Woodbridge, 2014), pp. 81–107

Rosser, G., 'Finding oneself in a medieval fraternity: individual and collective identities in the English guilds', in *Mittelalterliche Bruderschaften in Europäischen Städten: Funktionen, Formen, Akteure*, ed. M. Escher-Apsner (Frankfurt am Main and Oxford, 2009), pp. 29–46

———, 'Going to the fraternity feast: commensality and social relations in late medieval England', *Journal of British Studies*, xxxiii (1994), 430–46, doi:org/10.1086/386064

———, *Medieval Westminster: 1200–1540* (Oxford, 1989)

———, *The Art of Solidarity in the Middle Ages: Guilds in England, 1250–1550* (Oxford; New York, 2015)

———, 'Conflict and political community in the medieval town: disputes between clergy and laity in Hereford', in *The Church in the Medieval Town*, ed. T. R. Slater and G. Rosser (Aldershot, Hants, and Burlington, Vt., 1998), pp. 20–42

Roy, A., 'Slumdog cities: rethinking subaltern urbanism', *International Journal of Urban and Regional Research*, xxxv (2011), 223–38, doi:org/10.1111/j.1468-2427.2011.01051.x

Rubin, M., 'Small groups: identity and solidarity in the late middle ages', in *Enterprise and Individuals in Fifteenth-Century England*, ed. J. Kermode (Stroud, 1991), pp. 132–50

Schen, C. S., 'Strategies of poor aged women and widows in sixteenth century London', in *Women and Aging in British Society since 1500*, ed. P. Thane and L. Botelho (Harlow, 2001), pp. 13–30

Schofield, J., *Medieval London Houses* (New Haven, Conn., and London, 1995)

Schofield, J., and R. Lea, *Holy Trinity Priory, Aldgate, City of London: an Archaeological Reconstruction and History*, MoLAS Monograph, 24 (London, 2005)

Scribner, R.W., 'Wie wird man Außenseiter? Ein- und Ausgrenzung im frühneuzeitlichen Deutschland', in *Aussenseiter zwischen Mittelalter und Neuzeit: Festschrift für Hans-Jürgen Goertz zum 60. Geburtstag*, ed. N. Fischer and M. Kobelt-Groch (Leiden, 1997), pp. 21–46

Shepard, A., *Accounting for Oneself: Worth, Status and the Social Order in Early Modern England* (Oxford and New York, 2015)

Simon-Muscheid, K., 'Randgruppen, Bürgerschaft und Obrigkeit: der basler Kohlenburg, 14.–16. Jahrhundert', in *Spannungen und Widersprechen: Gedenkschrift für František Graus*, ed. S. Burghartz (Sigmaringen, 1992), pp. 203–25

Smith, L. B., 'A view from an ecclesiastical court: mobility and marriage in a border society at the end of the middle ages', in *From Medieval to Modern Wales: Historical Essays in Honour of Kenneth O. Morgan and Ralph A. Griffiths*, ed. R. R. Davies and G. H. Jenkins (Cardiff, 2004), pp. 64–80

Spindler, E., 'Between sea and city: portable communities in late medieval London and Bruges', in *London and Beyond: Essays in Honour of Derek Keene*, ed. M. P. Davies, J. A. Galloway and D. Keene (London, 2012), pp. 181–200

———, 'Marginality and social relations in London and the Bruges area, 1370–1440' (unpublished University of Oxford DPhil thesis, 2008)

———, 'Were medieval prostitutes marginals? Evidence from Sluis, 1387–1440', *Revue belge de philologie et d'histoire*, lxxxvii (2009), 239–72, doi:org/10.3406/rbph.2009.7673

Swanson, H., *Medieval Artisans: an Urban Class in Late Medieval England* (Oxford and New York, 1989)

Sweetinburgh, S., *The Role of the Hospital in Medieval England: Gift-Giving and the Spiritual Economy* (Dublin, 2004)

Swift, D., *Roman Burials, Medieval Tenements and Suburban Growth: 201 Bishopsgate, City of London* (London, 2003)

Thomas, C., *The Archaeology of Medieval London* (Thrupp, Stroud, Gloucestershire, 2002)

Thomas, C., B. Sloane and C. Phillpotts, *Excavations at the Priory and Hospital of St Mary Spital, London*, MoLAS Monograph (London, 1997)

Thornton, T., *Cheshire and the Tudor State, 1480–1560* (Woodbridge, 2000)

Tucker, P., *Law Courts and Lawyers in the City of London, 1300–1550* (Cambridge, 2007)

Wareham, A., 'The unpopularity of the hearth tax and the social geography of London in 1666', *Economic History Review*, lxx (2017), 452–82, doi:org/10.1111/ehr.12376

Wareing, J., 'Changes in the geographical distribution of the recruitment of apprentices to the London companies, 1486–1750', *Journal of Historical Geography*, vi (1980), 241–49

Wedell, M., 'Marginalität und Raumsemantik: Zur Einleitung', *Das Mittelalter: Perspektiven mediävistischer Forschung*, xvi (2011), 8–16

Wetherell, C., 'Historical social network analysis', *International Review of Social History*, xliii (1998), 125–44, doi:org/10.1017/S0020859000115123

Whipp, D., *The Medieval Postern Gate by the Tower of London*, MoLAS Monograph, 29 (London, 2006)

Whittle, J., 'Population mobility in rural Norfolk among landholders and others *c*.1440–*c*.1600', in *The Self-Contained Village? The Social History of Rural Communities, 1250–1900*, ed. C. Dyer, Explorations in Local and Regional History, 2 (Hatfield, 2006), pp. 28–45

Whittle, J., and M. Hailwood, 'The gender division of labour in early modern England', *Economic History Review*, lxxiii (2020), 3–32, doi:org/10.1111/ehr.12821

Winter, C. L., 'The Portsoken presentments: an analysis of a London ward in the 15th century', *Transactions of the London and Middlesex Archaeology Society*, lvi (2005), 97–162

Wood, R. A., 'Life and death: a study of the wills and testaments of men and women in London and Bury St Edmunds in the late fourteenth and early fifteenth centuries' (unpublished Royal Holloway, University of London PhD thesis, 2013)

———, 'Poor widows, *c.*1393–1415', in *Medieval London Widows, 1300–1500*, ed. C. M. Barron and A. F. Sutton (London and Rio Grande, Ohio, 1994), pp. 55–70

Wright, C., 'The Dutch in London: connections and identities, *c.*1660–*c.*1720' (unpublished University of London PhD thesis, 2015)

Wrightson, K., 'The "Decline of Neighbourliness" revisited', in *Local Identities in Late Medieval and Early Modern England*, ed. N. L. Jones and D. Woolf (London, 2007), pp. 19–49

Wunderli, R. M., *London Church Courts and Society on the Eve of the Reformation* (Cambridge, Mass., 1981)

Index

Note on indexing of places

In this book I have discussed places in London through multiple spatial and jurisdictional frames of reference. As a result, the same location may be indexed here under several headings. For instance, if looking for London's eastern extramural area, references would be found under London wards: Portsoken, London parishes: St Botolph Aldgate and London places: Aldgate, neighbourhood outside.

www.ingramcontent.com/pod-product-compliance
Lightning Source LLC
LaVergne TN
LVHW052016300826
846742LV00020B/77